Lecture Notes in Computer Science   12863

More information about this subseries at http://www.springer.com/series/7408

Alberto Lluch Lafuente ·
Anastasia Mavridou (Eds.)

Formal Methods for Industrial Critical Systems

26th International Conference, FMICS 2021
Paris, France, August 24–26, 2021
Proceedings

 Springer

Editors
Alberto Lluch Lafuente 🔟
Technical University of Denmark
Kongens Lyngby, Denmark

Anastasia Mavridou 🔟
KBR/NASA Ames Research Center
Moffett Field, CA, USA

ISSN 0302-9743 ISSN 1611-3349 (electronic)
Lecture Notes in Computer Science
ISBN 978-3-030-85247-4 ISBN 978-3-030-85248-1 (eBook)
https://doi.org/10.1007/978-3-030-85248-1

LNCS Sublibrary: SL2 – Programming and Software Engineering

This Springer imprint is published by the registered company Springer Nature Switzerland AG
The registered company address is: Gewerbestrasse 11, 6330 Cham, Switzerland

Preface

The International Conference on Formal Methods in Industrial Critical Systems (FMICS) is the ERCIM working group conference on Formal Methods for Industrial Critical Systems, and it is the key conference in the intersection of industrial applications and formal methods. The aim of the FMICS 2021 series is to provide a forum for researchers who are interested in the development and application of formal methods in industry. FMICS brings together scientists and engineers who are active in the area of formal methods and interested in exchanging their experiences in the industrial usage of these methods. FMICS also strives to promote research and development for the improvement of formal methods and tools for industrial applications.

This volume contains the papers presented at the 26th International Conference on Formal Methods in Industrial Critical Systems, which was held during August 24–26, 2021. The symposium was originally planned to be held physically in Paris, France. However, due to the COVID-19 pandemic and the associated travel restrictions, the conference was shifted to be completely online.

The conference was organized under the umbrella of QONFEST, alongside with the 32nd International Conference on Concurrency Theory (CONCUR 2021), the 18th International Conference on Quantitative Evaluation of Systems (QEST 2021), and the 19th International Conference on Formal Modeling and Analysis of Timed Systems (FORMATS 2021).

The main program contained three categories of papers: (1) Regular papers presenting fully developed original research work and complete results, (2) short papers presenting work-in-progress, and (3) tool papers presenting software artefacts. Tool papers were accompanied by a publicly available video.

FMICS 2021 received 34 abstract submissions, which ultimately resulted in 31 paper submissions. We selected a total of 16 papers (10 regular, 4 tool, and 2 short papers) for presentation during the conference and inclusion in these proceedings, resulting in an overall acceptance rate of 51.6% (45.4% for regular papers, 80% for tool papers, and 66.6% for short papers).

The submissions were reviewed by an international Program Committee (PC) of 27 members from a mix of academia, industry, and government. All submissions went through a rigorous single-blind review process overseen by the Program Committee Chairs. Each submission received at least 3 review reports and was actively and thoroughly discussed by in a forum.

The program of QONFEST 2021 included an FMICS invited keynote by Joe Kiniry of Galois Inc. and Free & Fair, USA.

We are grateful to all involved in FMICS 2021. We gratefully thank the authors for submitting and presenting their work at FMICS 2021 and the PC members and sub-reviewers for their accurate and timely reviewing. We also thank the invited speaker, session chairs, and attendees, all of whom contributed to making the virtual conference a success. We are also grateful to the providers of the EasyChair system, which was used to manage the submissions, to Springer LNCS for sponsoring the Best Paper Award and for publishing the proceedings, and to the Steering Committee of FMICS for their trust and support. We thank the General Chair of QONFEST, Benoît Barbot, for providing the logistics that enabled and facilitated the organization of FMICS.

July 2021

Alberto Lluch Lafuente
Anastasia Mavridou

Organization

FMICS Program Chairs

Alberto Lluch Lafuente	Technical University of Denmark, Denmark
Anastasia Mavridou	KBR, NASA Ames Research Center, USA

FMICS Program Committee

Erika Abraham	RWTH Aachen University, Germany
Massimo Bartoletti	University of Cagliari, Italy
Maurice ter Beek	ISTI-CNR, Italy
Simon Bliudze	Inria, France
Yu-Fang Chen	Academia Sinica, Taiwan
Silvia Crafa	University of Padova, Italy
Hubert Garavel	Inria, France
Diego Garbervetsky	University of Buenos Aires and CONICET, Argentina
Ákos Hajdu	Facebook Inc., UK
Klaus Havelund	NASA Jet Propulsion Laboratory, USA
Anne Haxthausen	Technical University of Denmark, Denmark
Fritz Henglein	University of Copenhagen/Deon Digital, Denmark
Fuyuki Ishikawa	National Institute of Informatics, Japan
Xiaoqing Jin	Apple Inc., USA
Joe Kiniry	Galois Inc. and Free & Fair, USA
Thierry Lecomte	ClearSy, France
Tiziana Margaria	CSIS, University of Limerick, and LERO, Ireland
Diego Marmsoler	University of Exeter, UK
Radu Mateescu	Inria, France
Dejan Nickovic	Austrian Institute of Technology, Austria
Corina Pasareanu	Carnegie Mellon University and NASA Ames Research Center, USA
Anna Philippou	University of Cyprus, Cyprus
Jaco van de Pol	Aarhus University, Denmark
Clara Schneidewind	Vienna University of Technology, Austria
Cristina Seceleanu	Mälardalen University, Sweden
Carolyn Talcott	SRI International, USA
Virginie Wiels	ONERA, DTIM, France

Additional Reviewers

Nikos Arechiga

Peter Backeman

Yun-Sheng Chang

Gianfranco Ciardo

Bence Graics

Christian Kalhauge

Georgia Kapitsaki

Tsutomu Kobayashi

Olga Kouchnarenko

Franco Mazzanti

Larisa Safina

Giorgio Oronzo Spagnolo

Kenji Taguchi

Andrea Turrini

Zhenya Zhang

FMICS Steering Committee

Maurice ter Beek	ISTI-CNR, Italy
Alessandro Fantechi	University of Florence, Italy
Hubert Garavel	Inria, France
Tiziana Margaria	University of Limerick and LERO, Ireland
Radu Mateescu	Inria, France
Jaco van de Pol	Aarhus University, Denmark

Haunting Tales of Applied Formal Methods from Academia and Industry (Abstract of Invited Talk)

Joe Kiniry

Galois Inc. and Free & Fair
kiniry@galois.com

Abstract. You learn a lot after being a formal methods researcher and practitioner for 25 years. Half of that time was spent in academia, creating formal processes, methodologies, and tools that I hoped I could secretly impact engineers. Half of that time has been spent in industry, working at companies to transition concepts, tools, and technologies in rigorous digital engineering (RDE) with applied formal methods. These days I work at two companies, Galois and Free & Fair, leading R&D in RDE that focus on problems in national security and nationally critical infrastructure. I also work with many of our other Galois spin-outs, such as Muse (now Sonotype Lift) and Niobium Microsystems on these same topics. In this talk I'll tell a small number of stories about these many years in the field, each of which has, I hope, an actionable nugget of wisdom for the audience at FMICS.

Biography. Dr. Joe Kiniry is a Principal Scientist at Galois and is the CEO and Chief Scientist at Free & Fair. Over the past twenty five years he has been everything from a tenured professor at several universities to a founder and chief scientist or CTO at several companies. He has been involved in security in some fashion since the early 80s when he hacked and wrote video games on 8 bit computers. These days, his day job is applying formal methods to hardware security for the DoD and trying to help the worlds' elections and democracies be more trustworthy.

Contents

Tools

Test Generation and Probabilistic Verification

Verification

Verification of Co-simulation Algorithms Subject to Algebraic Loops and Adaptive Steps

Simon Thrane Hansen[1]([✉])[ID], Cláudio Gomes[1][ID], Maurizio Palmieri[2][ID],
Casper Thule[1][ID], Jaco van de Pol[3][ID], and Jim Woodcock[1,4][ID]

[1] DIGIT, Department of Electrical and Computer Engineering, Aarhus University,
Aarhus, Denmark
sth@ece.au.dk

[2] DII, Department of Information Engineering, University of Pisa, Pisa, Italy

[3] DIGIT, Department of Computer Science, Aarhus University, Aarhus, Denmark

[4] Department of Computer Science, University of York, York, UK

Abstract. Simulation-based analyses of cyber-physical systems are increasingly vital. Co-simulation is one such technique that enables the coupling of specialized simulation tools through an orchestration algorithm. The orchestrator dictates how each simulation tool should simulate its corresponding subsystem. Obtaining correct simulation results requires an implementation-aware orchestration algorithm tailored to the specific scenario, without the orchestrator knowing each simulation tool's implementation. Such an algorithm should stabilize algebraic loops, perform time step negotiation, and adhere to each simulation tool's implementation. This paper describes an approach and implementation to prove that a given orchestration algorithm respects all contracts related to the simulation units' implementation. The approach has been applied to an industrial case study and other complex scenarios. The tool and results are available online.

Keywords: Co-simulation · Model-checking · Cyber-physical systems

1 Introduction

Cyber-physical systems (CPS) are omnipresent and embody physical processes being controlled by cyber elements. A CPS is typically developed in a distributed fashion using different tools and techniques. Such systems are becoming increasingly complex [18], which leads to the desire for techniques to assist in the development of these. One such technique is co-simulation: the study of how

We are grateful to the Poul Due Jensen Foundation, which has supported the establishment of a new Centre for Digital Twin Technology at Aarhus University. Maurizio Palmieri is also grateful to the Italian Ministry of Education and Research (MIUR) in the framework of the CrossLab project (Department of Excellence).

A. Lluch Lafuente and A. Mavridou (Eds.): FMICS 2021, LNCS 12863, pp. 3–20, 2021.
https://doi.org/10.1007/978-3-030-85248-1_1

to coordinate multiple black-box simulation units (SUs), each responsible for computing the behavior of a sub-system, in order to compute their combined behavior, and therefore produce the global behavior of a system, as a discrete trace (see, e.g., [8,17]).

Co-simulation allows iterative integration of constituents to explore the global system behavior without violating the constituents' intellectual property. The SUs are coupled by an orchestration algorithm that interacts with each SU through an interface. An example of such an SU is a Functional Mock-up Unit (FMU) defined by the Functional Mock-up Interface Standard [4] (FMI), which inspires the notion of an SU in this paper. FMI is a widely adopted standard used commercially and supported by many tools [7].

The overarching challenge of co-simulation is ensuring correct simulation results. Previous studies [11,12,19,21] have shown that obtaining a correct co-simulation result requires an algorithm specifically tailored to the scenario that respects the SUs' input approximation functions. Not considering such details can lead to hard to debug errors in the co-simulation results as highlighted in [11,19], where it is shown how contracts on the co-simulation algorithm could be constructed based on the SUs. Obeying such contracts leads to a substantial reduction of co-simulation errors (see also Sect. 3 for more related work). An even more challenging class of scenarios to simulate are complex scenarios subject to either algebraic loops or adaptive steps. Complex scenarios are simulated using a specific iterative algorithm [14]. The iterative algorithm solves the algebraic loop (cyclic dependencies between the SUs) and ensures that all SUs agree on a step; the latter is referred to as step negotiation. Step negotiation permits the SUs to implement error estimation and refuse certain future state evaluations to minimize the simulation error while ensuring that the SUs move in lockstep. We propose an approach that has been implemented as a tool. The tool lets users verify that their algorithm respects the contracts of the SUs.

Contribution: This paper describes an approach for verifying that a co-simulation algorithm satisfies the contracts of the scenario. The approach covers complex scenarios subject to algebraic loops and adaptive steps. It has been implemented in UPPAAL [3] and has been applied to several case studies, including an industrial case study from Boeing [9] and complex scenarios subject to algebraic loops and step negotiation.

Structure: The paper starts with introducing co-simulation and the verification challenge of co-simulation algorithms in Sect. 2. Section 3 describes other approaches for obtaining reliable and deterministic co-simulation results. Section 4 follows with a presentation of the verification technique. Section 5 discusses a case study and Sect. 6 concludes.

2   Background

Co-simulation is a technique enabling global simulation of a system consisting of multiple black-box SUs. An SU has its own solver that calculates the behavior trace of the dynamical system it represents. A dynamical system is a function from time and space into some often multi-dimensional and continuous space. Examples include population growth, water flow, and pendulums. The system interacts with the environment through inputs and outputs [9,17].

2.1 Simulation Units

SUs can be coupled through their inputs and outputs, indicating that the state of one SU is reliant on the state of another SU at all times - known as a coupling restriction. However, in practice, the coupling restrictions can only be satisfied at certain points in time, referred to as communication points. Furthermore, each SU makes assumptions about the evolution of the input values between the communication points, which can cause accumulable errors in the co-simulation [2].

A scenario is simulated using an orchestrator - an algorithm - that computes the behavior trace of all SUs trying to satisfy their coupling restrictions by exchanging values. The orchestrator's goal is to find the communication points that minimize the error introduced in the co-simulation and to ensure that the SUs move in lockstep. Studies [10–12,19,21] have shown that optimal communication points depend on the implementation of the SUs.

Definition 1 (Simulation Unit). *An SU with identifier c is represented by the tuple*

$$\langle S_c, U_c, Y_c, \mathsf{set}_c, \mathsf{get}_c, \mathsf{step}_c \rangle,$$

where:

- *S_c represents the state space.*
- *U_c and Y_c the set of input and output variables, respectively.*
- *$\mathsf{set}_c : S_c \times U_c \times \mathcal{V}_{\mathcal{E}} \to S_c$ and $\mathsf{get}_c : S_c \times Y_c \to \mathcal{V}_{\mathcal{E}}$ are functions to set the inputs and get the outputs, respectively (we abstract the set of values exchanged between input/output variables as $\mathcal{V}_{\mathcal{E}}$. The type of this set is the tuple $\langle t, \mathcal{V} \rangle$, where $\mathcal{V}$ denotes the value obtained at a given output port and $t : \mathbb{R}_{\geq 0}$ denotes the timestamp of c when the value was obtained by an action respecting the contracts).*
- *$\mathsf{step}_c : S_c \times \mathbb{R}_{>0} \to S_c \times \mathbb{R}_{>0}$ is a function that instructs the SU to compute its state after a given time duration. If an SU is in state $s_c^{(t)}$ at time t, $(s_c^{(t+h)}, h) = \mathsf{step}_c(s_c^{(t)}, H)$ approximates the state $s_c^{(t+h)}$ of the corresponding model at time $t + h$, where $h \leq H$.*

Definition 1 is inspired by [5,13] and represents a symbolic version of an SU. The state of SU A at time t is denoted $s_A^{(t)}$. We assume the last value set on an input/output port can be inspected, for example, the value of input u_x could be $u_x = \langle t, v_x \rangle$, where t is the timestamp when the value v_x set on u_x was obtained. The function step_c returns a step size because some SUs implement error estimation and may conclude that taking a step size of H will result in an intolerable error meaning the SU takes a smaller step than planned.

Definition 2 (Scenario). *A scenario is a structure* $\langle C, L, M, F, R, D \rangle$ *where each identifier* $c \in C$ *is associated with an SU, as defined in Definition 1, and* $L(u) = y$ *means that the output* y *is connected to input* u. *Let* $U = \bigcup_{c \in C} U_c$ *and* $Y = \bigcup_{c \in C} Y_c$, *then* $L : U \to Y$. $M \subseteq C$ *denotes the SUs that implement error estimation. The set of reactive components,* $R = \bigcup_{c \in C} R_c$, *where* $R_c(u_c) = true$ *means the function* $\mathtt{step}_c$ *assumes that the input* u_c *comes from an SU that has advanced forward relative to SU* c. *The set of delayed components,* $D = \bigcup_{c \in C} \neg R_c$, *where* $R_c(u_c) = false$ *means the function* $\mathtt{step}_c$ *assumes that the input* u_c *comes from an SU that is at the same time as SU* c. *Finally, the set of feed-through components,* $F = \bigcup_{c \in C} F_c$, *where the input* $u_c \in U_c$ *feeds through to output* $y_c \in Y_c$, *that is,* $(u_c, y_c) \in F_c$, *when there exists* $v_1, v_2 \in \mathcal{V_E}$ *and* $s_c \in S_c$, *such that* $\mathtt{get}_c(\mathtt{set}_c(s_c, u_c, v_1), y_c) \neq \mathtt{get}_c(\mathtt{set}_c(s_c, u_c, v_2), y_c)$.

The syntax in Fig. 1 is used to graphically present co-simulation scenarios. The couplings of SUs and feedthrough can introduce algebraic loops like the one seen in the scenario in Fig. 2a: The port variables in that scenario form a cyclic dependency, requiring that all their values are being set at the same time. The set of port variables involved in algebraic loops are the port variables of the non-trivial SCCs in the step operation graph, constructed based on Definition 15 in [13]. The set $algebraic_S$ denotes such variables in scenario S:

$$algebraic_S \triangleq \{s \mid \text{for each } s \in SCCs \land s \in U \cup Y\},$$

where $SCCs$: is the flatten set of all nontrivial SCCs in S.

The input variables involved in an algebraic loop in the scenario S are:

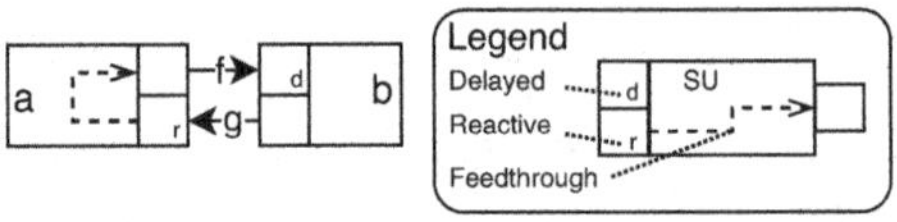

Fig. 1. A simple co-simulation scenario ($S1$).

$$U_{algebraic_S} \triangleq algebraic_S \cap U \tag{1}$$

Using the given definition of a scenario, we call a co-simulation scenario either simple or complex.

Definition 3. *A scenario* S *is simple if* $M = \emptyset \land algebraic_S = \emptyset$.

A scenario is complex if it is not simple. Using Definition 3 we conclude that the scenario ($S1$) in Fig. 1 is simple because $algebraic_{S1} = \emptyset$ and none of the SUs implement error estimation ($M_{S1} = \emptyset$). The scenario ($S2$) in Fig. 2a is complex since $algebraic_{S2} = \{u_f, u_g, y_f, y_g\}$ meaning that all variables are a part of a cyclic dependency that should be solved using a fixed point. The scenario ($S3$) in Fig. 2b is also complex because SU C implements error estimation ($M_{S2} = \{C\}$) and therefore can perform step rejection. Step rejection requires special attention since the orchestrator should backtrack the simulation and restart the simulation with a smaller step in case of a step rejection.

The reason for distinguishing between simple and complex scenarios is that the simulation strategy depends on the scenario type. This is treated in more

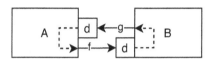

(a) Scenario $S2$ with an algebraic loop.

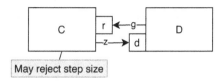

(b) Scenario $S3$ needs step negotiation.

Fig. 2. Complex co-simulation scenarios.

detail later in the paper. Next, we give a brief presentation of the contracts from [9] before describing how they can be used to verify a co-simulation algorithm.

The contracts are described as preconditions of the SU-actions `get`, `set` and `step`. It should be pointed out that each input and output has a timestamp referring to when it was last successfully activated by an action.

Definition 4 (Get Action). *The precondition of* $\mathtt{get}_c(s_c^{(t)}, y_c)$ *is:*
$\forall (u_\_, y_c) \in F_c \implies u_\_ = \langle t_h, \_\rangle \wedge t_h = t.$
Informally saying that all inputs that feeds through to y_c *should be set. This criterion is denoted as the predicate:* $\mathtt{preGet}_c : S_c \times Y_c \to \mathbb{B}.$

Definition 5 (Set Action). *The precondition of* $\mathtt{set}_c(s_c^{(t)}, u_c, v)$ *depends on the contract of the input:*

- *If* $u_c \in R$ *then the operation is valid if* $v = \langle t_h, \_\rangle$, *where* $t_h = t + H$
- *If* $u_c \in D$ *then the operation is valid if* $v = \langle t_h, \_\rangle$, *where* $t_h = t.$

This informally says that the value set on u_c *should be obtained at a meaningful point in time dictated by the input contract. We denote this as the predicate:* $\mathtt{preSet}_c : S_c \times U_c \times \mathcal{V}_{\mathcal{E}} \to \mathbb{B}.$

The criterion on a set-action will first have an effect when the SU is stepped. However, we found that it was easier to catch and correct an incorrect algorithm by moving this criterion to the set-action.

Definition 6 (Step Computation). *The precondition of* $\mathtt{step}_c(s_c^{(t)}, H)$ *is satisfied if all the following conditions are fulfilled:*

- $\forall u_c \in U_c . u_c \in D \implies u_c = \langle t_h, \_\rangle \wedge t_h = t.$
- $\forall u_c \in U_c . u_c \in R \implies u_c = \langle t_h, \_\rangle \wedge t_h = t + H.$

Informally, this is that all inputs should set with a new value since the last time the SU was stepped. This is denoted as the predicate: $\mathtt{preStep}_c : S_c \times \mathbb{R}_{>0} \to \mathbb{B}.$

Definition 7 (Preconditions of a Scenario). *The set of all preconditions Pre of a scenario is the union of the preconditions for each SU* $c \in C$:

$$Pre = \bigcup_{c \in C} \left\{ \bigcup_{i \in U_C} \mathtt{preSet}_c(\_, u_i, \_), \bigcup_{i \in Y_C} \mathtt{preGet}_c(\_, y_i), \mathtt{preStep}_c \right\} \quad (2)$$

The FMI-standard [4] also describes some contracts on the state-changing function. The implementation in UPPAAL enforces them, but they are not treated in this paper.

2.2 Co-simulation Algorithms

A scenario is simulated by a co-simulation algorithm that consists of state-changing functions, an initialization procedure, and a co-simulation step. This work concentrates on the co-simulation step, which we refer to as the algorithm throughout the paper. The other aspects of a co-simulation algorithm can trivially be derived from the method.

The purpose of the co-simulation step is to move all SUs C, and all inputs and outputs $(U \cup Y)$, from the initial times t to some future time $t + H$, where $H > 0$. We use function $\texttt{ftime} : S_C \to \mathbb{R}_{\geq 0}$ to obtain the current timestamp of an SU. This makes it possible to define the Hoare-triple of the co-simulation step P:

$$Hoare(P) \triangleq \{ \forall v \in U \cup Y. v = \langle t, \_ \rangle \wedge \forall c \in C. \texttt{ftime}(s_c^{(t)}) = t \} \quad P$$
$$\{ \forall v \in U \cup Y. v = \langle t + H, \_ \rangle \wedge \forall c \in C. \texttt{ftime}(s_c^{(t+H)}) = t + H \}$$

A co-simulation step P is a sequence of instructions using the SU's functions $\texttt{set}_c$, $\texttt{get}_c$, and $\texttt{step}_c$. Each index i of the sequence $P[i]$ represents an action in the algorithm, for example, if P is the co-simulation step in Algorithm 1 $P[0] = \texttt{step}_A(s_A^{(0)}, \_)$. Figure 3 shows three different co-simulation steps of the scenario in Fig. 1.

Algorithm 1	Algorithm 2	Algorithm 3
1: $(s_A^{(H)}, H) \leftarrow \texttt{step}_A(s_A^{(0)}, H)$	1: $(s_B^{(H)}, H) \leftarrow \texttt{step}_B(s_B^{(0)}, H)$	1: $(s_B^{(H)}, H) \leftarrow \texttt{step}_B(s_B^{(0)}, H)$
2: $(s_B^{(H)}, H) \leftarrow \texttt{step}_B(s_B^{(0)}, H)$	2: $(s_A^{(H)}, H) \leftarrow \texttt{step}_A(s_A^{(0)}, H)$	2: $g_v \leftarrow \texttt{get}_B(s_B^{(H)}, y_g)$
3: $f_v \leftarrow \texttt{get}_A(s_A^{(H)}, y_f)$	3: $g_v \leftarrow \texttt{get}_B(s_B^{(H)}, y_g)$	3: $s_A^{(0)} \leftarrow \texttt{set}_A(s_A^{(0)}, u_g, g_v)$
4: $g_v \leftarrow \texttt{get}_B(s_B^{(H)}, y_g)$	4: $s_A^{(H)} \leftarrow \texttt{set}_A(s_A^{(H)}, u_g, g_v)$	4: $f_v \leftarrow \texttt{get}_A(s_A^{(0)}, y_f)$
5: $s_B^{(H)} \leftarrow \texttt{set}_B(s_B^{(s)}, u_f, f_v)$	5: $f_v \leftarrow \texttt{get}_A(s_A^{(H)}, y_f)$	5: $s_B^{(H)} \leftarrow \texttt{set}_B(s_B^{(H)}, u_f, f_v)$
6: $s_A^{(H)} \leftarrow \texttt{set}_A(s_A^{(H)}, u_g, g_v)$	6: $s_B^{(H)} \leftarrow \texttt{set}_B(s_B^{(H)}, u_f, f_v)$	6: $(s_A^{(H)}, H) \leftarrow \texttt{step}_A(s_A^{(0)}, H)$

Fig. 3. Three algorithms conforming to the FMI standard (version 2.0) of the scenario in Fig. 1.

Although the three algorithms in Fig. 3 consist of the same actions, they are not equivalent, and simulating with one algorithm instead of one of the others could drastically change the co-simulation result as shown in [13]. They showed that by obeying the contracts, the scenario will be simulated correctly. We assume that the contracts in the scenario are constant through the simulation, which is the case for most commercially used SUs. At the end of Sect. 2.3, we show which of these algorithms is correct.

A co-simulation step P is executed using a configuration c. The configuration $c \triangleq \langle H, guess \rangle$ consists of the parameters of the co-simulation step P. $H \in \mathbb{R}_{>0}$ defines the step size, and $guess : U_{algebraic} \rightarrow \mathcal{V}_{\mathcal{E}}$ is a total function linking all inputs in $U_{algebraic}$ to a guess that tries to satisfy the algebraic loops. Using the example from Algorithm 1, the action at index 0 in P applied with the configuration $\langle 1, \_ \rangle$ is: $P[0](c) = \texttt{step}_A(s_A^{(0)}, 1)$. The configuration defines the step size (1) of the step-action.

The set *Configurations* denotes all the possible configurations of the co-simulation step for a given scenario. The execution of a co-simulation step P is the execution of each action in P. We define such execution of P using configuration c as:

$$P(c) \triangleq \text{for each } i \in dom(P). \, P[i](c) \tag{3}$$

An execution of $P(c_j)$ yields another configuration $c_{j+1} \in$ *Configurations* where $P(c_j) = c_{j+1}$. The configuration $c_{j+1} : \langle H_1, guess_1 \rangle$ is obtained from the algorithm P and configuration $c_j : \langle H, guess \rangle$ by updating H_1 to the smallest step accepted by an SU during the execution of $P(c_j)$. And the function $guess_1$ has the same domain as $guess$, but the range is updated to the new value of the output coupled to the associated input in the domain of $guess$ after executing $P(c_j)$.

$$guess_{j+1}(u) = value(u, P(c_j)) \text{ and } H_1 = minStep(P(c_j)) \tag{4}$$

The execution of a configuration $c : \langle H, guess \rangle$ has converged if all SUs accept the step H, and all algebraic loops are stabilized (all values in the range of $guess$ are fixed-points). The domain of $guess$ is all the inputs in $U_{algebraic}$ for the scenario; this means that all configurations of the same scenario have the same domain.

Definition 8. *Two configurations of the same scenario S $c_j : \langle H_1, guess_1 \rangle \in$ Configurations and $c_{j+1} : \langle H_2, guess_2 \rangle \in$ Configurations are convergent if:*

$$c_j \approx c_{j+1} \triangleq H_1 = H_2 \wedge (\forall i \in dom(guess). \, guess_1[i] \approx guess_2[i])$$

Two values $v1_E : (v_1, t_1)$ and $v2_E : (v_2, t_2)$ of type $\mathcal{V}_{\mathcal{E}}$ converge if:

$$v1_E \approx v2_E \triangleq |\, v_1 - v_2 \,| \leq \epsilon \wedge t_1 = t_2 \tag{5}$$

Formally an execution of a co-simulation step P of a configuration c_j is stable or has converged if $P(c_j) = c_{j+1} \implies c_j \approx c_{j+1}$.

A complex scenario is a scenario where not all configurations are stable. Such a scenario can only be correctly simulated by an algorithm P if a convergent configuration exists:

$$\exists c \in \textit{Configurations}, \exists j \in \mathbb{N}. \, P(c_j) = c_{j+1} \implies c_j \approx c_{j+1} \tag{6}$$

Some measures should be taken to handle cases where no convergent configuration exists.

2.3   Correct Co-simulation Algorithms

To optimally simulate a co-simulation scenario using an algorithm P requires more than a convergent configuration c. The algorithm P should also successfully satisfy all the preconditions/contracts. To describe this, we introduce the sequence $\mathcal{C}$, which is a permutation of the set Pre (cf. Definition 7). The sequence $\mathcal{C}$ is constructed by a function $\mathcal{C} = contracts(P, Pre)$ that for each action in P finds the corresponding precondition $pre \in Pre$ and adds it to $\mathcal{C}$ such that for an arbitrary index i in P, $\mathcal{C}[i]$ is the precondition of the action $P[i]$.

If an action at index i in P satisfies its precondition $\mathcal{C}[i]$ using the configuration c, it is denoted as:

$$P[i](c) \models \mathcal{C}[i] \tag{7}$$

A co-simulation step P using a configuration c satisfies $\mathcal{C}$ if all actions satisfy its precondition.

$$P(c) \models \mathcal{C} \triangleq \forall i \in dom(P).\, P[i](c) \models \mathcal{C}[i] \tag{8}$$

$P(c) \models \mathcal{C}$ means the algorithm respects the scenario's contracts. Based on previous studies it is well-known that a non-convergent configuration c does not respect all the contracts:

$$c_j \nsim c_{j+1} \implies P(c_j) \nvDash \mathcal{C} \tag{9}$$

Therefore we only check the contracts of the scenario if the current configuration is convergent. We can now describe what it means for an algorithm to be correct for a given scenario in the following Hoare triple.

Definition 9. *An algorithm P and configuration $c : \langle H, \_\rangle$ is correct if:*

$$P(c) \models \mathcal{C} \;\; \wedge \;\; \{\forall v \in U \cup Y.\, v = \langle t, \_\rangle \wedge \forall c \in C.\, \mathtt{ftime}(s_c^{(t)}) = t\} \;\; P(c)$$
$$\{\forall v \in U \cup Y.\, v = \langle t + H, \_\rangle \wedge \forall c \in C.\, \mathtt{ftime}(s_c^{(t+H)}) = t + H\}$$

Meaning all preconditions are satisfied and all SUs and inputs have moved from time t to time $t + H$ through the execution of $P(c)$.

Using Definition 9 we conclude that Algorithm 3 is correct while the others are incorrect since they break one or more of the defined preconditions. Algorithm 1 and 2 violate the precondition of $\mathtt{step}_b$ on line 2 by stepping it without having provided SU b with a value on the reactive input f. These definitions form the basis for describing the approach and implementation used to verify co-simulation algorithms in this work.

3   Related Work

The study of semantics and verification of co-simulation algorithms is presented in [5,9,13]. The paper [13] describes a formalization of an FMI-based co-simulation scenario where several correctness criteria are placed on the co-simulation algorithm to generate and verify a co-simulation algorithm. This paper extends their work by treating co-simulation scenarios subject to algebraic loops and adaptive steps. Thule et al. [22] studied how a co-simulation scenario's characteristics can be used to choose the correct simulation strategy for a given co-simulation algorithm. In [14], algorithms of complex scenarios are described, but this paper lacks the feature to verify the correctness of algorithms for complex scenarios.

Broman et al. describe in [5] an approach to achieve deterministic co-simulation results by placing constraints on the co-simulation scenario to avoid algebraic loops. They also propose a generic master algorithm for handling step negotiation. However, such generic algorithms do not consider other constraints on the SUs like reactive inputs or algebraic loops. This paper deals with all these constraints.

Formal methods have previously been successfully used in the area of co-simulation [1,6,23]. Amálio et al. [1] study how connections between simulation units can be formalized. They investigate how different formal tools can detect algebraic loops to obtain a deterministic co-simulation result. Cavalcanti et al. [6] claim to provide the first behavioral semantics of FMI. The paper shows how to prove essential properties of master algorithms, like termination and determinism. It also shows that the example provided in the FMI standard is not a valid algorithm. The paper [23] by Zeyda et al. formalizes models and proofs about co-simulation in Isabelle/UTP, illustrated by an industrial case study from the railway sector. However, their approach does not cover complex scenarios, unlike ours.

Nyman et al. in [16] examine how UPPAAL can analyze controller-based systems with FMUs and a master algorithm modeled in UPPAAL. UPPAAL was used to verify the properties of the controller used in the co-simulation. Palmieri et al. in [20] have used UPPAAL to provide sound guarantees on the interleaving between a graphical user interface and a generic FMI master algorithm. Our approach is more generic and relies on a parameterized template approach that can be applied to arbitrary co-simulation scenarios subject to both step negotiation and algebraic loops.

4   Verifying Complex Co-simulation Algorithms

This section describes our approach for verifying that a co-simulation algorithm respects the contracts of the scenario. The paper focuses on complex scenarios since the approach trivially covers simple scenarios. The section starts with an introduction of the UPPAAL-implementation. This is followed by some concrete examples of the approach using the scenarios in Figs. 2b and 8b.

4.1   Verifying an Algorithm Using UPPAAL

The approach is implemented in UPPAAL. A co-simulation is formalized as a collection of timed automata (TA) that formally describe a co-simulation as an orchestrator and some SUs. Two extra UPPAAL-templates are introduced to verify algorithms of complex scenarios by performing the search for a correct configuration. The structure of the UPPAAL model is fixed, however a translator (available online[1]) generates a unique model for each scenario and algorithm. The scenario and algorithm are expressed in a high-level domain-specific language similar to the algorithms in the paper. The tool can translate and verify all algorithms described by the grammar in Fig. 4. The tool checks both initialization procedures and co-simulation steps, but we only show the grammar of the co-simulation step due to space limitations.

⟨*cosim-step*⟩ ::= '['⟨*cosim-action*⟩*']'

⟨*SU-action*⟩ ::= ⟨*get : SU.Port*⟩ | ⟨*set: SU.Port*⟩ | ⟨*step: SU*⟩ | ⟨*restore-state: SU*⟩ |
        ⟨*save-state: SU*⟩

⟨*SU-step-action*⟩ ::= ⟨*SU-action*⟩ | '{' ⟨*algebraic*⟩ '}'

⟨*cosim-action*⟩ ::= ⟨*SU-action*⟩ | '{' ⟨*step-loop*⟩ '}' | '{' ⟨*algebraic*⟩ '}'

⟨*step-loop*⟩ ::= 'until-step-accept:' '['SU*']'
        'iterate:' '['⟨*SU-step-action*⟩*']'
        'if-retry-needed:' '['⟨*restore-state: SU*⟩*]'

⟨*algebraic*⟩ ::= 'until-converged:' '['SU.Port*']'
        'iterate:' '['⟨*SU-action*⟩*']'
        'if-retry-needed:' '['⟨*restore-state: SU*⟩*]'

Fig. 4. BNF Grammar for the specification of a co-simulation step

Notice, the tool does not allow nested fixed-point iteration procedures or step-negotiation inside a nested statement (step-loop or algebraic-loop). This is because the authors do not know any scenarios that such an algorithm should simulate. The following section explains the ideas behind the different UPPAAL-templates before describing how the verification of the algorithm is performed in UPPAAL.

The Interpreter orchestrates the behavior of the SUs by interpreting the supplied algorithm. It is responsible for executing the orchestration algorithm from *Instantiation* to *Termination*. A correct algorithm ensures that the Interpreter reaches the *Termination* state while an incorrect hits a deadlock. The Interpreter works deterministically by systematically picking an action of the algorithm and delegate it to one of the other automata using channel synchronization and shared variables.

---

[1] https://github.com/INTO-CPS-Association/Scenario-Verifier.

The preconditions described in Definitions 4 to 6 are encoded in UPPAAL as invariant functions of the states in the SU-template as shown in Fig. 5 by the function `preSet`, `preGet` and `preDostep`. The SU-template describes the interface (see Definition 1) and life-cycle of an SU. The values exchanged between the SUs are of the type $\mathcal{V}_\mathcal{E}$ (a status and a timestamp). Thus, the design contains enough information to check the contracts. However, nothing can be said about the numerical aspect of the co-simulation.

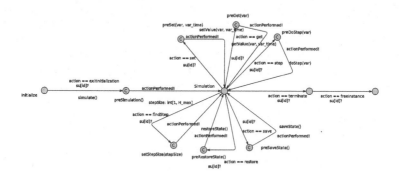

Fig. 5. Model of an SU in UPPAAL.

A violation of a guard or an invariant function results in a deadlock. A deadlock indicates that the algorithm either breaks a precondition or is not complete. A correct algorithm does not deadlock and reaches the state "Terminated", which means that all preconditions/contracts were satisfied and that the algorithm is complete. A complete algorithm correctly instantiates and informs all SUs that the simulation has ended. The automata in UPPAAL are designed, so all transitions are guarded except one identity transition in the trap state "Terminated" in the Interpreter-template. This ensures that all violations of the contracts result in a deadlock; furthermore, no deadlock can occur if the state "Terminated" is reached.

We
define the two CTL-formulas: $A\square$ not deadlock and $A\lozenge MasterA.Terminated$ for UPPAAL to verify. The first formula ensures that UPPAAL finds no deadlock. The second formula ensures that the Interpreter always reaches the state "Terminated", implying that the co-simulation is entirely executed and is not trapped into an infinite loop, which is not considered by the previous formula. Since the end time $(t + H$, where $H > 0)$ of the simulation is greater than the start time (t), it can be concluded that at least one co-simulation step was successfully executed/checked. Moreover, since the contracts are constant over time, it can be concluded using induction that all future/other steps also satisfy these contracts. This is the essential argument for describing how the tool verifies that an algorithm is correct concerning Definition 9.

The method is clarified through a couple of examples. First, looking back at the incorrect Algorithms 1 and 2, we can see that they violate both of the CTL-formulas since the broken precondition on line 2 is caught by the guard `preDostep` and results in a deadlock. Nevertheless, on the other hand, Algorithms 3 satisfies both CTL-formulas, and therefore also satisfies Definition 9.

4.2   Verifying Complex Simulation Scenarios in UPPAAL

Complex scenarios are, as previously described, simulated by an algorithm P that iteratively searches for a correct configuration, not violating any of the actions' preconditions. However, as described by Eq. (9) all unsuccessful search attempts violate some of the preconditions. Therefore, the implementation in UPPAAL tolerates such violations until a correct configuration is identified.

The approach is to temporarily turn off the preconditions for complex scenarios until a correct/convergent configuration is found (see Definition 8). Then, in between unsuccessful attempts, the co-simulation is backtracked, and a new search attempt is initiated where the configuration is updated as described in Sect. 2.2.

If the Interpreter finds a correct configuration, it backtracks the simulation, turns on the preconditions, and runs an extra iteration of the routine while checking the preconditions to ensure that the algorithm and configuration respect the contracts. To avoid state-space explosion and ensure termination, the number of search attempts is bounded. Thus, if the algorithm does not manage to find a correct configuration within the bound, the algorithm is considered incorrect. Since the simulation depends on the nature of the scenario, the next section is split to describe two different kinds of complex scenarios - step negotiation and algebraic loops.

Verifying a Step Negotiation Procedure.   Step negotiation is a mechanism for the SUs to agree on the step size. The procedure iteratively searches for a step using a sequence of SU-actions in each iteration. The step size is shrunken between unsuccessful iterations. The step negotiation for the scenario in Fig. 2b is presented in Algorithm 4. UPPAAL verifies that a common step can be found using a given algorithm. Furthermore, it ensures that all preconditions of the actions are satisfied using the found step.

UPPAAL first tries to establish a proper step without considering the contracts. UPPAAL confirms this by transforming the supplied algorithm to a similar one that initially turns off the preconditions while it searches for a step. The transformation is shown from the original Algorithm 4 to the modified Algorithm 5 that UPPAAL checks. The preconditions are disabled to circumvent the model from deadlocking on unsuccessful search attempts. For example, if SU C is not capable of performing a step of the same size as SU D, this would break the preconditions of $step_D$ in line 6 in Algorithm 4. However, violations are tolerated until the SUs agree on a step due to the backtracking. If a correct step is identified, the preconditions are turned back on (see line 16) and an extra iteration of the procedure is performed to verify that all contracts are respected. If a correct step is not establish within N-tries, the algorithm is declared incorrect, and the verification aborts (line 20). UPPAAL non-deterministically picks a maximal positive step for each SU in M to introduce the non-determinism of a step negotiation. We assume an SU accepts any step smaller or equal to its maximal step.

Algorithm 4 Step negotiation procedure of scenario in Fig. 2b.

1: $SaveSUs$ ▷ Save the SUs
2: **while** $!Step\_found$ **do**   ▷ Step negotiation
3:    $(s_D^{(s+h_D)}, h_D) \leftarrow \mathbf{step}_D(s_D^{(s)}, h)$
4:    $g_v \leftarrow \mathbf{get}_D(s_D^{(s+h_D)}, y_g)$
5:    $s_C^{(s)} \leftarrow \mathbf{set}_C(s_C^{(s)}, u_G, G_v)$
6:    $(s_C^{(s+h_C)}, h_C) \leftarrow \mathbf{step}_C(s_C^{(s)}, h_D)$
7:    $h \leftarrow min(h_C, h_D)$ ▷ Minimum step
8:    $Step\_found \leftarrow h == h_C \wedge h == h_D$
9:    **if** $!Step\_found$ **then**   ▷ Restore SUs
10:     RestoreSUs
11:    **end if**
12: **end while**

Algorithm 5 Modified Step negotiation procedure of scenario in Fig. 2b.

1: $SaveSUs$ ▷ Save the SUs
2: $TurnPreconditionsOff()$
3: $(I, isExtra) \leftarrow (0, false)$
4: **while** $!Step\_found$ **do**
5:    Line 3-8 from Algorithm 4
6:    **if** $!Step\_found$ **then**
7:     $I \leftarrow I + 1$
8:    **else**   ▷ Correct step found
9:     **if** $!isExtra$ **then**   ▷ Check contracts
10:      $TurnPreconditionsOn()$
11:      $isExtra \leftarrow true$
12:     **else**
13:      **return**$(true)$ ▷ Correct algorithm
14:     **end if**
15:    **end if**
16:    **if** $I == N$ **then**   ▷ Max attempt
17:     **return**$(false)$ ▷ Invalid algorithm
18:    **end if**
19:    $RestoreSUs$
20: **end while**

Verifying a Fixed-Point Procedure. The fixed-point procedure solves algebraic loops by finding fixed-points on the involved ports. Similar to step negotiation, a fixed-point procedure is an iterative search for a correct configuration. A fixed-point iteration procedure is shown in Algorithm 6.

The UPPAAL-model ensures the correctness of scenarios with algebraic loops that a fixed-point can be obtained using the algorithm without violating a single contract. However, the numerical aspect of finding a fixed-point is not included in our model since we restrict to a symbolic abstraction. However, the tool is still capable of checking that the contracts of the SUs are respected.

4.3 Debugging Algorithm Errors

When an algorithm is deemed incorrect by UPPAAL, the user needs to determine why. A model-checker (like UPPAAL) provides counter-examples. However, these are often hard to understand for a normal user. Therefore, a tool has been created to visualize the counter-example as an animation. The animation shows the violation found by UPPAAL. The animation shows which actions have been applied and which actions are enabled at any given time of the simulation. An example of the animation is shown in Fig. 8a.

5 Validation

The tool has been used to verify various algorithms and generate counter-examples for incorrect ones. The examples are publicly available[2]. The tested

---

[2] https://github.com/SimplisticCode/Co-simulation-Verifier.

scenarios include an industrial scenario from Boeing [11] of 4 SUs and 8 connections[3]. We have also tested it with what we believe to be the most common mistakes when implementing an algorithm to be confident that the tool catches these mistakes. The tests of the tool include abstract scenarios with multiple algebraic loops and more than 50 SUs and over 100 connections.

In this section, we show two examples: the first one, already introduced in Fig. 1, is designed to highlight the numerical errors that can happen when contracts are not satisfied, and the second one showcases an abstract scenario with all types of contracts described in the current manuscript.

5.1   Motivation Example

Our motivation example was introduced in Fig. 1, and its equations are displayed in Fig. 6. To highlight the numerical error caused by a mismatch in contracts, we conducted a series of experiments where the contracts were intentionally violated, i.e.; we applied the wrong algorithm to the contracts used. We studied this effect for multiple parameters' choices and selected two results representing the most common errors, illustrated in Fig. 7. Each plot shows the analytical solution, the correct co-simulation, and the incorrect co-simulation. Naturally, even the correct co-simulation will introduce errors. However, most of the results show an error caused solely by the contract mismatch, as shown on the left-hand side of Fig. 7. However, depending on the parameters and initial conditions of the experiment, some cases show that the mismatch is less important. This makes it very difficult to assess in practice whether some errors are caused by implementation mistakes or caused by the co-simulation discretization, and hence motivates our work. Some work has been carried out in [15] to characterize for which parameter values and initial conditions, the contracts are essential, but this is outside the scope of this paper.

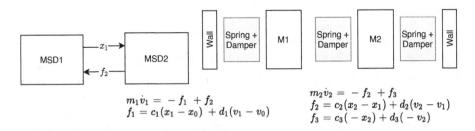

$$m_1 \dot{v}_1 = -f_1 + f_2$$
$$f_1 = c_1(x_1 - x_0) + d_1(v_1 - v_0)$$

$$m_2 \dot{v}_2 = -f_2 + f_3$$
$$f_2 = c_2(x_2 - x_1) + d_2(v_2 - v_1)$$
$$f_3 = c_3(-x_2) + d_3(-v_2)$$

Fig. 6. Structure and equations of motivational example. Legend: x_i, v_i represent the position and velocity, respectively; f_i represents force, c_i, d_i represent stiffness and damping parameters, m_i represents mass.

---

[3] https://github.com/SimplisticCode/Co-simulation-Verifier/blob/master/Scenario/examples/industrial_casestudy.conf.

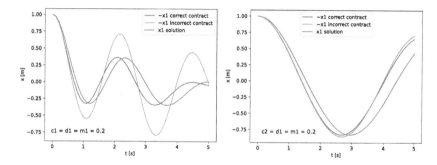

Fig. 7. Example results. Except when indicated in each plot, all parameters have the following default values: $m_i = c_i = 1$ and $d_i = 0$. The step used in the co-simulation is 0.1.

5.2 Complex Scenario

The scenario introduced here contains an algebraic loop between some SUs that may reject a step. The scenario is shown in Fig. 8b, and the algorithm of a valid co-simulation step is shown in Algorithm 6. The scenario is simulated using a

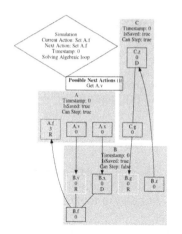

(a) Wrong algorithm of Fig. 8b highlighted by the animation.

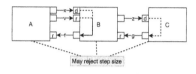

(b) Case study scenario - Loop within Loop.

Algorithm 6 Co-simulation Step of Fixed-point Iteration inside Step finding procedure.

1: Save SUs   ▷ Save all 3 SUs
2: $h \leftarrow H_{max}$
3: **while** !step_found **do**   ▷ Step negotiation
4:    **while** !converged **do**   ▷ FP procedure
5:       $s_A^{(s)} \leftarrow \mathsf{set}_A(s_A^{(s)}, u_f, f_v)$
6:       $s_B^{(s)} \leftarrow \mathsf{set}_B(s_B^{(s)}, [u_v, u_g], [v_v, g_v])$
7:       $(s_C^{(s+h_C)}, h_C), \leftarrow \mathsf{step}_C(s_C^{(s)}, h)$
8:       $(s_B^{(s+h_B)}, h_B), \leftarrow \mathsf{step}_B(s_B^{(s)}, h)$
9:       $(s_A^{(s+h_A)}, h_A), \leftarrow \mathsf{step}_A(s_A^{(s)}, h)$
10:      $[v_a, x_v] \leftarrow \mathsf{get}_A(s_A^{(s+h_A)}, [y_v, y_x])$
11:      $z_v \leftarrow \mathsf{get}_B(s_B^{(s+h_B)}, y_z)$
12:      $s_C^{(s+h_C)} \leftarrow \mathsf{set}_C(s_C^{(s+h_C)}, u_z, z_v)$
13:      $g_a \leftarrow \mathsf{get}_C(s_C^{(s+h_C)}, y_g)$
14:      $s_B^{(s+h_B)} \leftarrow \mathsf{set}_B(s_B^{(s+h_B)}, u_x, x_v)$
15:      $f_a \leftarrow \mathsf{get}_B(s_B^{(s+h_B)}, y_F)$
16:      $conv \leftarrow CheckConv((g_a, v_a, f_a), (g_v, v_v, f_v))$
17:      **if** !conv **then**
18:         Restore SUs   ▷ Restore all 3 SUs
19:      **end if**
20:      $(g_v, v_v, f_v) \leftarrow (g_a, v_a, f_a)$
21:    **end while**
22:    $h \leftarrow min(h_A, h_B, h_C)$
23:    $Step\_found \leftarrow h == h_A \wedge h == h_B \wedge h == h_C$
24:    **if** !Step_found **then**
25:       Restore SUs   ▷ Restore all 3 SUs
26:    **end if**
27: **end while**

Fig. 8. Advanced case study scenario (2b) and Algorithm (6). A counter-example is shown in 8a.

master algorithm consisting of a fixed-point iteration for solving the algebraic loop inside the step negotiation procedure like Algorithm 6.

Algorithm 6 is too complex to be analyzed with a simple visual inspection, showing the necessity of the UPPAAL tool created in this paper. The tool can analyze the algorithm in few seconds and has been used several times on intermediate versions of the algorithm to help the authors obtaining the correct version.

6   Concluding Remarks

This work proposed a model-checking approach to verify that an algorithm for an FMI-based co-simulation respects all the implementation contracts of the SUs. The contracts arose from previous work, which demonstrated that imposing them leads to better co-simulation results in the sense that the error introduced is caused only by the numerical discretization (as opposed to hard-to-debug contract mismatches, as Fig. 7 showed). In addition, the new approach can handle complex co-simulation scenarios containing both algebraic loops and step negotiation.

A tool generates a UPPAAL-model from a co-simulation scenario and an algorithm. The tool enables co-simulation practitioners to verify that their co-simulation algorithm is tailored to the scenario. Incorrect algorithms are presented using an animation of the simulation trace to clarify the problems. The approach inspires the work for synthesizing correct orchestration algorithms [14], and they together form the Scenario-Verifier.

Acknowledgements. We would like to thank Stefan Hallerstede, Tomas Kulik, Jalil Boudjadar, and the reviewers for providing valuable input to this paper.

References

1. Amálio, N., Payne, R., Cavalcanti, A., Woodcock, J.: Checking SysML models for co-simulation. In: Ogata, K., Lawford, M., Liu, S. (eds.) ICFEM 2016. LNCS, vol. 10009, pp. 450–465. Springer, Cham (2016). https://doi.org/10.1007/978-3-319-47846-3_28

2. Arnold, M., Clauß, C., Schierz, T.: Error analysis and error estimates for co-simulation in FMI for model exchange and co-simulation v2.0. In: Schöps, S., Bartel, A., Günther, M., ter Maten, E.J.W., Müller, P.C. (eds.) Progress in Differential-Algebraic Equations. DEF, pp. 107–125. Springer, Heidelberg (2014). https://doi.org/10.1007/978-3-662-44926-4_6

3. Behrmann, G., et al.: UPPAAL 4.0. In: Third International Conference on Quantitative Evaluation of Systems (QEST 2006), pp. 125–126 (2006)

4. Blockwitz, T., et al.: Functional mockup interface 2.0: the standard for tool independent exchange of simulation models. In: Proceedings of the 9th International MODELICA Conference, September 3-5, 2012, Munich, Germany. vol. 76, pp. 173–184. Linköping University Electronic Press (2012). https://doi.org/10.3384/ecp12076173

5. Broman, D., et al.: Determinate composition of FMUs for co-simulation. In: Eleventh ACM International Conference on Embedded Software. IEEE Press, Piscataway (2013). Article no. 2
6. Cavalcanti, A., Woodcock, J., Amálio, N.: Behavioural models for FMI co-simulations. In: Sampaio, A., Wang, F. (eds.) ICTAC 2016. LNCS, vol. 9965, pp. 255–273. Springer, Cham (2016). https://doi.org/10.1007/978-3-319-46750-4_15
7. FMI: Functional mock-up interface tools (2014). https://fmi-standard.org/tools/
8. Gomes, C., Broman, D., Vangheluwe, H., Thule, C., Larsen, P.G.: Co-simulation: a survey. ACM Comput. Surv. **51**(3), 49–49 (2018)
9. Gomes, C., Lucio, L., Vangheluwe, H.: Semantics of co-simulation algorithms with simulator contracts. In: 2019 ACM/IEEE 22nd International Conference on Model Driven Engineering Languages and Systems Companion (MODELS-C), pp. 784–789. IEEE (2019)
10. Gomes, C., et al.: Semantic adaptation for FMI co-simulation with hierarchical simulators. SIMULATION **95**(3), 241–269 (2019)
11. Gomes, C., et al.: HintCO - hint-based configuration of co-simulations. In: Proceedings of the 9th International Conference on Simulation and Modeling Methodologies, Technologies and Applications, pp. 57–68. Scitepress - Science and Technology Publications (2019)
12. Gomes, C., Thule, C., Lausdahl, K., Larsen, P.G., Vangheluwe, H.: Demo: stabilization technique in INTO-CPS. In: Mazzara, M., Ober, I., Salaün, G. (eds.) STAF 2018. LNCS, vol. 11176, pp. 45–51. Springer, Cham (2018). https://doi.org/10.1007/978-3-030-04771-9_4
13. Gomes, C., Thule, C., Lúcio, L., Vangheluwe, H., Larsen, P.G.: Generation of co-simulation algorithms subject to simulator contracts. In: Camara, J., Steffen, M. (eds.) SEFM 2019. LNCS, vol. 12226, pp. 34–49. Springer, Cham (2020). https://doi.org/10.1007/978-3-030-57506-9_4
14. Hansen, S.T., Gomes, C., van de Pol, J., Larsen, P.G.: Synthesizing co-simulation algorithms with step negotiation and algebraic loop handling (2021, to appear)
15. Inci, E.O., et al.: The effect and selection of solution sequence in co-simulation. In: The Annual Modeling and Simulation Conference, Virginia, USA (2021, to appear)
16. Jensen, P.G., Larsen, K.G., Legay, A., Nyman, U.: Integrating tools: co-simulation in UPPAAL using FMI-FMU. In: 2017 22nd International Conference on Engineering of Complex Computer Systems (ICECCS), pp. 11–19. IEEE (2017)
17. Kübler, R., Schiehlen, W.: Two methods of simulator coupling. Math. Comput. Model. Dyn. Syst. **6**(2), 93–113 (2000)
18. Lee, E.A.: Cyber physical systems: design challenges. In: 2008 11th IEEE International Symposium on Object and Component-Oriented Real-Time Distributed Computing (ISORC), pp. 363–369 (2008)
19. Oakes, B.J., Gomes, C., Holzinger, F.R., Benedikt, M., Denil, J., Vangheluwe, H.: Hint-based configuration of co-simulations with algebraic loops. In: Obaidat, M.S., Ören, T., Szczerbicka, H. (eds.) SIMULTECH 2019. AISC, vol. 1260, pp. 1–28. Springer, Cham (2021). https://doi.org/10.1007/978-3-030-55867-3_1
20. Palmieri, M., Bernardeschi, C., Masci, P.: A framework for FMI-based co-simulation of human-machine interfaces. Softw. Syst. Model. **19**(3), 601–623 (2020). https://doi.org/10.1007/s10270-019-00754-9
21. Schweizer, B., Li, P., Lu, D.: Explicit and implicit cosimulation methods: stability and convergence analysis for different solver coupling approaches. J. Comput. Nonlinear Dyn. **10**(5), 051007 (2015)

22. Thule, C., Gomes, C., Deantoni, J., Larsen, P.G., Brauer, J., Vangheluwe, H.: Towards the verification of hybrid co-simulation algorithms. In: Mazzara, M., Ober, I., Salaün, G. (eds.) STAF 2018. LNCS, vol. 11176, pp. 5–20. Springer, Cham (2018). https://doi.org/10.1007/978-3-030-04771-9_1
23. Zeyda, F., Ouy, J., Foster, S., Cavalcanti, A.: Formalising cosimulation models. In: Cerone, A., Roveri, M. (eds.) SEFM 2017. LNCS, vol. 10729, pp. 453–468. Springer, Cham (2018). https://doi.org/10.1007/978-3-319-74781-1_31

Automated Verification of Temporal Properties of Ladder Programs

Cláudio Belo Lourenço[1][ID], Denis Cousineau[2][ID], Florian Faissole[2][ID],
Claude Marché[1(✉)][ID], David Mentré[2][ID], and Hiroaki Inoue[3]

[1] Université Paris-Saclay, CNRS, Inria, LMF, 91405 Orsay, France
`Claude.Marche@inria.fr`
[2] Mitsubishi Electric R&D Centre Europe, Rennes, France
[3] Mitsubishi Electric Corporation, Amagasaki, Japan

Abstract. Programmable Logic Controllers (PLCs) are industrial digital computers used as automation controllers in manufacturing processes. The Ladder language is a programming language used to develop PLC software. Our aim is to prove that a given Ladder program conforms to an expected temporal behaviour given as a *timing chart*, describing scenarios of execution. We translate the Ladder code and the timing chart into a program for the Why3 environment, within which the verification proceeds by generating *verification conditions*, to be checked valid using automated theorem provers. The ultimate goal is two-fold: first, by obtaining a complete proof, we can verify the conformance of the Ladder code with respect to the timing chart with a high degree of confidence. Second, when the proof is not fully completed, we obtain a *counterexample*, illustrating a possible execution scenario of the Ladder code which does not conform to the timing chart.

Keywords: Ladder language for programming · PLCs · Timing charts · Formal specification · Deductive verification · Why3 environment

1 Introduction

Programmable Logic Controllers (PLCs) are industrial digital computers used as automation controllers in manufacturing processes, such as assembly lines or robotic devices. PLCs can simulate the hard-wired relays, timers and sequencers they have replaced, via software that expresses the computation of outputs from the values of inputs and internal memory. The Ladder language, also known as Ladder Logic, is a programming language used to develop PLC software. This language uses circuit diagrams of relay logic hardware to represent a PLC program by a graphical diagram. This language was one of the first available for programming PLCs, and is now standardised in the IEC 61131-3 standard [17].

This work has been partially supported by the bilateral contract ProofInUse-MERCE between Inria team Toccata and Mitsubishi Electric R&D Centre Europe, Rennes.

A. Lluch Lafuente and A. Mavridou (Eds.): FMICS 2021, LNCS 12863, pp. 21–38, 2021.
https://doi.org/10.1007/978-3-030-85248-1_2

It is one language among other languages for programming PLCs, and is still widely used and very popular among technicians and electrical engineers.

Because of the widespread usage of PLCs in industry, verifying that a given Ladder program conforms to its expected behaviour is of critical importance. In this work, we consider the description of the expected temporal behaviour under the form of a *timing chart*, describing scenarios of execution. Our approach consists in automatically translating the Ladder code and the timing chart into a program written in the WhyML language, which is the input language of the generic Why3 environment for deductive program verification [6]. In WhyML, expected behaviours of program are expressed using *contracts*, which are annotations expressed in formal logic. The Why3 environment offers tools for checking that the WhyML code conforms to these formal contracts. This verification process is performed using automated theorem provers, so that at the end, if the back-end proof process succeeds, the conformance of the Ladder code with respect to the timing chart is verified with a high degree of confidence. Yet, a complete formal proof is not the only expected feedback from our tool chain: we also want to obtain useful feedback when the proof does not succeed, our long-term goal being to build a tool that would be useful to regular Ladder programmers. More precisely, in such a case of proof failure, we aim at obtaining a *counterexample* which must illustrate a possible execution scenario of the Ladder code which does not conform to the timing chart.

This paper is organised as follows. We start in Sect. 2 by introducing the basics of Ladder programming, and the way their expected temporal behaviours are expressed using timing charts. The translation of Ladder code and timing charts into WhyML programs is described in Sect. 3. Section 4 presents our experiments and their results, both in the case of a complete proof success and in the case of a proof failure, where a counterexample is generated. We discuss related work and future work in Sect. 5. For sake of concision some technical details are omitted, such details are available in an extended research report [4].

2   Introduction to Ladder Programming

A Ladder program (a *diagram)* takes inputs values (*contacts*) that correspond to the fact that physical relays are either wired, not wired, pulsing (rising edge) or downing (falling edge), and other values stored in the internal memory of the PLC (Boolean values, integers, floating-point values, strings, *etc.*). A Ladder program can output Boolean values to the physical relays of the factory (*coils*) or it can call instructions, that may modify the values of the internal memory of the PLC (*devices*). Graphically, contacts are located at the left of the diagram. They can be combined in a serial way (Boolean conjunction) or in a parallel way (disjunction). Coils and instructions are activated when the combination of contacts at their left gives a wired value, and they can also be parallelised (in that case, they are either all activated or all deactivated). A line with contacts, coils and instructions is called a *rung*, and a program is composed of several rungs. Such a Ladder program is executed cyclically in a synchronous way: first inputs are read, then the program is executed and eventually outputs are written. One single execution of the program is called a *scan*.

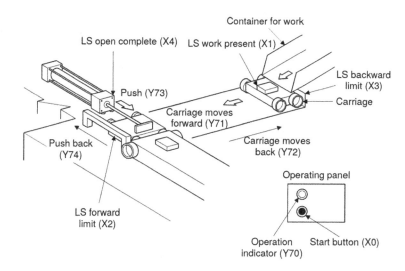

Fig. 1. Carriage line control: system description

Running Example. A rather simple example of a PLC controlling a carriage line is depicted in Fig. 1, with the corresponding Ladder program in Fig. 2. This example comes from a Mitsubishi Electric training manual for programming PLCs [14]. To our knowledge, timing charts are generally used to specify programs of comparable size, *e.g. Function Blocks*, which are kind of library functions that are shipped together with a PLC and a programming environment. We illustrate some principles of Ladder Logic on the first rung of this example: this rung expresses the fact that output Y70 receives the value of the Boolean formula $(X0 \lor Y70) \land (\neg M2)$, *i.e.* if the corresponding physical devices are activated such that the Boolean formula is true, then Y70 is activated, and is deactivated otherwise.

The program also makes use of the Ladder instructions SET, RST and PLS. The SET instruction activates its device argument (either an internal memory device or an output device) when its input is activated, and does nothing otherwise. For instance, in Fig. 2, Y71 is activated when both the common front $(X0 \lor Y70) \land (\neg M2)$ and the internal memory device M1 are activated. The RST instruction is the opposite: the device argument is deactivated when the input is activated. The PLS (pulse) instruction activates its device argument on a rising edge of its input, *i.e.* when the input has just been activated, then it deactivates its device argument on the next scan.

The diagram also uses a timer instruction on a special device T0 which is activated once the timer finishes. When its input is activated, the instruction

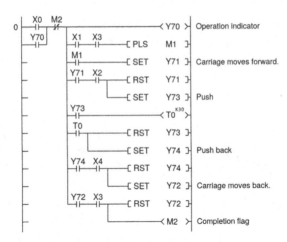

Fig. 2. Carriage line control: ladder program

sets the threshold (here 30) of the timer and increments a counter. After 30 consecutive scans in which both the common front and output Y73 are activated, the device T0 is activated (and it remains activated until the input of the timer instruction is deactivated).

Specification of Expected Temporal Behaviour. Because of its synchronous nature, the language hardly lends itself to exhaustive functional specifications. Since the work made on AutomationML [11] by an industrial and academic consortium, the practice, among PLC designers, is to use the *timing chart* paradigm, which describes the expected temporal behaviour of the PLC for a nominal execution scenario. A timing chart specifies the evolution of outputs over the execution of scans, according to the evolution of inputs. It is made of a succession of *events, i.e.* scans with either changes of inputs that may lead to changes of outputs, or endings of timers that lead to changes of outputs. Events are separated by *stable states, i.e.* arbitrary-length successions of scans in which the values of both inputs and outputs are unchanged.

Figure 3 depicts the timing chart specification of the carriage line control example. Events of the timing chart are depicted as ♯1, ♯2, . . . , ♯11. In the rest of the paper, we use the notation ♯(1 ↪ 2), . . . , ♯(10 ↪ 11) to depict stable states. The initial and final states of the timing chart are respectively depicted by ♯*idle* and ♯*end*. The timing chart of Fig. 3 also contains a fixed-duration sequence of events and stable states (represented by an arrow, between events ♯5 and ♯8), whose duration is 3 s. We call *fixed-duration sequence* the concerned sequence of events and stable states. Typically, the Ladder program is executed periodically every 100 ms, therefore, the fixed-time period of 3 s is made of 30 scans. Here, the given implementation uses the timer device T0 in order to satisfy this aspect of the specification.

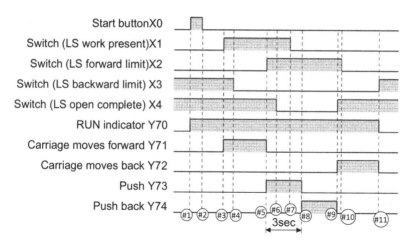

Fig. 3. Timing chart specification for the carriage line control

Our main goal is the verification that a Ladder diagram conforms to such a timing chart specification. A first idea would be to envision the use of deductive verification techniques, in the wake of our previous work on Ladder instruction-level verification [7]. However, not all variables used in the Ladder program of Fig. 2 are addressed by the timing chart. Indeed, internal memory devices (*e.g.* M1 and M2) and timers (*e.g.* T0) are introduced by the developer in order to make the program satisfy its specification, but do not belong to this specification. As an example, in the carriage line control program, the M2 device acts as a termination flag which stops the execution of the PLC as soon as it is activated. There is no doubt that M2 remains false during execution of the timing chart scenario. However, deductive verification would lack this information to check that outputs satisfy their specification. This kind of issue is at the heart of our strategy that is to integrate a method for *inferring loop invariants*.

3   Translation of Ladder Programs to WhyML

Our prototype automatically translates Ladder programs given as XML files and timing charts given as PlantUML [18] files into WhyML programs. After a short introduction to the Why3 environment in Sect. 3.1, we describe in Sect. 3.2 how we translate the Ladder program itself, and in Sect. 3.3 how we use this translation for modeling the successive executions of the program and verifying that it satisfies the given timing chart.

3.1   The Why3 Environment

Why3 is an environment for deductive program verification, providing the language WhyML for specification and programming [6]. A detailed introduction to Why3 is given in our extended report [4]. Among the recent features of Why3 of particular interest for our work are the ability to *generate loop invariants* and to *produce counterexamples* when a proof fails [8]. Indeed, the first of these features had to be improved in order to support our work on Ladder programs, this is a contribution that some of us made to Why3 [4].

```
val b : ref bool
val x : ref int

let toy () : unit
  requires { 0 <= !x <= 10 }
  writes { b, x }
  ensures { not !b }
  ensures { !x <= 200 }
= b := false;
  while (!x < 100) do
    b := (!x < 50);
    if !b then x := !x + 2
          else x := !x + 3;
  done;
  assert { !x >= 75 }
```

```
let set (input : bool)
        (device : ref bool) : unit
  writes  { device }
  ensures { !device ↔
            (input ∨ old !device) }
= if input then device := true
```

(a) Toy example of WhyML code   (b) the SET instruction in WhyML

Fig. 4. Examples of WhyML code

We illustrate those features on a toy WhyML program presented in Fig. 4a. This code involves two global variables, b of type Boolean and x of type integer (a mathematical, unbounded integer in WhyML). The function **toy** takes no arguments, and is equipped with a formal contract involving a pre-condition (keyword **requires**) stating that the value of x on function entry is required to lie between 0 and 10, and two post-conditions (keyword **ensures**) stating respectively that at exit, b is false and that x is smaller than 200. The clause **writes** expresses which global variables are potentially modified by that function. Notice the WhyML syntax for mutable variables, inspired by ML, requiring to write an exclamation mark to access their values. The body of that function is a simple imperative code involving a while loop and a conditional. This code ends by an other kind of formal annotation, namely a code assertion stating that the value of x must be greater or equal to 75 after the loop.

Given such an annotated code, the Why3 core engine generates three *verification conditions* (VCs), corresponding to the assertion and the two post-conditions. When calling provers for attempting to prove these VCs, only the assertion is proved valid: it directly follows from the negation of the loop condition. None of the post-conditions are proved valid, which is expected in the classical setting of deductive verification, because for proving properties about loops one should state appropriate *loop invariants*. These could be added by hand, but to make the process more automatic we rely on the automatic generation of such invariants. We use a technique based on *abstract interpretation*, for which an early prototype existed for Why3 [1], prototype that we extended in particular to support Boolean variables [4]. The generated loop invariant is then as follows:

```
(!b = false ∧ 0 <= !x <= 10) ∨ (!b = true  ∧ 2 <= !x <= 51) ∨
(!b = false ∧ 53 <= !x <= 102)
```

and with this loop invariant, the post-conditions are proved valid.

Assume now that we replace the loop condition with (!x < 300). Still assuming that we ask for generation of a loop invariant, all generated VCs are proved except the second post-condition. For this VC, Why3 proposes a *counterexample* where the values of b and x at loop exit are respectively false and 300. Indeed, these values satisfy the loop invariant, but with those the post-condition !x <= 200 is not valid.

3.2   Translation of Ladder Codes

The translation relies on models of Ladder instructions as WhyML functions, defined by some of the authors in a previous work [7]. For example, Fig. 4b depicts the function that corresponds to the SET instruction. This function takes two arguments, first the input of the instruction (whether it should be activated or not), and second the device on which it may have an effect. Both the code and the contract of the function state the intended behaviour of the SET function: if the instruction is activated then the considered device is activated (otherwise its value does not change). The WhyML functions modeling RST, PLS, and timer instructions are detailed in the extended research report [4].

Given this formalisation of Ladder instructions, we can now give, in Fig. 5b, the translation of the full Ladder program of Fig. 2. The translation makes use of auxiliary variables f1,...,f8 which corresponds to the common fronts depicted on Fig. 5a.

3.3   The Ladder Loop, and the Encoding of Timing Charts

By definition, timing charts are made of successive events and stable states. Checking that a program conforms to a timing chart means that, under the hypotheses on input values, the values of outputs are correct according to the order of appearance of events and stable states in the timing chart scenario. In addition, fixed-time duration information (timer-related sequence of events) also need to be verified. We propose and implement an automatic process that takes a Ladder diagram and a timing chart specification and returns the corresponding WhyML formalisation.

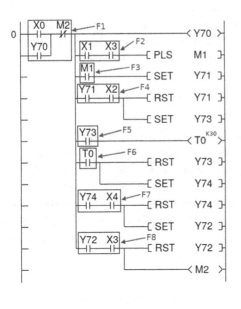

```
let f1 = (!x0 || !y70)
          && (not !m2) in
y70 := f1;
let f2 = !x1 && !x3 in
pls (f1 && f2) m1 cc0;
let f3 = !m1 in
set (f1 && f3) y71;
let f4 = !y71 && !x2 in
rst (f1 && f4) y71;
set (f1 && f4) y73;
let f5 = !y73 in
timer_coil (f1 && f5) t0 30;
let f6 = timer_contact t0 in
rst (f1 && f6) y73;
set (f1 && f6) y74;
let f7 = !y74 && !x4 in
rst (f1 && f7) y74;
set (f1 && f7) y72;
let f8 = !y72 && !x3 in
rst (f1 && f8) y72;
m2 := f1 && f8
```

(a) Ladder code with common fronts   (b) WhyML encoding

Fig. 5. Encoding of one scan of the Ladder program for the carriage line control

Events and Stable States as Loops. The formalisation is made of a succession of *do-while* style loops[1] (except for the initial stable state of the timing chart). The body of each loop corresponds to the WhyML formalisation of one scan of the Ladder program. Each do-while loop corresponds to a pair made of an event (the first iteration *do*) and the following stable state (*while*). The guard of the loop corresponds to the assumptions on inputs, *i.e.* the values taken by the inputs at the corresponding event and during the following stable states. The verification conditions on outputs are modelled as loop invariants: the invariant initialisation corresponds to the event while its preservation corresponds to the stable state.

The initial state of the timing chart (values of devices before the PLC starts) is handled in its own way. Basically, all outputs and internal memory devices are initially deactivated. The initial values of inputs are read at the beginning of the timing chart. The initial state is formalised as a while loop (and not a do-while loop) whose guard corresponds to the values of inputs at the initialisation of the timing chart. Indeed, the initial state of the timing chart is a stable state

---

[1] There are no *do-while* loops in WhyML, we just mean by *do-while* style loop a code piece of the following form with two occurrences of the loop body: "body; while cond do body done".

which does not begin with an event. The invariants to be proved for this loop correspond to the fact that outputs remain deactivated.

The events last during one scan, while stable states have an arbitrary duration and end when the next event is reached, *i.e.* when an input changes or a timer coils. In order to model this behaviour, the body of each loop iteration is enriched with an assignment of the concerned input to a random Boolean value, that may or may not update its value and lead to a new event.

```
< One scan of the Ladder program from Figure 5b >
x0 := randomb();
while (!x0 && not !x1 && not !x2 && !x3 && !x4) do
  invariant { !y70 && not !y71 && not !y72 && not !y73 && not !y74 }
  < One scan of the Ladder program from Figure 5b >
  x0 := randomb();
done
```

Fig. 6. WhyML formalisation of event ♯1 and stable state ♯(1 ↪ 2)

The WhyML code of Fig. 6 gives an example of formalisation of an event. It is for the event ♯1 and the stable state ♯(1 ↪ 2), the latter being terminated when event ♯2 is reached, *i.e.* when x0 is deactivated. The encoding of one scan (from Fig. 5b) is intentionally duplicated. Deductive verification is unfortunately not sufficient to directly prove the invariants on outputs. Indeed, as mentioned in Sect. 2, the specification used to generate the formalisation lacks information on internal memory devices. To bypass this difficulty, we rely on the invariant generation plug-in for Why3 (already presented in Sect. 3.1) to generate additional loop invariants for each while loop of the formalisation. For instance, in each loop of the formalisation, the inference of the invariant `not !m2` would be needed.

Timer-Related Sequences of Events. One of the most technical points of our work concerns the formalisation of fixed-duration sequences, *e.g.* events and stable states from ♯5 to ♯8 in the timing chart of the carriage line control (Fig. 3).

We have to capture the fact that the total duration of this sequence is exactly 3 s. Since timing charts specifications do not make explicit which timer device is used to implement this aspect, we cannot, in the general case, guess which timer device appearing in the code is used for any of the fixed-duration sequences appearing in the timing chart. That is why we introduce a fresh internal counter for each fixed-duration sequence of the timing chart, add the duration constraint in the guard of each loop associated to the concerned stable states and increment the value of that counter at each loop iteration. The timer is incremented accordingly, therefore, the counter is supposed to reflect the `current` value of the timer.

In addition, there are two ways to reach the end of the loops corresponding to intermediate stable states of the fixed-duration sequences: an input change or the

```
< One scan of the Ladder program from Figure 5b >
x4 := randomb();
c1 := !c1 + 1;
while (not !x0 && !x1 && !x2 && not !x3 && !x4 && !c1 < 29) do
    invariant { !y70 && not !y71 && not !y72 && !y73 && not !y74 }
    < One scan of the Ladder program from Figure 5b >
    x4 := randomb();
    c1 := !c1 + 1;
done;
assume { !c1 < 29 }
```

Fig. 7. WhyML formalisation of event ♯5 and stable state ♯(5 ↪ 6)

maximal number of scans being reached by the counter. We have to capture the fact that the termination of intermediate stable states (♯(5 ↪ 6) and ♯(6 ↪ 7) in our example) is due to an input update and not because the maximal number of scans has been reached. To enforce this property, we insert an **assume** clause after the loop end. In our example, we use c1 as a counter associated with the 3 s fixed-duration sequence. As an illustration, we give the shape of the formalisation of event ♯5 and stable state ♯(5 ↪ 6), ending with the deactivation of X4 while the number of elapsed scans of the fixed-duration sequence is not reached yet. The resulting WhyML code is given in Fig. 7. For stable state ♯(7 ↪ 8), *i.e.* the last stable state before the end of the fixed-duration sequence, there is only one way to end the loop (!c1 >= 29) so there is no need for any **assume** clause.

Note that the condition we use is !c1 < 29 and not !c1 <= 29 (or equivalently !c1 < 30). The reason is technical: at the end of the stable state ♯(7 ↪ 8), the counter reaches the value 29. The timer's current value is also equal to 29. The scan for event ♯8 begins and the current value of the timer is incremented during its execution (more precisely at rung 5), therefore, its value becomes equal to 30 and the timer coils.

At this stage, another pitfall remains. As explained previously, we cannot, in the general case, make explicit the equality between the introduced counter c1 and the **current** value of the timer in the formalisation of Fig. 7. Nonetheless, we can benefit from the invariant inference mechanism presented in Sect. 3.1. Indeed, this invariant generator does not only compute numerical domains for each variable independently: it makes use of relational domains (provided by the Apron library [13]) to infer logical relations between variables. In particular, we successfully obtain the invariant !c1 = t0.current that makes explicit the role of the introduced counter.

4   Implementation and Experimental Results

Our first goal is to be able to fully automatically prove that a Ladder program like our running example of in Fig. 2 is conforming to a timing chart. Our secondary goal is that we want to give back, to the users, meaningful and easy-to-use information when they try to prove an incorrect implementation.

In Sect. 4.1, we describe the workflow of the proprietary implementation of our approach. Then, Sect. 4.2 presents the results obtained when executing the analysis on a correct carriage line control implementation, *i.e.*, the implementation of Fig. 2. Finally, in Sect. 4.3, we present the feedback given by our toolbox when analysing one slight modification of the nominal program that makes the verification of conformance to the timing chart fail.

4.1 Overview of the Approach

The implemented approach proceeds as follows.

1. The tool takes two inputs: an XML representation of the Ladder program, and a timing chart specification written in the PlantUML language.
2. It translates the Ladder program as a WhyML program.
3. It derives, from the timing chart the different guard conditions (hypotheses on input values) and invariants (output values to prove) for formalising the successive events of the timing chart.
4. Then, for each event,
   - Why3 infers a loop invariant for the WhyML loop that models the state that is associated to the event, thus adding information on values of internal memory to the information on output values computed in the previous step.
   - Why3 computes the verification conditions that correspond both to the inferred invariants and the invariants that correspond to the timing chart specification, and dispatches them to SMT solvers.
5. The previous step is repeated for all events. Note that besides the hypotheses on the values of inputs and outputs at the start of the event, which are given by the timing chart, the proving process also needs hypotheses on the values of internal memory values at the beginning of the event. Those values are given by the loop invariant inferred for the previous event. Hence we store, during the process, the inferred invariants for each event in order to use them as preconditions for the next event.
6. If a proof obligation fails at event n, we build a WhyML program concatenating all the previous events and the faulty one, with loops enriched with the consecutively inferred invariants. Provers are called on this WhyML program and provide counterexamples (see Sect. 4.3).
7. On the contrary, if all events and stable states are proved, we conclude that the Ladder program satisfies the timing chart specification.

This approach of proving each event, one by one, until a specification violation is detected, is motivated by the fact that abstract interpretation, in our examples, is far more time-consuming than proving. In the case a violation is detected, our approach avoids to launch abstract interpretation for all the events that follow the one for which the violation has been detected.

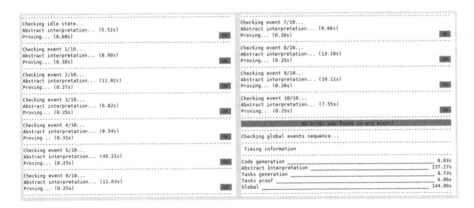

Fig. 8. Output of the tool on the nominal carriage line control program

4.2 Results on Correct Code

We apply our approach on the nominal Ladder program described in Fig. 2, for which we successfully verify the timing chart specification. Figure 8 depicts the result we obtain when running the analysis. In accordance with our strategy presented in Sect. 4.1, we consecutively infer invariants and then prove verification conditions for each pair (event, stable state), starting from the initial (*idle*) state of the timing chart. We observe that abstract interpretation is for now quite expensive, therefore, the proof time is negligible (6 s) compared to the time for inference of invariants (137 s).

4.3 Results on Incorrect Code

Let us assume the verification of a proof obligation fails for a faulty event (the case of a faulty stable state is similar). Our goal is to provide the most relevant information possible to the Ladder programmer, who may not be used to deductive verification. For that purpose, we propose an error scenario following the timing chart until the faulty event, mixing concrete values provided by counterexamples generated by Why3, and abstract domains provided by abstract interpretation.

Error Scenarios. When a proof obligation fails as assumed above, Why3 is able to provide a counterexample. Since such a proof obligation comes from the verification of the concatenation of the consecutive events from the very first one to the faulty one, the information we get provides the values of the inputs, outputs and internal devices at the beginning of each event until the faulty one. Due to the way Why3 handles loops during the computation of verification conditions for SMT-solvers (that is, the loop invariant is the only known fact for the code after the loop [4]), we do not have any information on the values the devices take during the stable states. We think that this lack of information concerning

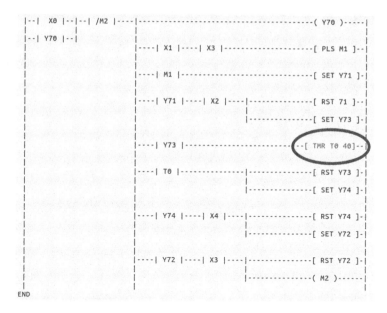

```
|--| X0 |--|--| /M2 |----|------------------------------------------( Y70 )-----|
|                       |                                                      |
|--| Y70 |--|           |                                                      |
|                       |----| X1 |----| X3 |---------------------[ PLS M1 ]--|
|                       |                                                      |
|                       |----| M1 |------------------------------[ SET Y71 ]-|
|                       |                                                      |
|                       |----| Y71 |----| X2 |----|---------------[ RST 71 ]--|
|                       |                         |                           |
|                       |                         |--------------[ SET Y73 ]-|
|                       |                                                      |
|                       |----| Y73 |--------------------------(--[ TMR T0 40]--)
|                       |                                                      |
|                       |----| T0 |----------------|---------------[ RST Y73 ]-|
|                       |                          |                          |
|                       |                          |--------------[ SET Y74 ]-|
|                       |                                                      |
|                       |----| Y74 |----| X4 |----|---------------[ RST Y74 ]-|
|                       |                         |                           |
|                       |                         |--------------[ SET Y72 ]-|
|                       |                                                      |
|                       |----| Y72 |----| X3 |----|---------------[ RST Y72 ]-|
|                       |                         |                           |
|                       |                         |--------------( M2 )------|
END
```

Fig. 9. An incorrect version of the carriage line control

values of devices during stable states may be an impediment to the understanding of the cause of the specification violation. That is why we propose to enrich the counterexample values with the domains of devices values given by abstract interpretation. This leads to the notion of *error scenario* that provides:

1. For each event that precedes the faulty one (including the faulty one), the values of devices before the beginning of the scan of this event, obtained from the counterexample trace provided by Why3.
2. For each stable state that precedes the faulty event, an over-approximation of domains of devices values, obtained by abstract interpretation.

In order to convince ourselves that this notion of error scenario should be useful to Ladder programmers, we implemented different slight modifications of the carriage line control program, introducing bugs. We present one of them in this article, another one is described in the extended research report [4]. The corresponding Ladder diagram is depicted in Fig. 9. The modification compared to the original code is circled.

The timer setting duration is here set to 40 scans instead of 30. We use our tool to get the reason of the proof failure, *i.e.* that Y73 is equal to true while it should be false. The obtained reason is rather intuitive: event 8 corresponds to 30 elapsed scans from timer's start. As the timer has a duration of 40 scans, it has not ended yet, therefore, Y73 is not reset yet, as highlighted by the error scenario of Fig. 10a.

The trace shows that the setting value of the timer (here 40) is not reached. In particular, the current value of the timer evolves between 3 and 29 in the stable

```
Values of devices at event 7 scan beginning:
  cc0 = false
  m1 = false
  m2 = false
  x1 = false
  y70 = true
  y71 = false
  y72 = false
  y73 = true
  y74 = false
  t0 = (current= 2, setting= 40): inactive
  c1 = 2


Values of devices between events 7 and 8:
  M1 = false
  M2 = false
  X0 = false
  X1 = false
  X2 = true
  X3 = false
  X4 = false
  Y70 = true
  Y71 = false
  Y72 = false
  Y73 = true
  Y74 = false
  T0.current ∈ [3; 29]
  T0.setting = 40


Values of devices at event 8 scan beginning:
  cc0 = false
  m1 = false
  m2 = false
  y70 = true
  y71 = false
  y72 = false
  y73 = true
  y74 = false
  t0 = (current= 29, setting= 40): inactive
  c1 = 29
```

(a) Output of the tool   (b) Violation of the timing chart

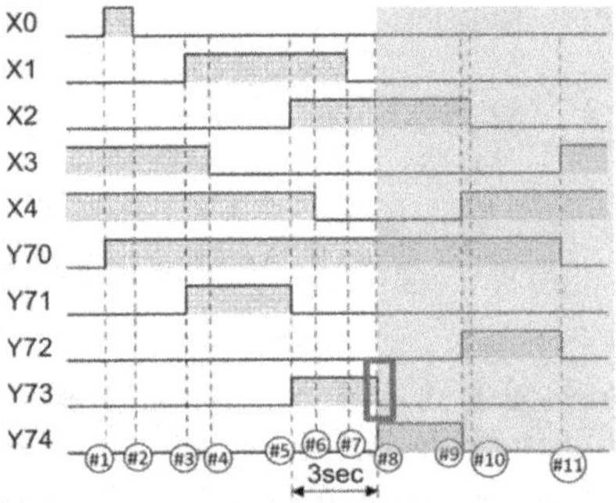

Fig. 10. Incorrect ladder program: analysis results

state between events 7 and 8, showing that the current event follows three other events in the fixed-duration sequence. Moreover, at the beginning of the scan of event 8, the current value of the timer and its associated counter $c1$ are both equal to 29, which is exactly the value we expect when leaving the fixed-duration sequence of events. The timing chart violation is depicted by Fig. 10b.

Qualitative Analysis of the Experiments. As a conclusion, we think that this notion of error scenario mixing concrete values provided by counterexamples to VCs, and abstract domains provided by abstract interpretation, should be useful to Ladder programmers in order to understand why a program does not conform to a given timing chart specification. A weakness of this approach is that in some cases, the concrete and abstract values might seem irrelevant. For example, for a timer counter c, we might have an abstract domain that states that c can take all the values between, say, 3 and 29 for a state, but the concrete value given for the next event might be 4. For that example, it means that the loop corresponding to the state is executed exactly once in the error scenario, before executing the next event. In that case, it might be very interesting to use the concrete values of counterexamples to refine the domain [3;29] into [3;4], and even make explicit to the programmer that there is exactly one execution of the program for the considered state.

5   Discussions, Related Work and Future Work

We presented a new method for formally verifying that a given Ladder code complies with an expected temporal behaviour expressed by a timing chart. By translating both the Ladder code and the timing chart to a WhyML program, and making use of the loop invariant generation capability of Why3, we are able to provide a fully automatic process to achieve such a verification, with a high level of confidence. Moreover, when this proof-based process fails at some point, we have a way to propose an error scenario which exposes why the Ladder code does not conform to the timing chart. Our method is implemented in a prototype which we experimented on a case study, demonstrating the effectiveness of our approach, both for formally proving the correct version and for providing counterexample scenarios on wrong mutants.

The level of confidence of our approach must be understood in terms of the trusted code base of the whole process. It first relies on the soundness of the translation from Ladder code and timing chart, which is described in Sect. 3. It also relies on the soundness of the VC generation process of Why3, which is not formally proven correct but validated on numerous applications [6]. Regarding trust in Why3, it is important to notice that the prototype implementation of loop invariant generation is *not* part of the trusted code base, because the loop invariants generated are later on checked for validity by the VC generation process. It is indeed fortunate to not have to rely on the soundness of this part of Why3 implementation, since we had to make significant extensions to it (mostly, support for Boolean variables, and adaptation of the API for external use) for the current purpose. The last part of the tool chain that must be trusted is the back-end SMT solver.

Regarding the generated errors scenarios, we have noticed that they are satisfactory on our case study, but due to the inherent incompleteness of countermodel generation with SMT solvers, we cannot guarantee that the generated scenarios are always valid. There are on-going work in the Why3 development team to increase the trust into the validity of generated counterexamples [3].

Related Work. PLC software verification is a vast domain and numerous works have been published on that subject. The majority of them use model-checking to verify functional and temporal properties. In 2014, Ovatman *et al.* [16] published a summary of those techniques. In 2016, Darvas *et al.* [9] proposed a newer model-checking based tool and compared with former similar tools. The general drawback of the model-checking approach is that the verification it provides cannot be exhaustive, it cannot model any possible number of executions during the states of a timing chart, contrary to deductive verification. On the other hand, abstract interpretation has also been used for a long time for verifying software, in particular microcontroller software [12,15] and PLC software [5] (in combination with model-checking). Contrary to model-checking, abstract interpretation gives a full guarantee when it detects no error in a program, but it is dedicated to compute the possible values of variables during the execution of a program, and is not suited for verifying temporal properties. Finally, in a previous work [7], some of us used the Why3 deductive verification platform for detecting run-time errors of Ladder programs. This work only considered one single execution of Ladder programs and was therefore also not suited for verifying temporal properties. To our knowledge, the present paper is the first one to combine abstract interpretation and deductive verification for verifying temporal properties of Ladder programs.

Outside the context of Ladder, Stouls and Groslambert proposed an approach for proving temporal properties of C code [19], based on a translation from LTL formulas into annotations in the ACSL language [2]. These LTL formulas express temporal properties of sequences of functions calls, which are very different from our kind of specifications. Their approach is similar to ours in the sense that they automatically translate temporal properties into annotated code, to be proved correct using deductive verification. They also identified a need for automatically generating extra intermediate annotations, for which they use their own variant of abstract interpretation. A successor of this work is the CaFE plug-in of Frama-C [10], which makes use of the Frama-C plug-in EVA for abstract interpretation. Unlike us, the approaches above do not provide any facilities for explaining errors.

Future Work. During our work, we had to improve the loop invariant generation feature of Why3, in particular the support for Boolean values. Even enough for our case study, there is clearly room for improvement in this implementation, required to make the tool chain more efficient. We plan to experiment our method on examples of Ladder programs that require WhyML translations involving arrays, and we have to ensure that the loop invariant generation could succeed when we are mixing all involving data-types: integers, Boolean, arrays, and also bounded integers in the future.

As mentioned at the end of Sect. 4.3, there is some need for improvement in the counterexample generation part of the chain. The inherent incompleteness of the SMT solvers implies that the proposed counterexample might be wrong. We are planning to incorporate in our tool-chain a recent technique that double-checks the validity of counterexamples *a posteriori* [3], which roughly amounts to symbolically executing the scenario it describes, and detect carefully at which step its behaviour diverges from what the timing chart allows.

On the error scenario side, as explained in the end of Sect. 4.3, the parts of a scenario that come from abstract interpretation domains, that correspond to the possible values of devices during states, could be refined using the concrete values given by the counterexamples for next events. This way, we might propose an even more understandable and useful error scenario to Ladder programmers, in case an error is detected in their code.

A longer-term goal is to augment the trust in the translation from Ladder to WhyML. We have some plans for designing a systematic and automatic validation process to confront our translation against existing test suites for Ladder programs.

References

1. Baudin, L.: Deductive verification with the help of abstract interpretation. Technical report, Université Paris-Saclay, November 2017. https://hal.inria.fr/hal-01634318
2. Baudin, P., et al.: ACSL: ANSI/ISO C specification language, version 1.16 (2020). https://frama-c.com/html/acsl.html
3. Becker, B., Belo Lourenço, C., Marché, C.: Explaining counterexamples with giant-step assertion checking. In: Creissac Campos, J., Paskevich, A. (eds.) 6th Workshop on Formal Integrated Development Environments (F-IDE 2021). Electronic Proceedings in Theoretical Computer Science, May 2021. https://hal.inria.fr/hal-03217393
4. Belo Lourenço, C., Cousineau, D., Faissole, F., Marché, C., Mentré, D., Inoue, H.: Formal analysis of Ladder programs using deductive verification. Research Report RR-9402, Inria, April 2021. https://hal.inria.fr/hal-03199464
5. Biallas, S., Kowalewski, S., Stattelmann, S., Schlich, B.: Efficient handling of states in abstract interpretation of industrial programmable logic controller code. In: Proceedings of the 12th International Workshop on Discrete Event Systems, pp. 400–405. IFAC, Cachan, France (2014)
6. Bobot, F., Filliâtre, J.C., Marché, C., Paskevich, A.: Let's verify this with Why3. Int. J. Softw. Tools Technol. Transf. (STTT) 17(6), 709–727 (2015). DOI: https://doi.org/10.1007/s10009-014-0314-5
7. Cousineau, D., Mentré, D., Inoue, H.: Automated deductive verification for ladder programming. In: Monahan, R., Prevosto, V., Proença, J. (eds.) Proceedings of the Fifth Workshop on Formal Integrated Development Environment, F-IDE@FM 2019, Porto, Portugal, 7th October 2019. Electronic Proceedings in Theoretical Computer Science, vol. 310, pp. 7–12 (2019). https://doi.org/10.4204/EPTCS.310.2
8. Dailler, S., Hauzar, D., Marché, C., Moy, Y.: Instrumenting a weakest precondition calculus for counterexample generation. J. Log. Algebraic Methods Program. **99**, 97–113 (2018). https://doi.org/10.1016/j.jlamp.2018.05.003
9. Darvas, D., Majzik, I., Blanco Viñuela, E.: Formal verification of safety plc based control software. In: Ábrahám, E., Huisman, M. (eds.) Integrated Formal Methods. Lecture Notes in Computer Science, vol. 9681, pp. 508–522. Springer (2016). https://doi.org/10.1007/978-3-319-33693-0_32
10. De Oliveira, S., Prévosto, V., Bardin, S.: Au temps en emporte le C. In: Baelde, D., Alglave, J. (eds.) Vingt-sixièmes Journées Francophones des Langages Applicatifs (JFLA 2015) (2015). https://hal.inria.fr/hal-01099128
11. Drath, R., Luder, A., Peschke, J., Hundt, L.: AutomationML - the glue for seamless automation engineering. In: ETFA - IEEE International Conference on Emerging Technologies and Factory Automation, pp. 616–623 (2008). https://doi.org/10.1109/ETFA.2008.4638461

12. Fehnker, A., Huuck, R., Schlich, B., Tapp, M.: Automatic bug detection in micro-controller software by static program analysis. In: Nielsen, M., Kučera, A., Miltersen, P.B., Palamidessi, C., Tůma, P., Valencia, F. (eds.) Theory and Practice of Computer Science (SOFSEM). Lecture Notes in Computer Science, vol. 5404, pp. 267–278. (2009). https://doi.org/10.1007/978-3-540-95891-8_26

13. Jeannet, B., Miné, A.: Apron: A library of numerical abstract domains for static analysis. In: Bouajjani, A., Maler, O. (eds.) Computer Aided Verification. pp. 661–667. Springer (2009)

14. Mitsubishi Electric Corporation: Mitsubishi programmable controllers training manual – MELSEC iQ-R Series basic course (for GX Works3). https://dl.mitsubishielectric.com/dl/fa/document/manual/school_text/sh081898eng/sh081898enga.pdf (2016). Accessed 30 March 2021

15. Nguyen, T., Aoki, T., Tomita, T., Endo, J.: Integrating static program analysis tools for verifying cautions of microcontroller. In: Asia-Pacific Software Engineering Conference (APSEC), pp. 86–93 (2019). https://doi.org/10.1109/APSEC48747.2019.00021

16. Ovatman, T., Aral, A., Polat, D., Ünver, A.: An overview of model checking practices on verification of PLC software. Softw. Syst. Model. **15**, 1–24 (2014). https://doi.org/10.1007/s10270-014-0448-7

17. Ramanathan, R.: The IEC 61131–3 programming languages features for industrial control systems. In: World Automation Congress (WAC), pp. 598–603 (2014). https://doi.org/10.1109/WAC.2014.6936062

18. Roques, A.: PlantUML standard library. https://plantuml.com/stdlib (2009). Accessed 24 March 2021

19. Stouls, N., Groslambert, J.: Vérification de propriétés LTL sur des programmes C par génération d'annotations. Research report (2011). https://hal.inria.fr/inria-00568947

Spatial Model Checking for Smart Stations
Research Challenges

Maurice H. ter Beek[(✉)], Vincenzo Ciancia, Diego Latella,
Mieke Massink, and Giorgio O. Spagnolo

Formal Methods and Tools (FMT) Laboratory, ISTI–CNR, Pisa, Italy
{terbeek,ciancia,latella,massink,spagnolo}@isti.cnr.it

Abstract. In this position paper, we discuss the introduction of spatial verification techniques in an application scenario from smart stations, viz. analysing the user experience with respect to the lighting conditions of station areas. This is a case study in industrial projects. We discuss three challenging use cases for the application of spatial model checking in this setting. First, we envision how to use the spatial model checker VoxLogicA, which can analyse both 2D and 3D voxel-based maps, to explore the areas that users can visit in a station area and to characterise them with respect to their illumination conditions. This is aimed at monitoring a smart station. We also ideate statistical spatio-temporal model checking of the design of energy-saving protocols, exploiting the modelling of user preferences. Finally, we discuss the idea of quantifying the impact of design changes, based on the logs of smart stations, to identify and measure the incidence of undesired events (e.g. non-illuminated platforms where a train is passing by) before and after each change.

1 Introduction and Outline

Spatial and spatio-temporal model checking have been introduced in [11–13], and have been used in case studies related to smart transportation [4,10,15] and medical image analysis [1,5,6]. For instance, in [6] a 10-lines logical specification was given, which can contour brain tumours in 3D magnetic resonance images with accuracy in par with the state of the art. Execution of such procedure using the newly defined spatial model checker VoxLogicA takes about 5 s on a quite standard desktop computer.

In this paper, we introduce and discuss three research challenges concerning the introduction of spatial verification techniques in a smart station lighting case study provided by industrial project partners. We show how the spatial verification methods defined so far in the literature can be used, and enhanced, in order to address such challenges. In Sect. 2, we introduce the context of our case study. In Sect. 3, we describe three research challenges that we plan to address in that context. In Sect. 4, we show how spatio-temporal model checking can be used to address such challenges. In Sect. 5, we provide an outlook on future research directions.

© Springer Nature Switzerland AG 2021
A. Lluch Lafuente and A. Mavridou (Eds.): FMICS 2021, LNCS 12863, pp. 39–47, 2021.
https://doi.org/10.1007/978-3-030-85248-1_3

2   Industrial Context and Case Study: Station Lighting

In this section, we provide a brief description of the case study from the railway domain and the industrial project it originates from. Traditionally, railway stations have a private energy distribution and communication system, mainly to ensure uninterrupted power supply and security. This isolation has two major drawbacks. First, it prohibits integration with smart cities which, ideally, exploit information between different transportation systems (e.g. bike sharing, car sharing, urban transport) in a synergic manner. Second, the station's system fails to benefit from modern energy-saving techniques.

STINGRAY (SmarT station INtelliGent RAilwaY) [16] is a regional project, funded by Regione Toscana, that aims at enhancing the integration of railway stations into smart cities of the future as well as to study advanced energy-saving techniques. The overall goals of the project are:

- to deploy a LAN over the station, using powerline and wireless technologies;
- to control and monitor station equipment via Supervisory Control And Data Acquisition (SCADA), in particular railroad switch heaters as studied in [3];
- to create value-added services for both customers and railway staff, such as connectivity, monitoring fault prediction service (FPS), video surveillance, environmental surveying and integration and access to smart city infomobility services, addressing in particular the energy management service (EMS);
- to optimise existing strategies for managing energy consumption within the station, in order to avoid wasting energy, as contemplated in this paper.

The case studies of STINGRAY provided by the industrial partners from the railway domain are station lighting and heating of the railroad switches in ice conditions. The latter was studied in [3]; in this paper we address the former. The follow-up project SmaRIERS (Smart Railway Infrastructures: Efficiency, Reliability and Safety), which has just been funded by Regione Toscana, will develop a monitoring system capable of handling huge amounts of data by combining Big Data and Analytics with AI in an attempt to increase energy efficiency.

Smart (station) lighting aims at reducing station illumination whenever (time) and wherever (space) possible, while guaranteeing minimum levels of illumination as requested by current legislation. Along the station platforms there are a number of LEDs, called (ceiling) lights. Each light is equipped with a data acquisition module called MADILL (Data Acquisition Module for ILLumination), which are in turn connected to a C-MAD (Data Acquisition Concentrator Module). Besides capturing the messages from each MADILL, the C-MAD is equipped with brightness sensors, and it transfers all collected data with the publish/subcribe messaging protocol MQTT [2] to a cloud service, which stores all data and makes it available in XML format by means of an HTTPS REST interface [17]. The same interface moreover allows to send commands to switch lights on, off, or dim them—either individually or for groups of lights.

So far, STINGRAY has achieved a 78% energy saving by replacing fluorescent tubes with LEDs and by using static rules to switch on, off, or dim groups of lights that are selected based on environmental brightness and railway traffic [23].

3   Challenges in User-Centric Design of Smart Stations

In this section, we present three relevant user-centric challenges in designing smart stations with efficient illumination. The questions we contemplate are related to the design of smart management applications in a spatial setting such as that of a smart station. We consider user-experience related requirements, like "passengers should always be able to rely on an illuminated pathway when getting off or on a train, from the main entrance, to the platform", or "there should be an illumination level greater than x on platforms where a train is about to arrive, even if the train is late", or "at any time, the areas with an illumination level less than x should be reachable only from paths controlled by an automatic gate". Such requirements are inherently spatial or spatio-temporal, as they deal with the possibly complex reachability relations and pathways of a train station.

At the technical/concrete level, mapping space and gathering real-time data can be challenging operations, whereas at the formal verification/abstract level, modelling space, and formalising the requirements in a mathematically sound, and unambiguous way, are the major difficulties.

In this work, we propose a modelling strategy in which space is mapped and formalised by exploiting previously available maps, in the form of digital images. This technique works quite well for 2-dimensional maps. For 3-dimensional structures, we envisage the adoption of *3D meshes*; since the technology for spatial verification of 3D meshes is relatively new (cf. the Conclusion), in this work we will mostly refer to 2-dimensional examples; however, the reader should keep in mind the results in [6], where 3D images based on *voxels* have been used.

Consider the requirements analysis and design phase of a smart management protocol (such as smart station lighting). The verification of a user-related requirement can be divided into the following three main verification challenges.

Challenges

Past: *Investigate whether the requirement has actually been violated in a specific period of time by the pre-existing implementation, and how frequently such violations have happened.*

Present: *Monitor an implementation (either the existing one or a new one) to promptly respond to new violations, and for quality assurance purposes.*

Future: *Verify that the new design can guarantee the requirement or improve on the previous situation.*

4   Methodology

Below, we show how we intend to address the challenges described in Sect. 3, using the tool VoxLogicA described in [6]. Our proposal is based on previous work in the area of spatial model checking for smart cities and smart transportation. To ease the presentation, we divide this work into subsections based on the analysis methodology, and in each subsection we establish the potential contribution of such a methodology to the challenges outlined in Sect. 3.

4.1 Spatial Model Checking

First presented in [13], spatial model checking is a method for automatically checking properties of points in a spatial structure. Abstractly, spatial structures are so-called *Closure Spaces*, a generalisation of Topological Spaces. Concretely, closure spaces can be continuous (e.g. topological, Euclidean spaces). However, in case studies such spatial structures have mostly been discrete, i.e. graphs. As a special case, graphs can take the shape of digital images whose nodes/points are pixels. In such setting, images are considered as (non-directed regular) graphs by using either 4-adjacency (pixels up, down, left, and right are connected to each pixel), 8-adjacency (also pixels reachable 'diagonally' count) or 27-adjacency in 3D space with *voxels* (viz. 3D pixels, also with 'diagonal' adjacency).

As we are discussing model checking, we first emphasise the logical language that we employ. This is SLCS, the *Spatial Logic of Closure Spaces*, a language interpreted on points of the space, encompassing atomic propositions, Boolean operators, a modal operator denoting 'nearness' (in images or graphs, one-step reachability), and a binary modal operator denoting *conditional reachability* via an arbitrary number of steps. Variants of reachability, and of its dual *surrounded*, have been defined in the literature. In [6], the operator ρ (standing for reach), with two parameters ψ and ϕ, is defined. Point x satisfies $\rho\,\psi[\phi]$ (read: "x can reach ψ passing by ϕ") if there is a path starting in x, ending in a point satisfying ψ, with all its intermediate points satisfying ϕ. An example user-centric, spatial requirement of lighting in a smart station is

All areas that are open to the public should be sufficiently illuminated   (1)

which indeed could be made more sophisticated, e.g. by adding points of interest, train timetables, actual train arrival and departure times, etc.

In this example, we aim at considering dimming of light in order to find the best trade-off between energy saving and providing enough light to users when needed. For instance, in principle, imagine dynamic policies in which the darkness caused by a broken lamp could be compensated by temporarily increasing the intensity of the lights nearby until the broken light is repaired. Spatial model checking provides means to check such policies. Another example could be that of *designing* the illumination system and producing, e.g., a map showing which areas (of interest to users) do not satisfy requirements that are related to the spatial distribution of features, which could then be described using SLCS.

In a simple scenario from Sect. 2, data from each MADILL, received via the C-MAD, can be linked to a spatial distribution of light based on distance by encoding light attenuation, for instance using the classical, well-known formula expressing the attenuation at each point x:

$$attenuation(x) = \frac{1}{c_1 + c_2 \times dst(src, x) + c_3 \times dst(src, x)^2}$$

where *src* is the position of the light source, c_1, c_2, and c_3 depend on the chosen illumination model, and *dst* is the Euclidean distance function. Such attenuation can be computed using VoxLogicA, exploiting its *distance transform* operation. More complex lighting simulations could be employed if needed (cf., e.g., [20]).

This allows one to use the reachability primitive in VoxLogicA to characterise insufficiently illuminated points that a user may reach, possibly refining the result by proximity to points of interest and presence/absence of trains at a platform. This basic design can be used to address the Challenge named Present: monitoring a smart station to promptly detect illumination failures in a user-centric way.

An illustration of the method is given in Fig. 1. The images were produced using VoxLogicA. In the figure, which is presented only for illustrative purposes, the light from different sources is not summed, so the method will need to be refined in future work. The full computation, starting from the image of the train station map, takes about 1 s on a desktop computer equipped with an Intel Core i7 CPU. The specification is quite small, 4 lines of text for the actual description of properties (cf. Code 1), and some 20 lines including loading, saving, macro definition, and identification of regions of interest via colour thresholding.

Fig. 1. Illustration of an experiment aimed at identifying poorly illuminated platform areas. **Top-left**: Pistoia station. Blue squares: a design with MADILL units, clearly, insufficient in number. Red squares: some C-MAD units. Green squares: indicate the platforms open to the public. **Top-right**: illumination computed using an attenuation formula with VoxLogicA (overlay is made with an external program). **Bottom-left**: by a threshold on the illumination value, areas that are sufficiently illuminated have been computed (output from VoxLogicA). **Bottom-right**: the parts of the platforms that are not sufficiently illuminated are computed using VoxLogicA (shown in white). (Color figure online)

```
let platform = grow(grow(platformSeed,platformArea),cmad|madill)
let attenuation = 1 ./ (1 .+ (0.01 .* dt(madill)) + (0.001 .* (dt(madill)*dt(madill))))
let threshold = attenuation >. 0.3
let nonIllumPlatform = platform \ threshold
```

Code 1. Part of VoxLogicA specification for our experiment. **Explanation.** platform: platform area, computed using a *region growing operator* starting from a seed, including the coloured squares overlayed on the image; attenuation: light attenuation formula, where dt(src) is the *distance transform* operator, returning an image-like map, containing at each point the Euclidean distance from src to that point; threshold: thresholding operation; nonIllumPlatform: final result. The results are shown in Fig. 1.

4.2 Statistical Spatio-Temporal Model Checking

Statistical spatio-temporal model checking was first demonstrated in [15], as implemented by a toolchain consisting of the spatial model checker Topochecker, the statistical analysis tool MultiVeStA[1] (cf. [18, 22, 24]), and a custom stochastic simulator for bike-sharing traffic, taking into account user preferences [14, 21].

The simulator produced traces of bike-sharing usage, in the form of an occupancy measure for each station. For each simulation, covering about one day of bike-sharing traffic, the model checker Topochecker identified and labelled (with a Boolean value) the bike-sharing stations satisfying specific formulas (e.g. the stations that eventually become part of a cluster of full docking stations, where it is no longer possible to leave a bike). MultiVeStA was used to schedule an appropriate number of such simulations, in order to compute a probability out of the Boolean values obtained. Finally, a heat map was produced, where each station was coloured according to the probability of satisfying each specific formula.

As a first step, with no simulator in place, the same methodology can be used for the smart station lighting scenario, to address the Challenge named Past. Past logs produced by C-MAD units can be analysed by linking VoxLogicA with MultiVeStA to compute the probability that each point of a map of a station satisfies a specific property. Such analyses can then be refined to, for instance, specific times of the day, specific situations (e.g. "all days that a disruption on the line has occurred", if such data is available), or considering points of interest.

Stochastic simulation can be used to study specific aspects of behaviour of the stations and/or users, similar to [15], which studies user preferences in a bike-sharing system, or [19], which presents a high-accuracy passenger-pedestrian model describing traveller dynamics in stations based on automated fare collection and train tracking data.

Furthermore, note that spatio-temporal model checking alone (without using MultiVeStA) could in principle be used to address the Challenge named Future. A model of the behaviour of the new design for a smart lighting system can be combined with the spatial map of the station to compute the violation of spatio-temporal requirements, e.g. using the timetable of the trains to identify points of interest in space-time. However, in order to produce more realistic data,

---

[1] https://github.com/andrea-vandin/MultiVeStA/wiki.

a (stochastic) simulation approach, possibly based on MultiVeStA, needs to be used also in this case, so as to take into account the probability of train delays and disruptions on the line, which need to be computed using a simulation.

5 Conclusion and Outlook

We introduced three research challenges based on an industrial case study on smart station lighting, explicitly considering user experiences; in particular, avoiding users ending up transiting or waiting in non-illuminated areas, with the associated risks (e.g. theft, injury). We envisioned how to tackle these concretely in the future by applying spatial model-checking techniques and tools. In this context, the statistical spatio-temporal model-checking framework of [15] could be of help. A technological advancement in this scenario is given by the recently defined extension of spatial model-checking techniques to 3D meshes [7]. In conjunction with statistical spatio-temporal model checking, the methodology can produce 3D meshes coloured according to heat maps related to spatio-temporal user-centric requirements, and at the same time demonstrate illumination issues on past system traces, simulation, or in real time, by classical means of 3D graphics, e.g. illumination and texturing. This provides a unique analysis and monitoring methodology, which can be complemented by the development of a suitable user interface for the analysis tool chain, focused on minimising the cognitive load and interference between different simultaneous tasks of the domain expert, along the lines of [8]. To make real-time analysis more effective, we plan to leverage on the *on-GPU* implementation of VoxLogicA proposed in [9].

Acknowledgments. Supported by the POR FESR 2014–2020 projects STINGRAY (SmarT station INtelliGent RAilwaY) and SmaRIERS (Smart Railway Infrastructures: Efficiency, Reliability and Safety), and by the MIUR PRIN 2017FTXR7S project IT MaTTerS (Methods and Tools for Trustworthy Smart Systems).

References

1. Banci Buonamici, F., Belmonte, G., Ciancia, V., Latella, D., Massink, M.: Spatial logics and model checking for medical imaging. Int. J. Softw. Tools Technol. Transf. **22**(2), 195–217 (2020). https://doi.org/10.1007/s10009-019-00511-9
2. Banks, A., Gupta, R.: MQTT version 3.1.1. OASIS standard, October 2014. http://docs.oasis-open.org/mqtt/mqtt/v3.1.1/os/mqtt-v3.1.1-os.html
3. Basile, D., ter Beek, M.H., Di Giandomenico, F., Fantechi, A., Gnesi, S., Spagnolo, G.O.: 30 years of simulation-based quantitative analysis tools: a comparison experiment between Möbius and Uppaal SMC. In: Margaria, T., Steffen, B. (eds.) ISoLA 2020. LNCS, vol. 12476, pp. 368–384. Springer, Cham (2020). https://doi.org/10.1007/978-3-030-61362-4_21
4. ter Beek, M.H., Gnesi, S., Knapp, A.: Formal methods for transport systems. Int. J. Softw. Tools Technol. Transf. **20**(3), 355–358 (2018). https://doi.org/10.1007/s10009-018-0487-4

5. Belmonte, G., Broccia, G., Vincenzo, C., Latella, D., Massink, M.: Feasibility of spatial model checking for nevus segmentation. In: Proceedings of the 9th International Conference on Formal Methods in Software Engineering (FormaliSE 2021), pp. 1–12. IEEE (2021). https://doi.org/10.1109/FormaliSE52586.2021.00007

6. Belmonte, G., Ciancia, V., Latella, D., Massink, M.: Voxlogica: a spatial model checker for declarative image analysis. In: Vojnar, T., Zhang, L. (eds.) TACAS 2019. LNCS, vol. 11427, pp. 281–298. Springer, Cham (2019). https://doi.org/10.1007/978-3-030-17462-0_16

7. Bezhanishvili, N., Ciancia, V., Gabelaia, D., Grilletti, G., Latella, D., Massink, M.: Geometric model checking of continuous space. http://arxiv.org/abs/2105.06194 [cs.LO], May 2021

8. Broccia, G., Milazzo, P., Ölveczky, P.C.: Formal modeling and analysis of safety-critical human multitasking. Innov. Syst. Softw. Eng. **15**(3–4), 169–190 (2019). https://doi.org/10.1007/s11334-019-00333-7

9. Bussi, L., Ciancia, V., Gadducci, F.: Towards a spatial model checker on GPU. In: Peters, K., Willemse, T. (eds.) FORTE 2021. LNCS, vol. 12719, pp. 188–196. Springer, Cham (2021). https://doi.org/10.1007/978-3-030-78089-0_12

10. Ciancia, V., Gilmore, S., Grilletti, G., Latella, D., Loreti, M., Massink, M.: Spatio-temporal model checking of vehicular movement in public transport systems. Int. J. Softw. Tools Technol. Transf. **20**(3) (2018). https://doi.org/10.1007/s10009-018-0483-8

11. Ciancia, V., Grilletti, G., Latella, D., Loreti, M., Massink, M.: An experimental spatio-temporal model checker. In: Bianculli, D., Calinescu, R., Rumpe, B. (eds.) SEFM 2015. LNCS, vol. 9509, pp. 297–311. Springer, Heidelberg (2015). https://doi.org/10.1007/978-3-662-49224-6_24

12. Ciancia, V., Latella, D., Loreti, M., Massink, M.: Model checking spatial logics for closure spaces. Log. Methods Comput. Sci. **12**(4) (2016). https://doi.org/10.2168/LMCS-12(4:2)2016

13. Ciancia, V., Latella, D., Loreti, M., Massink, M.: Specifying and verifying properties of space. In: Diaz, J., Lanese, I., Sangiorgi, D. (eds.) TCS 2014. LNCS, vol. 8705, pp. 222–235. Springer, Heidelberg (2014). https://doi.org/10.1007/978-3-662-44602-7_18

14. Ciancia, V., Latella, D., Massink, M., Paškauskas, R.: Exploring spatio-temporal properties of bike-sharing systems. In: Workshops Proceedings of the 9th International Conference on Self-Adaptive and Self-Organizing Systems (SASO 2015), pp. 74–79. IEEE (2015). https://doi.org/10.1109/SASOW.2015.17

15. Ciancia, V., Latella, D., Massink, M., Paškauskas, R., Vandin, A.: A tool-chain for statistical spatio-temporal model checking of bike sharing systems. In: Margaria, T., Steffen, B. (eds.) ISoLA 2016. LNCS, vol. 9952, pp. 657–673. Springer, Cham (2016). https://doi.org/10.1007/978-3-319-47166-2_46

16. Di Giandomenico, F., Gnesi, S., Spagnolo, G.O., Fantechi, A.: Smart services for railways. ERCIM News **117**, 34–35 (2019). https://ercim-news.ercim.eu/en117/r-i/smart-services-for-railways

17. Fielding, R.T.: Architectural styles and the design of network-based software architectures. Ph.D. thesis, University of California (2000). https://www.ics.uci.edu/~fielding/pubs/dissertation/top.htm

18. Gilmore, S., Reijsbergen, D., Vandin, A.: Transient and steady-state statistical analysis for discrete event simulators. In: Polikarpova, N., Schneider, S.A. (eds.) IFM 2017. LNCS, vol. 10510, pp. 145–160. Springer, Cham (2017). https://doi.org/10.1007/978-3-319-66845-1_10

19. Hänseler, F.S., van den Heuvel, J.P., Cats, O., Daamen, W., Hoogendoorn, S.P.: A passenger-pedestrian model to assess platform and train usage from automated data. Transp. Res. Part A: Policy Pract. **132**, 948–968 (2020). https://doi.org/10.1016/j.tra.2019.12.032

20. Lai, X., Dai, M., Rameezdeen, R.: Energy saving based lighting system optimization and smart control solutions for rail transportation: evidence from China. Results Eng. **5**, 100096 (2020). https://doi.org/10.1016/j.rineng.2020.100096

21. Massink, M., Paškauskas, R.: Model-based assessment of aspects of user-satisfaction in bicycle sharing systems. In: Proceedings of the 18th International Conference on Intelligent Transportation Systems (ITSC 2015), pp. 1363–1370. IEEE (2015). https://doi.org/10.1109/ITSC.2015.224

22. Sebastio, S., Vandin, A.: MultiVeStA: statistical model checking for discrete event simulators. In: Proceedings of the 7th International Conference on Performance Evaluation Methodologies and Tools (ValueTools 2013), pp. 310–315. ACM (2013). https://doi.org/10.4108/icst.valuetools.2013.254377

23. STINGRAY report: Algoritmi Innovativi. Deliverable D2.3.1, December 2020

24. Vandin, A., Giachini, D., Lamperti, F., Chiaromonte, F.: Automated and distributed statistical analysis of economic agent-based models. http://arxiv.org/abs/2102.05405 [econ.GN], February 2021

Program Safety and Education

Parametric Faults in Safety Critical Programs

Hamid Jahanian$^{(\boxtimes)}$

Macquarie University, Sydney, Australia
hamid.jahanian@hdr.mq.edu.au

Abstract. In the process industry, Safety Instrumented Systems (SIS) are mechanisms that protect against major plant accidents. A typical SIS consists of hardware components and a software part, the program. Failure Mode Reasoning (FMR) was originally designed for identifying failure modes of SIS inputs based on an analysis of its program. In this paper we introduce an extended version of the method that can be used as a diagnostic means for identifying systemic faults concerning incorrect parameters in the program. The proposed method can particularly help with SIS factory acceptance testing, which is a critical process in validating the integrity of SIS prior to its installation on site. The original FMR used the program architecture to reason about failure modes. Here we use test cases as an additional source of information for reasoning. We describe the concepts, formalize the method, and demonstrate its application in an industrial case study.

Keywords: Failure Mode Reasoning · Safety Instrumented Systems

1 Introduction

Plant accidents can have catastrophic consequences. An explosion at a chemical plant in eastern China in 2019 killed over 70 people and injured more than 600 [1]. Safety Instrumented Systems (SIS) are a critical component of large industrial plants, whose purpose is to monitor and protect against catastrophic process failures [10]. A typical SIS includes, among other parts, sensors for measuring the physical environment and an SIS program. The program takes inputs from the sensors and implements safety functions that determine whether any corrective intervention needs to be taken to ensure safe working of the plant.

Failure Mode Reasoning (FMR) was originally developed as a lightweight formal approach to the analysis of failure modes associated with random faults at the inputs of an SIS program [12–14]. In this paper we consider a similarly lightweight approach for identifying systemic faults within the SIS program; in particular concerning the errors in the setting of parameters. These faults may arise due to incorrect or inconsistent implementation of the safety requirements specification document [10], which is used as the benchmark for assessing the overall safety of the plant. Our primary goal is to provide a method which can

© Springer Nature Switzerland AG 2021
A. Lluch Lafuente and A. Mavridou (Eds.): FMICS 2021, LNCS 12863, pp. 51–66, 2021.
https://doi.org/10.1007/978-3-030-85248-1_4

assist engineers in their safety analyses by implementing, where possible, the parts of the safety assessment which are too large and complex to be performed accurately by hand. The method can be utilized in SIS factory acceptance tests, which are an important part of the SIS validation processes.

Our contributions in this paper are as follows:

1. We formulate the problem using a simple model based on sets and functions, and define inconsistency of parameters with respect to safety requirements.
2. We propose an algorithm that can automate the fault finding process.
3. We illustrate the implementation of our algorithm on a case study based on industrial settings.

The philosophy of our approach is inspired by the notion of Morgan's "informal methods" [16] (itself based on earlier work by Abrial [2]), that only sufficient formality to meet the needs of the problem is required to obtain a high return on impact. We propose a method that can help with real scenarios in industry, and we employ minimal formalism to prove the soundness of the method.

The rest of this paper is organized as follows: Sect. 2 provides an overview on FMR and its underlying ideas. Section 3 formalizes the concepts for identification of incorrect parameters, and proposes an algorithm for automating the analysis. The algorithm is applied in Sect. 4 to a medium-scale case study from the power generation industry. Section 5 discusses some aspects of the new method. Section 6 provides references to other research works in the field, and Sect. 7 closes the paper with some concluding remarks.

2 Background

We present a quick overview of FMR. Readers can refer to the original works [12,13] for more details.

SIS programs are designed to meet the safety requirements in terms of processing the information received from the sensors and translating those inputs into safety actions, such as raising alarms or shutting down parts of the plant. SIS programs are typically developed in graphical editors and in the form of Function Block Diagrams (FBD) [9]. Figure 1 illustrates a small example of an FBD. The program takes a single input i, and feeds it separately into two function blocks (FBs) $Gcom$ and $Lcom$[1], which together check whether the input i lies between an upper threshold p_1 and a lower threshold p_2. The final result r will be 1 if i lies outside the permissible range $[p_2, p_1]$, and 0 otherwise.

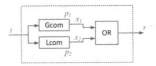

Fig. 1. A small SIS program

---

[1] *Gcom*: Greater Comparison, *Lcom*: Less Comparison.

Part of the safety assessment of an SIS is to determine when its output r can be trusted. One reason that r may *not* be trusted is because the inputs do not correctly report the state of the plant, perhaps because the sensors have unknowingly failed. FMR was originally developed to analyze this type of failures by using the SIS program. In a broad sense, FMR is a technique for analyzing *uncertain* deviations at the variables of an SIS program. Suppose x is the current, known, reported value at variable x, and x′ the desired, correct, yet unknown value at the same variable. By deviation at x we mean the (potential) difference between x and x′. Program variables include: parameters (e.g. p_1 and p_2), inputs (e.g. i), outputs (e.g. r), and intermediate variables (e.g. x_1 and x_2).

FMR uses an abstraction to categorize deviations into *failure modes*. This considerably simplifies the analysis by eliminating unnecessary numerical computations. We use the set $\mathcal{P} := \{\ell, m, \hbar\}$ for failure modes, in which $\hbar$, ℓ and m represent *higher*, *lower* and *matching* states[2], and we use function $\mathsf{md}_{\mathcal{P}} : \mathbb{R} \times \mathbb{R} \to \mathcal{P}$ to map numerical deviations to failure modes:[3]

$$\mathsf{md}_{\mathcal{P}}(\mathsf{x}, \mathsf{x}') := \hat{x} := \begin{cases} \hbar, & if \ \mathsf{x} > \mathsf{x}' \\ \ell, & if \ \mathsf{x} < \mathsf{x}' \\ m, & if \ \mathsf{x} = \mathsf{x}' \end{cases}$$

An FMR analysis begins with a given deviation at the SIS output. The objective is to identify the combinations of input faults that can lead to the given output fault. In doing so, the program is scanned from output to inputs, in the process of which the failure behavior of individual FBs are analyzed locally and then combined to model the global failure behavior.

For an output deviation $\hat{r} = \hbar$ in Fig. 1, the local failure models are:

$$\hat{r} = \hbar \Rightarrow (\hat{x}_1 = \hbar \vee \hat{x}_2 = \hbar)$$
$$\hat{x}_1 = \hbar \Rightarrow \hat{i} = \hbar$$
$$\hat{x}_2 = \hbar \Rightarrow \hat{i} = \ell$$

By combining these statements we obtain the failure model of the whole program, which is solely based on input/output failure modes:

$$\hat{r} = \hbar \Rightarrow (\hat{i} = \hbar \vee \hat{i} = \ell) \tag{1}$$

Statement (1) simply suggests that if output r becomes 1 by fault, that must be because input i is reading either higher ($\hbar$) or lower (ℓ) than what it should.

The failure models of individual FBs vary depending on their mathematical functions. However, for the particular category of monotonic functions a generic model can be derived:

---

[2] The original works [12–14] use t and f specifically for Boolean variables. In this paper we use the 0/1 convention for Boolean variables, instead of $false/true$, and thus $\hbar$ and ℓ will cover both $\mathbb{R}$ and $\mathbb{B}$ domains. Also note that m is actually not a failure and it is only used to express the no-fault states.

[3] Here, symbol ˆ separates between program variables and failure mode variables. As an example, $\hat{x}$ represents the failure modes at variable x.

Axiom 1. *Let* $f : \mathbb{R} \to \mathbb{R}$ *be a monotonic function. Let* $x, y \in \mathbb{R}$ *and* $y := f(x)$. *If* f *is increasing, i.e.* $x_1 > x_2 \Rightarrow f(x_1) \geq f(x_2)$, *then:* $(\hat{y} = \hbar \lor \hat{y} = \ell) \Rightarrow \hat{x} = \hat{y}$. *If* f *is decreasing, i.e.* $x_1 > x_2 \Rightarrow f(x_1) \leq f(x_2)$, *then:* $\hat{y} = \hbar \Rightarrow \hat{x} = \ell$ *and* $\hat{y} = \ell \Rightarrow \hat{x} = \hbar$.

The original FMR analyzes the random faults at SIS inputs. In this paper, we study the kind of systemic faults that are caused by incorrect settings of parameters. Such analyses lead to outcomes such as: $\hat{r} = \hbar \Rightarrow \hat{p}_1 = \ell$. Compared to (1), which expresses *all* the possible failure modes of *inputs*, the latter result solely depends on the faults of *parameters* and it is *minimized* to those parameters that have caused the deviation.

3   Identifying Incorrect Parameters

Let $\mathcal{I}$ be the (finite) set of (real-valued) input variables. Let Θ be a (finite) set of parameters in an SIS program. Let $\mathcal{R}$ be the (finite) set of (Boolean-valued) result variables. Let $f \in \mathbb{R}^{|\mathcal{I}|} \to \mathbb{R}^{|\Theta|} \to \mathbb{B}^{|\mathcal{R}|}$ be the mathematical model of an SIS program. The safety analysis we study here is a technique to identify faults in the current setting of parameters. Let $T \subseteq \mathbb{R}^{|\mathcal{I}|} \times \mathbb{B}^{|\mathcal{R}|}$ be a finite set of input/output test cases. A test case $(\iota, \rho) \in T$ consists of test input ι, injected at the input of SIS program; and output ρ, which is the response of the program to input ι in the absence of faults.

Definition 1. *Given are* T *a test set,* $\theta \in \mathbb{R}^{|\Theta|}$ *a parameter setting, and* f *a model of an SIS program. We say that* $(\iota, \rho) \in T$ *is consistent wrt.* θ *in* f *if* $\rho = f(\iota, \theta)$. *Conversely we say that* $(\iota, \rho) \in T$ *is inconsistent wrt.* θ *in* f *if* $\rho \neq f(\iota, \theta)$.

Definition 2. *A parameter setting* θ *is inconsistent with test set* T *and SIS program* f *if there is some* $(\iota, \rho) \in T$ *that is inconsistent wrt.* θ *in* f.

Definition 3. *Given are a parameter setting* θ, *test set* T *and SIS program* f. *Further, let* θ *be inconsistent wrt.* T *and* f. *A subset of parameters* $P \subseteq \Theta$ *are incorrectly set if there is some* θ' *parameter setting such that: (i)* θ' *is consistent wrt.* T *and* f, *and (ii)* $\theta'_j \neq \theta_j$ *implies that* $p_j \in P$.[4] *If* P *is also a minimal, then we say that the parameters in* P *are a potential cause of inconsistencies in* T.

A major class of SIS program architectures is the Disjunctive Normal Form (DNF), where each conjunctive clause represents a hazardous scenario that should lead to a 1 at the output of the program, regardless of the states of other scenarios. We model such programs in the following form:[5]

$$r = f(i, p) = \bigvee_{l=1}^{L} f_l(i_l, p_l) = \bigvee_{l=1}^{L} \bigwedge_{k=1}^{K} f_{lk}(i_{lk}, p_{lk}) \tag{2}$$

---

[4] Here, θ_j and θ'_j mean the current and correct settings at parameter p_j.

[5] In this paper we only formulate the analysis for DNF. Similar approach can be taken to formulate the CNF-based analysis.

where $r \in \mathbb{B}$ is the output variable, f the model of SIS program, $i \in \mathbb{R}^{|g|}$ the input variables, $p \in \mathbb{R}^{|\Theta|}$ the parameter variables and $f_{lk}(i_{lk}, p_{lk})$ an arbitrary expression on a subset of inputs $i_{lk} \subseteq i_l \subseteq i$ and a subset of parameters $p_{lk} \subseteq p_l \subseteq p$.

An incorrect parameter may cause a failure at the output of an f_{lk} literal, which can in turn lead to a failure at the final output r. The impact of faulty parameters on individual f_{lk}s depends on the function of these literals individually; and can be determined by using the original FMR. The impact of faulty f_{lk}s on r, on the other hand, is always in accordance with DNF architecture, and is independent from the individual f_{lk}s. So, let us first examine the propagation of faults through a generic DNF.

Lemma 1. *Let* $r = f(i, p)$ *be the DNF model of an SIS program as defined in* (2). *Let* $\hat{r}$, $\hat{f}_l$ *and* $\hat{f}_{lk}$ *represent the failure modes at the outputs of* f, f_l *and* f_{lk} *respectively. Then:*

$$(\hat{r} = \ell \vee \hat{r} = \hbar) \Rightarrow \bigvee_{l=1}^{l=L} (\hat{f}_l = \hat{r}) \tag{3}$$

$$(\hat{r} = \ell \vee \hat{r} = \hbar) \Rightarrow \bigvee_{l=1}^{l=L} \bigvee_{k=1}^{k=K} (\hat{f}_{lk} = \hat{r}) \tag{4}$$

Proof. We begin with the disjunctive part $r = \vee_l f_l$:

$$\hat{r} = \ell \Rightarrow (r = 0 \wedge r' = 1) \Rightarrow \bigwedge_{j=1}^{j=L} (f_j = 0) \wedge \bigvee_{l=1}^{l=L} (f_l' = 1)$$

$$\Rightarrow \bigvee_{l=1}^{l=L} (\hat{f}_l = \ell) \bigwedge_{\substack{j=1 \\ j \neq l}}^{j=L} (f_j = 0) \Rightarrow \bigvee_{l=1}^{l=L} (\hat{f}_l = \ell) \tag{5}$$

$$\hat{r} = \hbar \Rightarrow (r = 1 \wedge r' = 0) \Rightarrow \bigvee_{l=1}^{l=L} (f_l = 1) \wedge \bigwedge_{j=1}^{j=L} (f_j' = 0)$$

$$\Rightarrow \bigvee_{l=1}^{l=L} (\hat{f}_l = \hbar) \bigwedge_{\substack{j=1 \\ j \neq l}}^{j=L} (f_j' = 0) \Rightarrow \bigvee_{l=1}^{l=L} (\hat{f}_l = \hbar) \tag{6}$$

(5) and (6) together prove (3). Further, each conjunctive clause in DNF is defined by $f_l = \wedge_k f_{lk}$. Similar to the disjunctive part, we can say:

$$\hat{f}_l = \ell \Rightarrow (f_l = 0 \wedge f_l' = 1) \Rightarrow \bigvee_{k=1}^{k=K} (f_{lk} = 0) \wedge \bigwedge_{j=1}^{j=K} (f_{lj}' = 1)$$

$$\Rightarrow \bigvee_{k=1}^{k=K} (\hat{f}_{lk} = \ell) \bigwedge_{\substack{j=1 \\ j \neq k}}^{j=K} (f_{lj}' = 1) \Rightarrow \bigvee_{k=1}^{k=K} (\hat{f}_{lk} = \ell) \tag{7}$$

$$\hat{f}_l = \hbar \Rightarrow (f_l = 1 \wedge f_l' = 0) \Rightarrow \bigwedge_{j=1}^{j=K} (f_{lj} = 1) \wedge \bigvee_{k=1}^{k=K} (f_{lk}' = 0)$$

$$\Rightarrow \bigvee_{k=1}^{k=K} (\hat{f}_{lk} = \hbar) \bigwedge_{\substack{j=1 \\ j \neq k}}^{j=K} (f_{lj} = 1) \Rightarrow \bigvee_{k=1}^{k=K} (\hat{f}_{lk} = \hbar) \qquad (8)$$

By substituting (7) in (5) and (8) in (6) we will have:

$$\hat{r} = \ell \Rightarrow \bigvee_{l=1}^{l=L} \bigvee_{k=1}^{k=K} (\hat{f}_{lk} = \ell) \qquad (9)$$

$$\hat{r} = \hbar \Rightarrow \bigvee_{l=1}^{l=L} \bigvee_{k=1}^{k=K} (\hat{f}_{lk} = \hbar) \qquad (10)$$

which together prove (4).

Lemma 1 shows the minimum condition: if the output of a DNF is deviated in either ℓ or $\hbar$ direction, at least one f_{lk} literal is deviated in the same direction. We will see later how test cases can help minimize (4); but let us first describe how a test case is typically used in a real test scenario.

SIS "Factory Acceptance Tests" are often done in a black-box setting, where only the inputs to and outputs of the system are used to validate its functionality. In such settings, not only do we need to confirm that the system produces the expected output, but we also need to ensure that the output is indeed *caused* by the given test input. This is the causality condition. Further, the test input ι may only be a subset of all SIS inputs i. There may remain a number of inputs $\delta := i \setminus \iota$ that are not specified as part of a test case, simply because they are not related to the hazardous scenario under test. Such inputs should remain unchanged during the test. To include both the causality condition and the finiteness of test inputs, we need to agree on a key assumption here.

Assumption 1. *Given the SIS program f as defined in (2) and a test case (ι, ρ) proposed for testing f, we assume that:*

- *If $\rho = 1$, there is at least one $f_l(i_l, p_l)$ clause in f such that $i_l \subseteq \iota$ and if p_l is correct then $f_l(\iota_l, p_l) = \rho$.*
- *If $\rho = 0$ and $i_l \cap \iota \neq \emptyset$, there is at least one $f_{lk}(i_{lk}, p_{lk})$ in f_l such that $i_{lk} \subseteq \iota$ and if p_{lk} is correct then $f_{lk}(\iota_{lk}, p_{lk}) = \rho$.*

Corollary 1. *Given the SIS program with DNF architecture defined in (2) and the test case (ι, ρ), if $i_l \cap \iota = \emptyset$ then p_l cannot be incorrect (wrt. to (ι, ρ)).*

Assumption 1 is particularly important in identifying the f_{lk} literals with incorrect parameters. If an f_{lk} is not a part of a successful response at the output of program, it obviously cannot be a part of the failure either. This Assumption also implies a minimum level of consistency between a chosen test case and the implemented program architecture. This is particularly important in factory acceptance tests in the process industry, where test cases are typically decided by hand and based on informal requirement specifications; which is very different to test case generation scenarios in generic software engineering [3].

We can now set out the rules that we will use for simplifying disjunction (4).

Lemma 2. *Given are the SIS program with DNF architecture defined in (2) and the test case (ι, ρ). Let δ be the set of unspecified inputs $\delta := i \setminus \iota$. A literal f_{lk} can only be considered as a potential cause of an output deviation $\hat{r} = \ell$ or $\hat{r} = \hbar$ if the following conditions are all met: 1) $p_{lk} \neq \emptyset$; 2) $i_{lk} \cap \delta = \emptyset$; 3) $f_{lk}(\iota, \theta) \neq \rho$; and 4) if there is a f_{lm} such that $m \neq k$ and $p_{lm} = \emptyset$, then $f_{lm}(\iota, \theta) \neq 0$.*

Proof. Condition 1: f_{lk} is a function of inputs i_{lk} and parameters p_{lk}. Given that inputs are specified and the function is correctly implemented (Assumption 1), the only reason for a deviation at the output of f_{lk} would be its parameters.

Condition 2: $i_{lk} \cap \delta \neq \emptyset$ would mean that some inputs in f_{lk} are unspecified. Thus, the output of f_{lk} cannot be judged as a certain cause of fault or success.

Condition 3: From $\hat{r} = \ell \vee \hat{r} = \hbar$ it implies that $r = \neg \rho$. Recall (4) from Lemma 1. For $\hat{f}_{lk} = \hat{r}$ to hold, we need to have $f_{lk} = r = \neg \rho$, which requires $f_{lk}(\iota, \theta) \neq \rho$.

Condition 4: $p_{lm} = \emptyset$ and $f_{lm}(\iota, \theta) = 0$ would together imply that $f_l(\iota, \theta) = \wedge_{k=1}^{K} f_{lk}(\iota, \theta) = 0$, which means f_l is producing its intended output; because it is set to 0 by a specified input. Thus, no other f_{lm} can lead to a fault at the output of f_l or at r.

Lemma 2 helps eliminate those literals in (4) that cannot be true. Once these literals are eliminated, the remaining sentences can be extended to expressions of parameter's failure modes by applying the original FMR. The complete method is outlined in Algorithm 1.

The algorithm is divided into two separate parts for better clarity. In the first part the f_{lk} literals with potentially incorrect parameters are identified and labeled. At the end of this part, an entry $w_{lk} = 0$ in the labels matrix w indicates that the corresponding $\hat{f}_{lk}$ is ruled out and can be eliminated from the failure mode expression ϕ. In the second part, the original FMR is applied to the remaining f_{lk}s to compose a failure mode expression with respect to the parameters. The last step of this part uses basic rules of propositional logic, e.g. De Morgan's laws [7] to simplify the resultant ϕ.

Algorithm 1 produces an understanding of failure modes with respect to one test case. One would expect that more test cases should help narrow down these findings even further.

Theorem 1. *Given are the SIS program with DNF architecture defined in (2) and the test set $T = \{(\iota^n, \rho^n) \mid 1 \leq n \leq N\}$. Let ϕ^n be the failure mode expression produced by Algorithm 1 wrt. test case n. The intersection between all ϕ^n expressions represents the minimal set of potentially incorrect parameters.*

Proof. We proved Lemmas 1 and 2, on which Algorithm 1 is based. Hence, ϕ^n corresponds the potentially incorrect parameters related to test case n. We also know that all ϕ^n expressions should hold at the same time; because there is only one set of current parameters setting. Therefore, the overall failure mode expression ϕ should satisfy all the ϕ^ns, and thus ϕ is the intersection of all ϕ^ns.

Algorithm 1: FMR4SP

Input: SIS program DNF as defined in (2)
Input: Current parameter settings θ
Input: Test case (ι, ρ)
Output: Failure modes disjunction ϕ
`// Identifying suspicious` f_{lk}`s:`
$\hat{r} := \mathrm{md}_\wp(f(\iota, \theta), \rho);$
forall the *elements of* w **do**
  | $w_{lk} := 0;$ `//` w `is an` $L \times K$ `matrix`
end
for $l := 1$ **to** L **do**
  | **for** $k := 1$ **to** K **do**
  | | **if** $i_{lk} \cap (i \setminus \iota) \neq \emptyset$ **then** continue;
  | | $z := f_{lk}(\iota_{lk}, \theta_{lk});$
  | | **if** $p_{lk} = \emptyset$ **then**
  | | | **if** $z = 0$ **then**
  | | | | **forall the** *elements of* w_l **do** $w_{ln} := 0;$
  | | | | break; `// To next` l
  | | | **else** continue; `// To next` k
  | | **else if** $z = \rho$ **then** continue;
  | | $w_{lk} := 1;$ `//` p_{lk} `potentially faulty`
  | **end**
end
`// Composing the FMR expression:`
$\phi := \vee_l \vee_k (\hat{f}_{lk} = \hat{r});$
for $l := 1$ **to** L **do**
  | **for** $k := 1$ **to** K **do**
  | | **if** $w_{lk} = 1$ **then**
  | | | Use original FMR to convert $(\hat{f}_{lk} = \hat{r})$ to an expression depending on $\hat{p}_{lk};$
  | | **else** Remove $(\hat{f}_{lk} = \hat{r})$ from ϕ
  | **end**
end
Simplify the resultant ϕ by using logic rules;

---

4   Case Study

In this section we will demonstrate the implementation of our method in an industrial case study from a medium-scale power plant project. In this project the SIS was installed to protect a heat recovery steam generator (HRSG) and its supplementary burner. Simply put, an HRSG is an industrial boiler that uses recycled heat from another source, e.g. a gas turbine, to generate super-heat steam, which can then be used in a downstream process, e.g. a steam turbine. Some HRSGs utilize supplementary burners to expand their capacity.

The SIS we study here performs 30 safety functions for the burner, 11 of which are shared with the HRSG. For our case study, we analyze a shared safety function; that of "extreme level of water in boiler". This function receives readings from level and pressure sensors as its inputs. Pressure measurement is used to modify the level readings[6]. The corrected level readings are then compared to a preset threshold and, if it is determined that the water level is above the permissible range, a trip will be initiated at the SIS outputs to close the gas valves. A failure to initiate the trip may lead to catastrophic damages to the steam turbine and potential risk to the personnel working in the area.

An overview of the SIS program with a focus on drum level safety function is shown in Fig. 2. The SIS program as a whole receives almost 200 inputs from sensors, and produces 25 hardwired outputs. The program comprises over 2170 function blocks, with thousands of parameters. Here, we are only interested in output r and the FBs and parameters that link r to the nominated inputs.

In Fig. 2, parameters are named by p_js and intermediate variables by x_js. Drum level is measured by inputs $i_1, i_2, i_3 \in [-380\,\text{mm}, 755\,\text{mm}]$ and pressure by $i_7, i_8 \in [0\,\text{MPa}, 20\,\text{MPa}]$. The other six inputs $i_4, i_5, i_6, i_9, i_{10} \in \mathbb{B}$ indicate the detected faults of their corresponding sensors. Each box in the diagram represents an FB. Details of some of the functions is given below with some simplifications.

$$x_0 = (x_1 \wedge x_2) \vee (x_2 \wedge x_3) \vee (x_3 \wedge x_1) \qquad x_1 = i_4 \vee (\neg i_4 \wedge x_{13}) \vee (x_{19} \wedge x_{22})$$
$$x_{19} = Abs(i_1 - Avg(i_1, i_2, i_3)) > p_{22} \qquad x_{22} = \neg(i_4 \vee i_5 \vee i_6)$$
$$x_{13} = (x_{16} - p_7) > p_1 \qquad x_{16} = Corr(x_{23}, x_{27}, p_{10})$$
$$x_{23} = i_1 + p_{13} \qquad x_{27} = x_{28} \times p_{19}$$
$$x_{28} = Max(p_{18}, Min(p_{17}, x_{29})) \qquad x_{30} = \begin{cases} i_7, & if\ x_{31} = 0 \\ i_8, & if\ x_{31} = 1 \end{cases}$$

Here, Abs, Avg, Min and Max calculate the absolute, average, maximum and minimum values respectively. The correction FB $Corr$ reads the level and pressure sensors and a "distance" parameter (e.g. p_{10}), and it produces the corrected value of level based on complex thermodynamic formulas and look-up tables. Also, $PT1$ and OFF are time delay functions and do not alter the values of their inputs. Therefore, for the purpose of FMR: $x_{29} = x_{30}$ and $x_{31} = i_9$.

Consider now a factory setup where the SIS program is to be tested and validated. The test engineers know from the requirements specification that the burner should trip if any two out of the three level sensors are healthy and their

---

[6] Water drum pressure can vary within a wide range, causing considerable changes to water density and thus to the level measurement. High pressure drums usually use pressure readings to compensate the impact of water density on level measurements.

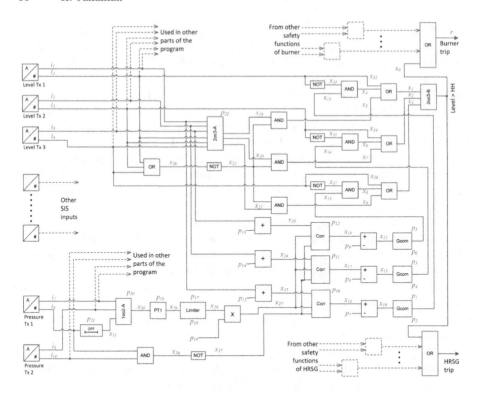

Fig. 2. SIS program for the burner case study

corrected values read over 260 mm. So, the engineers set the pressure measurement to the arbitrary value of 0.5 MPa by injecting $i_7 = 0.5$ and $i_9 = 0$. Then, they inject and adjust level measurements such that the corrected values of level show > 260 mm on the operator screen. At this point the injected inputs are 243 mm; however, given that the corrected level is above the specified threshold, we expect to see a 1 at output r. Based on the selected test cases, which are in turn selected based on the requirement specification, we have encountered the following cases where the observed and expected outputs do not match:

$$\text{Test case 1: } ([\iota_1^1 \ \iota_2^1 \ \iota_4^1 \ \iota_5^1 \ \iota_7^1 \ \iota_9^1], \rho^1) = ([243 \ 243 \ 0 \ 0 \ 0.5 \ 0], 1), \quad r = 0$$
$$\text{Test case 2: } ([\iota_2^2 \ \iota_3^2 \ \iota_5^2 \ \iota_6^2 \ \iota_7^2 \ \iota_9^2], \rho^2) = ([243 \ 243 \ 0 \ 0 \ 0.5 \ 0], 1), \quad r = 0$$
$$\text{Test case 3: } ([\iota_1^3 \ \iota_3^3 \ \iota_4^3 \ \iota_6^3 \ \iota_7^3 \ \iota_9^3], \rho^3) = ([243 \ 243 \ 0 \ 0 \ 0.5 \ 0], 1), \quad r = 0$$

These test cases constitute an input to Algorithm 1. A second input to Algorithm 1 is the current settings of parameters. The current values of those parameters that are related to our case study is given here:

$\theta_1 = 270$	$\theta_5 = 260$	$\theta_9 = 380$	$\theta_{13} = 380$	$\theta_{17} = 25$	$\theta_{21} = 20$
$\theta_2 = 15$	$\theta_6 = 15$	$\theta_{10} = 490$	$\theta_{14} = 380$	$\theta_{18} = 0$	$\theta_{22} = 100$
$\theta_3 = 270$	$\theta_7 = 380$	$\theta_{11} = 490$	$\theta_{15} = 380$	$\theta_{19} = 10$	
$\theta_4 = 15$	$\theta_8 = 380$	$\theta_{12} = 490$	$\theta_{16} = 5$	$\theta_{20} = 2$	

As a last input to Algorithm 1, we need to define the program DNF. We use Corollary 1 as a basis for an initial screening, in order to reduce the large SIS program into a smaller version, containing only those parts that are relevant to a nominated set of inputs. In this SIS program, r is the output of a DNF with over 450 f_{lk} literals; however, as can be seen in Fig. 2, only a small portion of this DNF is relevant to the drum level inputs. All other clauses can be filtered out, and the SIS program can be reduced to:

$$
\begin{aligned}
x_0 &= (\neg i_4 \wedge x_{19} \wedge \neg i_5 \wedge x_{20} \wedge \neg i_6) \vee (\neg i_4 \wedge x_{19} \wedge \neg i_5 \wedge \neg i_6 \wedge x_{21}) \vee \\
&\quad (\neg i_4 \wedge \neg i_5 \wedge x_{20} \wedge \neg i_6 \wedge x_{21}) \vee (x_{19} \wedge \neg i_5 \wedge x_{14}) \vee (\neg i_4 \wedge x_{13} \wedge x_{20}) \vee \\
&\quad (x_{19} \wedge \neg i_6 \wedge x_{15}) \vee (\neg i_4 \wedge x_{13} \wedge x_{21}) \vee (x_{20} \wedge \neg i_6 \wedge x_{15}) \vee \\
&\quad (\neg i_5 \wedge x_{14} \wedge x_{21}) \vee (x_{13} \wedge i_5) \vee (x_{13} \wedge x_{14}) \vee (x_{13} \wedge i_6) \vee (x_{13} \wedge x_{15}) \vee \\
&\quad (i_5 \wedge i_6) \vee (i_5 \wedge x_{15}) \vee (x_{14} \wedge i_6) \vee (x_{14} \wedge x_{15}) \vee (i_4 \wedge i_5) \vee (i_4 \wedge x_{14}) \vee \\
&\quad (i_4 \wedge i_6) \vee (i_4 \wedge x_{15}) \\
&\equiv \vee_{l=1}^{21} \wedge_{k=1}^{5} f_{lk}
\end{aligned}
\tag{11}
$$

We now get into the processing part of Algorithm 1, which consists of two separate loops for identifying the irrelevant literals and composing the failure mode expression. Effectively, the process begins with a maximal disjunction (see Lemma 1), which is then reduced to a minimal one by applying the elimination rules given in Lemma 2. Consider the test case no. 1 where the output deviation is $\hat{r} = \ell$. The maximal failure mode expression for this test case will be:

$$
\begin{aligned}
\phi^1 &\equiv (\hat{i}_4 = \ell \vee \hat{x}_{13} = \ell \vee \hat{x}_{19} = \ell \vee \hat{i}_5 = \ell \vee \hat{x}_{14} = \ell \vee \hat{x}_{20} = \ell \vee \\
&\quad \hat{i}_6 = \ell \vee \hat{x}_{15} = \ell \vee \hat{x}_{21} = \ell)
\end{aligned}
\tag{12}
$$

The first group of literals that can be eliminated from ϕ^1 includes $\hat{i}_4$, $\hat{i}_5$ and $\hat{i}_6$; because these sentences do not depend on any parameters. Next, $\hat{x}_{19}, \hat{x}_{20}, \hat{x}_{21}$ and $\hat{x}_{15}$ can be eliminated too; because x_{19}, x_{20}, x_{21} and x_{15} depend on unspecified inputs i_3 and i_6. Therefore, the failure mode expression will be simplified to:

$$
\phi^1 \equiv (\hat{x}_{13} = \ell \vee \hat{x}_{14} = \ell)
\tag{13}
$$

We now use the original FMR method to expand $\hat{x}_{13} = \ell$ and $\hat{x}_{14} = \ell$ with respect to parameters. This can be done based on the program architecture and its constituting FBs. x_{13} is the output of a *Gcom* FB. Therefore:

$$
\hat{x}_{13} = \ell \Rightarrow (\hat{p}_1 = \hbar \vee \hat{x}_{10} = \ell)
\tag{14}
$$

Moving backward in the program, from $x_{10} = x_{16} - p_7$ we can reason that $\hat{x}_{10} = \ell \Rightarrow (\hat{p}_7 = \hbar \vee \hat{x}_{16} = \ell)$, and thus:

$$
\hat{x}_{13} = \ell \Rightarrow (\hat{p}_1 = \hbar \vee \hat{p}_7 = \hbar \vee \hat{x}_{16} = \ell)
\tag{15}
$$

Sentence $\hat{x}_{16} = \ell$ depends on the *Corr* FB. As mentioned earlier, this FB uses complex calculations that cannot be expressed in simple mathematical forms.

However, thanks to FMR's abstraction, we do not need to directly deal with such complexities. We know from the description of *Corr* [19] that, for almost the entire operation range, this function has an increasing behavior with respect to its level and pressure inputs, and a decreasing behavior with respect to its "distance" parameter. Therefore, based on Axiom 1:

$$\hat{x}_{16} = \ell \Rightarrow (\hat{x}_{23} = \ell \vee \hat{x}_{27} = \ell \vee \hat{p}_{10} = \hbar) \tag{16}$$

By substituting (16) in (15), we will have:

$$\hat{x}_{13} = \ell \Rightarrow (\hat{p}_1 = \hbar \vee \hat{p}_7 = \hbar \vee \hat{p}_{10} = \hbar \vee \hat{x}_{23} = \ell \vee \hat{x}_{27} = \ell)$$
$$\Rightarrow (\hat{p}_1 = \hbar \vee \hat{p}_7 = \hbar \vee \hat{p}_{10} = \hbar \vee \hat{p}_{13} = \ell \vee \hat{x}_{27} = \ell) \tag{17}$$

Variable x_{27} is the output of a multiplication function. It can be shown that when the current values of both inputs are greater than zero and the output fault is $\hat{x}_{27} = \ell$, the input faults will be: $\hat{x}_{28} = \ell \vee \hat{p}_{19} = \ell \vee (\hat{x}_{28} = \hbar \wedge \hat{p}_{19} = \hbar)$. Therefore, (17) can be changed to:

$$\hat{x}_{13} = \ell \Rightarrow (\hat{p}_1 = \hbar \vee \hat{p}_7 = \hbar \vee \hat{p}_{10} = \hbar \vee \hat{p}_{13} = \ell \vee$$
$$\hat{x}_{28} = \ell \vee \hat{p}_{19} = \ell \vee (\hat{x}_{28} = \hbar \wedge \hat{p}_{19} = \hbar)) \tag{18}$$

Variable x_{28} is the output of a limiter (i.e. min/max) function, which is also a monotonic function with respect to its input and its parameters. The input to this function is x_{29}, which is directly linked to SIS inputs, and thus cannot be faulty. Therefore, the only possible cause for $\hat{x}_{28} = \ell$ can be $p_{18} = \ell$ and the cause for $\hat{x}_{28} = \hbar$ can be $p_{17} = \hbar$. As a result:

$$\hat{x}_{13} = \ell \Rightarrow (\hat{p}_1 = \hbar \vee \hat{p}_7 = \hbar \vee \hat{p}_{10} = \hbar \vee \hat{p}_{13} = \ell \vee$$
$$\hat{p}_{18} = \ell \vee \hat{p}_{19} = \ell \vee (\hat{p}_{17} = \hbar \wedge \hat{p}_{19} = \hbar)) \tag{19}$$

Similarly, we can interpret $\hat{x}_{14} = \ell$ to an expression on parameters:

$$\hat{x}_{14} = \ell \Rightarrow (\hat{p}_3 = \hbar \vee \hat{p}_8 = \hbar \vee \hat{p}_{11} = \hbar \vee \hat{p}_{14} = \ell \vee$$
$$\hat{p}_{18} = \ell \vee \hat{p}_{19} = \ell \vee (\hat{p}_{17} = \hbar \wedge \hat{p}_{19} = \hbar)) \tag{20}$$

which, together with (19), will lead to:

$$\phi^1 \equiv (\hat{p}_1 = \hbar \vee \hat{p}_7 = \hbar \vee \hat{p}_{10} = \hbar \vee \hat{p}_{13} = \ell \vee$$
$$\hat{p}_3 = \hbar \vee \hat{p}_8 = \hbar \vee \hat{p}_{11} = \hbar \vee \hat{p}_{14} = \ell \vee$$
$$\hat{p}_{18} = \ell \vee \hat{p}_{19} = \ell \vee (\hat{p}_{17} = \hbar \wedge \hat{p}_{19} = \hbar)) \tag{21}$$

Using Algorithm 1 for test cases no. 2 and 3 we will lead to the following results:

$$\phi^2 \equiv (\hat{p}_3 = \hbar \vee \hat{p}_8 = \hbar \vee \hat{p}_{11} = \hbar \vee \hat{p}_{14} = \ell \vee$$
$$\hat{p}_{18} = \ell \vee \hat{p}_{19} = \ell \vee (\hat{p}_{17} = \hbar \wedge \hat{p}_{19} = \hbar)) \tag{22}$$
$$\phi^3 \equiv (\hat{p}_1 = \hbar \vee \hat{p}_7 = \hbar \vee \hat{p}_{10} = \hbar \vee \hat{p}_{13} = \ell \vee$$
$$\hat{p}_{18} = \ell \vee \hat{p}_{19} = \ell \vee (\hat{p}_{17} = \hbar \wedge \hat{p}_{19} = \hbar)) \tag{23}$$

As we showed earlier in Theorem,1, ϕ^1, ϕ^2 and ϕ^3 should all hold at the same time, and thus the final failure expression will be their intersection:

$$\phi \equiv (\hat{p}_{18} = \ell \vee \hat{p}_{19} = \ell \vee (\hat{p}_{17} = \hbar \wedge \hat{p}_{19} = \hbar) \vee$$
$$((\hat{p}_1 = \hbar \vee \hat{p}_7 = \hbar \vee \hat{p}_{10} = \hbar \vee \hat{p}_{13} = \ell) \wedge$$
$$(\hat{p}_3 = \hbar \vee \hat{p}_8 = \hbar \vee \hat{p}_{11} = \hbar \vee \hat{p}_{14} = \ell))) \qquad (24)$$

The resultant expression indicates two possibilities of fault: a conjunction of parameters in the paths of sensors 1 and 2; and parameters set $\{p_{17}, p_{18}, p_{19}\}$, which constitute a common cause to all the three sensor paths. We know from (22) and (23) that the cause of fault in our program cannot be a common cause; otherwise both tested channels would indicate faults, as they did in (21). Hence, the final result will be:

$$\phi \equiv ((\hat{p}_1 = \hbar \vee \hat{p}_7 = \hbar \vee \hat{p}_{10} = \hbar \vee \hat{p}_{13} = \ell) \wedge$$
$$(\hat{p}_3 = \hbar \vee \hat{p}_8 = \hbar \vee \hat{p}_{11} = \hbar \vee \hat{p}_{14} = \ell)) \qquad (25)$$

Our search for incorrect parameters cannot be adjusted any further. This is mainly because a group of parameters (e.g. p_1, p_7, p_{10}, p_{13}) have a cascade impact on the same variable (in this case x_{13}). However, considering the total number of parameters, which is in the range of thousands, having to manually recheck only 8 parameters against the specification is a considerable advantage. Most importantly, the result does include the actual combination of fault that we had simulated for the purpose of this case study: $\hat{p}_1 = \hbar \wedge \hat{p}_3 = \hbar$. The result also shows the capability of our method in identifying concurring faults.

5   Discussion

When using FMR for input faults, the objective is to *maximize* the results, to include all possible failure causes coming into the system. When fault finding parameters, we try to *minimize* the results because we are looking for an existing fault within the system. In the former scenario we are interested in how the SIS *may* fail in the future. In the latter we try to locate an existing, *certain* fault. In studying input failure modes, program architecture alone is sufficient for reasoning; since we look for external faults. When searching for incorrect parameters, we utilize test cases as an additional source of information; since we look for internal faults. These functional differences make the two methods suitable for two different applications: the former is suitable in the early stage of design when safety engineers analyze the modes and probability of SIS failure. The latter is helpful in pre-installation factory acceptance testing and, similarly, in regular validation tests during plant operation.

We introduced a method that can serve in parameter diagnostics scenarios. Our add-on to the original FMR included the elimination process and the use of test cases. We also added to the reasoning process of the original FMR by formulating a generic DNF architecture, which is commonly used in SIS programs in the process industry.

Our intention in this paper was not to introduce a tool, but rather to propose and formalize the method. We are currently working towards incorporating Algorithm 1 into our existing FMR tool so that we can utilize it for detecting failure modes of parameters too. We are also working on generalizing the elimination phase based on dynamic program slicing [15] and graph reachability [18] in order to extend the analysis capacity of our method to non-DNF architectures.

In using FMR for parameters, the main objective is to diagnose the fault. However, the reasoning process can be extended to include estimating boundary conditions for correct values of parameters. The logic is simple: if ϕ indicates that the current setting of a parameter is lower (or higher) than what it should be, then that parameter should be adjusted to a higher (or lower) value than what it currently is. A proposed correction for (25), for instance, will be: $(\theta'_1 < \theta_1 \vee \theta'_7 < \theta_7 \vee \theta'_{10} < \theta_{10} \vee \theta'_{13} > \theta_{13}) \wedge (\theta'_3 < \theta_3 \vee \theta'_8 < \theta_8 \vee \theta'_{11} < \theta_{11} \vee \theta'_{14} > \theta_{14})$. One may however ask whether such rough solutions are of practical help. In our experience, once the suspicious parameters are located, it is often easier to check them against the requirement specification, rather than to recalculate them.

6 Related Works

Diagnostics based on systematic inference was extensively studied in the 1980's. Some of the frequently cited articles include [5,8,17]. Generally speaking, these studies were aimed to answer one question: given an observed deviation at the output of a system, how can we identify the faulty components by reasoning based on the knowledge of system structure and/or system function? Logic circuits in particular made an interesting application as they typically consist of complex yet well-defined logical structures. Unlike inference-based diagnostics, FMR was primarily designed to target probable input faults, rather than faulty system components. Moreover, FMR is specialized in analyzing SIS programs, rather than hardware systems. In searching for faulty parameters we used the existing FMR platform to solve a diagnostics problem for a specific application context; i.e. SIS programs.

Finding faulty parameters may also be compared to program debugging, provided we include the correction steps that the user would take after the incorrect parameters are identified. Going by the definitions in [11], FMR is a method for debugging by deduction, where we create a list of possible causes of the bug and then narrow them down by reasoning. Readers can find a useful historical and methodological summary of debugging functional programs in [21], which also proposes its own method based on interpretation. Compared to functional programs in general [4], debugging an SIS program is a simpler problem to solve. The functions (i.e. FBs) are developed by technology suppliers and undergo independent certification processes that are then followed by systematic revision control and patching processes. For an SIS system integrator (who would be the main target user of our method) FBs are deemed to be correct, and the main concerns in developing an SIS application program are selecting, interconnecting, and parameterizing the FBs. The method we presented here is specific to

SIS programs, and it uses the advantage of their specific logical structure to gain benefits in other aspects of debugging, such as speed and scalability.

A well-established approach in debugging is "program slicing", where a large, complex program is reduced to a small, yet relevant slice of the program in order to make the fault finding easier [15,20]. Our Corollary 1 and Lemma 2 in fact constitute a slicing method specific to DNF programs. It should be noted, however, that slicing alone is not a fault finding process; and it is only used to reduce the search area. In the method we presented here the actual fault reasoning process happens in the second half of Algorithm 1 and by using the FMR techniques.

As a diagnostic approach, our focus in FMR is on detecting faults; and in this paper we focused on detecting faults of parameters. Although the outcome of our fault finding can essentially help with correcting the right parameters in the right directions, our method is not aimed to provide any calculation or optimization of exact values for parameters. Calculating the optimum settings of parameters is rather a design question, for which optimization methods, such as parameter synthesis [6], may be employed.

7   Conclusion

We formalized the application of FMR for identifying incorrect parameters and their failure modes. We demonstrated the implementation of the method through a case study from the process industry.

The case study that we used here illustrated that our method can correctly narrow down the fault to the smallest possible set of suspicious parameters, given the architecture of the program and the test cases. While the final results may not always be limited to certainly faulty parameters, the final set of candidates is dramatically smaller than the complete set of parameters in the program. This can substantially reduce the time and effort that safety engineers would otherwise need to spend on visually reviewing the program. The case study also showed that our algorithm efficiently operates in scenarios where multiple incorrect parameters exist in the program.

For future research works, we aim to expand the FMR prototype tool to include automated identification of incorrect parameters. Other areas for further research include generalizing the method to non-DNF programs and incorporating the "prior states". The latter topic is particularly helpful in programs with hysteresis elements, in which the validity of an expected output also depends on the status of SIS output prior to applying a test input. Lastly, we would like to examine the potential for cross-reasoning between test cases. Currently each test case is analyzed independently. A cross comparison between the findings of test cases may provide a better visibility to common cause failure, and help further narrow down the final results.

References

1. Wikipedia: 2019 Xiangshui chemical plant explosion. https://en.wikipedia.org/wiki/2019_Xiangshui_chemical_plant_explosion. Accessed 28 Jun 2021
2. Abrial, J.R., Abrial, J.R.: The B-Book: Assigning Programs to Meanings. Cambridge University Press, Cambridge (2005)
3. Anand, S., et al.: An orchestrated survey of methodologies for automated software test case generation. J. Syst. Softw. **86**(8), 1978–2001 (2013)
4. Chitil, O.: Functional programming. In: Wah, B.W. (ed.) Encyclopedia of Computer Science and Engineering, pp. 1334–1344. Wiley, Hoboken (2009)
5. Davis, R.: Diagnostic reasoning based on structure and behavior. Artif. Intell. **24**(1–3), 347–410 (1984)
6. Dehnert, C., et al.: Prophesy: a probabilistic parameter synthesis tool. In: International Conference on Computer Aided Verification, pp. 214–231 (2015)
7. Genesereth, M., Kao, E.: Introduction to Logic. Synthesis Lectures on Computer Science, vol. 4, no. 1, pp. 1–165. Routledge, London (2013)
8. Genesereth, M.R.: The use of design descriptions in automated diagnosis. Artif. Intell. **24**(1–3), 411–436 (1984)
9. IEC: IEC 61131: Programmable Controllers - Part 3: Programming Languages (2013)
10. IEC: IEC 61511: Functional Safety-safety Instrumented Systems for the Process Industry Sector - Part 1: Framework, Definitions, System, Hardware and Application Programming Requirements (2016)
11. Glenford, J.M., Tom, B., Corey, S.: Debugging. In: Art of Software Testing, 3rd edn, pp. 157–174. Wiley, Hobobken (2012)
12. Jahanian, H.: Failure mode reasoning. In: 2019 4th International Conference on System Reliability and Safety (ICSRS), pp. 295–303. IEEE (2019)
13. Jahanian, H., McIver, A.: Reasoning with failures. In: Lin, S.W., Hou, Z., Mahony, B. (eds.) ICFEM 2020. LNCS, vol. 12531, pp. 36–52. Springer, Cham (2020). https://doi.org/10.1007/978-3-030-63406-3_3
14. Jahanian, H., Parker, D., Zeller, M., McIver, A., Papadopoulos, Y.: Failure mode reasoning in model based safety analysis. In: Zeller, M., Höfig, K. (eds.) IMBSA 2020. LNCS, vol. 12297, pp. 130–145. Springer, Cham (2020). https://doi.org/10.1007/978-3-030-58920-2_9
15. Korel, B., Laski, J.: Dynamic program slicing. Inf. Process. Lett. **29**(3), 155–163 (1988)
16. Morgan, C.: (In-)formal methods: the lost art - a users' manual. In: Liu, Z., Zhang, Z. (eds.) SETSS 2014. LNCS, vol. 9506, pp. 1–79. Springer, Cham (2014). https://doi.org/10.1007/978-3-319-29628-9_1
17. Reiter, R.: A theory of diagnosis from first principles. Artif. Intell. **32**(1), 57–95 (1987)
18. Reps, T.: Program analysis via graph reachability. Inf. Softw. Technol. **40**(11–12), 701–726 (1998)
19. Siemens: SPPA T3000 Rel 8.2 - Engineering Help. Siemens (2018)
20. Weiser, M.: Program slicing. IEEE Trans. Softw. Eng. (4), 352–357 (1984)
21. Whitington, J.: Debugging functional programs by interpretation. Ph.D. thesis, University of Leicester (2020)

Modular Transformation of Java Exceptions Modulo Errors

Robert Rubbens(✉), Sophie Lathouwers, and Marieke Huisman

Formal Methods and Tools, University of Twente, Enschede, The Netherlands
r.b.rubbens@utwente.nl

Abstract. Deductive verifiers are used more and more in both academia and industry to prevent costly bugs. Their capabilities of verifying concurrent programs are getting better, but they are still lagging behind with regard to many major programming language features such as exceptions. To improve the situation, this work presents a semantics of Java exceptions which reduces the annotation burden on the user, while still allowing verification of exceptions. This is accomplished by ignoring sources of errors which are irrelevant to functional verification. Additionally, to deal with the complex control flow introduced by `finally`, a transformation is proposed that simplifies verification of exceptional postconditions and `finally` into postconditions and `goto`. We implement the approach and evaluate it against several common exception patterns.

Keywords: Deductive verification · Java · VerCors · Exceptions · Finally · Errors

1 Introduction

For programs which require high reliability and robustness, such as nuclear power plant, railroad, or tunnel software, bugs are not acceptable. To ensure that a program complies with the highest standards of correctness, deductive verifiers have been developed. Deductive verifiers implement logics to reason about programs mathematically, and can ensure adherence to a specification. This guarantee increases the chance that bugs will be caught before software is deployed.

If we have tools that can verify if a program is free of bugs, why do we still have bugs? Part of the answer is that industry uses language features that are often unsupported by deductive verifiers. An example of such a feature is the Java exceptions mechanism, which is the primary tool to identify and handle failures of many kinds in Java code. Osman et al. indicate that for four mature Java projects the proportion of exception-related code remains around 1%, even after 6 years of ongoing development [27]. For code bases like Hadoop and Tomcat, which contain millions of lines of code, these are significant numbers [4,5]. We do not know of any efforts to fully verify code bases such as these, but to accomplish this, support for exceptions is mandatory.

A. Lluch Lafuente and A. Mavridou (Eds.): FMICS 2021, LNCS 12863, pp. 67–84, 2021.
https://doi.org/10.1007/978-3-030-85248-1_5

There are several projects that allow verification of Java, and some support exceptions. For example, OpenJML [7] can verify sequential Java. Another example, VerCors [2], can verify concurrent Java, but does not have support for exceptions at all. Finally, Verifast [19] can verify concurrent Java with exceptions, but does not support finally. Therefore, when verifying Java, a choice must be made. Either sequential Java can be verified with full support for exceptions, or concurrent Java can be verified with limited exception support. What is surprising is that this dichotomy is not necessary: concurrent execution and exceptional control flow are orthogonal concerns.

In this work, we try to improve the state of the art by implementing full support for exceptions in VerCors, a verifier of concurrent Java.

Java itself has some facilities for checking at compile time if some exceptions are handled. Particularly, "checked exceptions" are required to be handled when they occur. "Unchecked exceptions" are not required to be handled. Exceptions are intended to make error handling more structured and robust, but there are signs they currently fail at the latter. According to a study done by Sena et al. 20% of the bugs in 656 Java projects are related to improper exception usage [31].

One way of solving this is only using checked exceptions, as Java requires each checked exception to be handled. Unfortunately, Java ignores unchecked exceptions, so this rule is easily broken. Furthermore, various parts of the standard library use unchecked exceptions, so it is easy to break this rule accidentally, and hard to manually ensure only checked exceptions are used. This is where deductive verifiers can help: verifying exception handling code automatically could help with reducing bugs related to exception handling, as the verifier can guarantee that an exception is always handled correctly.

Verifying exceptions poses three problems. First, supporting finally entails handling complex control flow. To avoid a monolithic implementation, a modular transformation must be designed that decomposes the control flow as much as possible. Second, according to *The Java Language Specification* [14] (JLS), exceptions can come from many places, not just the throw statement, but also from e.g. allocating memory. Requiring the user to create annotations for all these cases is unfeasible. A subset of Java exceptions must be chosen such that the annotation burden is reduced, while still allowing verification of common exception patterns. Third, standard library code that throws checked and unchecked exceptions must be annotated with exceptional specifications.

In this work, we try to resolve the first and second problem, and leave the third for future work. First, to decompose complex control flow introduced by exceptions, we transform all control flow in the program into exceptions. The exceptional control flow is then transformed into goto statements. This approach splits up the transformation into multiple steps, making it more modular. It also reduces the number of different kinds of control flow, which simplifies the semantics in the intermediate stages.

Second, to relieve the user of the annotation burden, we define a subset of Java exceptions called "exceptions modulo errors". This view allows exceptions to originate from throw statements and method calls with throws attributes, and ignores exceptions caused by memory allocation failures or other low-level implementation details. Reducing the annotation burden this way has a cost: guarantees of verification are weaker because some errors are ignored. However, since the assumption of exceptions modulo errors is often made in commercial software development, we argue it is a reasonable simplification.

Contributions. The main contributions of this work are:

- A simplified semantics of exceptions allowing verification of functional properties which ignores a number of specific errors.
- An evaluation of the simplified semantics with common exception patterns.
- An encoding of exceptional postconditions and `finally` into postconditions and `goto`.
- An implementation of support for exceptions in the VerCors verifier.

The files used for evaluating exceptions modulo errors, as well as instructions for running jStar, Krakatoa, and VerCors, can be found in the package accompanying this paper. The package can be found here: [30].

Paper Structure. Section 2 discusses the background on Java verification in VerCors. Section 3 discusses related work. Section 4 discusses the definition of exceptions modulo errors. Section 5 discusses how `finally` complicates Java verification, and how this can be resolved by transforming all control flow into exceptional control flow. Section 6 evaluates the approach presented in this work against common exception patterns. Section 7 reflects on the presented approach. Section 8 contains the conclusions and future work.

2 Background

This section discusses background necessary to understand how VerCors verifies Java programs. We first discuss the notion of abrupt termination in Java. Then we discuss how VerCors verifies Java programs.

2.1 Abrupt Termination

Abrupt termination [22, p. 14] is a grouping term for control flow that does not go from one statement to the next, like regular control flow. Instead, abrupt termination is when a statement terminates not because it is completed, but because it is terminated sooner than normal and control flow is redirected to another program point. Abrupt termination is sometimes also referred to as non-local or non-linear control flow.

One example of abrupt termination is the `throw` statement, as it aborts execution of the current block and redirects control flow to the nearest `catch` block. Other abrupt termination keywords are: `break`, `continue` and `return`. They all terminate the current block earlier than normal, and redirect control flow to another program point.

The labelled `break` and `continue` statements are an extra source of complexity as they allow the user to specify which loop to `break` from or `continue`. These constructs can be useful when nested loops are used. Furthermore, labelled `break` can also be used within `if`, `switch` or labelled blocks.

2.2   VerCors

VerCors is verifier for concurrent software [2]. It can verify programs written in Java, OpenCL, C, and PVL. VerCors uses separation logic to reason about concurrent access to data.

It is a deductive verifier, which means it uses a system of proof rules to establish correctness of the input. When VerCors reports an input program to be correct, it means it has found a proof using logical inference. For more information about deductive verification, we refer the reader to "Deductive Software Verification: From Pen-and-Paper Proofs to Industrial Tools" by Hähnle and Huisman [16].

It is also a modular verifier, which means that verification of each method only depends on the contract of other methods, and not on their implementation. This also holds for concurrency: threads are verified "thread-modularly", which implies that adding another thread does not invalidate the correctness of previously verified threads.

Figure 1 presents the architecture of VerCors. The general principle is that an input program is parsed and converted into the internal AST called Common Object Language (COL). Then various passes are applied to the COL AST depending on the input language and provided flags. Finally, after applying all necessary passes, the COL AST is converted into Silver, the input language of Viper [24]. Viper reports if there are any failed assertions by translating the input into SMT and calling the Z3 SMT solver [23]. These errors are translated back by VerCors to the level of the input file. For more details on the architecture and implementation of VerCors, we refer the reader to "The VerCors Tool Set: Verification of Parallel and Concurrent Software" by Blom et al. [6].

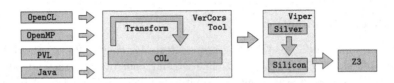

Fig. 1. The architecture of the VerCors tool.

VerCors exposes deductive logic through pre- and postconditions. These are added to the program through annotations, after which VerCors verifies the program if the program adheres to the annotations. Pre- and postconditions are sometimes transformed into assertions, but the semantics remain unchanged.

Listing 1. An implementation of a method computing the maximum of two integers.

```
1  //@ ensures (a > b ? a : b) == \result;
2  //@ signals (ArithmeticException e) a < 0 || b < 0;
3  int max(int a, int b) {
4    if (a < 0 || b < 0) { throw new ArithmeticException(); }
5    return a > b ? a : b; }
```

The VerCors pre- and postcondition syntax is inspired by JML [21]. In the example given in Listing 1, the `max` method is given a contract on line 1 that specifies that its result has to be equal to the maximum of `a` or `b`. Note how the contract is preceded with `//@`, indicating that this comment is in fact a verification annotation. The `ensures` keyword indicates this is a postcondition.

One example of a more complicated contract is the `signals` clause, which first appeared in JML [21]. It is similar to a regular `ensures` postcondition, but only holds if a certain type of exception is thrown. In Listing 1 on line 2 a `signals` clause specifies that if the method throws an `ArithmeticException` it can be assumed that the arguments are negative. Note that the `signals` clause does not impose an obligation to throw when `a < 0 || b < 0`. It *only* indicates that *if* an exception is thrown, the given exceptional postcondition holds.

3   Related Work

There are several tools that support exceptions, each with their own level of support. The following tools support separation logic: Nagini, Gillian-JS, Verifast and jStar. These other tools do not: KeY, OpenJML and Krakatoa. Table 1 summarizes the tools discussed in this section.

Nagini. Nagini fully supports exceptions in the Python language, including the Python equivalents of the statements `break`, `continue`, `return`, `try`, `catch`, and `finally`. This is done by encoding the control flow into an auxiliary state variable that indicates the type of control flow. This approach is documented in the code documentation of Nagini [10].

At first sight it seems that the Python exception model is identical to the exception model of Java. However, there is one subtle difference: Python does not allow labelled breaks. As labelled `breaks` complicate the verification of `finally` (explained in Sect. 5), the implementation strategy employed by Nagini is not directly usable for verifying exceptions in Java and would have to be extended.

Gillian-JS. Gillian-JS [13], formerly known as JaVerT [11], supports exceptions as defined in ECMAScript 5 Strict mode fully. Strict mode is a restricted version of JavaScript where pitfalls of original JavaScript are interpreted as errors.

Table 1. Related work summary

Name	Language	Separation logic	Exceptions
Nagini	Python	Yes	Yes
Gillian-JS	JavaScript	Yes	Yes
Verifast	Java	Yes	Up to `finally`
jStar	Java	Yes	Trivial `finally`
KeY	Java	No	Yes
OpenJML	Java	No	Yes
Krakatoa	Java	No	Up to `finally`

Through private communication with the authors of Gillian-JS we have concluded that Gillian-JS uses the inlining approach. This makes Gillian-JS susceptible to blow-up of the AST size when nested `finally` blocks occur, but the authors of Gillian-JS say they have had no problems with this in practice.

One interesting aspect of Gillian-JS is that internally it keeps track of the following four pieces of information while processing commands: the current error variable, the current return value variable, and the nearest `break` and `continue` labels. This could be simplified by using the approach presented in this work, which, if used, would only need the following two pieces of information: the current exception variable, and the nearest `try-catch-finally` block.

Verifast. Verifast [19] almost fully supports Java exceptions. This means `break`, `return`, `continue`, `throw`, `try`, and `catch` are all supported. These are encoded directly into SMT. The only language feature missing is `finally`. As mentioned in [18], the authors of Verifast are not sure how to encode `finally` clauses.

jStar. jStar [8] has some support for exceptions. Specifically, it allows use of the `try-finally` statement if it can be optimized away trivially. Otherwise jStar crashes. This optimizing is done by Soot [33], an analysis framework for Java.

Soot can parse Java bytecode into its internal representation Jimple. Then, it can apply transformations to this internal representation. Soot can also do a degree of static analysis, which allows it to remove parts of the program if it can detect that it is never executed. For example, if it can detect that the condition of an `if` statement is always true, it will remove the false branch of the `if`. This simplified Jimple code is processed by jStar for analysis.

For convenience we have included a test setup with instructions for running jStar in the package accompanying this paper [30].

KeY. KeY supports sequential Java exceptions. KeY is based on the JavaDL logic, as described in "The KeY Book" [1]. JavaDL provides axiomatic rules for dealing with exceptions, `return`, and labelled `break`. Support for `continue` is implemented by transforming it into **break**. Within these axiomatic rules, control flow is encoded through control flow flags, as described in [32].

Steinhöfel and Wasser present the loop scopes approach that will soon replace the control flow flags approach [32]. Loop scopes reduce the number of proof obligations KeY generates in most cases when dealing with abrupt termination in loops. This is achieved by generalizing the various notions of abrupt termination into the concept of a loop scope.

OpenJML. OpenJML [7] also supports sequential Java exceptions, as well as extensive JML support for specifying the behaviour of exceptions. Steinhöfel and Wasser mention that exceptions and abrupt termination are implemented in OpenJML by encoding the control flow in **goto** [32, Sec. 6].

Krakatoa. Krakatoa [22] supports exceptions, but not **finally**. It achieves this by compiling Java exceptions into the more limited exception model of WhyML. By running the latest version of Krakatoa with **finally** in the input, we have concluded that it does not support **finally**. A test setup with instructions to check this is included in the package accompanying this paper [30].

Krakatoa takes a similar approach to this work by encoding Java exceptions into the cleaner exception model of WhyML. Also similar to our work, they use this approach to implement the abrupt termination semantics of **continue** and **break**. Surprisingly, the developers of Krakatoa seem to have missed the insight that the approach of encoding abrupt termination into exceptions can be applied to **finally**. Since Krakatoa uses an architecture based on an intermediate representation that is passed through various transformations, we expect that applying this insight could simplify the implementation of Krakatoa.

4 Semantics of Exceptions

In this section we describe the semantics of exceptions that we have implemented in VerCors. First we define how we separate error types from error causes. Then, we describe what the ideal semantics is, and why we have not implemented it. Finally, we describe the approximation semantics that we have settled on.

4.1 Errors and Sources of Errors

In Java, an exception of a subclass of **Error** is thrown when a runtime problem occurs. It is important to separate the error types from the error sources, i.e. the exception types that are thrown from the events that cause them to be thrown. We define operations that can cause an **Error** to be thrown as "sources of errors".

For example, when allocating a new object, it can occur that the system is out of memory. In response to this, the allocation terminates abruptly, and throws an exception of type **OutOfMemoryError**. In this case, the error type is **OutOfMemoryError**. The source of the error is the system running out of memory while allocating a new object. Some other Java `Error` types and their sources are: `OutOfMemoryError` caused by loading a new class, and `NoClassDefFoundError` if a class that needs to be loaded is absent. Note that a single error type, e.g. `ClassFormatError`, can be caused by many sources of errors.

4.2   Ideal Semantics

An ideal static analysis tool would follow the semantics outlined in the JLS to the letter. Taking this approach would result in a tool that can analyse the behaviour of a program close to its actual runtime behaviour. Unfortunately, this is not a useful approach for two reasons.

First, the annotation overhead would be enormous. This is because of `OutOfMemoryError`, which occurs when there is no more free memory. Java programs do many allocations, e.g. incrementing an Integer object allocates a new Integer. Since deductive verification requires annotating for exceptions, the ideal semantics would require every method that allocates an object to specify a contract for `OutOfMemoryError`. However, this is often a meaningless contract, because the system would crash in that case, and no recovery is possible. Therefore, formalizing error sources such as the system being out of memory in a tool will require many superfluous annotations in programs, to be specified by the user.

Second, some exceptions cannot be verified at compile time. For example, `ClassFormatError` can be thrown while loading or linking improperly formatted code. `VirtualMachineError` can be thrown because of bugs in the virtual machine. Because some errors depend on the runtime environment, static analysis tools cannot guarantee their absence. Additionally, the design rationale behind `Error` types is that regular programs do not recover from them. Paraphrasing the JLS [15, Sec. 11.1.1]: "Error is the superclass of all the exceptions from which ordinary programs are not ordinarily expected to recover.".

4.3   Semantics Modulo Errors

To avoid the problems with the ideal semantics, we define a simplified view of exceptions where only a subset of the ideal exceptions semantics is included. We refer to this view of exceptions as "exceptions modulo errors". In this view, exceptions can only come from the `throw` statement and method calls.

Formally, if VerCors does not report any problems when verifying a program it implies the following guarantee:

Definition 1 (Exception guarantee). *Any exception from a `throw` statement or a method call is handled in a surrounding `catch`, or the method declares the exception type in a `signals` or a `throws` clause. In addition, during execution the following errors will not occur:*

- *`NullPointerException` when a `null` reference is dereferenced.*
- *`ArithmeticException` when division by zero or modulo zero takes place.*
- *`ArrayIndexOutOfBoundsException` for out of bounds array accesses.*

This definition does not guarantee if an exception will be thrown at all. Therefore it is similar to the notion of partial correctness, which states that a postcondition of a program only holds *if* a program terminates at all.

In short, the exception guarantee implies that all exceptions originating from most common operations, or where the users specify them, are handled through `catch`, `signals`, or `throws`.

While the exception guarantee reduces the annotation burden on the user, it must be emphasised that this is a trade-off. In other words, the guarantee is weaker than what happens in practice. For example, some allocations may fail, but these are not modelled by the exception guarantee. Therefore, the exception guarantee will allow some bugs to go unnoticed. We leave annotation and verification of error sources for future work.

5   The `finally` Encoding Problem

In the previous section we have introduced the semantics that VerCors uses for reasoning about exceptions. In this section, we discuss how VerCors implements this semantics as several program transformations. Specifically, we discuss how the combination of regular control flow and exceptional control flow in `finally` clauses complicates the transformation, and how we resolve this.

Encoding abrupt termination into `goto` is straightforward if `finally` is not present. This is because the description of the semantics as given in the JLS can be interpreted literally. An overview of the transformation is as follows.

- `throw` redirects control flow to the nearest handler or exits the method.
- After a `catch` clause execution continues after the `try`.
- `break` redirects control flow to after the nearest loop.
- `return` redirects control flow to the end of a method.
- When method calls throw an exception, control flow is redirected to the nearest handler or to the end of the method.
- If `try` terminates normally execution should continue after the `try` block.

However, when `finally` is introduced, a more intricate transformation is needed. This is because contrary to all other abrupt termination primitives, at the end of a `finally` clause, it is not directly clear where to jump to.

Consider the example in Listing 2. The lines indicate how control flow would progress. The `break` statements on lines 5 and 7 both redirect control flow to the `finally` block, as it must be executed before leaving the inner `while` loop. Then, at the end of the `finally` block, control flow continues to either directly after the inner, or directly after the outer `while` loop. The control flow after the `finally` splits because the `break` statements are subtly different. The first `break` statement is unlabelled, which means it breaks from the most recently entered `while` loop. The second `break` statement is labelled, which means it breaks from the `while` loop that has that label.

Listing 2. Breaks can introduce ambiguous code paths.

```
1     L: while (p) {
2        while (q) {
3           try {
4              if (r) {
5                 break;
6              } else if (s) {
7                 break L;
8              }
9           } finally {
10             /* Ambiguity */
11          }
12       }
13
14    }
15
```

With the control flow explicitly drawn, reasoning about the control flow is easy. However, without the lines it is less clear what exactly must happen on line 10. If **break** was just executed, control flow needs to jump to after the **while** on line 13. If **break L** was just executed, control flow needs to jump to after the outer while loop on line 15. Without any further information, there is an ambiguity on line 10 which can only be resolved by knowing what kind of statement was previously executed. Hence, we argue that **finally** is non-modular in the sense that its semantics can only be determined when taking into account multiple parts of a method, and not just the **finally** clause itself.

To encode **finally** blocks, what "kind" (returning, breaking, or throwing) of control flow currently applies needs to be encoded. Furthermore, once labelled breaks are added to the language it becomes even more complicated since which *specific* loop is to be broken out of also needs to be tracked.

5.1   Candidate Encodings

Several candidate encodings for **finally** and the rest of the abrupt termination primitives are possible. We discuss the three encodings known to us next. These are: using inlining, using control flow flags, and using exceptions.

While the first and second of these encodings have appeared in some form in an implementation before this work, we have not yet seen an effort to categorize and compare the approaches.

Inlining. The first option that comes to mind is to inline all **finally** blocks in places where normally control flow would jump to the next place of interest. For example, before a throwing method call would jump to a handler, the **finally** clause could be executed by inlining it right there.

Listing 3. Before transformation.

```
try { m1();
      m2();
} finally {
  try { m3();
        m4();
  } finally { inner(); } }
```

Listing 4. After transformation.

```
m1(); if (exc) {
    m3(); if (exc) inner();
    m4(); if (exc) inner(); }
m2(); if (exc) {
    m3(); if (exc) inner();
    m4(); if (exc) inner(); }
```

Fig. 2. Transformation of inlining `finally`. m1-4 are assumed to be throwing. Pseudo exception handling syntax is used in Listing 4, where *exc* evaluates to **true** if the previous line threw an exception.

This option is interesting because it is conceptually straightforward. It is also used in Java compilers [17, p. 3], informally showing that the approach works. The downside of this encoding is possibly exponential code duplication. Figure 2 shows a practical example of the inlining approach where this exponential duplication happens. Notice how the call to **inner** is duplicated four times. This is because the number of times the inner finally is duplicated is equal to the product of the number of times it must be inlined in the inner and outer **try**.

The blow-up caused by inlining was shown to be minimal for regular Java code by Stephen Freund [12]. However, for Java code containing verification annotations, it is unknown if this is also the case, as verification annotations can contain proof steps. Therefore, this cannot be assumed to be the case for verification code as well. Moreover, it is bad for the prover backend, as duplicated code might cause duplicated proof obligations, which will increase the time needed to prove the program correct. We have performed an informal experiment that shows this could be the case for VerCors. This experiment is discussed in [29].

Gillian-JS, as discussed in Sect. 3, uses the inlining approach.

Control Flow Flags. The second option is the optimized version of the first option: **finally** blocks are not inlined, but instead a flag is set whenever the mode of control flow changes. For example, when a **return** is executed, the flag is set to a constant called MODE_RETURN. This flag can then be queried at the end of a **finally** clause to determine where next to jump to. There should be values for each available mode of abrupt termination (i.e. **break**, **return**, **throw**), as well as a mode for every label that can be broken from.

As far as we can tell this is technically possible, but keeping track of all the labels and modes available seems error-prone. Furthermore, at the end of every **finally** clause there has to be an **if** statement determining where to jump next. In a way, this **if** statements encodes all possible origins of the **finally** block, and all possible destinations. This means the **if** statement is non-modular, as it needs information from various places in the method. This introduces unnecessary complexity and increases the chances for bugs.

Listing 5. Before transformation.

```
L: while (c) {
... break L; ...
}
```

Listing 6. After transformation.

```
try { while (c) {
... throw new L(); ...
} } catch (L e) { }
```

Fig. 3. Transformation of break to throw and catch.

This approach has been proposed before, but formulated differently, by Freund [12]. He proposes to encode finally into goto by transforming each finally into a subroutine. Before such a subroutine is called, a unique number is pushed on the stack. This unique number corresponds to the return address of the subroutine, which is recorded in a table. Even though this formulation is different than ours, the downsides of the control flow flag approach still apply.

Nagini, as discussed in Sect. 3, uses the control flow flag approach.

Exceptions. The third option is to consider abrupt termination from an exceptional point of view. When only exceptional control flow is considered, the question of where to continue at the end of a finally clause is simplified:

- If an exception is currently being thrown, execution should continue at the next nearest catch or finally. If there is no such clause, execution should go to the end of the method.
- Otherwise, execution continues after the try-finally block.

Note that the choice of where to jump after a finally clause becomes more local: it does not matter how many exceptions or labels are in scope. Only the next finally or catch clause needs to be known. Homogenizing control flow into the exceptional model simplifies the choice at the end of a finally clause.

A requirement of this encoding is the requirement for this simplification to apply: all other abrupt termination must be removed or transformed into exceptional control flow. This is extra work, but we argue that it is not difficult. An example of how break can be encoded as throw can be seen in Fig. 3.

The translation is similar for continue and return:

- For a statement continue L, the body of the while loop that is the target of the continue must be wrapped in a try { ... } catch (ContinueL e) {} block. The continue statement is replaced by throw new ContinueL().
- For a statement return, the body of the method must be wrapped in try { ... } catch (Return e) {}. The return statement is replaced by throw new Return(). For return statements that return a value, the Return exception type thrown can be augmented with a field to store the value.

Other control-flow related statements, such as throw, if, try, catch and while are not transformed. Extended forms of try-catch, such as try-with-resources, can be supported by transforming the statement into try-finally, as described in the JLS [15, Sec. 14.20.3.1]. try-with-resources is currently not supported in VerCors.

After this step, the remaining throw and try-catch-finally statements can be transformed into goto following the approach outlined at the beginning of Sect. 5, with two differences:

1. throw is converted into a goto to the nearest finally or catch clause. Throwing methods are handled similarly.
2. At the end of a finally, if the current control flow is exceptional, control flow must jump to the next nearest catch or finally clause. Otherwise, control flow must continue after the try-finally.

Because the exceptions approach results in a less error-prone encoding we have implemented it in VerCors. The encoding is used if finally is present in a method. If finally is not present, the basic encoding into goto (which was discussed at the beginning of Sect. 5) is used for a cleaner back-end output. The implementation can be found via the VerCors homepage [34].

A downside of compiling to exceptions is that information is lost, because all control flow is exceptional after the transformation. If this information is needed it can be encoded in the AST. This ensures that synthetic try-catch and throw can be discerned from authentic ones. Additionally, by adding an extra flag the current control flow can be identified as synthetic or authentic.

Another downside is that this approach is not suitable for a single-pass architecture, and only works in verifiers with multiple passes. Therefore the approach is less flexible and cannot be straightforwardly applied to all verifiers.

A verifier that uses a comparable approach is Krakatoa. We discuss the differences with our encoding in Sect. 3.

6 Evaluation

Next, we evaluate if the view of exceptions modulo errors can handle exception patterns from commercial software. We answer the following research questions:

1. What are common exception patterns that occur in commercial software? (Discussed in Sect. 6.1)
2. Can VerCors verify common exception patterns? (Discussed in Sect. 6.2)

6.1 Common Exception Patterns in Commercial Software

Methodology. To find common exception patterns that occur in commercial software, we do an informal survey of the literature through a search on Google Scholar using the keywords "java", "exceptions", and "usage". We look for research that is at most 5 years old, presents a categorization of exception patterns, and considers fifteen or more Java projects.

Table 2. Exception pattern overview.

Used in catch	Used in finally
Empty	Empty
Log, stack trace	Log
if, while, switch, continue, break, return	continue, return
throw e, throw new E(), throw new E(e)	throw new E()
Nested try	Nested try

Results. From this search, four works are selected [3, 20, 25, 28]. We have aggregated the patterns from these works, combining them into common categories. The complete table, listing each category per paper and the elements of the categories, is included in the package accompanying this paper [30]. The aggregated categories can be seen in Table 2. Columns "Used in catch" and "Used in finally" contain patterns that are used in those clauses. "Empty" means the respective clause is used without any statements.

Discussion. While all four studies categorize the use of exceptions and catch clauses extensively, they do not discuss the use of finally thoroughly. More specifically, only Bicalho de Pádua and Purohit et al. include finally in their measurements [3, 28]. Kery et al. and Nakshatri et al. do not include finally [20, 25], because they do their measurements using the Boa tool [9], which does not support the finally clause. As a result, finally is less represented in the table, and some patterns could be missing. However, as completeness was not the goal of this evaluation, this is not a major issue.

6.2 Verification with VerCors

Methodology. To show that VerCors can verify each of the common exception patterns in Sect. 6.1, an example program containing the pattern has been created for each pattern in Table 2. This yields 19 example programs. Where relevant, we added annotations for stronger guarantees, e.g., in some programs we added assert false to indicate control flow cannot reach that part of the program. In other programs we added postconditions to indicate what kinds of normal and exceptional control flow are possible. All of these programs are included in the package accompanying this paper [30].

Results. VerCors verifies all of the annotated example programs. In Listing 7 we show the test program contained in the file CatchStackTrace.java. With regard to Table 2, the program corresponds to the "Used in catch" column and "stack trace" entry. Particularly, in this program there are no further assertions, as printing the stack trace does not require specific pre- or postconditions.

Listing 7. Example program `CatchStackTrace.java`.

```
1  class CatchStackTrace {
2      void m () {
3          try {
4              throw new Exception ();
5          } catch (Exception e) {
6              e.printStackTrace ();
7      } } }
```

Discussion. An aspect of Table 2 that was ignored in the evaluation is that exception patterns can occur simultaneously within a `catch` or `finally`. We are confident this is handled correctly. However, because the purpose of this evaluation was to determine if common patterns are verifiable, we leave the aspect of combinations of patterns for future work.

7 Discussion

We will briefly discuss backend requirements and performance.

7.1 Backend Requirements

Our approach imposes two requirements on the backend: support for `goto` and support for conditional permissions.

Goto. To encode exceptional control flow within a method, the approach presented in this work relies on `goto`. Therefore, if `goto` would not be available in the backend, our transformation to `goto` would not work.

Conditional Permissions. Exceptional postconditions result in conditional permissions. Permissions are a construct used in separation logic with permissions. A permission allows reading or writing from a data location on the heap. For a more thorough introduction to separation logic, we refer the reader to [26]. Conditional permissions are permissions that apply if a condition is met. For example, the postcondition `ensures b ==> Perm(x, write)` yields a `write` permission for x whenever b holds. Exceptional postconditions cause these kinds of permissions because they are encoded as *RuntimeException is thrown ==>* P, where P is an arbitrary postcondition containing permissions.

Conditional permissions are not problematic for separation logic, as they are well defined. However, they might lead to unclear or verbose specifications because permissions are only usable once certain conditions have been met.

One way to avoid conditional permissions is through an "exceptional invariant". This is a user-defined invariant that holds both at entry and exit of a `try-catch` block, and at the end of `catch` clauses. This could simplify the handling of permissions.

7.2   Performance

During the usage of the implementation, we have not seen performance issues. However, there might be three causes of performance problems in the future: bigger encoded output, complex control flow, and conditional permissions.

Bigger Encoded Output. The size of code produced for the backend (the "encoded output") increases when exceptions are used. This is mostly due to an increase of trivial statements. Specifically, more labels, `goto`, and `if` statements for typechecks are emitted. As no complex proof obligations are introduced, we do not think the increase in encoded output will be problematic.

Complex Control Flow. When using exceptions, many jumps are introduced that target few destinations, compared to programs without exceptions. This is because every call that can throw introduces a conditional jump. All these jumps go to either a `catch` block, `finally`, or the end of the method. This seems unavoidable, as this kind of control flow is the core of exceptions in Java. If complex control flow causes longer verification times, a different format for the output encoding can be investigated, for example continuation passing style.

Conditional Permissions. When the proposed transformation is applied, more conditional permissions are produced compared to programs that do not use exceptions. We have not seen evidence that this increases verification times. If conditional permissions become a cause of performance problems, the "exceptional invariant" mentioned in the subsection above could also help with this.

8   Conclusion

We presented an approach for supporting exceptional control flow that makes it easier to support `finally`. This is achieved by first transforming all occurrences of abrupt termination into exceptional control flow. This simplifies encoding `finally` and leads to a modular transformation that can be split up into several steps. Moreover, to avoid the annotation burden caused by exceptions as defined in the JLS, we propose a simplified view called exceptions modulo errors. This view focuses on the primary sources of exceptions, `throw` statements and `throws` clauses, and disregards exceptions that are ignored in practice, such as out of memory errors or other low-level details. Finally, we have evaluated the exceptions modulo errors semantics, and conclude that exceptions modulo errors can handle common exception patterns that appear in practice.

Future work will go in several directions. It would be useful to further validate the view of exceptions modulo errors by doing an empirical study of the catching and throwing of `Error` exceptions. This can be combined by researching how to annotate for `Error` exceptions, and what kinds of contracts would be specified in the context of `Error` exceptions. Possibly the implementation in this work can also be used to design and implement support for exceptional specifications of the standard library.

References

1. Ahrendt, W., Beckert, B., Bubel, R., Hähnle, R., Schmitt, P.H., Ulbrich, M.: Deductive Software Verification - The KeY Book. LNCS, vol. 10001. Springer, Cham (2016). https://doi.org/10.1007/978-3-319-49812-6
2. Amighi, A., Blom, S., Huisman, M., Zaharieva-Stojanovski, M.: The VerCors project: setting up basecamp. In: Proceedings of the Sixth PLPV Workshop. ACM (2012). https://doi.org/10.1145/2103776.2103785
3. Bicalho de Pádua, G.: Studying and Assisting the Practice of Java and C# Exception Handling. Masters, Concordia University, February 2018
4. Black Duck Open Hub: The Apache Hadoop Open Source Project on Open Hub: Languages Page (2018). https://www.openhub.net/p/Hadoop/analyses/latest/languages_summary
5. Black Duck Open Hub: The Apache Tomcat Open Source Project on Open Hub: Languages Page (2018). https://www.openhub.net/p/tomcat/analyses/latest/languages_summary
6. Blom, S., Darabi, S., Huisman, M., Oortwijn, W.: The VerCors tool set: verification of parallel and concurrent software. In: iFM, vol. 10510, pp. 102–110 (2017). https://doi.org/10.1007/978-3-319-66845-1_7
7. Cok, D.R.: OpenJML: software verification for Java 7 using JML, OpenJDK, and Eclipse. EPTCS (2014). https://doi.org/10.4204/EPTCS.149.8
8. Distefano, D., Parkinson, M.J.: jStar: towards practical verification for Java. In: Proceedings of the 23rd ACM SIGPLAN OOPSLA Conference. ACM (2008). https://doi.org/10.1145/1449764.1449782
9. Dyer, R., Nguyen, H.A., Rajan, H., Nguyen, T.N.: Boa: a language and infrastructure for analyzing ultra-large-scale software repositories. In: 2013 35th ICSE. IEEE (2013). https://doi.org/10.1109/icse.2013.6606588
10. Eilers, M.: Shortened github link to code-level documentation of `get_finally_var` method (2021). https://edu.nl/8a9qe
11. Fragoso Santos, J., Maksimović, P., Naudžiūnienė, D., Wood, T., Gardner, P.: JaVerT: JavaScript verification toolchain. In: Proceedings of the ACM Programming Language 2(POPL) (2017). https://doi.org/10.1145/3158138
12. Freund, S.N.: The costs and benefits of Java bytecode subroutines. In: Formal Underpinnings of Java Workshop at OOPSLA 98 (1998)
13. Gillian Team: Gillian - a multi-language platform for compositional symbolic analysis (2020). https://gillianplatform.github.io/
14. Gosling, J., Joy, B., Steele, G., Bracha, G.: The Java language specification, Java SE 7th edn. (2000)
15. Gosling, J., et al.: The Java language specification, Java SE 16th edn. (2021)
16. Hähnle, R., Huisman, M.: Deductive Software Verification: From Pen-and-Paper Proofs to Industrial Tools. Springer (2019)
17. Hamilton, J., Danicic, S.: An evaluation of current java bytecode decompilers. In: Ninth IEEE SCAM (2009). DOI: 10.1109/SCAM.2009.24
18. Jacobs, B.: Verifast & Java's "finally" clause (2020). https://groups.google.com/forum/#!topic/verifast/56uhVmdERwA
19. Jacobs, B., Smans, J., Piessens, F.: A Quick Tour of the VeriFast Program Verifier. In: Programming Languages and Systems, vol. 6461. Springer (2010). https://doi.org/10.1007/978-3-642-17164-2_21

20. Kery, M.B., Le Goues, C., Myers, B.A.: Examining programmer practices for locally handling exceptions. In: Proceedings of the 13th MSR Conference. ACM (2016). https://doi.org/10.1145/2901739.2903497
21. Leavens, G.T., et al.: JML reference manual (2008). https://www.cs.ucf.edu/~leavens/JML/jmlrefman/jmlrefman_toc.html
22. Marché, C., Paulin-Mohring, C., Urbain, X.: The Krakatoa tool for certification of Java/JavaCard programs annotated in JML. Journal of Logic and Algebraic Programming 58, 89-106 (2004). https://doi.org/10.1016/j.jlap.2003.07.006
23. de Moura, L., Bjørner, N.: Z3: an efficient smt solver. In: TACAS. Springer (2008)
24. Müller, P., Schwerhoff, M., Summers, A.J.: Viper: A verification infrastructure for permission-based reasoning. In: VMCAI. Springer (2016)
25. Nakshatri, S., Hegde, M., Thandra, S.: Analysis of exception handling patterns in java projects: an empirical study. In: Proceedings of the 13th MSR Conference (2016). https://doi.org/10.1145/2901739.2903499
26. O'Hearn, P.: Separation logic. Commun. ACM **62** (2019). https://doi.org/10.1145/3211968
27. Osman, H., Chiş, A., Schaerer, J., Ghafari, M., Nierstrasz, O.: On the evolution of exception usage in Java projects. In: 2017 IEEE 24th SANER Conference (2017). https://doi.org/10.1109/SANER.2017.7884646
28. Purohit, P., Tokekar, V.: An investigation of exception handling practices in.NET and Java environments. Int. J. Appl. Eng. Res. **13**, 2130–2140 (2018)
29. Rubbens, R.: Improving support for Java exceptions and inheritance in VerCors. Master's thesis, University of Twente (2020). https://essay.utwente.nl/81338/
30. Rubbens, R.: Modular Transformation of Java Exceptions Modulo Errors: accompanying package (2021). https://doi.org/10.4121/14905251
31. Sena, D., Coelho, R., Kulesza, U., Bonifácio, R.: Understanding the exception handling strategies of Java libraries: an empirical study. In: Proceedings of the 13th MSR Conference. ACM (2016). https://doi.org/10.1145/2901739.2901757
32. Steinhöfel, D., Wasser, N.: A New Invariant Rule for the Analysis of Loops with Non-standard Control Flows. In: IFM, vol. 10510. Springer (2017). https://doi.org/10.1007/978-3-319-66845-1_18
33. Vallée-Rai, R., Co, P., Gagnon, E., Hendren, L., Lam, P., Sundaresan, V.: Soot: a java bytecode optimization framework. CASCON First Decade High Impact Papers (2010). https://doi.org/10.1145/1925805.1925818
34. VerCors Team: VerCors homepage (2020). https://vercors.ewi.utwente.nl/

On Education and Training in Formal Methods for Industrial Critical Systems

Bernd Westphal$^{(\boxtimes)}$ (iD)

Albert-Ludwigs-Universität Freiburg, Freiburg, Germany
`westphal@informatik.uni-freiburg.de`

Abstract. The 2020 expert survey on formal methods has put one topic into the focus of the formal methods for industrial critical systems community: education and training. Of three overall conclusions, the first one finds the survey to indicate "a consensus about the essential role of education". At the same time, survey results and individual expert statements indicate largely open challenges. In this work, we analyse the 2020 expert survey results from an education and training perspective, and we discuss the proposal of an integrative approach with respect to these challenges. A central enabler for the integrated approach is the modern, inclusive interpretation of formal methods as put forth in the survey report and a differentiated understanding of roles (or stakeholders) in formal methods for industrial critical systems.

1 Introduction

The '2020 Expert Survey on Formal Methods' [28] reports results from a survey among a selection of internationally renowned scientists from inside the formal methods for industrial critical systems (FMICS) community and from outside. The authors "report on [the experts'] collective vision on the past, present, and future of formal methods with respect to research, industry, and education". Of these three aspects, the expert statements from the survey and the reported findings [28] put education at the very heart of FMICS. The introduction draws the somewhat gloomy conclusion that "we cannot lean back" and that "the transmission of our knowledge to the next generation is not guaranteed" [28]. The situation of FMICS education is characterised as "the formal verification landscape in higher education is scattered" followed by stating that "at many universities, formal methods courses are shrinking."

The aspect of education and training reappears throughout the report, both explicitly and implicitly, and the results, quotes, and conclusions do not paint the brightest possible picture If we, for example, jump to the overall conclusion of [28], we find education and training at the top of a list of three. "The results of the survey indicate a consensus about the essential role of education to give the next generations of students a sufficient background and practical experience in formal methods." On Question 5.5 (*What are the limiting factors for a wider adoption of formal methods by industry?*), four of the top six answers are

© Springer Nature Switzerland AG 2021
A. Lluch Lafuente and A. Mavridou (Eds.): FMICS 2021, LNCS 12863, pp. 85–103, 2021.
https://doi.org/10.1007/978-3-030-85248-1_6

"obstacles arising from human factors" and "reflect educational problems". Of the answers to Question 6.2 (*What is your opinion on the level of importance currently attributed to teaching of formal methods at universities?*), only 9.3% of the answers with an opinion see the level as "right" or "too much". How do these two observations go together with the successes in formal methods education and training that are consistently reported at respective conferences and workshops (such as FMTea, FMT, etc.) where students reportedly formalise and analyse the wildest system designs, with the broad availability of reflections and recommendations on what to do (e.g., [20,50,64]) and what not (e.g., [49]), with the increasing availability of textbooks ([8,51,53,58], to name only a few), with the existence of a formal methods teaching committee[1], etc.? (Fig. 1)

Parosh Abdulla: "vital", Erika Ábrahám: "strongest possible weight", Jean-Raymond Abrial: "fundamental", Gérard Berry: "above all", Erik Poll: "biggest challenge", Markus Roggenbach: "second challenge", Jun Sun: "the challenge".

Fig. 1. High-profile experts on FMICS education and training [28].

In this work, we elaborate on a view that is able to support both observations and provides us with new starting points to improve education and training in formal methods for industrial critical systems. The view hinges on the differentiation of terms and roles. Following [28], we need to differentiate meanings of the term 'formal method'. The *modern, inclusive interpretation* (as proposed in [28] for FMICS) is not always identical to the interpretation that underlies the above named courses and textbooks, hence they may not necessarily provide custom-fit education and training in formal methods *for industrial critical systems*. Secondly, and this is one of the main contributions of this article, we advocate for a differentiation of roles so to better understand what custom-fit education and training in formal methods *for industrial critical systems* is. We propose to distinguish two roles which, in a first approximation, differ in that one focuses on the theoretical and technical side of formal methods and the other focuses on the application side. The first role largely coincides with the educational objectives of classical formal methods courses, the new and second role could be able to fill gaps that the 2020 survey indicates.

The paper is structured as follows. Section 2 recalls some terminology and Sect. 3 introduces the new roles. Section 4 proposes learning objectives for the new role and Sect. 5 discusses how the two moves, in terminology and role definition, open a design space for FMICS education and training. Section 6 reports experience from an implementation and Sect. 7 concludes.

2   Terminology

The discussion of education and training in formal methods for industrial critical systems is at times hindered by the fact that there is no universally agreed upon

---

[1] https://www.fmeurope.org/teaching/.

understanding of the term *formal methods*. The 2020 expert survey report [28] alone offers five interpretations: The *extensive mathematical* one, the *extensive theoretical* one, the *light-* and the *heavyweight* interpretation, and the *modern, inclusive* one. The two first ones (including any use of mathematics in computer science, and fundamental, theoretical computer science concepts such as grammars and automata, respectively) are considered too wide by Garavel et al. [28] and we agree from the perspective of FMICS education and training.

The lightweight interpretation refers to "language features [...] for defensive programming [and] related verifications" and the heavyweight one includes "only those approaches that are fully mathematical and based on proofs". Garavel et al. [28] propose to consider the heavyweight interpretation alone as too restrictive for FMICS purposes and offer the following interpretation (to which the survey participants were obviously able to agree for the scope of the survey):

> "Mathematics-based techniques for the specification, development, and (manual or automated) verification of software and hardware systems." [28]

Conceptually, this modern, inclusive interpretation is less new than the name 'modern' may suggest. We find similar views, e.g., with Cerone et al. [19], Bjørner and Havelund [9][2], Gries [12], and Wing [63]. The strong point of these interpretations is their inclusiveness, which has a very modern and useful effect on education and training: Included are, as Garavel et al. [28] elaborate, "multiple, diverse artefacts, such as the description of the environment in which the system operates, the requirements and properties that the system should satisfy, the models of the system used during the various design steps, the (hardware or software) code embedded in the final implementation, etc." Hence formal methods (in the modern, inclusive sense) include textual requirements specification patterns (with a proper formal semantics and analysis method, like FRET [29] or Hanfor [44]), Decision Tables (cf. [6]), visual formalisms including (proper subsets of) UML languages [54,55] (with a precise, formal semantics and analysis tools such as USE [17] for structural models and for behavioural models, (formal) variants of Statecharts [34] and sequence diagrams [22,42]), model-based test generation, etc.

What these examples have in common is that they provide us with common ground to students and engineers alike: having used, e.g., a visual formalism in an informal or semi-formal way can be half the way to the formal view that we aim for in FMICS education and training, and then a stepping stone towards, e.g., formal methods in the heavyweight interpretation.

3   Roles in Formal Methods for Industrial Critical Systems: *Engineer/Conduct* and *Engineer/Utilise*

If we accept the thought that FMICS education and training is not identical to classical formal methods courses, then one aspect of distinction is the interpre-

---

[2] "A method is called *formal method* if and only if its techniques and tools can be explained in *mathematics*." We have adopted this one for our course (cf. Sect. 6).

Table 1. The six top-frequent answers to Question 5.5 (*What are the limiting factors for a wider adoption of formal methods by industry?*) [28].

Engineers lack proper training in formal methods	71.5%
Academic tools have limitations and are not professionally maintained	66.9%
Formal methods are not properly integrated in the industrial design life cycle	66.9%
Formal methods have a steep learning curve	63.8%
Developers are reluctant to change their way of working	62.3%
Managers are not aware of formal methods	57.7%

tation of the term 'formal methods, that, by the 2020 survey [28], is immediately the modern, inclusive one for the area of formal methods in industrial critical systems (see Sect. 2). This distinction alone does not yield a concept for FMICS education and training, first of all because a more inclusive interpretation asks for more content to be presented.

Yet there is a second, equally important distinction that the 2020 survey [28] suggests, though it does not have an own section like the first one. Best visible is the second distinction in Section 5.5, *'Limiting Factors'* and Section 5.6, *'Research-Industry Gap'* of [28]. Section 5.5 (cf. Table 1) concludes that "obstacles arising from human factors predominate, as the 1st, 4th, 5th, and 6th most selected answers[3] reflect educational problems, namely a lack of knowledge from managers and developers, and their difficulties to learn and deploy formal methods." Sect. 5.6 reports the comment "if you always need the academic doctor working in formal methods for a real industrial project, then something is wrong." Note that in Table 1, we see mentioned the roles *engineer*, *developer*, and *manager*[4], and all three do not sound as if their intention is to denote the proverbial 'academic doctor' (which we may also associate with classical formal methods courses). So a second distinction between the FMICS education and training that the experts ask for in Section 5.9, *'Academic Policies'* ("updat[e] curricula in ICT professionals at bachelor level", "teach[...] students on a large scale") and classical formal methods teaching can be the professional role that the education and training aims to develop.

3.1 FMICS Roles and Activities

The survey report does not further elaborate on capabilities and responsibilities of the roles introduced in Sect. 5.5, so we take a step back and propose an analysis of roles in formal methods for industrial critical systems based on the literature and our own experience. Keeping students aside for a moment (cf. Fig. 2), we distinguish the roles *scientist* and *engineer* (corresponding to stakeholders 'academia' and 'industry', cf. Section 5.8, *'Dissemination Players'* [28]), and in addition the role *client*.

---

[3] Where we would not exclude the 3rd row, as we shall add (cf. Sect. 3.1).

[4] Also see Manfred Broy's individual statement on managers [28].

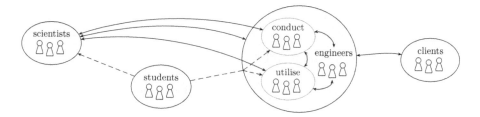

Fig. 2. Stakeholders in formal methods for industry critical systems. Solid arrows indicate communication paths, dashed arrows indicate career paths of students.

People in the role *scientist* may work in academic institutions or research-oriented institutes (MPI, etc.), develop formal methods and tools, and conduct case studies. People in this role typically value novelty over consolidation, and focus on "most difficult and challenging problems" rather than "'real world' issues" (cf. Section 4.3, *'Main Criticisms'* [28]). People in the role *engineer* work in the industry or in transfer-oriented institutes (such as Fraunhofer, OFFIS, etc.) and use formal methods to develop products in branches such as transportation, or formal methods products like Astree [1]. Incentives for *engineers* are strongly affected by economic consideration: a typical goal is to develop a product of the required quality with an adequate amount of effort (cf. [37]).

People in the *engineer* role may work together and communicate with *scientists* on case studies. This communication can be different from the communication within a role group due to different incentives, in particular if domain and formal methods expertise is diametrical on both sides, and it can be difficult.[5] People in the role *engineer* may also need to communicate with people in the role *client* (or product owner). The background of a person in the role *client* may be comparable to the *engineer* (for example, in the automotive industry, we find people with similar capabilities as *client* on the side of an OEM and as *engineer* on the side of a supplier; the difference lies in their responsibilities) or vastly different (e.g., electrical or communication engineers as *client* and system or software engineers as *engineer*). In the latter case, the communication is in general of a different quality than towards *scientist* in, e.g., a case study cooperation and needs explicit consideration in FMICS education and training.

To reflect the evolution of capabilities and responsibilities of engineers in the area of formal methods over the last 25 years, we propose to consider two specialisations of role *engineer*: The role *engineer/conduct* and the role *engineer/utilise*. We distinguish these two roles according to the following set of activities (cf. Fig. 3, from right to left):

- The *Construct* activity includes the development and investigation of formalisms, theories, proof systems, analysis algorithms and data-structures,

---

[5] Woodcock et al. [65] already report "a difficulty in communication between the verifiers and the signalling engineers, [...]" (solved by an ad-hoc solution) in the SACEM project; a problem that *eng./utilise* people are supposed to substantially mitigate.

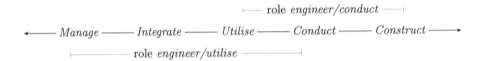

Fig. 3. Role competencies over a scale of depth of formal methods knowledge.

etc. to enable or support the use of formal methods. This activity needs a
deep understanding of the formal method that is worked on and may commonly be associated with research institutions and scientists, although today
it has its place in the industry as well. Note that people who work on such
activities need not necessarily be able to create good, elegant formal models
at appropriate levels of abstraction.

- In the *Conduct* activity, we see all work where an existing formal method is
applied to formally analyse properties of a formal model. This activity needs
good training with the employed formalism in order to create formal models,
and familiarity with proof methods or tools in order to obtain analysis results.
Note that people who work on such activities need not be able to, e.g., repair
the tools they use, and they need not necessarily know the details of how
the results from their formal analyses contribute to the overall dependability
case [40] for the system under development.

- The *Utilise* activity is concerned with the product. In this activity, formal
models and analyses are used for a certain purpose and the specification of
a formal analysis (what does the obtained report say about the presence
or absence of which issues with the product) is more important than, e.g.,
the theory and the implementation of the analysis. This activity comple-
ments *Conduct*, and both can be performed in an integrated way, possibly by
the same person, but we see an increasing demand for a separation [25, 27]
because, e.g., small to medium sized enterprises can not afford permanent
positions for *Conduct*.

When performed separately, *Conduct* can be offered by a department (or even
an external agency, or 'dedicated service companies' [28]) with lower domain
knowledge but expertise in formal methods, and *Utilise* is the complementary
counterpart with higher domain and lower formal methods knowledge. People
who work on *Utilise* activities should be able to read and understand formal
models, they need to understand analysis results such as counter-examples
in model-checking with respect to to the product under development, and
they may need to be able to communicate about models and results with
clients. People who work on this activity need not be able to, e.g., overlook
the whole business case of a product under development and take decisions
on which formal methods to use when, but they should be able to support
such decisions.

- The *Integrate* activity is concerned with the integration of formal methods
into system and software engineering processes (cf. Section 5.2, *'Technology
Readiness'* [28]). The integration may be on more conceptual levels (such as

the process of subcontracting a semantical review for informal requirements documents) or on more technical levels (e.g., the integration of lightweight formal methods such as compiler checks or static analyses into continuous integration tool-chains). People who work on this activity may not be the ones who decide, which method and which tool to use, but they should be able to support such decisions.

– The *Manage* activity is concerned with decisions, e.g., on which methods and which tools to use, whether to conduct formal methods internally or subcontracted, and with putting all other activities into place.

These five activities provide a refined view on the survey results [28]. Engineers (Table 1, 1st row) work on *Conduct* or *Utilise*, and would assume the role *eng./conduct* or *eng./utilise* depending on their focus and goals.[6] Integration into industrial life cycles (3rd row) is part of *Integrate*, developers (4th row) work on *Utilise*, and managers (5th row) on *Manage*, hence we see integrators, developers and managers in the role *eng./utilise* rather than *eng./conduct*.

Note that the concept of roles in the context of formal methods has been raised before, e.g., in the survey on the state of formal methods in industry by Woodcock et al. [65]. The results are somewhat inconclusive because the 56 respondents (plus 6 data points from the literature) were asked which roles were part of the project team and all answers but 'other' name standard software engineering roles with no hint of a formal methods aspect to them. As most of the eight highlighted projects (including Transputer, Train Control, Airbus, etc.) seem to have strong contributions from scientists, the question may have been answered in the understanding of who else, next to the formal methods people, were part of the project teams.

3.2   Consequences on Education and Training

Table 2. Section 7.2, *'Future users'* [28]. Of 130 respondents, twelve commented 'both'.

A large number of mainstream software engineers	42.3%
A small number of skilled experts	43.8%
Others	13.8%

Our differentiation of two roles is in line with answers from the survey. Section 7.2, *'Future Users'* reports beliefs on likely future users of formal methods. The survey offered the answers shown in Table 2. We position the role *eng./conduct* in the group of skilled experts (towards the end of higher or more specialised formal methods skills), and the role *eng./utilise* in the intersection ('both') because the role clearly needs strong system and software engineering skills as well as formal methods skills, yet the latter not as deep as *eng./conduct*. Note that role

---

[6] We feel that the 'formal methods engineer' proposed in Frank de Boer's individual statement [28] is positioned in the intersection yet a bit stronger on *eng./conduct*, while Stefan Kowalewski and Antti Valmari [28] seem to tend to *eng./utilise*.

eng./utilise is not identical to the 'mainstream software engineer' but a bit narrower: many software engineers will not fit the role *eng./utilise* but still *use* "lightweight formal methods, particularly the automated ones, which are hidden in standard development tools" as the survey report puts it.

Implications for education and training become visible by also considering career paths of students (cf. Fig. 2). Students can join the academic world, work as a *scientist*, and become the proverbial 'academic doctor' that we began the section with. Afterwards they may join the industry and work as *eng./utilise* or *eng./conduct* with some industry-specific training. People who follow this path can in particular bring a deep understanding of the academic world to the industry and, e.g., resolve misunderstandings caused by the different constellation of incentives (cf. Section 4.3, *'Main Criticism'*).[7]

The way to the industry via academia may have been the main career path of engineers who are active in the area of formal methods (cf. Orna Grumberg's individual statement [28]), but it may not scale in a way that yields the increased quantities of people that are qualified for FMICS that the survey experts ask for (cf. Section 5.9, *'Academic Policies'*). Hence there is a need to update education for career paths that directly lead from higher education institutes to industry positions that match roles *eng./utilise* or *eng./conduct*. Knowledge, that would otherwise be picked up with the career path over *scientist*, needs to be provided as part of the education in order to, e.g., understand the main criticisms concerning the placement of efforts of academic researchers.

4   Learning Objectives: *Eng./Utilise* vs. *Eng./Conduct*

The new differentiation of engineers who are active in the area of formal methods allows us to revisit learning objectives for eduction and training of the two roles. We see the role *eng./conduct* as the target audience of existing, well-developed, dedicated courses and textbooks on (heavyweight) formal methods as mentioned in the introduction. Learning objectives of these courses typically include to know and understand a formalism to its full extent, to be familiar with corresponding properties, to understand analysis methods and algorithms, and to be able to create formal models of the structure and behaviour of industrial critical systems and to apply analysis tools. An often reported assessment of learning success (see [26], for example) is that students show the ability to create a substantial formal model of a complex system from a specification and prove certain properties for the model using at least one of the formal methods introduced in the course.

The role *eng./utilise* needs different competences and capabilities according to Sect. 3, some more and some less compared to classical formal methods courses. The survey report [28] offers the quote "'every bachelor in computer science/informatics should know about formal methods' and 'be trained in applying [them]'" but what could 'know about' mean? Colloquially put, we propose the top-level learning objective to make the experts opinions and beliefs from the 2020 survey *plausible* and *comprehensible* for bachelor students. To us, it sounds

---

[7] See Jan Friso Groote's individual statement on "change the (industrial) society" [28].

Table 3. Formal methods-specific learning objectives [62].

O1	Students have a broad overview of interpretations of the term 'formal methods' in the software engineering context and know examples of such methods
O2	Students have basic capabilities of using (understanding, analysing, and (to a certain amount, cf. [23]) creating) formal specifications of requirements and designs, and apply program verification
O3	Students are able to discuss which and in how far formal methods address common, well-known problems and issues in the software engineering process, and are aware of the advantages and limitations of formal methods

like a major step forward if students get the information and experience that makes plausible, e.g., the survey finding that 81.5% of the respondents believe that formal methods together with formal analysis tools definitely can deliver the promise of better software quality.

We have proposed the learning objectives recalled in Table 3. With learning objective (O1), we advocate for the presentation of an explicit definition of 'formal methods' (in the modern, inclusive interpretation) and an explicit elaboration of the common principles of formal methods, and against 'weaving' [64], 'ninja' [41], 'hero' [50] 'religion' (sic!) [28] or 'stop calling it formal methods' [28] recommendations. The reason is that when our graduates join a workplace, they may need to work and communicate with colleagues who have 10, 20, or 30 years of work experience. These colleagues will have finished their studies around the 2010's, 2000's, or 1990's and may probably have come across the term 'formal methods', maybe in a less modern and inclusive interpretation or together with a contemporary fashion of (mis)conceptions along the lines of the Hall/Bowen/Hinchey series of 'myths' papers [13,33]. In other words, these experienced colleagues may be well familiar with the heritage and history of formal methods (also cf. Section 5.1, 'Impact Evaluation') and bring up the term at the workplace. The student who has an explicit definition and multiple examples of the own interpretation should be able to clarify on which interpretation of the term the own impression is based; then the communication need not fail due to an unresolved case of different interpretations of the term.

Objective (O2) addresses the aspect that people in role *eng./utilise* need to communicate with *eng./conduct* and *client*. To this end, *eng./utilise* should know examples of formal specifications as used in different activities of system and software engineering (requirements, designs, programs, etc.). The emphasis is on understanding the *purpose* of formalisations in these activities, the ability to read and understand existing formalisations, and to interpret analysis results in terms of the product under development. This learning objective also includes basics of the communication towards non-technical *clients*.

Learning objective (O3) revisits the previous ones from the perspective of management activities, including the important message that, quoting Edward

A. Lee's individual statement: "[The role of formal methods] is not, as is often stated, to prove a system correct." [28] Formal methods also do not necessarily make a design or a requirements set better, but using formal methods can lower the average risk of systems to fail due to design or requirements issues. Using formal methods also has costs and benefits, which, as well as advantages and limitations, need to be discussed in particular engineering contexts and projects (cf. [14,15]; also see the individual statement of Matthias Güdemann [28]). Note that the we do not imply that courses that address *eng./conduct* necessarily do not address learning objectives (O1)–(O3). We do state that education towards *eng./utilise* should address them.

An alternative formulation of the overall learning objective behind (O1)–(O3) is to provide students with knowledge and competences that can serve a 'common ground' and 'connection points' at the workplace.[8] Here we also see a strong potential to mitigate some risks as discussed in Section 5.3, *'Return on Investment'*: In our experience, providing specialisation training (in a particular method or tool) is easier, faster, and comes with a lower risk of disappointment when the audience is familiar with the underlying concepts.

5   Curriculum and Course Construction

Given a set of learning objectives, the next question is how much workload at which time in the study plan should be used to reach them. Regarding the level of courses that teach formal methods, the survey answers clearly favour universities (80.0% master, 79.2% bachelor) over training (70.8% engineering schools, 70.0% continuing education), and only 31.5% see the doctorate level fit (cf. Section 6.1, *'Course Level'*). Our following discussion targets the undergraduate level.

The literature has proposals on how to present formal methods to a broader audience. One obvious approach is a classical course on formal methods in the heavyweight interpretation (cf. Fig. 4a). Such a course would build on content from introductions to system or software engineering and relate formal methods to that content, yet typically does not have enough workload to address both, *eng./conduct* and *eng./utilise*. Gibson and Méry [31], for example, reports on how to conceptionally connect a formal methods course in a graduate program to software engineering knowledge. Other proposals consider formal methods education in the broader context of the whole (undergraduate) curriculum. Wing [64], for example, proposes to spread formal methods education all over the curriculum (cf. Fig. 4b) and gives suggestions on where to add which aspect. Mandrioli [49] sketches a curriculum design where a series of formal methods courses is scheduled in parallel to other courses. For both, it is unclear from the literature whether they have ever been realised to the extent of the proposal, and if not, for which reasons. Yet for reflections on curriculum and course design, we need to keep in mind that there are more aspects and constraints than optimal didactics. Educational units may be equally reluctant to change as the industry

---

[8] Also see Radu Mateescu's statement on "'formal methods culture'" [28].

(as perceived by many experts in the survey). So the curriculum-oriented proposals may be much harder to realise than a few courses, or, possibly the easiest case, to (re-)position a single specialisation course (cf. Fig. 4a). Liu et al. [46] in contrast, report on a successfully realised curriculum design, yet tailored to the SOFL (Structured Object-based Formal Language) methodology.

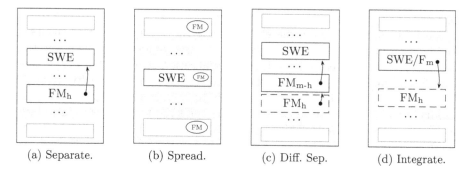

(a) Separate.   (b) Spread.   (c) Diff. Sep.   (d) Integrate.

Fig. 4. Schematic illustrations of four curricula (duration not specified, can be viewed as only undergraduate, or consecutive B.Sc. and M.Sc.). Flat rectangles represent courses (or modules), solid and dashed outlines indicate compulsory and elective, respectively. Labels indicate topics (or content; also inside ovals), and arrows represent a puts-into-perspective relation (see running text below).

An in-between proposal is to devise one compulsory formal methods course (which may take the modern, inclusive interpretation) and subsequent specialisations courses (which may address the *eng./utilise* role), cf. Fig. 4c. Examples are reported by Larsen [11] (in a graduate program), and Robinson [57]. Similar ideas of sequences of formal methods courses (cf. Fig. 4c) are found in curricula for professional education (see Ishikawa et al. [38] and Davies [23], for example), and summer schools as in [20].

We propose to implement the opposite direction: Integrate the content for *eng./utilise* into 'otherwise completely ordinary' introductions to systems or software engineering [7,48,59] (cf. Fig. 4d).[9] In the remainder of this section, we discuss advantages, feasibility, and related work. Integrating formal methods (in the modern, inclusive interpretation) into an introduction to system or software engineering comes with the following advantages. Firstly, such courses come with obvious and natural motivations (also see [47,56]): Subject of the course is the goal to contribute to the development of a system or software (in any form, e.g., with requirements, design, programming, quality assurance, etc.). The system is supposed to have a defined reliability or dependability, and this goal is not reached 'for free' (otherwise, e.g., certain aircraft models would not be grounded by regulators for the reason of software issues). Secondly, such courses allow a natural progression from an informal to a formal view. The

---

[9] Also see Stefan Kowalewski, Martin Leucker, and Cesare Tinelli in [28].

typical systems/software engineering course is bound to introduce informal and semi-formal means to mitigate risks of software issues. An integrated course completes the picture with a discussion of how formal methods can lower the risk for system failures if used in, e.g., requirements engineering, design, programming, etc. Notably, the envisioned integration is not at all in contradiction to the well-known SWEBOK [10] that covers formal methods as a topic of its own and enriches knowledge areas like requirements engineering or modelling with pointers to formal approaches.

Specialist courses can immediately connect to the 'bridgeheads' that the integrated approach provides and can consider the basics of formal methods and the engineering context given.[10] Even if the specialisation course elaborates on one of the formalisms that did occur in the introduction to system or software engineering, the overlap will be low and probably tolerated as a 'recap' because the introduction course will spend at most two lectures per formalisms to introduce the fragment that it needs. This is perfectly in line with the vast majority of expert answers of which 83.8% are reported in Section 6.3, *'Course Format'* to have answered "both: specialist courses taught to a limited number of students, and gentle introduction to formal methods for a larger number of students."

How is an integrated course feasible in a curriculum with a fixed workload and where, by Fig. 4c, we need two courses for a similar sounding goal? We obtain feasibility from two observations: (1) In education for *eng./utilise*, we can focus on lower competence levels of Bloom's revised taxonomy of educational learning objectives [4] (apply, analyse (a.k.a. *reading* formal specifications)), we can consider simpler or smaller formalisms for *examples of* writing tasks, and we can highlight an interface (or input/output) perspective onto formal methods that abstracts from the algorithms inside. The proposed separate constructions, in contrast, still sound like education for role *eng./conduct* and thus different learning objectives. A main difference is that education for role *eng./conduct* needs to establish proficiency in *creating* formal models of complex systems and *conducting* complex analysis tasks. Creating artefacts is of the highest competence level [4] and *takes time* to develop. (2) In education for role *eng./utilise*, we can exploit the fact that the survey report [28] advocates for the modern, inclusive interpretation of formal methods (cf. Sect. 2). With the modern, inclusive interpretation, we can use formal variants of Decision Tables (cf. [6]), subsets of UML languages with a precise, formal semantics and analysis tools (such as formal state machine or sequence diagram dialects), etc. These formalisms are already present in many introductions to systems and software engineering in an informal (neither syntax nor semantics well-defined) or a semi-formal (syntax only) form. We only need to present a formal semantics to complete the picture. Still, adding a formal semantics needs time which may not be provided in the schedule of a classical introduction to systems or software engineering. On second sight we can see that the time that we need is usually already there: Popular software engineering textbooks allocate a lot of time to tell informal meanings

---

[10] We feel that Benjamin Monate's note on "be modest with formal methods" and incremental training [28] points into the exact same direction.

of oversized fragments of semi-formalisms, with artificial or oversimplified examples. This telling time we can trade for precise semantics of useful fragments of formalisms illustrated with scaled-down examples from the industrial practice.

Figure 5 contrasts our approach to education for role *eng./utilise* with classical formal methods courses on three axes. Classical formal methods courses aim at *writing* complex formal models (darker gray area), which implies the capa-

Fig. 5. *Eng./utilise* education focus illustrated on the axes competence level (left), inside vs. outside view (middle), formalism.

bilities to modify and read models. For *eng./utilise*, we focus on the latter (lighter gray area). Classical formal methods courses present a complete theory and analysis algorithms, the view towards the engineering context is often a view from the inside to the outside. We focus on the interface from the engineering perspective. Finally, many classical formal methods courses work with the heavyweight interpretation, from which it is easy to acquire knowledge on less heavyweight methods, in particular small fragments thereof. For *eng./utilise*, we focus on the latter.

Integrative approaches to formal methods education have been proposed before but for different purposes. Noble et al. [52] report on a first year course on software modelling yet allocates one third of the workload to Alloy. This course design does not provide the overview over formal methods that role *eng./utilise* should have. Similar thoughts are found in the high-level reflections [50] of which the majority of claims and observations are backed by the 2020 survey results. Overall, [50] does not present a solution but rather an abstract specification of side-conditions (or principles [20]) that formal methods teaching should satisfy.

6   Exemplary Implementation

We have implemented the integrated approach (cf. Fig. 4d) with the re-design of an undergraduate introduction to software engineering [62]. A cornerstone is the explicit introduction of a concept of formal methods using one as-simple-as-possible (but not trivial) example of a formal method (in the modern, inclusive interpretation) in the topic area requirements engineering (cf. Table 4).

Essential for role *eng./utilise* is to see the relation between a formal description and the system under design. The formal description is a model [60] (also see Edward A. Lee's statement in [28]) and analysis results obtained on the model need to be interpreted with respect to the original. A result of a formal analysis on a model can be *true* or *false*, depending on whether the formalisation is *valid*. Engineers in the role *eng./utilise* need to be able to take appropriate actions or communicate appropriate actions to other engineers. This topic is re-occurring all over the course, e.g., for design models, program verification [5], etc. Similarly essential to role *eng./utilise* are the principles behind dependability cases (cf. [40]): A dependability case is a transparent argument of what a

Table 4. High-level course design: role *eng./utilise* in Software Engineering.

Lecture	Topic area	Key content
2–4	Project management	Semi-formal process models
5–9	Requirements engineering	Formal methods concept, validation, interpretation
10–13	Architecture & design	Structural and behavioural models, model-checking
14–16	Code quality assurance	Testing, program verification (manual and tools)

formal analysis (like a correctness proof) does and does not imply about the product under construction.[11] Formal methods is not, as Lee puts it, "to prove a system correct."

As already recommended in the Ten Principles [20], we reinforce the aspects of concrete syntax, abstract syntax, and semantics. The aspect of concrete syntax needs particular attention for the visual formalisms that enter the discussion with the modern, inclusive interpretation of formal methods. By complementing existing software description languages with formal semantics, we cover different examples for each of the aspects formalism simplicity, concrete syntax, modelled aspect, constructive vs. reflective view [35], formality, and paper & pencil vs. tool (see [61] for details). Hereby, we reach (O1) and (O2), satisfy the needs stated in Section 6.3, *'Course Format'* [28], and avoid the concerns raised ibid.: Our approach is not about giving flavours or impressions, but we introduce self-contained, well-defined formal software description languages and offer meaningful exercises. Regarding examples, we have decided against a running one, against toy examples (in line with, e.g., Anne Haxthausen [28]), and against games and puzzles (see [18]). Instead, we follow, e.g., [16,36] (and Section 7.3, *'Promising Applications'* [28]) in presenting scaled down versions of examples for formal methods for industrial critical systems and discuss how and in how far formal methods are assumed to have contributed to product quality. In addition (and in line with [28] and also [14,15]), we take care to present each formal method with examples for which the method is known to work particularly well.[12] Regarding tool use, we follow [32] in valuing concepts over tools. For the formal modelling languages of which we only present small fragments, it is usually not economic to learn any tool to solve the exercises. Still, we perfectly agree to the majority of expert answers in the 2020 survey (cf. Section 6.5, *'Tool Usage'*) that tool experience is important. For behavioural models, we use Uppaal [45] for reasons also detailed in [2,3]. Even small models of concurrent systems are sufficient to vividly demonstrate the value of tools. For the same reason, we use, e.g., VCC [21] to demonstrate that practical program verification is possible.

---

[11] Also see individual statement of Joseph Sifakis [28].
[12] Also see the individual statement of Edward A. Lee [28].

As a measure for the adequacy of our course design for the education of role *eng./utilise*, we can check which phases of the design life cycle that the expert answers in the 2020 survey consider most likely to attract formal are touched upon by the course design. Table 5 recalls the 10 (of 12) most frequently given answers. Our course explicitly addresses six

Table 5. Section 5.7, *'Design life-cycle'* [28].

(a)	Generate test cases, esp. corner cases	77.7%
(b)	Capture and formalise requirements	75.4%
(c)	Check whether models are correct	69.2%
(d)	Build models of the system	64.6%
(e)	Validate the requirements	53.8%
(f)	Generate code from models	53.1%
(g)	Certify correctness of the final code	45.4%
(h)	Monitor deployed software at run time	43.1%
(i)	Maintain consistency between models	42.3%
(j)	Detect mistakes in handwritten code	39.2%

of these ten: (b)–(e), (g), and (j). Mentioned in the lectures are (a) (yet more in the sense of model-based testing), (f), and (h). The only phase that we leave to the specialisation courses is phase (i), consistency between models.

Experiences with teaching the course over five seasons so far[13] are encouraging with respect to to the course goals and student feedback. There are no indications of overstraining students in the aspects difficulty and workload. In contrast to reports on classical formal methods courses, we do not have any indications of 'mathphobia' [49], possibly resulting from a combination of our use of mathematics on a strict as-needed basis and overall lower demands that the interface view has. We also find few preconceptions (like Hall/Bowen/Hinchey 'myths') with the majority of the students. Formal methods are named in the same breath with '(over-)selling' in the 2020 survey (cf. Section 3.5, *'Missed Opportunities'*) and so do some software engineering textbooks. Our take is that we do not sell anything at all (also see [43]): We present, where possible with evidence, available theories and technologies for the development of industrial critical systems.

7   Conclusion

The 2020 survey report [28] recalls a dilemma with the topic of formal methods for industrial critical systems: The topic does neither exclusively classify as 'cs.LO' (logic) nor as 'cs.SE' (software engineering) but is a well-understood topic area somewhere in the intersection. It would be surprising if the same would not hold for education and training in formal methods for industrial critical systems: It is neither exclusively formal methods teaching nor software engineering education, hence neither a conference or workshop like FMTea or SEET can be expected to solve the education and training problems of the FMICS community that the survey [28] has brought to light in striking clarity.

---

[13] Mainly as undergraduate compulsory course, majority of audience on B. Sc. in C.S. study plan, 4th semester/2nd year, open to students on M. Sc. and other study plans; heterogeneous previous knowledge; also offered as graduate block course at NM-AIST, Tanzania, with very heterogeneous previous knowledge; see [62] for details.

It needs key conferences in the intersection of industrial applications and formal methods (in Marieke Huisman's words, "the scientific community"), venues that bring together 'providers' and 'consumers' of FMICS education and training, to improve the situation and come to a positive answer on Pedro Merino's question "Are we are still on time?" [28].

In this article, we move from the survey-recommended starting point [19] towards a concretisation of the discussion. The most striking observation to us is that the 2020 survey does not only name and pinpoint problems but it also includes valuable hints on possible solutions. To us, FMICS education differs from classical formal methods education in two aspects: Firstly, we can work with the modern, inclusive interpretation of FM (that the survey report has thankfully established at FMICS), and secondly, we aim to develop a different role, of which we propose a first definition. These two differences open an intriguing design space for new course concepts that build on the state of the art of formal methods teaching and software and system engineering education.

References

1. AbsInt: Astreé software (2020). http://www.absint.com/astree
2. Aceto, L., Ingólfsdóttir, A., Larsen, K.G., Srba, J.: Reactive Systems: Modelling, Specification and Verification. Cambridge University Press, Cambridge (2007)
3. Aceto, L., Ingólfsdóttir, A., Larsen, K.G., Srba, J.: Teaching concurrency: theory in practice. In: Gibbons et al. [30], pp. 158–175
4. Anderson, L.W., Krathwohl, D.R., et al. (eds.): A Revision of Bloom's Taxonomy of Educational Objectives. Longman, New York (2001)
5. Apt, K.R., de Boer, F.S., Olderog, E.: Verification of Sequential and Concurrent Programs. Texts in Computer Science. Springer, London (2009). https://doi.org/10.1007/978-1-84882-745-5
6. Balzert, H.: Lehrbuch der Softwaretechnik: Basiskonzepte und Requirements Engineering, 3rd edn. Spektrum (2009)
7. Bauer, F.L.: Software engineering. In: IFIP Congress, no. 1, pp. 530–538 (1971)
8. Bjørner, D.: Software Engineering: Abstraction and Modelling. EATCS, vol. 1. Springer, Heidelberg (2006). https://doi.org/10.1007/3-540-31288-9
9. Bjørner, D., Havelund, K.: 40 years of formal methods - some obstacles and some possibilities? In: Jones, C.B., Pihlajasaari, P., Sun, J. (eds.) FM 2014. LNCS, vol. 8442, pp. 42–61. Springer, Cham (2014). https://doi.org/10.1007/978-3-319-06410-9_4
10. Bourque, P., Fairley, R. (eds.): Guide to the Software Engineering Body of Knowledge, Version 3.0. IEEE (2014)
11. Boute, R.T., Oliveira, J.N. (eds.): Formal Methods in the Teaching Lab, Workshop Preprints (2006)
12. Bowen, J.P., et al.: An invitation to formal methods. IEEE Comput. 29(4), 16–30 (1996)
13. Bowen, J.P., Hinchey, M.G.: Seven more myths of formal methods. IEEE Softw. 12(4), 34–41 (1995)
14. Bowen, J.P., Hinchey, M.G.: Ten commandments of formal methods. Computer 28(4), 56–63 (1995)

15. Bowen, J.P., Hinchey, M.G.: Ten commandments of formal methods ...ten years later. Computer **39**(1), 40–48 (2006)
16. Brakman, H., Driessen, V., Kavuma, J., Bijvank, L.N., et al.: Supporting formal method teaching with real-life protocols. In: Boute and Oliveira [11], pp. 59–68
17. Burgueño, L., Vallecillo, A., Gogolla, M.: Teaching UML and OCL models and their validation to software engineering students: an experience report. Comput. Sci. Educ. **28**(1), 23–41 (2018)
18. Cerone, A., Roggenbach, M. (eds.): Formal Methods - Fun for Everybody, FMFun, Proceedings. CCIS, vol. 1301. Springer, Cham (2020). https://doi.org/10.1007/978-3-030-71374-4
19. Cerone, A., Roggenbach, M., Davenport, J., Denner, C., Farrell, M., et al.: Rooting formal methods within higher education curricula for computer science and software engineering - a white paper. CoRR abs/2010.05708 (2020)
20. Cerone, A., Roggenbach, M., Schlingloff, B.H., et al.: Teaching formal methods for software engineering - ten principles. informatica didactica **9** (2011)
21. Cohen, E., et al.: VCC: a practical system for verifying concurrent C. In: Berghofer, S., et al. (eds.) TPHOLs. LNCS, vol. 5674, pp. 23–42. Springer, Heidelberg (2009). https://doi.org/10.1007/978-3-642-03359-9_2
22. Damm, W., Harel, D.: LSCs: Breathing life into Message Sequence Charts. FMSD **19**(1), 45–80 (2001)
23. Davies, J., Simpson, A., Martin, A.P.: Teaching formal methods in context. In: Dean and Boute [24], pp. 185–202
24. Dean, C.N., Boute, R.T. (eds.): TFM. LNCS, vol. 3294. Springer, Heidelberg (2004). https://doi.org/10.1007/978-3-540-30472-2
25. Dietsch, D., Langenfeld, V., Westphal, B.: Formal requirements in an informal world. In: FORMREQ, pp. 14–20. IEEE (2020)
26. Dongol, B., Petre, L., Smith, G. (eds.): FMTea, LNCS, vol. 11758. Springer, Cham (2019). https://doi.org/10.1007/978-3-030-32441-4
27. Feo Arenis, S., Westphal, B., Dietsch, D., Muñiz, M., Andisha, A.S., Podelski, A.: Ready for testing: ensuring conformance to industrial standards through formal verification. Form. Asp. Comput. **28**(3), 499–527 (2016)
28. Garavel, H., ter Beek, M.H., van de Pol, J.: The 2020 expert survey on formal methods. In: ter Beek, M.H., Nickovic, D. (eds.) FMICS. LNCS, vol. 12327, pp. 3–69. Springer, Cham (2020). https://doi.org/10.1007/978-3-030-58298-2_1
29. Giannakopoulou, D., Pressburger, T., Mavridou, A., Rhein, J., Schumann, J., Shi, N.: Formal requirements elicitation with FRET. In: Sabetzadeh, M., Vogelsang, A., et al. (eds.) REFSQ Workshops. CEUR, vol. 2584. CEUR-WS.org (2020)
30. Gibbons, J., et al. (eds.): TFM, LNCS, vol. 5846. Springer, Heidelberg (2009). https://doi.org/10.1007/978-3-642-04912-5
31. Gibson, J.P., Méry, D.: Teaching formal methods: lessons to learn. In: Flynn, S., Butterfield, A. (eds.) 2nd Irish Workshop on Formal Methods, Cork, Ireland, 2–3 July 1998. Workshops in Computing, BCS (1998)
32. Glinz, M.: The teacher: "concepts!" the student: "tools!". Softwaretechnik-Trends **16**(1) (1996)
33. Hall, A.: Seven myths of formal methods. IEEE Softw. **7**(5), 11–19 (1990)
34. Harel, D.: Statecharts: a visual formalism for complex systems. SCP **8**(3), 231–274 (Jun 1987)
35. Harel, D.: Some thoughts on statecharts, 13 years later. In: Grumberg, O. (ed.) CAV. LNCS, vol. 1254, pp. 226–231. Springer, Cham (1997). https://doi.org/10.1007/978-3-030-58298-2_1

36. Heitmeyer, C.L.: On the need for practical formal methods. In: Ravn, A.P., Rischel, H. (eds.) FTRTFT. LNCS, vol. 1486, pp. 18–26. Springer, Heidelberg (1998). https://doi.org/10.1007/BFb0055332

37. Holloway, C.M.: Why engineers should consider formal methods. In: 16th Digital Avionics Systems Conference, Proceedings. vol. 1, pp. 1.3–16 (1997)

38. Ishikawa, F., Taguchi, K., Yoshioka, N., Honiden, S.: What top-level software engineers tackle after learning formal methods: experiences from the Top SE project. In: Gibbons et al. [30], pp. 57–71

39. Istenes, Z. (ed.): Formal Methods in Computer Science Education, FORMED2008, Budapest, Hungary, 29 March 2008, Proceedings (2008)

40. Jackson, D.: A direct path to dependable software. CACM **52**(4) (2009)

41. Kiniry, J.R., Zimmerman, D.M.: Secret ninja formal methods. In: Cuéllar, J., Maibaum, T.S.E., et al. (eds.) FM. LNCS, vol. 5014, pp. 214–228. Springer, Heidelberg (2008). https://doi.org/10.1007/978-3-540-68237-0_16

42. Klose, J., Wittke, H.: An automata based interpretation of live sequence charts. In: Margaria, T., Yi, W. (eds.) TACAS. LNCS, vol. 2031, pp. 512–527. Springer, Heidelberg (2001). https://doi.org/10.1007/3-540-45319-9_35

43. Lamport, L.: Who builds a house without drawing blueprints? CACM **58**(4), 38–41 (2015)

44. Langenfeld, V., Dietsch, D., Westphal, B., Hoenicke, J.: Scalable analysis of real-time requirements. In: Damian, D., et al. (eds.) RE, pp. 234–244. IEEE (2019)

45. Larsen, K.G., Pettersson, P., Yi, W.: Uppaal in a nutshell. Int. J. Softw. Tools Technol. Transf. **1**(1), 134–152 (1997)

46. Liu, S., Takahashi, K., Hayashi, T., Nakayama, T.: Teaching formal methods in the context of software engineering. SIGCSE Bull. **41**(2), 17–23 (2009)

47. Loomes, M., Christianson, B., Davey, N.: Formal systems, not methods. In: Dean and Boute [24], pp. 47–64

48. Ludewig, J., Lichter, H.: Software Engineering, 3rd edn. dpunkt (2013)

49. Mandrioli, D.: Advertising formal methods and organizing their teaching: yes, but ... In: Dean and Boute [24], pp. 214–224

50. Mandrioli, D.: On the heroism of really pursuing formal methods. In: Gnesi, S., Plat, N. (eds.) FormaliSE, pp. 1–5. IEEE (2015)

51. Nielson, F., Nielson, H.R.: Formal Methods. Springer, Heidelberg (2019). https://doi.org/10.1007/978-3-030-05156-3

52. Noble, J., Pearce, D.J., Groves, L.: Introducing alloy in a software modelling course. In: Istenes [39], pp. 81–90

53. Ölveczky, P.C.: Designing Reliable Distributed Systems - A Formal Methods Approach Based on Executable Modeling in Maude. Undergraduate Topics in Computer Science, Springer, London (2017). https://doi.org/10.1007/978-1-4471-6687-0

54. OMG: OCL, Version 2.4. OMG Document Number formal/2014-02-03 (2014)

55. OMG: UML, Version 2.5.1. OMG Document Number formal/2017-12-05 (2017)

56. Reed, J.N., Sinclair, J.: Motivating study of formal methods in the classroom. In: Dean and Boute [24], pp. 32–46

57. Robinson, K.: Reflecting on the future: objectives, strategies and experiences. In: Istenes [39], pp. 15–24

58. Roggenbach, M., Cerone, A.: Formal Methods for Software Engineering. Springer, Cham (2021, to appear)

59. Sommerville, I.: Software Engineering, 9th edn. Pearson, London (2010)

60. Stachowiak, H.: Allgemeine Modelltheorie. Springer, New York (1973)

61. Westphal, B.: Teaching software modelling in an undergraduate introduction to software engineering. In: Burgueño, L., Pretschner, A., Voss, S., et al. (eds.) EduSymp@MODELS, pp. 690–699. IEEE (2019)
62. Westphal, B.: On complementing an undergraduate software engineering course with formal methods. In: Daun, M., et al. (eds.) CSEE&T, pp. 1–10. IEEE (2020)
63. Wing, J.M.: A specifier's introduction to formal methods. IEEE Comput. **23**(9), 8–24 (1990)
64. Wing, J.M.: Invited talk: weaving formal methods into the undergraduate computer science curriculum. In: Rus, T. (ed.) AMAST. LNCS, vol. 1816, pp. 2–9. Springer, Heidelberg (2000). https://doi.org/10.1007/3-540-45499-3_2
65. Woodcock, J., Larsen, P.G., Bicarregui, J., Fitzgerald, J.S.: Formal methods: practice and experience. ACM Comput. Surv. **41**(4), 19:1–19:36 (2009)

(Event-)B Modeling and Validation

Improving SMT Solver Integrations for the Validation of B and Event-B Models

Joshua Schmidt$^{(\boxtimes)}$ (ID) and Michael Leuschel (ID)

Institut für Informatik, Universität Düsseldorf,
Universitätsstr. 1, 40225 Düsseldorf, Germany
{joshua.schmidt,michael.leuschel}@hhu.de

Abstract. PROB provides a constraint solver for the B-method written in Prolog and optionally can make use of different backends based on SAT or SMT solving. One such solver integration translates B and Event-B operators to SMT-LIB using the C interface of the Z3 solver. This translation uses quantifiers to axiomatise operators when translating to SMT-LIB, which are not well-handled by Z3. Several relational constraints such as the transitive closure are not supported since their translations were too involved.

In this paper, we substantially improve the translation to SMT-LIB by employing a more constructive rather than axiomatised style using Z3's lambda functions. Thereby, we are able to translate more set-theoretic B and Event-B operators to SMT-LIB, and improve the overall performance. We further extend PROB's interface to Z3 to run different solver configurations in parallel, *e.g.*, either using the former or new translation. Empirical results show that the new translation to SMT-LIB and the parallel integration of different configurations of the Z3 solver have improved the performance of constraint solving.

1 Introduction

The B-method [2] is a correct-by-construction approach for software development based on refinement. Its foundation is an expressive formal language rooted in set-theory, integer arithmetic, and first-order logic. The B language supports higher order data types such as functions or arbitrarily nested relations, and is nowadays referred to as classical B. Event-B [3] is the successor of B which improves the language in several aspects and puts the focus on systems modelling, in particular by extending refinement. In the following we only refer to the B language which covers predicates and expressions in classical B and Event-B.

PROB [27,28] is an animator, model checker, and constraint solver for the B-method. The constraint solver is used for many tasks and is the foundation of the PROB tool. For instance, the constraint solver has to compute the effect of state changes during animation, find counter examples to proof obligations during disproving, or solve constraints for symbolic model checking or program synthesis. One key feature of PROB is that it computes all solutions of a constraint. For instance, this is important for a complete state-space exploration during model

© Springer Nature Switzerland AG 2021
A. Lluch Lafuente and A. Mavridou (Eds.): FMICS 2021, LNCS 12863, pp. 107–125, 2021.
https://doi.org/10.1007/978-3-030-85248-1_7

checking or when computing set comprehensions. This search is performed using backtracking. The core of PROB is implemented in SICStus Prolog [10] using its CLP(FD) library for constraint solving over the finite domain integers [11], and other features such as co-routines for deterministic propagation and constraint reification. PROB handles integer overflows by custom implementations and supports constraints over unbounded domains by using symbolic representations. Of course, PROB might fail to solve constraints over unbounded domains, *e.g.*, due to a timeout or a virtual timeout (when PROB detects that a domain cannot be enumerated exhaustively and all solutions are required).

Other prominent constraint solvers such as Z3 [13] implement a CDCL(T) architecture based on a conflict driven clause learning scheme which combines SAT and theory solving called Satisfiability Modulo Theories (SMT). In contrast to PROB and CLP(FD), SMT solvers are able to learn from contradictions [34,35] and possibly leave dead-end parts of the search tree earlier and more aggressively by applying backjumping. The SMT-LIB standard [5,6] defines the input language for SMT solvers.

In prior work, Krings and Leuschel present a high-level translation from B to SMT-LIB to integrate the Z3 SMT solver into PROB [24]. The authors have shown that, on the one hand, Z3 is often superior to PROB in disproving formulas especially over unbounded domains. On the other hand, Z3 often fails to find solutions for satisfiable constraints involving relations or set comprehensions. The suggested translation uses existing operators of SMT-LIB or Z3 wherever possible. Yet, for instance, SMT-LIB does not have native support for set comprehensions, which are frequently used in the B language. The authors thus suggested translating B set comprehensions to SMT-LIB using a universal quantification which constrains all members of a set variable. Unfortunately, this axiomatic translation often leads to complex constraints for which Z3 fails to find a solution. Other B operators which are not supported by the SMT-LIB standard are the relational composition, iteration and closure, as well as the general or quantified union $\bigcup_{x \in S}$ and intersection $\bigcap_{x \in S}$ of a nested set S. As the axiomatic translation to SMT-LIB using universal quantifiers was too complex, the authors decided to not support these operators.

When revising the translation of satisfiable B constraints which can not be solved by Z3, we noted that the axiomatic translation using universal quantifiers can be replaced by a more constructive translation using lambda functions which can considerably improve performance. For instance, the integration of Z3 is able to solve the constraint $f = \{1 \mapsto 2\} \wedge g = f \mathbin{\lhd\!\!\!-} \{2 \mapsto 3\}$ when using a lambda function for the translation of the overwrite operator but is not able to do so when using quantifiers. Z3 supports such lambda functions, even though they are not part of the latest SMT-LIB standard 2.6. Note that from version 3.0 lambda functions will be part of the SMT-LIB standard as well. Nevertheless, we observed that the axiomatic translation from B to SMT-LIB has benefits as well. In order to achieve the best performance, we decided to run several configurations of the Z3 solver with both translations in parallel.

This paper has three main contributions. First, we provide a new translation for most operators from B to SMT-LIB as understood by Z3 as well as a parallel integration of different Z3 solver configurations in PROB. Second, we provide a formal description of our translation which was not the case for the former translation [24] integrated in PROB. Third, we conclude the results with an empirical evaluation in the field of bounded model checking.

2 Former Z3 Integration

In the following we revise the workflow of the former integration of Z3 in PROB as well as the high-level translation from B to SMT-LIB presented in [24].

2.1 High-Level Translation

The former high-level translation [24] uses corresponding operators of SMT-LIB wherever possible. B sets are translated as characteristic functions in SMT-LIB mapping set elements to either true or false as defined by the array theory [12]. All logical B predicates ($\land$, $\lor$, $\Rightarrow$, $\Leftrightarrow$), all integer expressions except of division ($+$, $-$, mod, $**$, $\geq$, $>$, $<$, $\leq$), simple set expressions ($\in$, $\subset$, $\subseteq$, $\cup$, $\cap$, $-$), and quantifiers ($\forall$, $\exists$) can be translated to corresponding operators in SMT-LIB.

While B has a strict type system, there is no distinction between sets of pairs, relations, functions and sequences. For instance, the sequence $[-1]$ is the function $\{1 \mapsto -1\}$, which is also a relation, which in turn is a set of pairs. All these datatypes are thus translated as sets of pairs as is defined in B. Unfortunately, this prevents using certain features of Z3 which would probably be more efficient. For instance, B sequences could be directly translated as arrays in SMT-LIB instead of rewriting them to sets of pairs beforehand. Since B set operators can be called on sequences yielding a relation which is not a sequence anymore, e.g., $[-1] \cup \{5 \mapsto 3\} = \{1 \mapsto -1, 5 \mapsto 3\}$, this translation to arrays could only be performed if sequences only interoperate with other sequences.

Another difference between B and SMT-LIB is that B implements a concept of well-definedness [4] which is not present in SMT-LIB. Axioms for well-definedness ensure that certain operators are only applied when they make sense and that proof rules of classical two-valued logic can be applied. For instance, B prohibits the division by zero while in SMT-LIB the integer division is a total function, e.g., $(= (\mathbf{div}\ 1\ 0)\ (\mathbf{div}\ 1\ 0)$ is true in SMT-LIB and not well-defined in B. Another difference is that B's integer division rounds towards zero while SMT-LIB follows Boute's euclidean definition [8]. B's integer division a/b is thus translated to SMT-LIB as follows:

- $(\mathbf{ite}\ (\mathbf{or}\ (= (\mathbf{rem}\ a\ b)\ 0)\ (>\ a\ 0))\ (\mathbf{div}\ a\ b)$
  $(\mathbf{ite}\ (>\ b\ 0)\ (+\ (\mathbf{div}\ a\ b)\ 1)\ (-\ (\mathbf{div}\ a\ b)\ 1)))$

For the well-definedness of a/b, we assert that b is not equal to zero. Other operators with a well-definedness condition are, e.g., B's function application or minimum and maximum of a set of integers. For the translation of these operators, additional well-definedness conditions are added as well.

A frequently used construct of B is the set comprehension which has no direct counterpart in SMT-LIB. Set comprehensions are thus axiomatised using quantifiers in [24]. In particular, an existentially quantified variable is defined for each quantified variable of a set comprehension. For instance, the set comprehension $\{x \mid x > 0\}$ is encoded as a fresh existential variable tmp alongside the axiom $\forall v.(v \in \text{tmp} \Leftrightarrow v > 0)$ [24].

Several B set operators which can not be directly translated to SMT-LIB such as the domain of a relation are rewritten as set comprehensions. For instance, $\text{dom}(r)$ is rewritten to $\{x \mid \exists y.(x \mapsto y \in r)\}$. Yet, the operators $\min(s)$, $\max(s)$, and $\text{card}(s)$ can not be rewritten as set comprehensions. These operators are instead translated as identifiers which are axiomatised accordingly. For instance, the minimum of an integer set $\min(s)$ is replaced by an identifier m which is axiomatised by $\forall x.(x : s \Rightarrow m \leq x) \wedge \exists x.(x \in s \wedge m = x)$. The maximum of an integer set is encoded analogously.

Computing the cardinality of a set in SMT-LIB is expensive due to the employed encoding of sets. Hereby, a total bijection has to be computed mapping sets to their cardinalities since no set cardinality constraint is available in SMT-LIB. For instance, the B predicate $c = \text{card}(s)$ is encoded as $\exists t.(t \in s \rightarrowtail 1 \mathbin{..} c)$ [24]. The authors refer to such rewritten predicates as normalised B. A normalised predicate is then passed to the actual translator to SMT-LIB.

B supports user-defined types in the form of deferred sets and enumerated sets. Such B types are translated to corresponding sorts in SMT-LIB. Deferred sets are not limited in size, but assumed to be finite and non-empty for proof and animation in PROB. For enumerated sets, the actual instances are given which are defined as identifiers in SMT-LIB and axiomatised to be distinct.

The authors point out that several operators such as the relational closure, or the general union and intersection of a nested set can not be translated effectively to SMT-LIB using quantifiers [24].

2.2   Workflow

The former integration [24] of Z3 in PROB provides two interfaces. First, full B predicates can be translated to SMT-LIB and be solved by Z3. As described in Sect. 2.1, several B operators are not supported by the former translation to SMT-LIB and thus are filtered before the translation. If a predicate uses unsupported operators, the result of Z3 can thus only be used if a contradiction has been found. The second interface intertwines PROB's constraint solver with Z3 by setting up constraints simultaneously and sharing intermediate results. In particular, clauses learned by Z3 are fed to PROB as well, which lifts PROB's search capabilities from backtracking to backjumping. Since PROB generally shows better performance in model finding over B constraints than Z3, the call to Z3 is delayed after the deterministic propagation phase of PROB [24]. During this phase, PROB might infer new constraints which are then added to Z3.

3   New Z3 Integration

In the following we describe the new high-level translation from B to SMT-LIB as supported by Z3 as well as the new parallel solver integration.

3.1   High-Level Translation

For the formal description of the translation, we provide two semantic functions for B *expressions* representing values and *predicates* representing a truth value. In particular, $E[\![e]\!]i$ is the Z3 encoding of the B expression e, and $M[\![p]\!]i$ is the Z3 encoding of the B predicate p. The following example shows a series of rewriting steps, applying the rules of $E[\![e]\!]i$ and $M[\![e]\!]i$ (shown further below):

$$
\begin{aligned}
- \ M[\![x{>}y \wedge y{>}x]\!]i \ &\hat{=}\ (\textbf{and }E[\![x{>}y]\!]i\ E[\![y{>}x]\!]i) \\
&\hat{=}\ (\textbf{and }({>}\ E[\![x]\!]i\ E[\![y]\!]i)\ ({>}\ E[\![y]\!]i\ E[\![x]\!]i)) \\
&\hat{=}\ (\textbf{and }({>}\ x\ y)\ ({>}\ y\ x))
\end{aligned}
$$

B variables such as $E[\![x]\!]i$ are translated as functions using the same name. That means, $E[\![x]\!]i \ \hat{=}\ x$ but as a side effect a function for x has been introduced in the SMT-LIB model.

The variable i is an environment which stores specific information of a translation. This comprises a list of translated Z3 expressions and function declarations, a mapping from Z3 expressions to Z3 sorts Φ_i, e.g., $\Phi_i(-1) = \textbf{Int}$, and a mapping from B expressions to B types Ψ_i, e.g., $\Psi_i(-1) = \mathbb{Z}$. Furthermore, the environment stores a mapping from B tuple types to Z3 tuple sort projection functions Ω_i. For instance, $\Omega_i(\Psi_i(1 \mapsto 2)) = \{\text{``}x\text{''} : \textbf{get\_x}, \text{``}y\text{''} : \textbf{get\_y}\}$, where $\textbf{get\_x}$ and $\textbf{get\_y}$ are the projection functions of the Z3 tuple sort corresponding to the B type $\Psi_i(1 \mapsto 2)$ which have been defined by Z3 automatically. For the sake of readability, we use the abbreviations $\textbf{first}_{i,\Phi_i(c)}$ and $\textbf{second}_{i,\Phi_i(c)}$ with $c = E[\![x \mapsto y]\!]i$ for the projection functions of the Z3 tuple sort that has been introduced for the B type $\Psi_i(x \mapsto y)$. For instance, $\textbf{first}_{i,\Phi_i(E[\![1\mapsto2]\!]i)} = \Omega_i(\Psi_i(1 \mapsto 2))[\text{``}x\text{''}]$ and $\textbf{second}_{i,\Phi_i(E[\![1\mapsto2]\!]i)} = \Omega_i(\Psi_i(1 \mapsto 2))[\text{``}y\text{''}]$. Furthermore, we drop the type information of the projection functions if their argument is given. For instance, $(\textbf{first}_{i,\Phi_i(c)}\ c) = (\textbf{first}_i\ c)$ with $c = E[\![x \mapsto y]\!]i$. Last but not least, we allow to call the semantic functions on partially defined B operators, e.g., $E[\![\text{dom}(s)]\!]i \ \hat{=}\ (E[\![\text{dom}]\!]i\ E[\![s]\!]i)$.

Tuples. In B, tuples are encoded as nested pairs. Thus, several encodings of tuples exist and the modeller has to know which one is being used. For instance, a triple can be represented as either $(x \mapsto (y \mapsto z))$ or $((x \mapsto y) \mapsto z)$. We use the first left-associative encoding and introduce a unique Z3 sort for each tuple type occurring in a B predicate when translating to SMT-LIB. B tuples are then translated using their corresponding Z3 sort's constructor which is defined as follows:

$$
\begin{aligned}
- \ E[\![(x_1,\ldots,x_n)]\!]i \ &\hat{=}\ (\textbf{tuple}_{i,\Phi_i(E[\![x_1]\!]i),\ldots,\Phi_i(E[\![x_n]\!]i)}\ E[\![x_1]\!]i\ \ldots\ E[\![x_n]\!]i) \\
&=\ (\textbf{tuple}_i\ E[\![x_1]\!]i\ \ldots\ E[\![x_n]\!]i)
\end{aligned}
$$

The Z3 function $\mathbf{tuple}_{i,\Phi_i(E[\![x_1]\!]i),\ldots,\Phi_i(E[\![x_n]\!]i)}$ is the constructor of the Z3 tuple sort which has been introduced for B tuples of type $\Psi_i(x_1 \times \cdots \times x_n)$, where $n \in \mathbb{N}$. For the sake of readability, we drop the type information of the tuple constructor since the types are implicitly given by the constructor's arguments.

B provides two projection functions to access the elements of a tuple which are translated as follows:

- $E[\![\mathrm{prj}_1(\Psi_i(x), \Psi_i(y))(x \mapsto y)]\!]i \; \widehat{=} \; (\mathbf{first}_i \; E[\![x \mapsto y]\!]i)$
- $E[\![\mathrm{prj}_2(\Psi_i(x), \Psi_i(y))(x \mapsto y)]\!]i \; \widehat{=} \; (\mathbf{second}_i \; E[\![x \mapsto y]\!]i)$

Set Notation. As described in Sect. 2.2, the former high-level translation rewrites many set operators to B set comprehensions since they are not directly supported by SMT-LIB. The set comprehensions themselves are then rewritten using B quantifiers which can be directly translated to SMT-LIB. However, using many quantifiers can lead to unnecessarily complex constraints for which Z3 is not able to find a model. Fortunately, Z3 provides lambda functions which allow to define a set of variables that are constrained by an expression. In general, a lambda function (**lambda** sorts body) in Z3 returns an expression of the sort (**Array** sorts range) where range is the sort of body. For instance, (**lambda** $((x \; \mathbf{Int}))$ (**and** $(>= x \; 0)$ $(<= x \; 2)))$ is a lambda function that describes the set of integers $\{0, 1, 2\}$ as an array that maps integers to either true or false, *i.e.*, the output has the sort (**Array Int Bool**). For our translations, we consistently use lambda functions that constrain a single variable by a boolean expression.

First and foremost, we suggest translating B set comprehensions using Z3's lambda function which we define as follows:

- $E[\![\{x \mid \mathrm{p}\}]\!]i \; \widehat{=} \; (\mathbf{lambda} \; ((E[\![x]\!]i \; \Phi_i(E[\![x]\!]i))) \; M[\![\mathrm{p}]\!]i)$
- $E[\![\{x_1,\ldots,x_n \mid \mathrm{p}\}]\!]i \; \widehat{=}$
$\qquad (\mathbf{lambda} \; ((c \; \Phi_i(E[\![x_1 \times \cdots \times x_n]\!]i)))$
$\qquad\qquad (\mathbf{exists} \; ((E[\![x_1]\!]i \; \Phi_i(E[\![x_1]\!]i)) \; \ldots \; (E[\![x_n]\!]i \; \Phi_i(E[\![x_n]\!]i)))$
$\qquad\qquad\qquad (\mathbf{and} \; M[\![\mathrm{p}]\!]i \; (= c \; E[\![(x_1,\ldots,x_n)]\!]i))))$

The first case is a special case for a B set comprehension with a singleton result variable since no tuple constructor has to be called here.

Although this improved the performance of Z3 regarding model finding for set comprehensions, we decided to provide specialised translations for most set operations such as the range of a relation instead of rewriting operators into set comprehensions. We thus prevent unnecessary uses of existential quantifiers at the top-level of lambda functions, which would always be introduced by the second translation rule. Furthermore, the general set union and intersection were not supported by the prior translation since their axiomatisations were too involved. Both operators can be encoded efficiently using lambda expressions. We provide the following syntax-directed translation rules for a subset of set operators:

- $E[\![m..n]\!]i \;\widehat{=}\;$ (**lambda** $((k$ **Int**$))$ (**and** $(>= k\; E[\![m]\!]i)\; (<= k\; E[\![n]\!]i)))$
- $E[\![\mathbb{P}(S)]\!]i \;\widehat{=}\;$ (**lambda** $((x\; \Phi_i(x)))$ (**subset** $x\; E[\![S]\!]i))$
- $E[\![\mathbb{P}_1(S)]\!]i \;\widehat{=}\;$ (**lambda** $((x\; \Phi_i(x)))$ (**and** (**subset** $x\; E[\![S]\!]i)$
  (**not** $(= x\;$ **emptySet**$))))$
- $E[\![\mathrm{id}(S)]\!]i \;\widehat{=}\;$ (**lambda** $((c\; \Phi_i(c)))$ (**exists** $((x\; \Phi_i(x)))$
  (**and** (**in** $x\; E[\![S]\!]i)\; (= c\;$ (**tuple**$_i\; x\; x)))))$
- $E[\![S \times T]\!]i \;\widehat{=}\;$ (**lambda** $((c\; \Phi_i(c)))$
  (**and** (**in** (**first**$_i\; c)\; E[\![S]\!]i)$ (**in** (**second**$_i\; c)\; E[\![T]\!]i)))$
- $E[\![\mathrm{dom}(r)]\!]i \;\widehat{=}\;$ (**lambda** $((x\; \Phi_i(x)))$ (**exists** $((y\; \Phi_i(y)))$
  (**in** (**tuple**$_i\; x\; y)\; E[\![r]\!]i)))$
- $E[\![\mathrm{ran}(r)]\!]i \;\widehat{=}\;$ (**lambda** $((y\; \Phi_i(y)))$ (**exists** $((x\; \Phi_i(x)))$
  (**in** (**tuple**$_i\; x\; y)\; E[\![r]\!]i)))$
- $E[\![r^{-1}]\!]i \;\widehat{=}\;$ (**lambda** $((c\; \Phi_i(c)))$
  (**in** (**tuple**$_i\;$ (**second**$_i\; c$) (**first**$_i\; c$)) $E[\![r]\!]i))$
- $E[\![S \lhd r]\!]i \;\widehat{=}\;$ (**lambda** $((c\; \Phi_i(c)))$
  (**and** (**in** $c\; E[\![r]\!]i)$ (**in** (**first**$_i\; c)\; E[\![S]\!]i)))$
- $E[\![S \lhd\!\!\!- r]\!]i \;\widehat{=}\;$ (**lambda** $((c\; \Phi_i(c)))$
  (**and** (**in** $c\; E[\![r]\!]i)$ (**not** (**in** (**first**$_i\; c)\; E[\![S]\!]i))))$
- $E[\![r \rhd T]\!]i \;\widehat{=}\;$ (**lambda** $((c\; \Phi_i(c)))$
  (**and** (**in** $c\; E[\![r]\!]i)$ (**in** (**second**$_i\; c)\; E[\![T]\!]i)))$
- $E[\![r \rhd\!\!\!- T]\!]i \;\widehat{=}\;$ (**lambda** $((c\; \Phi_i(c)))$
  (**and** (**in** $c\; E[\![r]\!]i)$ (**not** (**in** (**second**$_i\; c)\; E[\![T]\!]i))))$
- $E[\![r_1 \Leftarrow\!\!\!- r_2]\!]i \equiv E[\![r_2 \cup (\mathrm{dom}(r_2) \lhd\!\!\!- r_1)]\!]i$
- $E[\![r[S]]\!]i \;\widehat{=}\;$ (**lambda** $((y\; \Phi_i(y)))$ (**exists** $((x\; \Phi_i(x)))$
  (**and** (**in** $x\; E[\![S]\!]i)$ (**in** (**tuple**$_i\; x\; y)\; E[\![r]\!]i))))$
- $E[\![\mathrm{union}(S)]\!]i \;\widehat{=}\;$ (**lambda** $((e\; \Phi_i(e)))$ (**exists** $((\mathrm{sub}\; \Phi_i(\mathrm{sub})))$
  (**and** (**in** sub $E[\![S]\!]i)$ (**in** e sub))))
- $E[\![\mathrm{inter}(S)]\!]i \;\widehat{=}\;$ (**lambda** $((e\; \Phi_i(e)))$ (**forall** $((\mathrm{sub}\; \Phi_i(\mathrm{sub})))$
  (**implies** (**in** sub $E[\![S]\!]i)$ (**in** e sub))))
- $E[\![\lambda z.(\mathrm{Pred} \mid \mathrm{Expr})]\!]i \;\widehat{=}\;$ (**lambda** $((c\; \Phi_i(c)))$ (**exists** $((z\; \Phi_i(z)))$
  (**and** $M[\![\mathrm{Pred}]\!]i\; (= c\;$ (**tuple**$_i\; z\; E[\![\mathrm{Expr}]\!]i)))))$

Finite Subsets. The finite set operators min, max, and card can not be expressed efficiently using lambda functions. We thus stick to the axiomatic translation using universal quantifiers for these operators as defined by Krings and Leuschel [24] and described in Sect. 2.1. The same applies for the Event-B operator finite as is formalised in the following.

- $E[\![\mathrm{finite}(S)]\!]i \equiv E[\![\exists(b, f).(b \in \mathbb{N} \wedge f \in S \to 0 .. b)]\!]i$
- $E[\![\mathbb{F}(S)]\!]i \;\widehat{=}\;$ (**lambda** $((x\; \Phi_i(x)))$ (**and** (**subset** $x\; E[\![S]\!]i)\; (E[\![\mathrm{finite}]\!]i\; x)))$
- $E[\![\mathbb{F}_1(S)]\!]i \;\widehat{=}\;$ (**lambda** $((x\; \Phi_i(x)))$ (**and** (**subset** $x\; E[\![S]\!]i)\; (E[\![\mathrm{finite}]\!]i\; x)$
  (**not** $(= x\;$ **emptySet**))))

Rewriting Cardinality. Since Z3 often lacks performance when solving quantified formulas [24], we provide special rewriting rules for B cardinality constraints to equivalent representations which do not lead to quantified formulas in SMT-LIB. In particular, we provide the following rewriting rules:

- $\text{card}(\{x_1, \ldots, x_n\}) = n \equiv \text{all\_different}(\{x_1, \ldots, x_n\})$, where all_different sets up a pairwise distinction between all elements
- $q \in 1 \mathinner{\ldotp\ldotp} n \rightarrow 1 \mathinner{\ldotp\ldotp} n \wedge \text{card}(\text{ran}(q)) = n \equiv \bigwedge_{i \in 1 \mathinner{\ldotp\ldotp} n-1} q(i) \neq q(i+1)$

Furthermore, we replace cardinality constraints of enumerated sets by integer values. For instance, we can simplify the B constraint $s = 1 \mathinner{\ldotp\ldotp} 4 \wedge \text{card}(s) > 1 \wedge i = \text{card}(s) - 1$ to $s = 1 \mathinner{\ldotp\ldotp} 4 \wedge i = 3$ to prevent sending any cardinality constraint to Z3. Such formulas might not be written by hand but do often occur when using an automated translation backend of PROB such as the integration [18] of TLA$^+$ [26] in B.

Relational Composition, Iteration, and Closure. Some relational B operators such as the transitive and reflexive closure are more complex to translate to SMT-LIB and will be discussed in the following. The transitive and reflexive closure r^* of a relation $r \in S \leftrightarrow S$ can be mathematically defined as $\bigcup_{n \in \mathbb{N}} r^n$, and the transitive and not reflexive closure r^+ as $\bigcup_{n \in \mathbb{N}_1} r^n$. Here, the transitive and reflexive closure is defined by the union of a relation's iterations for all natural numbers.

The iteration of a relation $r \in S \leftrightarrow S$ can be defined recursively using B's forward composition. This conforms the formula $r^n = r^{n-1}; r^1$, where the base case is $r^1 = r$. One special case of the relational iteration in B is $r^0 = \text{id}(S)$, which is rewritten before the translation. B's forward composition of two relations $p; q$ is defined by the set comprehension $\{x, y \mid \exists z.(x \mapsto z \in p \wedge z \mapsto y \in q)\}$ which can be straightforwardly translated to SMT-LIB using lambda functions:

- (**define-fun fcomp** (($p\ \Phi_i(p)$) ($q\ \Phi_i(q)$)) (**Array** $\Phi_i(c)$ **Bool**)
    (**lambda** (($c\ \Phi_i(c)$)) (**exists** (($z\ \Phi_i(z)$)) (**and**
        (**in** (**tuple**$_i$ (**first**$_i$ c) z) p) (**in** (**tuple**$_i$ z (**second**$_i$ c)) q)))))
- $E[\![p; q]\!]i \mathrel{\widehat{=}} (\textbf{fcomp}\ E[\![p]\!]i\ E[\![q]\!]i)$

Note that a relational backward composition can be described by a forward composition, i.e., $p \circ q \equiv q; p$. We are able to define the iteration of a relation r as a recursive function using the encoding of B's forward composition in SMT-LIB as follows:

- (**define-fun-rec iterate** (($r\ \Phi_i(r)$) (n **Int**)) $\Phi_i(r)$
    (**ite** (= n 1) r (**fcomp** (**iterate** r (- n 1)) r)))
- $E[\![r^n]\!]i \mathrel{\widehat{=}} (\textbf{iterate}\ E[\![r]\!]i\ E[\![n]\!]i)$

Due to the employed encoding of sets in SMT-LIB which introduces a sort for each type of set, e.g., a set of the integers or a set of the booleans, we have to define the functions **iterate** and **fcomp** for each type they are applied to. We

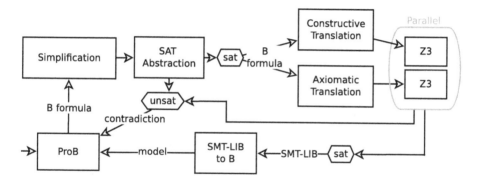

Fig. 1. A workflow diagram of the new Z3 integration in PROB.

thus define unique names for the different functions differing in the relation's type and case split on these types before translating to SMT-LIB.

Let **union** be a function passing its only argument to the lambda function for the translation of B's general union as defined before. The transitive and reflexive closure of a relation r can now be translated to SMT-LIB straightforwardly:

- $E[\![r^*]\!]i \;\hat{=}\;$ (**union** (**lambda** $((s\ \Phi_i(s)))$ (**exists** $((n\ \textbf{Int}))$
$$\textbf{(and} \;(>=\; n\ 0)\; (=\; s\; (\textbf{iterate}\; E[\![r]\!]i\; n)))))$$

B's transitive and not reflexive closure r^+ is translated analogously but using $n \in \mathbb{N}_1$.

3.2 New Workflow

The new workflow of PROB's Z3 interface is supposed to replace the former interface which sends full predicates to Z3 as described in Sect. 2.2. Note that PROB also has an interface to Z3 where both solvers share constraints which we do not consider here. A diagram of the workflow is presented in Fig. 1.

Preprocessing. First, a formula is simplified by PROB as was the case for the former integration [24] of Z3. For instance, formulas are rewritten to use a subset of operators such as only using $\leq$ but not $\geq$.

We decided to apply a static analysis to check syntactically for contradictions before translating to SMT-LIB. The goal is to prevent that those are no longer detected by Z3, e.g., after adding quantifiers. For this, we extended the simplification rules of PROB to more aggressively replace variables by their value if this value is explicitly given. For instance, the formula $s = \varnothing \wedge \text{card}(s) > 1$ can be rewritten to $s = \varnothing \wedge \text{card}(\varnothing) > 1$ in a first phase. Afterwards, the cardinality constraint can be replaced by the integer 0 which makes it obvious that the integer comparison is not satisfied. We thus prevented the translation of a cardinality constraint to SMT-LIB.

To further extend the static syntax analysis, we decided to abstract a B formula to a SAT formula as is done by lazy SMT solvers [31] and only translate a formula to SMT-LIB if its SAT abstraction is satisfiable as can be seen in Fig. 1. If it is not satisfiable, we have avoided the overhead of translating B to SMT-LIB and calling the external solvers. For instance, the formula $x = y \wedge x \neq y$ can be abstracted to $A \wedge \neg A$ where $A \equiv x = y$. Note that this is not an eager SMT solving [31] where all semantics are translated to SAT. We are now able to call a SAT solver to find a solution for an abstracted B formula. For this, we implemented a SAT solver for propositional B formulas in Prolog as proposed by Howe and King [21].

Z3 Solver Integration. If the SAT abstraction is satisfiable, we apply both translations from B to SMT-LIB: the pre-existing one from [24] (Sect. 2.1), as well as the new one described in Sect. 3.1.

The former integration of Z3 always used the *incremental* solver where constraints can be pushed on the solver stack. While this was required when both PROB and Z3 run simultaneously, this is not the case for the integration presented in this paper, where we send full predicates to Z3 only. In particular, using the incremental solver incurs an additional overhead since constraints are internalised. We thus decided to run two non-incremental Z3 solvers in parallel with the two different translations, as described above. Unfortunately, Z3's incremental solver does not support an existential quantifier at the top-level of a lambda expression.[1] This makes our new translation not applicable for running PROB and Z3 simultaneously and sharing constraints.

We use the result of the solver which answers first if a solution or a contradiction has been found. The other solvers are then interrupted. If the fastest solver answers unknown, we do not use this result but wait for another solver. The solver integration returns unknown if all solvers did so as well, or if a formula can not be translated to SMT-LIB, *e.g.*, because of a missing implementation. The return of unknown is not shown in Fig. 1.

Note that it is simple to add an additional Z3 solver configuration to the workflow. Our implementation is able to create a deep copy of a translation with all of its referenced Z3 objects. We then just have to create a new solver object and set the desired options.

Postprocessing of Models. A model found by Z3 is represented in SMT-LIB. We parse a model and translate it to B as was the case for the former workflow integration described in Sect. 2.2. Unfortunately, Z3 often fails to compute explicit values from lambda functions or quantifiers while it is able to find contradictions. For instance, for the formula $s = \text{union}(\{\{1\}, \{2\}\})$, Z3 returns a model containing the translated lambda function of the general union defined in Sect. 3.1 while s could be set to $\{1, 2\}$. However, Z3 is able to find contradictions using the general union such as for the formula $\{1\} = \text{union}(\{\{1\}, \{2\}\})$.

---

[1] Z3 throws the error "internalization of exists is not supported".

We thus extend the translation from SMT-LIB to B and the processing of found models to compute remaining quantifiers and lambda functions with PROB's constraint solver. For instance, the lambda function in above example's model returned by Z3 is translated as a set comprehension in B which results in $s = \{e \mid \exists f.(e \in f \land (f = \{1\} \lor f = \{2\}))\}$. The PROB constraint solver is then called to compute an explicit value which results in $s = \{1, 2\}$.

4   Empirical Evaluation

In the following we present an empirical evaluation of the new Z3 solver interface including the new translation from B to SMT-LIB. We split the evaluation in three categories. First, we focus on the downsides of our employed translation of selected language constructs which we deem to be responsible for a possibly bad performance when solving constraints. Second, we present selected constraints for which the integration of Z3 is superior to PROB regarding constraint solving. Third, we evaluate the performance of our translation using a variety of benchmarks from bounded model checking.

4.1   Weaknesses of the Integration of Z3

The weaknesses of the integration of Z3 are mainly caused by the employed encoding of sets. Most of B's set theoretic operators are not supported by SMT-LIB such as computing a power set or the cardinality of a set. As discussed in Sects. 2.1 and 3.1, this can lead to involved quantified constraints for which Z3 is not able to find a solution. We thus employ several rewriting rules and a preprocessing to prevent sending quantified formulas to Z3 if this is not necessary. The benefit of this preprocessing is discussed in the following.

Finite Sets. The former and new translation from B to SMT-LIB both support infinite sets. Krings and Leuschel have shown that Z3 is able to solve a variety of B constraints over infinite domains which PROB is not able to solve especially when a formula is a contradiction [24]. However, the support of infinite domains leads to involved translations for finite set constraints such as the minimum, maximum or the cardinality of a finite set. For instance, the current translation searches for a total bijection mapping sets to their cardinalities to compute the cardinality of a set [24]. A total bijection is rewritten using B quantifiers before the translation to SMT-LIB.

Since Z3 lacks performance when solving quantified formulas, Z3 often fails to find a solution for translated B constraints using set cardinalities. For instance, Z3 is not able to solve the translation of $q \in 1 .. 3 \rightarrow 1 .. 3 \land \text{card}(\text{ran}(q)) = 3$. With the use of the rewriting rule for the cardinality of range constraints defined in Sect. 3.1, Z3 is able to solve the constraint in several milliseconds as is PROB. The rewriting rule replaces the cardinality constraint with $q(1) \neq q(2) \land q(1) \neq q(3) \land q(2) \neq q(3)$. Of course, not all cardinality constraints can be replaced by equivalent constraints and remaining quantifiers are still one of the main culprits for a possibly bad performance of the presented translation from B to SMT-LIB.

The translation of set constraints to SMT-LIB such as card, max, or min could be improved by focussing on finite sets only, *e.g.*, as presented by Plagge and Leuschel [33] for B by translating to Kodkod [36] or by Konnov et al. [22] for TLA$^+$ [26] by translating to SMT-LIB [5].

Static Contradictions. Translations which result in quantifiers in SMT-LIB can become too involved to be solved by Z3. In some cases this means that Z3 cannot find obvious contradictions in a formula. For instance, Z3 is not able to find the contradiction in the formula $r \in \mathbb{Z} \rightarrowtail \mathbb{Z} \land r \notin \mathbb{Z} \rightarrowtail \mathbb{Z}$. Here, both partial functions are translated as quantified formulas in SMT-LIB leading Z3 to report unknown. We are able to detect the contradiction by abstracting the formula to propositional logic and using a SAT solver as described in Sect. 3.2. In particular, we lift negations from B operations before the abstraction which results in $A \land \neg A$ where $A \equiv r \in \mathbb{Z} \rightarrowtail \mathbb{Z}$. It can be seen that no translation to SMT-LIB is necessary in such cases. Such constraints do often occur in bounded model checking, where invariants are negated to check for counterexamples.

4.2 Strengths of the Integration of Z3

Weaknesses of PROB are often caused by the use of unbounded integer domains. One motivating example which speaks in favor of the Z3 constraint solver is the constraint $x > y \land y > x$. PROB is not able to solve this constraint with its default CLP(FD) backend since the integer domains of x and y cannot be narrowed down. Although PROB is able to solve this constraint by using its additional CHR backend, the example shows a benefit of using Z3 for unbounded integer domains, in particular for linear integer arithmetic. For example, Z3 is able to solve the constraint $\forall(x, y).(x \in \mathbb{Z} \land y \in \mathbb{Z} \Rightarrow \exists z.(x - z = y))$ while PROB is not. The constraint is taken from the 14th SMT competition for quantified integer difference logic [38]. Another constraint which can not be disproven by PROB is $\neg((s2 = s0 \land s3 = s \cup \{1\} \land s4 = s2 \cup \{1\} \land s5 = s3 \cup \{0\}) \Rightarrow s4 = s5)$, which stems from a computation that occurred during partial order reduction for B. Again, both constraints contain unbounded sets of the integers which can not be enumerated exhaustively by PROB. The constraints further indicate that this issue affects model finding as well as the disproving of formulas.

We further observed strengths of the integration of Z3 regarding the disproving of constraints involving infinite relations. For instance, the integration of Z3 is able to solve the constraint $f \in \mathbb{N} \rightarrowtail \mathbb{N} \land x \in \mathbb{N} \land g = f \lhd \{x \mapsto x+1\} \land \neg(g \in \mathbb{N} \rightarrowtail \mathbb{N})$ which can not be solved by PROB. Furthermore, this constraint can only be solved when using the new translation which uses Z3's lambda expressions.

The integration of Z3 is also able to solve several constraints faster than is PROB. Such constraints do not necessarily involve unbounded domains but are related to the enumeration of domains as performed by PROB. For instance, the integration of Z3 is able to find a model for the constraint $f = \lambda x.(x \in 1 \mathbin{..} n \mid$

Table 1. Bounded model checking (BMC) constraints from TLA$^+$ benchmarks compiled by Konnov et al. [22], and B benchmarks compiled by Krings and Leuschel [23, 25]. BMC uses a bound of 25 and sets up 26 constraints for each benchmark.

Nr	Name	PROB	PROB-Z3 [24]	PROB-Z3-Par
1	Prisoners-4	**13/432.591** s	0/733.875 s	0/766.105 s
2	Bakery	**3/699.099** s	0/800.109 s	1/796.406 s
3	SimpleTwoPhase	**26/0.160** s	26/1.635 s	26/1.989 s
4	Lightbot	2/720.352 s	0/280.375 s	**11/493.477** s
5	LargeBranching	**26/0.116** s	26/29.633 s	26/40.105 s
6	SearchEvents	3/690.355 s	**20/184.992** s	20/185.989 s
7	ABZ16_m4	**26/1.061** s	26/3.658 s	26/2.474 s
8	ABZ16_m5	0/1.457 s*	26/4.080 s	**26/3.105** s
9	ABZ16_m7	0/2.306 s*	15/359.713 s	**16/369.549** s
10	R3_Sensors	**12/456.854** s	2/11.736 s	2/19.906 s
11	R4_Handle	**4/362.064** s	1/551.389 s	1/570.001 s
12	R5_Switch	**8/550.870** s	3/37.233 s	3/46.487 s
13	R6_Lights	**6/606.375** s	3/44.841 s	3/64.622 s

Solved constraints / Runtime s

*unknown due to the use of deferred sets

$x + 1) \cup \{n + 1 \mapsto (n/2)\} \wedge x = f[x] \wedge x \neq \varnothing \wedge n = 20$ in around 0.166 s while PROB is not able to solve the constraints within 60 s. The reason is that CLP(FD) enumerates many values before finding a solution which does not seem to be the case for Z3.

4.3 Symbolic Model Checking

For a more sophisticated performance evaluation we decided to use constraints from bounded model checking (BMC)[2]. In particular, we use the monolithic bounded model checking implementation [25] of PROB which sends a single formula to a selected constraint solving backend. Hereby, we solve 26 constraints for each model and compare the amount of constraints that can be solved by a specific solver, as well as the time needed to decide for the satisfiability of all constraints. That means, the presented runtimes are the sum of the times needed to solve all 26 constraints. We use a maximum solver timeout of 30 s for each constraint and compare the PROB constraint solver, its integration of Z3 using the former translation [24], as well as the parallel integration of Z3 as described in Sect. 3.2. We did not investigate the effects of a larger timeout since the results already show an overall trend. Furthermore, Z3 often answers unknown rather than exceeding the solver timeout.

---

[2] The benchmarks can be found in the following repository to reproduce the results: https://github.com/Joshua27/fmics2021_benchmarks.

The evaluated benchmarks can be seen in Table 1. We use two TLA$^+$ [26] benchmarks compiled by Konnov et al. [22]. The authors used the benchmarks to evaluate the performance of their symbolic model checker APALACHE for TLA$^+$ which translates to SMT-LIB. We use the translation from TLA$^+$ to B [18] to load TLA$^+$ models in PROB. Unfortunately, the integration of Z3 is not able to solve many constraints of these benchmarks. We thus only use these two benchmarks which already exhibit this trend. Additionally, we use a set of B benchmarks compiled by Krings and Leuschel [25]. The benchmarks number 7 to 9 are taken from a submission to the ABZ 2016 case study [30] by Hoang et al. [20], and the benchmarks 10 to 13 from a submission to the ABZ 2014 landing gear case study [7] by Hansen et al. [17].

The benchmarks were run on a system with an Intel Core I7-8750H CPU (2.2 GHz) and 16 GB of RAM using PROB version 1.10.2, SICStus Prolog version 4.6.0, and Z3 version 4.8.10.

In general, the benchmarks show that the PROB constraint solver is superior to the integration of Z3. The main reason are cardinality constraints whose translation to SMT-LIB results in quantified formulas. Unfortunately, quantifiers often cause Z3 to immediately answer with unknown or to exceed the defined solver timeout. Yet, this is not the case for the benchmarks number 4, 6, 8 and 9 presented in Table 1. In particular, the 2nd, 4th, and 9th benchmark also show that the new translation is benificial since more constraints can be solved. PROB is not able to disprove the constraints for the 8th and 9th benchmark because of unfixed deferred sets, which is not the case for Z3.

The 4th benchmark shows clear benefits of the integration of Z3 compared to PROB. Here, PROB exceeds the maximum solver timeout for most constraints. The constraints use many bounded integer domains, total functions, and function applications.

Note that all but one constraint of the benchmarks 7 and 8 can be disproven by static rewriting rules which is the case for both integrations of Z3. These constraints should thus not be put in relation with SMT solving too much. A general comparison of the runtimes of the former and new integration of Z3 indicate that the additional static syntax analysis described in Sect. 3.2 does not add too much overhead.

5   Related Work

Déharbe et al. [14] presented an integration of SMT solvers for B and Event-B by translating to SMT-LIB. The goal was to support automated theorem provers by disproving single proof-obligations. The authors presented two translations which support a subset of the B language. One translation specifically interfaces an SMT solver and uses its lambda expressions. Sets are translated as characteristic functions as is the case for our implementation, but only basic sets are supported in this case. In the other translation, sets are translated as uninterpreted functions which are axiomatised. The axiomatic translation presented by Krings and Leuschel [24] and described in Sect. 2.1 is similar to this translation, but uses Z3's set theory [12] and characteristic functions instead of uninterpreted functions. Empirical results by Déharbe et al. have shown that the amount of proof obligations which can be proven automatically has improved [15]. Krings and Leuschel have shown that their derived high-level translation improves the one by Déharbe et al. regarding constraint solving [24].

The mathematical foundations of TLA$^+$ and B have quite a few similarities, and translations between both formalisms exist [18,19]. TLC [39] is an explicit state model checker for TLA$^+$ that relies on simple domain enumeration. Konnov et al. [22] presented a translation from TLA$^+$ to SMT-LIB to improve symbolic model checking by interfacing SMT solvers. The translation only supports finite sets, which avoids many downsides of our translation from B to SMT-LIB. For instance, the authors suggest translating a set membership as a disjunction of equalities, which is feasible for finite sets only. Furthermore, quantifiers are unfolded, *e.g.*, an existential quantification is replaced by a disjunction. In the future, we plan to conduct an empirical comparison with APALACHE's SMT solver integration [22], which will require a fair translation of TLA$^+$ constraints to B and backwards, and isolating the constraint solving performed by APALACHE from the symbolic verification algorithms.

El Ghazi and Taghdiri [16] presented a translation from Alloy to SMT-LIB. Abbazzi et al. [1] presented an integration of SMT solvers in the Alloy analyzer, as well as an evaluation of different translations from Alloy to SMT-LIB. The Alloy analyzer usually translates Alloy to Kodkod [36] which applies SAT solving. Yet, this eager approach to SMT solving can result in large propositional formulas depending on the size of domains. This possibly leads to a bad performance. For instance, sets can be translated as bit vectors where one bit is reserved for each domain element. The authors have shown performance improvements of model finding for Alloy by translating to SMT-LIB. Furthermore, the translation enables to reason over infinite sets.

Weber [37] presented an SMT solver integration for the HOL4 theorem prover which supports the first-order subset of the language. The translation to SMT-LIB employs an axiomatised style for operators that are not supported by SMT-LIB such as the minimum of a set of integers.

Bride et al. [9] conducted an empirical evaluation and comparison of SMT solving and constraint logic programming for workflow nets. In particular, they interface Z3 and SICStus Prolog as is the case for our implementation. Their results show benefits of SMT solving for unsatisfiable formulas, and benefits of constraint logic programming for satisfiable ones, which fits also with our experience.

6   Future Work

In the future, we plan to provide alternative translations for B functions and sequences using lambda expressions as well. Furthermore, the translation of B sequences to SMT-LIB can be improved if sequences only interact among themselves guaranteeing the well-definedness of resulting sequences. This is not necessarily the case since B sequences are relations and might interact with other relations which are not sequences as described in Sect. 2.1.

As discussed in Sect. 4.1, the support of infinite sets entails several suboptimal translations, *e.g.*, for cardinality constraints. If only finite sets are used in a formula, we are able to translate sets to a more concise representation, *e.g.*, using a bit vector encoding. Of course, we then have to provide translations for all set operators for this new type which requires some implementation effort.

Furthermore, we plan to compile other configurations of the Z3 constraint solver to run in parallel, *e.g.*, using different solver tactics.

Another future work is to use other SMT solvers to solve SMT-LIB models. Currently, the new translation presented in this paper uses Z3 specific lambda functions. Once the SMT-LIB standard officially supports lambda functions we should be able to interface other SMT solvers as well for the new translation. Hereby, it is worth to mention that the implementation of an automated translation which interfaces a solver specific programming API is a tedious and error-prone task. Mann et al. [29] presented a solver-agnostic programming API for SMT solving which should be considered for future implementations.

Finally, we currently implement techniques from SMT solving in PROB to tightly connect the PROB constraint solver with a learning scheme based on the DPLL(T) algorithm [32]. The goal is to combine the strengths of SMT solving and constraint logic programming. Furthermore, we can overcome the performance drawbacks of the integration of Z3 regarding cardinality constraints when using PROB as a theory solver in a conflict-driven clause learning scheme.

7   Conclusion

In conclusion, we have presented a formal description and implementation of a new translation from B to SMT-LIB as well as a parallel SMT solver integration in PROB. Empirical results have shown that the new translation improves performance and completeness compared to the prior integration in PROB [24] by utilising Z3's lambda functions. Furthermore, we were able to identify a bug in Z3 using PROB's regression tests which occured when using Z3's lambda function with a specific solver option.

Unfortunately, the overall performance on large constraints as selected from bounded model checking is still often bad compared to using only PROB. The main reason is the use of cardinality constraints which can not be translated to SMT-LIB concisely for the employed encoding of sets. Nevertheless, the empirical results have also shown that the new solver integration can solve some constraints better than PROB. In the most cases, such constraints contain bounded or unbounded integer domains and function applications.

Acknowledgements. We would like to thank the reviewers of FMICS'2021 for their useful feedback.

References

1. Abbassi, A., Day, N.A., Rayside, D.: Astra version 1.0: evaluating translations from alloy to SMT-LIB. CoRR, abs/1906.05881 (2019)
2. Abrial, J.-R.: The B-Book: Assigning Programs to Meanings. Cambridge University Press, New York (1996)
3. Abrial, J.-R.: Modeling in Event-B: System and Software Engineering, 1st edn. Cambridge University Press, New York (2010)
4. Abrial, J.-R., Mussat, L.: On using conditional definitions in formal theories. In: Bert, D., Bowen, J.P., Henson, M.C., Robinson, K. (eds.) ZB 2002. LNCS, vol. 2272, pp. 242–269. Springer, Heidelberg (2002). https://doi.org/10.1007/3-540-45648-1_13
5. Barrett, C., Fontaine, P., Tinelli, C.: The Satisfiability Modulo Theories Library (SMT-LIB) (2016). www.SMT-LIB.org
6. Barrett, C.W., Sebastiani, R., Seshia, S.A., Tinelli, C.: Satisfiability modulo theories. In: Biere, A., Heule, M., van Maaren, H., Walsh, T. (eds.) Handbook of Satisfiability. Frontiers in Artificial Intelligence and Applications, vol. 185, pp. 825–885. IOS Press (2009)
7. Boniol, F., Wiels, V.: The landing gear system case study. In: Boniol, F., Wiels, V., Ait Ameur, Y., Schewe, K.-D. (eds.) ABZ 2014. CCIS, vol. 433, pp. 1–18. Springer, Cham (2014). https://doi.org/10.1007/978-3-319-07512-9_1
8. Boute, R.: The Euclidean definition of the functions div and mod. ACM Trans. Program. Lang. Syst. **14**, 127–144 (1992)
9. Bride, H., Kouchnarenko, O., Peureux, F., Voiron, G.: Workflow nets verification: SMT or CLP? In: ter Beek, M.H., Gnesi, S., Knapp, A. (eds.) AVoCS 2016, FMICS 2016. LNCS, vol. 9933, pp. 39–55. Springer, Cham (2016). https://doi.org/10.1007/978-3-319-45943-1_3
10. Carlsson, M., Mildner, P.: SICStus prolog-the first 25 years. Theory Pract. Log. Program. **12**(1–2), 35–66 (2012)
11. Carlsson, M., Ottosson, G., Carlson, B.: An open-ended finite domain constraint solver. In: Glaser, H., Hartel, P., Kuchen, H. (eds.) PLILP 1997. LNCS, vol. 1292, pp. 191–206. Springer, Heidelberg (1997). https://doi.org/10.1007/BFb0033845
12. de Moura, L., Bjørner, N.: Generalized, efficient array decision procedures. In: 2009 Formal Methods in Computer-Aided Design, pp. 45–52 (2009)
13. de Moura, L.M., Bjørner, N., Z3: an efficient SMT solver. In: Ramakrishnan, C.R., Rehof, J. (eds.) TACAS 2008. LNCS, vol. 4963, pp. 337–340. Springer, Heidelberg (2008). https://doi.org/10.1007/978-3-540-78800-3_2
14. Déharbe, D., Fontaine, P., Guyot, Y., Voisin, L.: SMT solvers for Rodin. In: Derrick, et al. (eds.) ABZ 2012. LNCS, vol. 7316, pp. 194–207. Springer, Heidelberg (2012). https://doi.org/10.1007/978-3-642-30885-7_14
15. Déharbe, D.: Integration of SMT-solvers in B and Event-B development environments. Sci. Comput. Program. **78**(3), 310–326 (2013). Abstract State Machines, Alloy, B and Z - Selected Papers from ABZ 2010
16. El Ghazi, A.A., Taghdiri, M.: Relational reasoning via SMT solving. In: Butler, M., Schulte, W. (eds.) FM 2011. LNCS, vol. 6664, pp. 133–148. Springer, Heidelberg (2011). https://doi.org/10.1007/978-3-642-21437-0_12
17. Hansen, D., Ladenberger, L., Wiegard, H., Bendisposto, J., Leuschel, M.: Validation of the ABZ landing gear system using ProB. In: Boniol, F., Wiels, V., Ait Ameur, Y., Schewe, K.-D. (eds.) ABZ 2014. CCIS, vol. 433, pp. 66–79. Springer, Cham (2014). https://doi.org/10.1007/978-3-319-07512-9_5

18. Hansen, D., Leuschel, M.: Translating TLA$^+$ to B for validation with ProB. In: Derrick, J., Gnesi, S., Latella, D., Treharne, H. (eds.) IFM 2012. LNCS, vol. 7321, pp. 24–38. Springer, Heidelberg (2012). https://doi.org/10.1007/978-3-642-30729-4_3

19. Hansen, D., Leuschel, M.: Translating B to TLA$^+$ for validation with TLC. In: Ait Ameur, Y., Schewe, K.D. (eds.) ABZ 2014. LNCS, vol. 8477, pp. 40–55. Springer, Heidelberg (2014). https://doi.org/10.1007/978-3-662-43652-3_4

20. Hoang, T.S., Snook, C., Ladenberger, L., Butler, M.: Validating the requirements and design of a hemodialysis machine using iUML-B, BMotion Studio, and co-simulation. In: Butler, M., Schewe, K.-D., Mashkoor, A., Biro, M. (eds.) ABZ 2016. LNCS, vol. 9675, pp. 360–375. Springer, Cham (2016). https://doi.org/10.1007/978-3-319-33600-8_31

21. Howe, J.M., King, A.: A pearl on SAT solving in Prolog. In: Blume, M., Kobayashi, N., Vidal, G. (eds.) FLOPS 2010. LNCS, vol. 6009, pp. 165–174. Springer, Heidelberg (2010). https://doi.org/10.1007/978-3-642-12251-4_13

22. Konnov, I., Kukovec, J., Tran, T.-H.: TLA$^+$ model checking made symbolic. Proc. ACM Program. Lang. **3**(OOPSLA), 1–30 (2019)

23. Krings, S.: Towards infinite-state symbolic model checking for B and event-B. Ph.D. thesis, University of Düsseldorf, Germany (2017)

24. Krings, S., Leuschel, M.: SMT solvers for validation of B and event-B models. In: Ábrahám, E., Huisman, M. (eds.) IFM 2016. LNCS, vol. 9681, pp. 361–375. Springer, Cham (2016). https://doi.org/10.1007/978-3-319-33693-0_23

25. Krings, S., Leuschel, M.: Proof assisted bounded and unbounded symbolic model checking of software and system models. Sci. Comput. Prog. **158**, 41–63 (2018)

26. Lamport, L.: Specifying Systems: The TLA$^+$ Language and Tools for Hardware and Software Engineers. Addison-Wesley Longman Publishing Co., Inc, Boston (2002)

27. Leuschel, M., Butler, M.: ProB: a model checker for B. In: Araki, K., Gnesi, S., Mandrioli, D. (eds.) FME 2003. LNCS, vol. 2805, pp. 855–874. Springer, Heidelberg (2003). https://doi.org/10.1007/978-3-540-45236-2_46

28. Leuschel, M., Butler, M.: ProB: an automated analysis toolset for the B method. Int. J. Softw. Tools Technol. Transf. **10**(2), 185–203 (2008)

29. Mann, M., Wilson, A., Tinelli, C., Barrett, C.W.: SMT-switch: a solver-agnostic C++ API for SMT solving. CoRR, abs/2007.01374 (2020)

30. Mashkoor, A.: The hemodialysis machine case study. In: Butler, M., Schewe, K.-D., Mashkoor, A., Biro, M. (eds.) ABZ 2016. LNCS, vol. 9675, pp. 329–343. Springer, Cham (2016). https://doi.org/10.1007/978-3-319-33600-8_29

31. Nieuwenhuis, R., Oliveras, A., Tinelli, C.: Abstract DPLL and abstract DPLL modulo theories. In: Baader, F., Voronkov, A. (eds.) LPAR 2005. LNCS, vol. 6452, pp. 36–50. Springer, Heidelberg (2005). https://doi.org/10.1007/978-3-540-32275-7_3

32. Nieuwenhuis, R., Oliveras, A., Tinelli, C.: Solving SAT and SAT modulo theories: from an abstract Davis-Putnam-Logemann-Loveland procedure to DPLL(T). J. ACM **53**(6), 937–977 (2006)

33. Plagge, D., Leuschel, M.: Validating B, Z and TLA$^+$ using ProB and Kodkod. In: FM 2012. LNCS, vol. 7436, pp. 372–386. Springer, Heidelberg (2012). https://doi.org/10.1007/978-3-642-32759-9_31

34. Silva, J.P.M., Lynce, I., Malik, S.: Conflict-driven clause learning SAT solvers. In: Biere, A., Heule, M., van Maaren, H., Walsh, T. (eds.) Handbook of Satisfiability. Frontiers in Artificial Intelligence and Applications, vol. 185, pp. 131–153. IOS Press (2009)

35. Silva, J.P.M., Sakallah, K.A.: GRASP - a new search algorithm for satisfiability. In: Proceedings of the 1996 IEEE/ACM International Conference on Computer-Aided Design, ICCAD 1996, USA, pp. 220–227. IEEE Computer Society (1997)
36. Torlak, E., Jackson, D.: Kodkod: a relational model finder. In: Grumberg, O., Huth, M. (eds.) TACAS 2007. LNCS, vol. 4424, pp. 632–647. Springer, Heidelberg (2007). https://doi.org/10.1007/978-3-540-71209-1_49
37. Weber, T.: SMT solvers: new oracles for the HOL theorem prover. Int. J. Softw. Tools Technol. Transf. (STTT) 13(5), 419–429 (2011)
38. Weber, T., Conchon, S., Déharbe, D., Heizmann, M., Niemetz, A., Reger, G.: The SMT competition 2015–2018. J. Satisf. Boolean Model. Comput. 11(1), 221–259 (2019)
39. Yu, Y., Manolios, P., Lamport, L.: Model checking TLA$^+$ specifications. In: Pierre, L., Kropf, T. (eds.) CHARME 1999. LNCS, vol. 1703, pp. 54–66. Springer, Heidelberg (1999). https://doi.org/10.1007/3-540-48153-2_6

Standard Conformance-by-Construction with Event-B

Ismail Mendil[1(✉)], Yamine Aït-Ameur[1], Neeraj Kumar Singh[1], Dominique Méry[2], and Philippe Palanque[3]

[1] INPT-ENSEEIHT/IRIT, University of Toulouse, Toulouse, France
`{ismail.mendil,yamine,nsingh}@enseeiht.fr`
[2] Telecom Nancy, LORIA, Université de Lorraine, Nancy, France
`dominique.mery@loria.fr`
[3] IRIT, Université de Toulouse, Toulouse, France
`palanque@irit.fr`

Abstract. Checking the conformance of a system design to a standard is a central activity in the system engineering life cycle, *a fortiori* when the concerned system is deemed critical. Standard conformance checking entails ensuring that a system or a model of a system faithfully meets the requirements of a specification of a standard improving the robustness and trustworthiness of the system model. In this paper, we present a formal framework based on the correct-by-construction Event-B method and related theories for formally checking the conformance of a formal system model to a formalised standard specification by construction. This framework facilitates the formalization of standard concepts and rules as an ontology, as well as the formalization of an engineering domain, using an Event-B theory consisting of data types and a collection of operators and properties. Conformance checking is accomplished by annotating the system model with typing conditions. We address an industrial case study borrowed from the aircraft cockpit engineering domain to demonstrate the feasibility and strengths of our approach. The ARINC 661 standard is formalised as an Event-B theory. This theory formally models and annotates the safety-critical real-world application of a weather radar system for certification purposes.

Keywords: Standard conformance · Safety properties ·
Correctness-by-construction · Event-B and theories · ARINC 661 · Critical Interactive Systems

1 Introduction

Checking the standard conformance of a system design is a central activity in the system engineering life cycle, *a fortiori* when the concerned system is deemed critical. Standard compliance checking entails ensuring that a system or a model of a system faithfully meets the requirements of a standard, in particular domain and certification standards, improving the robustness and trustworthiness of the system model.

In many cases, conformance of system design models and/or implementation to a standard is achieved by informal or semi-formal processes like argument-based

A. Lluch Lafuente and A. Mavridou (Eds.): FMICS 2021, LNCS 12863, pp. 126–146, 2021.
https://doi.org/10.1007/978-3-030-85248-1_8

reports produced through model reviews, testing and simulation, experimentation, and so on [28]. Although, these qualification methods have proven to be valuable for system engineering in areas like transportation systems, medical devices, power plants, etc., formal checking of conformance, as advocated by the DO178-C, is more trustworthy and has many advantages, including extensive case coverage and availability of automatic verification capabilities such as model-checking and theorem proving.

Context of the Work. As part of the French ANR FORMEDICIS[1] project, we have studied the problem of ARINC 661 [8] standard conformance for CIS (Critical Interactive Systems). ARINC 661 is a standard for the development of flight deck display interfaces. In fact, modern cockpit designs increasingly rely on the ARINC 661 standard series used in several airplane development programs, e.g. Airbus A380, A350, and A400M, as well as the Boeing 787, 737MAX, KC-46A, and B777X[2].

Our Claim is that it is possible to check that a formal design model complies with domain standards formalised as a theory with data types, operators, axioms and theorems.

Standard Conformance addressed by our approach consists in transferring, to formal design models, theorems proved, once and for all, in the theory formalising a domain standard specification. The conformance is checked by proving the well-definedness proof obligations generated when using the theory operators. Note that we do not address the process of building these theories which requires to move from text-based standard documents to formal theories. Building such theories is out of the scope of this paper. Such processes have been addressed in [12–14] to link text-based standards with formalised theories expressed in Isabelle/HOL.

So, the *goal of this Paper* is to demonstrate how to check the compliance of formal design models with domain standards expressed as theories. The overall approach is exemplified on ARINC 661 standard and weather radar system application.

Our Contribution. In this paper, we present a formal framework based on the correct-by-construction Event-B method and related theories for formally checking, by construction, the conformance of a formal system model to a formalised standard specification. This framework formalises engineering standard concepts and rules as an ontological Event-B theory. To demonstrate the feasibility and strengths of our approach, we report on our experiments, from the FORMEDICIS project, addressing an interactive system available in aircraft cockpits. Relying on domain ontologies as a ground knowledge model, the ARINC 661 standard is formalised as an Event-B theory which formally *annotates* the model of the real-world weather radar system.

Organisation of this Paper. Next section is a brief review related to conformance and certification and Sect. 3 is devoted to a summary of the Event-B method. Section 4 contains the description of the CIS and the ARINC661 standard. Our framework is presented in Sects. 5 and 6 and its application is given in Sect. 7. Section 8 provides an assessment of the approach. Last, Sect. 9 concludes this paper.

---

[1] FORmal MEthods for the Development and the engIneering of Critical Interactive Systems (CIS) https://anr.fr/Projet-ANR-16-CE25-0007.

[2] https://www.aviation-ia.com/activities/cockpit-display-systems-cds-subcommittee.

2 Certification and Conformance

According to ISO, a standard is defined as: *Standards are documented agreements containing technical specifications or other precise criteria to be used consistently as rules, guidelines or definitions of characteristics, to ensure that materials, products, process and services are fit for their purpose* [26].

The use of standards has a number of potential advantages. It plays an important role for the development of complex systems, including both product-based and process-based developments. This process is both time-consuming and difficult. Some work focuses on integrating standards into process development. In [17], the authors propose a model for standards conformance by introducing lightweight mechanisms. In [9], a framework based on Natural Language Semantics techniques is presented. It assists in the processing of legal documents and standards through building a knowledge base that includes logical representations. In [16], the authors propose a step-by-step process for conformance checking that includes process modeling and execution. Similarly, [34] shows how to implement the conformance relation on transition systems. Nair et al. [35] provide a detailed survey how practitioners deal with safety evidence management for critical systems and they also draw the conclusion that there is a limited use of safety evidence in industries based on empirical evaluation.

In recent years, assurance cases have been used in critical domains to establish system safety by presenting appropriate arguments and evidences [30, 39]. The chosen evidences are always questionable, regardless of how they are established or how much confidence we have in them. There are several approaches to justifying confidence, such as eliminative induction [19], quantitative estimation [22], provided as claims in the assurance case [20]. Wassyng et al. [42, 43] propose an *Assurance Case Template* used in the development of critical systems and their certification within a domain model.

Regarding Event-B [2] and B [1] methods, Fotso et al. [41] present a specification of the hybrid ERTMS/ETCS level 3 standard, in which requirements are specified using SysML/KAOS [32] goal diagrams that are translated into B, and domain-specific properties are specified by ontologies using the SysML/KAOS domain modeling language, which is based on OWL [7] and PLIB [27]. Last, we mention the work of [10, 11] which uses the RSL language to model engineering domains.

The interest and motivation of handling domain knowledge has been discussed and argued in [5]. In this paper, we propose to use the capability of Event-B theories to improve the explicitation and integration of domain knowledge in design models. A key advantage of our proposed approach is that the proof of domain properties holding in the design models is explicit since a Well-Definedness (WD) proof obligation (PO) is generated. Such WD POs are generated for each theory defined operator, it states that each parameter belongs to the domain operator. This is particularly relevant for partial operators. Obviously, the approach exempts from explicitly specifying domain properties on the model side. Compared to our approach which relies on an ontology modelling language referenced by formal design models, none of the mentioned work use a shared modelling language.

3   Event-B

Event-B [2] is a *correct-by-construction* method based on set theory and first-order logic. It relies on state-based modelling where a set of events allows for state changes.

3.1   Contexts and Machines (Tables 1b and 1c)

The `Context` component describes the static properties of a model. It introduces the definitions, axioms and theorems needed to describe the required concepts using *carrier sets s, constants c, axioms A* and *theorems T_{ctx}*. `Machine` describes the model behaviour as a transition system. A set of guarded events is used to modify a set of states using Before-After Predicates (*BAP*) to record variable changes. They use *variables x, invariants I(x), theorems $T_{mch}(x)$, variants V(x)* and *events evt* (possibly guarded by *G* and/or parameterized by α) as core components.

Refinements. Refinement (not used in this paper) decomposes a *machine* into a less abstract one with more design decisions (refined states and events) moving from an abstract level to a less abstract one (simulation relationship). Gluing invariants relating abstract and concrete variables ensure property preservation.

Table 1. Global structure of Event-B theories, contexts and machines

Theory	Context	Machine
THEORY Th	**CONTEXT** Ctx	**MACHINE** M
IMPORT Th1, ...	**SETS** s	**SEES** Ctx
TYPE PARAMETERS $E, F, ...$	**CONSTANTS** c	**VARIABLES** x
DATATYPES	**AXIOMS** A	**INVARIANTS** $I(x)$
Type1($E, ...$)	**THEOREMS** T_{ctx}	**THEOREMS** $T_{mch}(x)$
constructors	**END**	**VARIANT** $V(x)$
cstr1($p_1: T_1, ...$)		**EVENTS**
OPERATORS		**EVENT** *evt*
Op1 <nature> ($p_1: T_1, ...$)		**ANY** α
well−definedness $WD(p_1,...)$		**WHERE** $G(x, \alpha)$
direct definition D_1		**THEN**
AXIOMATIC DEFINITIONS		$x:\mid BAP(\alpha,x,x')$
TYPES $A_1, ...$		**END**
OPERATORS		...
AOp2 <nature> ($p_1: T_1, ...$): T_r		**END**
well−definedness $WD(p_1,...)$		
AXIOMS $A_1, ...$		
THEOREMS $T_1, ...$		
END		
(a)	(b)	(c)

Proof Obligations (PO) and Property Verification. Table 2 provides a set of, automatically generated, POs to guarantee Event-B machines consistency.

Table 2. Relevant Proof Obligations

(1)	Ctx Theorems (ThmCtx)	$A(s,c) \Rightarrow T_{ctx}$ (For contexts)
(2)	Mch Theorems (ThmMch)	$A(s,c) \wedge I(x) \Rightarrow T_{mch}(x)$ (For machines)
(3)	Initialisation (Init)	$A(s,c) \wedge G(\alpha) \wedge BAP(\alpha,x') \Rightarrow I(x')$
(4)	Invariant preservation (Inv)	$A(s,c) \wedge I(x) \wedge G(x,\alpha) \wedge BAP(x,\alpha,x') \Rightarrow I(x')$
(4)	Event feasibility (Fis)	$A(s,c) \wedge I(x) \wedge G(x,\alpha) \Rightarrow \exists x' \cdot BAP(x,\alpha,x')$
(5)	Variant progress (Var)	$A(s,c) \wedge I(x) \wedge G^A(x,\alpha) \wedge BAP(x,\alpha,x') \Rightarrow V(x') < V(x)$

Core Well-Definedness (WD). In addition, WD POs are associated to all built-in operators of the Event-B modelling language. Once proved, these WD conditions are used as hypotheses to prove further proof obligations.

3.2   Event-B Extensions with Theories

In order to handle more complex and abstract concepts beyond set theory and first-order logic, an Event-B extension for supporting externally defined mathematical objects has been proposed in [3, 15]. This extension offers the capability to introduce new data types by defining new types, operators, theorems and associated rewrite and inference rules, all bundled in so-called *theories*. Close to proof assistants like Isabelle/HOL [36] or PVS [37], they are convenient when modelling *concepts unavailable in core Event-B*.

Theory Description (See Table 1a). Theories define and make available new data types, operators and theorems. Data types (DATATYPES) are associated with *constructors*, i.e. to build inhabitants of the defined type that may be inductive. A theory defines various *operators* further used in Event-B expressions. They may be *FOL predicates* or *expressions* producing actual values (<nature> tag). Operator applications can be used in other Event-B theories, contexts and/or machines. They *enrich the modelling language* as they may occur in axioms, theorems, invariants, guards, assignments, etc.

Operators may be defined either explicitly using an explicit ("direct") equivalent definition, in the `direct definition` clause, (case of a constructive definition), or defined axiomatically in the `AXIOMATIC DEFINITIONS` clause (a set of axioms). Last, a theory defines axioms, completing the definitions, and theorems. Theorems are proved from the definitions and axioms.

Many theories have been defined for sequences, lists, groups, reals, differential equations, etc. Theories can be extended (`Imports`) to define more complex theories and instantiated (in `context`) by providing concrete type parameters.

Well-Definedness (WD) in Theories. An important feature provided by Event-B theories is the possibility to define *well-definedness* (WD) conditions. Each defined operator (partially defined) is associated to a condition guaranteeing its correct definition.

When it is applied (in an Event-B expression), this WD condition generates a PO requiring to establish that this condition holds, i.e. the use of the operator is correct. The theory developer defines these WD conditions for the partially defined operators. All the WD POs and theorems are proved using the Event-B proof system.

Event-B Proof System and its IDE Rodin. Rodin[3] is an open source IDE for modelling in Event-B. It offers resources for model editing, automatic PO generation, project management, refinement and proof, model checking, model animation and code generation. Event-B's theories extension is available under the form of a plug-in. Theories are tightly integrated in the proof process. Depending on their definition (direct or axiomatic), operators definitions are expanded either using their direct definition (if available) or by enriching the set of axioms (hypotheses in proof sequents) using their axiomatic definition. Theorems may be imported as hypotheses and used in proofs. Many provers like predicate provers, SMT solvers, are plugged to Rodin as well. In addition to the known success of the Event-B and B methods in dealing with complex formal system developments, the choice of Event-B as a ground modelling formal method is motivated by the provided abstract modelling level. Indeed, it offers first a built-in mechanism (state and transitions) associated to an inductive proof process for invariants and second an extension mechanism to define theories with operators associated to WD conditions that generate POs when applied. These WD POs are fundamental for our approach to conformance checking. In addition, animators and model checkers like ProB [33] are useful to validating the defined theories over model instances. Finally, other techniques could have been used as long as they could check the correctness of operator applications and they are connected to the Rodin platform.

4 Case Study: ARINC 661 + Multi-purpose Interactive Application

4.1 ARINC 661 Standard Specification: An Extract

ARINC 661 [8] is the Cockpit Display System (CDS) standard for communication protocols between interface objects and aircraft systems. It has been used for the development of interactive applications in, for instance, Airbus A380 and Boeing B787. In ARINC 661 specification standard, an interactive application is called a User Application (UA) that receives input from the CDS and triggers actions in aircraft systems. Such input are produced by the flying crew manipulating specific input devices such as a KCCU (Keyboard Cursor Control Unit). UAs also receive information flow from aircraft systems that is presented to the flying crew using interactive objects which behaviour and parameters are described in the standards. The current version of the standard (called supplement 7 for part 1) describes in about 800 pages a set of definitions and requirements for the CDS and its graphical objects (called widgets).

   Communication between the CDS and UA is defined based on the identification of widgets defined in the Widget Library. Different levels widget states are available. 1) *Visibility* level indicating whether the widget is visible or not. 2) *Inner level specific states of a widget* which represents the core of the widget behavior as well as

---

[3] Rodin Integrated Development Environment http://www.event-b.org/index.html.

its functional objectives. Examples of inner states for a *CheckButton*, are two stable inner states: *Selected* and *Unselected*. 3) *Interactivity levels* are: *enabled* or *disabled*. An enabled widget is ready to receive input from crew member interaction. Last, 4) *visual* level (visual representation) internal behavior of the widget inside the CDS. Examples are "Normal" and "Focus" denoting different interactions style (e.g. in the "Focus" state a standard interaction such as spacebar keypress would trigger the widget). Usually, implementations of CDS present different graphical appearances for the widgets depending on their state. It is important to note that such rendering is outside the scope of the standard.

4.2   Multi-purpose Interactive Application and Weather Radar System

We demonstrate the relevance of the approach on the formal development of a real-world case study: the multi-purpose interactive application (MPIA)—See Fig. 1, focusing on one of its sub-parts: the weather radar system (WXR). MPIA consists of three pages or tabs: WXR (weather radar system and information), GCAS (Ground Collision Avoidance System) and AIRCOND (setting of AIR CONDitioning). A crew member navigates and switches to a desired page using the corresponding button on the menu bar at the bottom. Each page of the MPIA user interface is made of two distinct parts: an interaction area and the menu bar for selecting one of the three interfaces (bottom of Fig. 1).

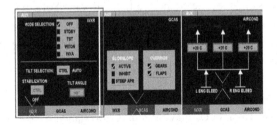

Fig. 1. Tabbed MPIA user interface: WXR, GCAS and AIRCOND

In this paper, we focus on WXR system which is designed to display and modify the mode of the weather radar system (top of the page) and to modify the orientation of the tilt angle in the weather radar system (middle of the page). There are three means for modifying the tilt angle: auto adjustment, auto stabilization, and setting up manually the tilt angle. WXR user interface provides different interactive widgets (PicturePush-Buttons, RadioButtons, EditBoxNumeric) in order to trigger commands to the weather radar system. The information received from the weather radar (e.g. density of clouds ahead of the aircraft) is not displayed in the WXR page but on another Display Unit (the Navigation Display). The information area displays the current state of the UA, by default the right part is blank but shows errors messages, actions in progress or bad manipulation when necessary. Workspace area controls the corresponding application.

5   Standards Formalised as Ontologies ((1) on Fig. 2)

Ontologies, as explicit knowledge models [21], have been extensively studied in the literature and applied in several domains spanning semantic web, artificial intelligence, information systems, system engineering etc. Approaches for designing and formalising ontologies for these domains have been proposed. Most of them rely on XML-based formats and pay lot of attention to *web knowledge* which may limit the scope of models.

The challenge of linking domain knowledge and design models is clearly stated in [25]. It includes a mathematical analysis of models and meta models, ontologies, modelling and meta-modelling languages. Design models annotation by domain-specific knowledge has been studied for state-based methods [5] as well. More recently, the textbook [6] reviewed many cases of exploiting explicit models of domain knowledge by system models spanning medical [31,40], e-voting [18], distributed systems etc.

Last, focusing on Event-B, a proposal of simplified ontology description language was put forward and illustrated on case studies in [23,24].

While [5,23,24] and our approach share the same objective and motivation, the two approaches are different. In [5,23,24], Event-B contexts are used to formalise domain knowledge in terms of axioms and theorems. However, our approach relies on the theory extension of Event-B providing operators endowed with WD conditions and data types for defining the objects of the knowledge domain. Moreover, they use set-theoretic operators when our approach advocates the exclusive usage of domain-specific operators provided by the theory bearing standard properties together with their WD conditions that need to be discharged when applied in the design model. In addition, the use of data types allowed us to encode an ontology modelling language as an Event-B theory providing a *unified ontological framework* to formalise the various domain knowledge modules. Consequently, WD POs permits a formalisation and integration of domain constraints into design models automatically when used by design models features.

In this paper, we rely on engineering domain ontologies in the view of [4,29,38] to model domain knowledge as Event-B theories and on typing to annotate Event-B design models. While [5] use set-theory based contexts where designers explicitly borrow domain standards constraints in the design model, the approach we develop here avoids the developer having to explicitly describe these constraints for each design model.

In the spirit of the OWL [7] ontology modeling language, Listing 1 represents an extract of the OntologiesTheory generic Event-B theory parameterised by C, P and I type parameters for classes, properties and Instances, respectively.

```
THEORY OntologiesTheory
TYPE PARAMETERS C,P,I
DATA TYPES Ontology(C,P,I)
CONSTRUCTORS
consOntology(classes:P(C),properties:P(P),instances:P(I),classProperties:P(C ×
    P),
classInstances:P(C×I),classAssociations:P(C×P×C),instancePropertyValues:P(I×P
    ×I))
OPERATORS
isWDgetInstancePropertyValues <predicate> (o: Ontology(C, P, I))
   well−definedness isWDClassProperites(o) ∧ isWDClassInstances(o) ∧
       isWDClassAssociations(o)
   direct definition
     instancePropertyValues(o) ⊆ { i1 ↦ p ↦ i2 | i1 ∈ I ∧ p ∈ P ∧ i2∈I∧i1↦p↦i2
       ∈instances(o)×properties(o)×instances(o) ∧ ( ∃c1, c2 · c1 ∈ C ∧c2∈C∧
       ...)}
getInstancePropertyValues <expression> (o: Ontology(C, P, I))
   well−definedness isWDgetInstancePropertyValues(o)
   direct definition instancePropertyValues(o)
isWDOntology <predicate> (o: Ontology(C, P, I))
   direct definition isWDClassProperties(o) ∧ isWDClassInstances(o) ∧
       isWDClassAssociations(o) ∧ isWDInstancesAssociations(o)
CheckOfSubsetOntologyInstances <predicate> (o:Ontology(C,P,I),ipvs:P(I×P×I))
       well−definedness isWDOntology(o)
       direct definition
       ipvs ⊆ { i1 ↦ p ↦ i2 | i1 ∈ I ∧ p ∈ P ∧ i2 ∈ I ∧ i1 ↦ p ↦ i2 ∈
           instances(o) × properties(o) × instances(o) ∧ ...}
isA <predicate> (o: Ontology(C, P, I),c1: C,c2: C) ···
...
THEOREMS
thm1 : ∀o,c1,c2,c3·o∈Ontology(C,P,I)∧isWDOntology(o)∧c1 ∈C∧c2∈C∧c3∈C∧
       ontologyContainsClasses(o,{c1,c2,c3})⇒(isA(o,c1,c2)∧isA(o,c2,c3)⇒isA(o,c1,
       c3))
END
```

Listing 1. Ontology Modelling Language

This theory describes a constructor consOntology for ontologies with a set of classes (classes), properties (properties), instances (instances) and associations of properties to classes (classProperties), instances to classes (classInstances) and classes to classes (classAssociations) and property values (instance PropertyValues). Expression and predicate operators allowing to manipulate classes, properties and instances are also defined. Predicate operators are used to define WD conditions. For example, the getInstancePropertyValues operator retrieving all the properties values is defined under the WD isWDGetInstancePropertyValues. The two important operators isWDOntology and CheckOfSubsetOntologyInstances respectively check that an ontology is well built and a subset of instances is conform to a given ontology. Last, theorems are formalised and proved, e.g. thm1 for transitivity of IsA relationship.

6   Our Approach

First, standards are formalised as ontology Event-B theories and, second, these theories should provide data types bundled with a collection of operators to be used by Event-B system models. Note that conformance is achieved under the *closure* condition stating that *solely the operators supplied by the theory formalising a standard are used for state variables changes in design models* . The operators WD POs shall be proved.

Obviously, all the theorems entailed by every theory operator also hold for all models that use theory operators. So, conformance-by-construction is guaranteed since 1) models type and manipulate state variables using standard data types and operators and 2) theory safety properties and rules formalising a standard are conveyed by all operators.

Conformance is achieved following the three-step methodology depicted in Fig. 2 *Conceptualisation*, *Instantiation*, and *Annotation*. First, standard concepts and operators are formalised in theories (2) using OntologiesTheory (see Listing 1) (1). Second, theories are instantiated for a particular system to design (3), and last system model is annotated with data types and operators (4) to enforce the constraints and rules, expressed as theorems, establishing standard conformance. Note that OntologiesTheory (1) is formalised once and for all, while standard concepts, rules and properties (2) are formalised in stable theories evolving with standard updates. In Fig. 2, Instantiates and Imports links correspond to Event-B built-in constructs (generic type parameters instantiation is automatically achieved by type synthesis), and Annotation is implemented by typing model concepts with theories data-types using the Sees Event-B construct.

Note.
A key requirement to set up our approach is the exclusive use of data types and operators provided by the Event-B theory formalising the standard specification. In fact, this condition is necessary to ensure that theorems entailed by operators are transferred and then provable in the Event-B model.

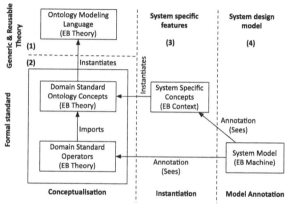

Fig. 2. Standard conformance-by-construction framework

Last, all the developments and Event-B models discussed in this paper are accessible at https://www.irit.fr/~Ismail.Mendil/recherches/.

6.1   Domain Standards as Ontology-Based Theories ((2) on Fig. 2)

The first phase consists in formalising the standard as an ontology using OntologiesThe – ory (see Listing 1). Type parameters C, P and I are instantiated with the standard objects and properties. Furthermore, rules and conformance criteria (i.e. WD condition predicate isWDOntology) are formalised as a set of axioms. In a design model, operators allow the modification of the system state variables. A set of theorems, stating that all the defined operators entail standard desired requirements and properties, is also expressed and proved. When these operators are applied in models, these theorems are used to prove model invariants and thus safety properties.

6.2 Standard Theory Instantiation ((3) on Fig. 2)

At this level, the classes are filled with instances and the associations between instances are specified taking into account the WD conditions required by ontology instantiation, i.e. `isWDgetInstancePropertyValues`. Three components of the ontology are valued by theory instantiation: `instances`, `classInstances` and `instance PropertyValues`. The definitions of these components are *system-dependent* and represent the elements of the system as instances of the standard classes. The `CheckOfSubsetOntologyInstances` operator ensures that system-specific concepts comply with defined standard ontology.

6.3 Model Annotation for Conformance ((4) on Fig. 2)

Model annotation consists in typing model variable with instance-related ontology components, generally `instancePropertyValues`, to comply with data types originated from the formalised standard. When state changes are done by theory operators, its already proven theorems are transferred to models.

In Event-B, this means that the formalised standard requirements and safety properties expressed as theorems are discharged by deduction as POs of the model. However, this assertion necessitates that the system-specific model state changes to *be realised, exclusively, with the operators provided by the theory describing the domain standard.* Obviously, since the operators are conditional, their WD POs need to be discharged.

7 Standard Conformance-by-Construction: The Case of ARINC 661

In this section, we showcase the approach of Sect. 6 on a part of ARINC 661 and WXR user interface. `ARINC661Theory` is built upon the ontology description theory, which in turn is used to develop the `WXRTheory` theory. Last, the two theories are used to model the WXR user interface as an Event-B machine. Due to space limitation, only an extract of the models covering relevant elements of the WXR case study is presented.

7.1 ARINC 661 Standard Formalisation ((2) on Fig. 2)

ARINCARINC 661 Concepts. After an in-depth analysis of the ARINC 661, many concepts are identified and formalised using `OntologiesTheory`. Table 3 shows some identified correspondences between ARINC 661 concepts and their formal counterparts.

ARINC 661 defines a collection of widgets intended to define the user interfaces. `ARINC661Theory` is described in Listing 2. The formalisation follows the structure of the ARINC 661 widget library and is guided by the ontology description theory. C, P and I of `OntologiesTheory` are instantiated by three abstract types: `ARINC661Classes`, `ARINC661Properties` and `ARINC661Instances`. Constants are defined as well.

Table 3. Correspondence between Event-B formalisation and ARINC 661 standard

ARINC 661 element	Reference (page)	Event-B formal element
Label	3.3.20 (p114)	Label
RadioBox	3.3.34 (p184)	RadioBox
CheckButton	3.3.5 (p80)	CheckButton
SELECTED, UNSELECTED	3.3.5-1 (p81)	SELECTED, UNSELECTED
CheckButtonState	3.3.5-1 (p81)	hasCheckButtonState
LabelString	3.3.5-1(p81)	hasLabelStringForCheckButton
Textual paragraph	3.3.34 (p185)	isWDRadioBox
...	...	...

```
THEORY  ARINC661Theory
IMPORT THEORY PROJECTS  OntologiesTheory
AXIOMATIC DEFINITIONS  ARINC661Axiomatisation :
TYPES ARINC661Classes , ARINC66Properties , ARINC661Instances
OPERATORS
ARINC661_BOOL <expression> ()  :  ARINC661Classes
A661_TRUE <expression> ()  :  ARINC661Instances
A661_FALSE <expression> ()  :  ARINC661Instances
A661_EDIT_BOX_NUMERIC_ADMISSIBLE_VALUES<expression>():ℙ(ARINC661Instances)
CheckButtonState <expression> ()  :  ARINC661Classes
Label <expression> ()  :  ARINC661Classes
RadioBox <expression> ()  :  ARINC661Classes
CheckButton <expression> ()  :  ARINC661Classes
hasChildrenForRadioBox <expression> ()  :  ARINC66Properties
hasCheckButtonState <expression> ()  :  ARINC66Properties
SELECTED <expression> ()  :  ARINC661Instances
UNSELECTED <expression> ()  :  ARINC661Instances
isWDRadioBox <predicate> (o:  Ontology(ARINC661Classes , ARINC66Properties ,
     ARINC661Instances ) )  :
    well−definedness isWDOntology(o)
isWDARINC661Ontology <predicate> (o:  Ontology(ARINC661Classes , ARINC66Properties
     , ARINC661Instances ) )  :
```

Listing 2. ARINC 661 theory concept declarations

ARINC 661 Theory Operators. Axiomatic definitions introduce ontology operators and predicates defining WD conditions. In Listing 4, consARINC661Ontology operator completes the construction of the ontology, this operator returns a well-defined ontology provided correct arguments are used. Moreover, CkeckOfSubset A661Ontology Instances enforces ontology rules on machine variables if supplied with a well-defined ontology, e.g. isWDRadioBox operator encodes a key safety property. It states that *only one child widget can be selected in a given RadioBox at a time*[4].

---

[4] More details are available in Sect. 3.3.34 page 184 of ARINC 661 standard [8].

```
consARINC661Ontology <expression> (ii : ℙ(ARINC661Instances), cii : ℙ(
      ARINC661Classes×
ARINC661Instances), ipvs:ℙ(ARINC661Instances×ARINC66Properties×
      ARINC661Instances)):        Ontology(ARINC661Classes, ARINC66Properties,
      ARINC661Instances)
      well-definedness isWDARINC661Ontology(consOntology(ARINC661Classes,
            ARINC66Properties, ii, wellBuiltClassProperties,
            wellbuiltTypesElements ∪ cii, wellBuiltClassAssociations, ipvs))
CkeckOfSubsetA661OntologyInstances <predicate> (o: Ontology(ARINC661Classes,
      ARINC66Properties, ARINC661Instances), ui: ℙ(ARINC661Instances ×
      ARINC66Properties × ARINC661Instances)) :
      well-definedness isWDOntology(o)
...
```

Listing 3. ARINC 661 theory operator declarations

ARINC 661 Axioms. In Listing 4, `ARINC661ClassesDef` axiom defines all the elements of `ARINC661Classes`. For example, `Label` is a widget and `CheckButtonState` corresponds to `SELECTED` and `UNSELECTED` states. Similarly, identified ARINC 661 properties are defined in `ARINC66PropertiesDef` axiom.

```
AXIOMS
ARINC661ClassesDef: partition(ARINC661Classes, {Label},{RadioBox},{CheckButton},{
      CheckButtonState}, ...)
ARINC66PropertiesDef: partition(ARINC66Properties, {hasLabelStringForLabel},
{hasChildrenForRadioBox},{hasCheckButtonState},{hasLabelStringForCheckButton
      },...)
ARINC661InstancesDef: partition(ARINC661Instances,{A661_TRUE},{A661_FALSE},{SELECTED
      },
{UNSELECTED}, LabelInstances, RadioBoxInstances, CheckButtonInstances, ...)
consARINC661OntologyDef: ∀ii, cii, ipvs · ii ∈ ℙ(ARINC661Instances) ∧
      cii ∈ ℙ(ARINC661Classes × ARINC661Instances) ∧
      ipvs ∈ ℙ(ARINC661Instances × ARINC66Properties × ARINC661Instances) ∧
      wellbuiltTypesElements ∩ cii = ∅ ∧ ii ⊆ WidgetsInstances ⇒
            consARINC661Ontology(ii, cii, ipvs)=consOntology(...)
isWDRadioBoxDef:∀o· o ∈ Ontology(ARINC661Classes, ARINC66Properties,
      ARINC661Instances) ⇒ ( isWDRadioBox(o) ⇔ ( ∀ ... )
isWDARINC661OntologyDef:
      ∀o· o ∈ Ontology(ARINC661Classes, ARINC66Properties, ARINC661Instances) ⇒
      (isWDOntology(o)∧isWDRadioBox(o)∧isWDEditBoxNumeric(o)⇒isWDARINC661Ontology(
            o))
CheckOfSubsetA661OntologyInstancesDef:∀o, ipvs·o∈Ontology(ARINC661Classes,
      ARINC66Properties,
ARINC661Instances)∧ipvs∈ℙ(ARINC661Instances×ARINC66Properties×
      ARINC661Instances)⇒
(isWDARINC661Ontology(consOntology(...))⇒CkeckOfSubsetA661OntologyInstances
      (...))
...
```

Listing 4. ARINC 661 theory definitions

ARINC 661 Relevant Theorems. The correctness of the ontology is ensured by theorems `thm1` and `thm2`. They describe two important properties: classes are related to already defined properties (`thm1`) and class associations relate provided classes and properties (`thm2`). Their proofs are achieved using intermediate abbreviations and proved lemmas.

```
THEOREMS
thm1:  ∀ii , cii , ipvs ·
   ii ∈ ℙ(ARINC661Instances) ∧ cii ∈ ℙ(ARINC661Classes × ARINC661Instances) ∧
   ipvs ∈ ℙ(ARINC661Instances × ARINC66Properties × ARINC661Instances) ∧
   wellbuiltTypesElements ∩ cii = ∅ ∧ ii ⊆ WidgetsInstances
         ⇒ isWDClassProperites(consARINC661Ontology(ii , cii , ipvs))
thm2:  ∀ii , cii , ipvs ·
   ii ∈ ℙ(ARINC661Instances) ∧ cii ∈ ℙ(ARINC661Classes × ARINC661Instances) ∧
   ipvs ∈ ℙ(ARINC661Instances × ARINC66Properties × ARINC661Instances) ∧
   wellbuiltTypesElements ∩ cii = ∅ ∧ ii ⊆ WidgetsInstances
         ⇒ isWDClassAssociations(consARINC661Ontology(ii , cii , ipvs))
...
END
```

Listing 5. ARINC 661 theory theorems

Ontology Building Process. The ontology introduced above formalises the concepts of the ARINC 661 standard. This ontology (theory) has been built for the purpose of the FORMEDICIS project and to process the different addressed case studies. The selection of axioms and the formalisation and proofs of theorems have been performed according to the studied case study. In case of a wide and shared usage, as with any standard, the designed theory requires consensus among the stakeholders of the ARINC 661 standard.

7.2 System-Specific Concepts Describing WXR Widgets ((3) on Fig. 2)

WXRTheory Concepts Declaration. WXRTheory encompasses constants and operators dealing with instance information (not defined in ARINC661Theory as instances are system specific) and allowing to manipulate the user interface. WXRFeature gathers the instances used by the WXR design model.

```
THEORY  WXRTheory
IMPORT THEORY PROJECTS  ARINC661Theory
AXIOMATIC DEFINITIONS   WXRUIDescriptoinAxiomatisaiton :
OPERATORS
A661WXROntology<expression>: Ontology(ARINC661Classes , ARINC66Properties ,
      ARINC661Instances)
WXRInstances <expression>    : ℙ(ARINC661Instances)
WXRClassInstances <expression>   : ℙ(ARINC661Classes × ARINC661Instances)
WXRInstancePropertyValues<expression>:ℙ(ARINC661Instances×ARINC66Properties×
      ARINC66Instances)
MODESELECTIONLabel <expression>   : ARINC661Instances
OFFLabel <expression>    : ARINC661Instances
OFFCheckButton <expression>    : ARINC661Instances
...
WXRFeatures<expression>(o: Ontology(ARINC661Classes ,... , ARINC661Instances)) :
            ℙ(ARINC661Instances × ARINC66Properties × ARINC661Instances)
well−definedness  isWDARINC661Ontology(o)
```

Listing 6. WXR theory constant declarations

WXR Concepts Definitions. In Listing 7, ARINC 661 ontological class instances are used for defining constants of the type ℙ (ARINC661). For example, WXRinstances is a set of all possible widgets of user interface: WXRLabels, WXRCheckButtons, etc. The WXRFeatures operator restricts ARINC661 ontology to the instances needed to design the WXR user interface i.e. *none of these instances is outside ARINC 661 theory*.

```
AXIOMS
WXRLabelsDef :  partition(WXRLabels, {MODESELECTIONLabel}, {OFFLabel}, ... )
WXRcheckButtonsDef :  partition(WXRcheckButtons, {OFFCheckButton}, ...)
WXRradioBoxesDef :  partition(WXRradioBoxes, {WXRradioBoxModeSelection },...)
WXRInstancesDef :  partition(WXRInstances, WXRLabels, WXRcheckButtons, WXRradioBoxes,
    ...)
WXRClassInstancesDef :  WXRClassInstances = ({Label} × WXRLabels) ∪ ({CheckButton} ×
    WXRcheckButtons) ∪ ...
iaCheckBttonsDef : iaCheckBttons=({OFFCheckButton ,...}×{hasVisible ,hasEnable}×{
    A661_TRUE})∪({OFFCheckButton , ...} × {hasCheckButtonState} × {UNSELECTED
    }) ∪
        ({OFFCheckButton} × {hasCheckButtonState} × {SELECTED}) ∪
    ({OFFCheckButton ,...}×{hasParentIdent}×{WXRradioBoxModeSelectionWidgetIdent})∪
    ...
WXRInstancePropertyValuesDef : WXRInstancePropertyValues=iaCheckBttons∪ioRadioBoxes∪
    ...
A661WXROntologyDef :  A661WXROntology = consARINC661Ontology(Instances ,
    ClassInstances ,              WXRInstancePropertyValues)
WXRFeaturesDef :  ∀o · o ∈ Ontology(ARINC661Classes ,ARINC66Properties ,
    ARINC661Instances) ∧ isWDARINC661Ontology(o) ⇒ WXRFeatures(o) =
    WXRInstancePropertyValues
```

Listing 7. WXR theory constant definitions

WXRTheory Operators. The user interface provides user interactions operators: choosing a mode selection, switching between the two states of the stabilization and tilt section feature and finally input a new tilt angle value. Each interaction is modelled by two operators: a WD predicate and an interactions modelling operators. For example, isWDChangeModeSelection and changeModeSelection pair of operators deals with mode selection change (see Listing 8).

```
AXIOMATIC DEFINITIONS    EventsAffectingWidgetsAxiomatisation :
OPERATORS
isWDChangeModeSelection <predicate> (o: Ontology(ARINC661Classes ,
    ARINC66Properties , ARINC661Instances) ,ui: ℙ(ARINC661Instances ×
    ARINC66Properties × ARINC661Instances) ,mode: ARINC661Instances) :
changeModeSelection <expression> (o: Ontology(ARINC661Classes , ARINC66Properties ,
    ARINC661Instances) ,ui:  ℙ(ARINC661Instances × ARINC66Properties ×
    ARINC661Instances) ,mode: ARINC661Instances) : ℙ(ARINC661Instances ×
    ARINC66Properties × ARINC661Instances)
well−definedness isWDChangeModeSelection(o, ui , mode)
```

Listing 8. WXR theory operator declarations

In the AXIOMS clause, several operators are defined (see Listing 9). For example, changeModeSelection operator is associated to a WD operator isWDChangeMode Selection stating that *crew members may select only specified modes in* WXRcheck Buttons and CkeckOfSubsetA661OntologyInstances ensures that the ui parameter complies with ontology rules and constraints. This principle applies to all operators.

```
AXIOMS
isWDChangeModeSelectionDef : ∀o , ui , mode · o ∈ Ontology(ARINC661Classes ,
     ARINC66Properties , ARINC661Instances) ∧ ui ∈ ℙ(ARINC661Instances ×
     ARINC66Properties × ARINC661Instances) ∧ mode ∈ ARINC661Instances ⇒
     (isWDChangeModeSelection(o , ui , mode) ⇔ CkeckOfSubsetA661OntologyInstances
          (o , ui) ∧ mode ∈ WXRcheckButtons)
changeModeSelectionDef : ∀o , ui , mode · o ∈ Ontology(ARINC661Classes ,
     ARINC66Properties , ARINC661Instances) ∧ ui ∈ ℙ(ARINC661Instances ×
     ARINC66Properties × ARINC661Instances) ∧ mode ∈ ARINC661Instances ⇒
(changeModeSelection(o , ui , mode)=(ui∖{i↦hasCheckButtonState ↦ UNSELECTED | i ↦
     hasCheckButtonState ↦ SELECTED ∈ ui ∧
     i∈(WXRcheckButtons∖{mode})})∪{mode↦hasCheckButtonState↦SELECTED})
...
```

Listing 9. WXR theory operator definitions

WXRTheory Theorems. In WXRTheory, important safety properties (e.g. theorem WXR FeaturesSafety) assert that the selection of the buttons under radio boxes are exclusive ($\Rightarrow b1 = b2$) (Listing 10). All theorems have been proved on the Rodin Platform.

```
THEOREMS
isWDARINC661Ontology :  isWDARINC661Ontology(A661WXROntology)
WXRFeaturesSafety : ∀o , ipvs · CkeckOfSubsetA661OntologyInstances(o , ipvs )∧(ipvs =
     WXRFeatures(o)) ⇒ (∀rb , b1 , b2··· ⇒ b1 = b2) ) ∧ ...
WXRFeaturesCkeckOfSubsetA661OntologyInstances :  ∀o , ipvs·isWDARINC661Ontology(o)
∧ipvs∈ℙ(ARINC661Instances × ARINC661Properties × ARINC661Instances) ∧
(ipvs = WXRFeatures(o)) ⇒
          changeModeSelectionCkeckOfSubsetA661OntologyInstances(o , ipvs)
changeModeSelectionSafety :  ...
changeModeSelectionCkeckOfSubsetA661OntologyInstances :  ...
   ...
END
```

Listing 10. WXR theory theorems

7.3   Annotated Event-B Model of WXR Application ((4) on Fig. 2)

The WXR user interface is modelled as an Event-B machine and uses elements defined in WXRTheory. In Listing 11, the state of the user interface is modelled by uiStateVar variable. The event changeMode Selection models the interaction on the mode selection radio box where only one check box shall be selected. The safety properties are entailed by theorems, WXRFeaturesCkeck

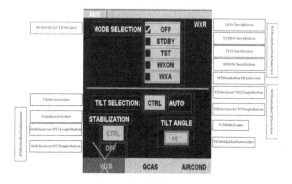

Fig. 3. WXR annotated with Event-B concepts

OfSubsetA661OntologyInstancesInst and SafetyInst, establishing at the same time the conformance of WXR specification to ARINC 661. However, the approach requires to use the theory operator to update the variable as uiStateVar as prescribed by inv2.

Listing 11 shows an extract of WXR model. In particular, changeModeSelection Evt event uses changeModeSelection operator to select a mode from the mode selection radio box, like *STDBY* (see Fig. 3). Note that this event is guarded with WD conditions of `WXRTheory`. In Fig. 3, correspondences between WXR widgets and their standard formal counterparts are depicted.

```
MACHINE   WXRModel
VARIABLES   uiStateVar
INVARIANTS
inv1 :  uiStateVar ∈ ℙ(ARINC661Instances × ARINC66Properties ×
                      ARINC661Instances)
inv2 :  ∃uiArg · ((uiStateVar = WXRFeatures(A661WXROntology)) ∨
              ∃m · isWDChangeModeSelection(A661WXROntology, uiArg, m) ∧
                      uiStateVar = changeModeSelection(A661WXROntology, uiArg, m)) ∨
                ...
SafetyInst :  CkeckOfSubsetA661OntologyInstancesDef(A661WXROntology, uiStateVar)
WXRFeaturesCkeckOfSubsetA661OntologyInstancesInst :
    (∀rb, b1, b2· rb ∈ RadioBoxInstances ∧ b1 ∈ CheckButtonInstances ∧
        b2 ∈ CheckButtonInstances ∧ rb ↦ hasChildrenForRadioBox ↦ b1 ∈
            uiStateVar∧
        rb ↦ hasChildrenForRadioBox ↦ b2 ∈ uiStateVar⇒
            (b1↦hasCheckButtonState↦SELECTED∈ui∧
             b2↦hasCheckButtonState↦SELECTED∈ uiStateVar ⇒b1=b2)) ∧ ...)
EVENTS
  INITIALISATION
  THEN
      act1 :  uiStateVar := WXRFeatures(A661WXROntology)
  END
  changeModeSelectionEvt
  ANY    mode
  WHERE
      grd1 :  mode ∈ WXRcheckButtons
      grd2 :  isWDChangeModeSelection(A661WXROntology, uiStateVar, mode)
  THEN
      act1 :  uiStateVar := changeModeSelection(A661WXROntology, uiStateVar, mode)
  END
    ...
END
```

Listing 11. Event-B machine modelling the WXR user interface

8   Assessment

Achieving Standard Conformance. Provided that the domain knowledge is formalised as a theory and supplied with data types and operators that preserve the safety properties prescribed by the standard specification, the models can be proven to entail desired theorems achieving conformance with the formalised standard.

Enhanced System Models. WXR model has been greatly improved as a result of extensive outsourcing of safety properties to the theory level and the use of ontology description theory. The use of a theory validated by experts led to trustworthy models. In addition, this approach enabled domain-specific (standards) models to be validated, once and for all, independently of the systems design models.

Reduction of Modelling and Proving Effort. Although the description of the domain-specific theory, `ARINC661Theory`, requires a significant amount of modelling effort, the specification of the models is simplified as a result of the formalisation of interaction by theory operators. At theory level, the properties (theorems) are proved once and for all. The design models rely on the defined data types and operators *conveying* all desired WD and safety properties expressing the domain constraints encoded in the theory of the standard. Here, the proving process is eased as, on the one hand, the

WD POs are discharged thanks to WD predicates associated with each operator and, on the other hand, INV POs are discharged automatically. Indeed, inv1 is a typing invariant and inv2 states that no other operator, except those provided by the theory, is used. Table **??** shows 88 automatically generated POs for the theories and WXRmodel. Theories related POs are discharged using a mix of automatic and interactive proofs, whereas WXRMode POs are discharged by simplifying predicates, instantiating theorems and using proof tactics. System invariants are proved as theorems in one proof step (modusponens rule), and the invariants representing our working hypothesis (exclusive use of theory operators) are trivially proved as model events use the operators of WXRTheory exclusively.

Deploying the Approach in Engineering Contexts. The work presented in this paper has been conducted in the FORMEDICIS project. As mentioned in Sect. 7.1, the ARINC 661 standard has been formalised following our understanding of the informal descriptions of [8]. However, as the obtained theories play the role of a standard, we believe that this formalisation requires consensus among the stakeholders, engineers and developers. From the development process point of view, this formalisation and the proofs of theorems are achieved once and for all. When, design models are produced, the conformance consists in discharging POs consisting in instantiating the theorems and using proof tactics. Therefore, we believe that the deployment of the approach, in its current form, is not a heavy task compared to the benefits of the provided proofs.

Standard Theories Validation. The formalisation of standards relies on axiomatised theories. The quality of these formalisations consist in checking 1) the consistency of the axioms and 2) the validation of these axioms and entailed theorems with respect to the informal descriptions. Fortunately, formal methods such as Event-B, Isabelle/HOL or CoQ come with tools like SMT solvers, animators and model checkers capable to instantiate such axioms with specific values and check axiom consistency or testing instances validity.

Table 4. Proof statistics

Event-B models and theories	Proof obligations
OntologiesTheories	21
ARINC661Theory	10
WXRTheory	39
WXRModel	18

Enabling Evolution of Standard. Last but not least, the approach enables the nondestructive standards evolution. Indeed, the neat separation of the common domain knowledge from system specifics fosters separation of concerns principle and orthogonality of evolution principle. In fact, both domain models and system design models may evolve asynchronously with limited impact on the each other. From a proof perspective, only POs caused by the evolution need to discharged.

9 Conclusion

The approach presented in this paper proposes a generic framework for formalising standard conformance through formal modelling of standards as ontologies. Data types and operators associated to the modelled features become accessible to system design models. We have shown how this approach applies to a real-world case study of aircraft cockpit. This approach is completely formalised using Event-B and relies on three steps: conceptualisation of the domain standard, instantiation to describe the system specific features and finally model annotation through typing of state variables and use of operators for state changes. The approach starts from an already formalised standard. It does not address the process of deriving these theories from text-based standards. It exploits the WD conditions POs that raise when applying theory operators.

The work presented in this paper addressed the issue of standard conformance. It needs to be extended to provide the required safety assurances to meet certification standards, where assurance cases are used in the development of critical systems. The formally proved properties and the generated formal artifacts can be used as evidence in assurance cases, which can aid in the certification process by guiding both the development and regulatory evaluation of CIS. Last, from the standardisation point of view, industry consortium and standardisation bodies shall define formal processes (not studied in this paper) addressing consensual agreement on the definition and consistence of the formal theories modelling domain standards i.e. the process consisting in analysing text-based standards in order to derive domain standard theories and in validating these derived theories. In addition, this work shall be completed by the study of other type of domain standards related to temporal properties, real-time scheduling, common criteria for security etc. and application domains like avionics, transportation systems.

References

1. Abrial, J.R.: The B-Book: Assigning Programs to Meanings. Cambridge University Press, New York (1996)
2. Abrial, J.R.: Modeling in Event-B: System and Software Engineering. Cambridge University Press, New York (2010)
3. Abrial, J.R., Butler, M., Hallerstede, S., Leuschel, M., Schmalz, M., Voisin, L.: Proposals for mathematical extensions for event-B. Technical report (2009)
4. Aït Ameur, Y., Baron, M., Bellatreche, L., Jean, S., Sardet, E.: Ontologies in engineering: the OntoDB/OntoQL platform. Soft. Comput. 21(2), 369–389 (2017)
5. Aït Ameur, Y., Méry, D.: Making explicit domain knowledge in formal system development. Sci. Comput. Program. Elsevier J. 121, 100–127 (2016)
6. Aït Ameur, Y., Nakajima, S., Méry, D.: Implicit and Explicit Semantics Integration in Proof-Based Developments of Discrete Systems. Springer, Singapore (2021). https://doi.org/10.1007/978-981-15-5054-6
7. Antoniou, G., van Harmelen, F.: Web ontology language: OWL. In: Staab, S., Studer, R. (eds.) Handbook on Ontologies. International Handbooks on Information Systems, pp. 67–92. Springer, Heidelberg (2004). https://doi.org/10.1007/978-3-540-24750-0_4
8. ARINC: ARINC 661 specification: Cockpit Display System Interfaces to User Systems, Prepared by AEEC, Published by SAE, Melford Blvd., Bowie, Maryland, USA, June 2019
9. Bartolini, C., Giurgiu, A., Lenzini, G., Robaldo, L.: A framework to reason about the legal compliance of security standards. In: 10th International Workshop on Juris-Informatics (2016)
10. Bjørner, D.: Manifest domains: analysis and description. Formal Aspects Comput. 29(2), 175–225 (2017)
11. Bjørner, D.: Domain analysis and description principles, techniques, and modelling languages. ACM Trans. Softw. Eng. Methodol. 28(2), 8:1–8:67 (2019)

12. Brucker, A.D., Ait-Sadoune, I., Crisafulli, P., Wolff, B.: Using the Isabelle ontology framework. In: Rabe, F., Farmer, W.M., Passmore, G.O., Youssef, A. (eds.) CICM 2018. LNCS (LNAI), vol. 11006, pp. 23–38. Springer, Cham (2018). https://doi.org/10.1007/978-3-319-96812-4_3

13. Brucker, A.D., Wolff, B.: Isabelle/DOF: design and implementation. In: Ölveczky, P.C., Salaün, G. (eds.) SEFM 2019. LNCS, vol. 11724, pp. 275–292. Springer, Cham (2019). https://doi.org/10.1007/978-3-030-30446-1_15

14. Brucker, A.D., Wolff, B.: Using ontologies in formal developments targeting certification. In: Ahrendt, W., Tapia Tarifa, S.L. (eds.) IFM 2019. LNCS, vol. 11918, pp. 65–82. Springer, Cham (2019). https://doi.org/10.1007/978-3-030-34968-4_4

15. Butler, M., Maamria, I.: Practical theory extension in event-B. In: Liu, Z., Woodcock, J., Zhu, H. (eds.) Theories of Programming and Formal Methods. LNCS, vol. 8051, pp. 67–81. Springer, Heidelberg (2013). https://doi.org/10.1007/978-3-642-39698-4_5

16. Carmona, J., van Dongen, B., Solti, A., Weidlich, M.: Introduction to Conformance Checking, pp. 3–20. Springer, Cham (2018). https://doi.org/10.1007/978-3-319-99414-7_1

17. Emmerich, W., Finkelstein, A., Montangero, C., Stevens, R.: Standards compliant software development. In: Proceedings of the International Conference on Software Engineering Workshop on Living with Inconsistency, pp. 1–8. IEEE CS Press (1997)

18. Gibson, J.P., Raffy, J.-L.: Modelling an E-voting domain for the formal development of a software product line: when the implicit should be made explicit. In: Ait-Ameur, Y., Nakajima, S., Méry, D. (eds.) Implicit and Explicit Semantics Integration in Proof-Based Developments of Discrete Systems, pp. 3–18. Springer, Singapore (2021). https://doi.org/10.1007/978-981-15-5054-6_1

19. Goodenough, J., Weinstock, C., Klein, A.: Toward a theory of assurance case confidence. Technical report. CMU/SEI-2012-TR-002, Software Engineering Institute, CMU, Pittsburgh (2012)

20. Grigorova, S., Maibaum, T.S.E.: Argument evaluation in the context of assurance case confidence modeling. In: 25th IEEE ISSRE Workshops, pp. 485–490. IEEE CS (2014)

21. Gruber, T.R.: Towards principles for the design of ontologies used for knowledge sharing. In: Guarino, N., Poli, R. (eds.) Formal Ontology in Conceptual Analysis and Knowledge Representation. Kluwer Academic Publisher's, Deventer (1993)

22. Guiochet, J., Do Hoang, Q.A., Kaaniche, M.: A model for safety case confidence assessment. In: Koornneef, F., van Gulijk, C. (eds.) SAFECOMP 2015. LNCS, vol. 9337, pp. 313–327. Springer, Cham (2015). https://doi.org/10.1007/978-3-319-24255-2_23

23. Hacid, K., Ait-Ameur, Y.: Strengthening MDE and formal design models by references to domain ontologies. A model annotation based approach. In: Margaria, T., Steffen, B. (eds.) ISoLA 2016. LNCS, vol. 9952, pp. 340–357. Springer, Cham (2016). https://doi.org/10.1007/978-3-319-47166-2_24

24. Hacid, K., Aït Ameur, Y.: Handling domain knowledge in design and analysis of engineering models. Electron. Commun. Eur. Assoc. Softw. Sci. Technol. **74**, 1–21 (2017)

25. Henderson-Sellers, B.: On the Mathematics of Modelling, Metamodelling, Ontologies and Modelling Languages. Springer Briefs in Computer Science, Springer, Heidelberg (2012). https://doi.org/10.1007/978-3-642-29825-7

26. IEC 62304: Medical Device Software - Software Life Cycle Processes, May 2006

27. ISO: Industrial automation systems and integration - parts library - part 42: Description methodology: Methodology for structuring parts families. ISO ISO13584-42, International Organization for Standardization, Geneva, Switzerland (1998)

28. Information technology - Open Systems Interconnection - Conformance testing methodology and framework - Part 1: General concepts (1991)

29. Jean, S., Pierra, G., Ait-Ameur, Y.: Domain ontologies: a database-oriented analysis. In: Filipe, J., Cordeiro, J., Pedrosa, V. (eds.) Web Information Systems and Technologies. LNBIP, vol. 1, pp. 238–254. Springer, Heidelberg (2007). https://doi.org/10.1007/978-3-540-74063-6_19

30. Kelly, T.: Arguing safety - a systematic approach to managing safety cases. Ph.D. thesis, University of York, September 1998

31. Singh, N.K., Ait-Ameur, Y., Méry, D.: Formal ontological analysis for medical protocols. In: Ait-Ameur, Y., Nakajima, S., Méry, D. (eds.) Implicit and Explicit Semantics Integration in Proof-Based Developments of Discrete Systems, pp. 83–107. Springer, Singapore (2021). https://doi.org/10.1007/978-981-15-5054-6_5

32. van Lamsweerde, A.: Requirements Engineering - From System Goals to UML Models to Software Specifications. Wiley, Hoboken (2009)

33. Leuschel, M., Butler, M.: ProB: a model checker for B. In: Araki, K., Gnesi, S., Mandrioli, D. (eds.) FME 2003. LNCS, vol. 2805, pp. 855–874. Springer, Heidelberg (2003). https://doi.org/10.1007/978-3-540-45236-2_46

34. Luong, H.-V., Lambolais, T., Courbis, A.-L.: Implementation of the conformance relation for incremental development of behavioural models. In: Czarnecki, K., Ober, I., Bruel, J.-M., Uhl, A., Völter, M. (eds.) MODELS 2008. LNCS, vol. 5301, pp. 356–370. Springer, Heidelberg (2008). https://doi.org/10.1007/978-3-540-87875-9_26

35. Nair, S., de la Vara, J.L., Sabetzadeh, M., Falessi, D.: Evidence management for compliance of critical systems with safety standards: a survey on the state of practice. Inf. Softw. Technol. **60**, 1–15 (2015)

36. Nipkow, T., Wenzel, M., Paulson, L.C.: Isabelle/HOL: A Proof Assistant for Higher-order Logic. Springer, Heidelberg (2002). https://doi.org/10.1007/3-540-45949-9

37. Owre, S., Rushby, J.M., Shankar, N.: PVS: a prototype verification system. In: Kapur, D. (ed.) CADE 1992. LNCS, vol. 607, pp. 748–752. Springer, Heidelberg (1992). https://doi.org/10.1007/3-540-55602-8_217

38. Pierra, G.: Context representation in domain ontologies and its use for semantic integration of data. J. Data Semant. **10**, 174–211 (2008)

39. Rushby, J.: The interpretation and evaluation of assurance cases. Technical report. SRI-CSL-15-01, Computer Science Laboratory, SRI International, Menlo Park, CA, July 2015

40. Singh, N.K., Aït Ameur, Y., Méry, D.: Formal ontology driven model refactoring. In: 23rd International ICECCS, pp. 136–145. IEEE CS (2018)

41. Tueno Fotso, S.J., Frappier, M., Laleau, R., Mammar, A.: Modeling the Hybrid ERTMS/ETCS Level 3 standard using a formal requirements engineering approach. In: Butler, M., Raschke, A., Hoang, T.S., Reichl, K. (eds.) ABZ 2018. LNCS, vol. 10817, pp. 262–276. Springer, Cham (2018). https://doi.org/10.1007/978-3-319-91271-4_18

42. Wassyng, A., Joannou, P., Lawford, M., Maibaum, T.S.E., Singh, N.K.: New standards for trustworthy cyber-physical systems. In: Romanovsky, A., Ishikawa, F. (eds.) Trustworthy Cyber-Physical Systems Engineering, pp. 337–368. Taylor & Francis Group (2016)

43. Wassyng, A., et al.: Can product-specific assurance case templates be used as medical device standards? IEEE Des. Test **32**(5), 45–55 (2015)

Formal Analysis

Randomized Reachability Analysis in Uppaal: Fast Error Detection in Timed Systems

Andrej Kiviriga[✉], Kim Guldstrand Larsen, and Ulrik Nyman

Aalborg University, Selma Lagerløfs Vej 300, 9220 Aalborg, Denmark
{kiviriga,kgl,ulrik}@cs.aau.dk

Abstract. We introduce Randomized Reachability Analysis – an efficient and highly scalable method for detection of "rare event" states, such as errors. Due to the under-approximate nature of the method, it excels at quick falsification of models and can greatly improve the model-based development process: using lightweight randomized methods early in the development for the discovery of bugs, followed by expensive symbolic verification only at the very end. We show the scalability of our method on a number of Timed Automata and Stopwatch Automata models of varying sizes and origin. Among them, we revisit the schedulability problem from the Herschel-Planck industrial case study, where our new method finds the deadline violation three orders of magnitude faster: some cases could previously be analyzed by statistical model checking (SMC) in 23 h and can now be checked in 23 s. Moreover, a deadline violation is discovered in a number of cases that where previously intractable. We have implemented the Randomized Reachability Analysis – and made it available – in the tool UPPAAL.

Keywords: Model-checking · Randomized · State-space explosion · Schedulability analysis · Timed automata · Stopwatch automata

1   Introduction

Formal verification of system designs in the form of model checking requires that reliable formal models of a system are created. Apart form the ability to verify formal queries, many model checking tools also give the modeller access to a simulator in order to understand the model behavior. Throughout the process of developing the models, a number of sanity queries can be used in the same way as unit tests in software development. Verifying these queries repeatedly between each addition to the model can be prohibitively time consuming, especially for

Supported by the ERC Advanced Grant Project: LASSO: Learning, Analysis, Synthesis and Optimization of Cyber-Physical Systems, and by the Villum Investigator project S4OS: Synthesis of Safe, Small, Secure and Optimal Strategies for Cyber-Physical Systems.

A. Lluch Lafuente and A. Mavridou (Eds.): FMICS 2021, LNCS 12863, pp. 149–166, 2021.
https://doi.org/10.1007/978-3-030-85248-1_9

complex systems that often grow large and become difficult to analyze. In this paper we present a solution to this problem.

The main contribution of this paper is the implementation of randomized reachability analysis in the tool UPPAAL. Randomized reachability analysis is a non-exhaustive efficient technique for the detection of "rare event" states, such as errors. The work is a continuation of [13] where similar randomized analysis was applied to refinement checking. The method can analyse Timed Automata and Stopwatch Automata models with the features already supported by UPPAAL. The randomized approach is based on repeated exploration of the model by means of *random walks* and was inspired by [10]. It explores the state-space in a light and under-approximate manner; hence, it can only perform conclusive verification when a single trace can demonstrate a property. However, our randomized method excels at reachability checking and in many cases outperforms existing model-checking techniques by up to several orders of magnitude. The benefits are especially notable in large systems where traditional model-checking is often intractable due to the state-space explosion problem. Randomized reachability analysis is particularly useful for an *efficient development process*: running cheap, randomized methods early in the development to discover violations and performing an expensive and exhaustive verification at the very end. Randomized reachability analysis supports the search for *shorter* traces which improves the usability of discovered traces in debugging the model. We have implemented randomized reachability analysis – and made it available – in the tool UPPAAL [1].

Timed Automata models can also be used in the domain of schedulability, which deals with resource management of multiple applications ranging from warehouse automation to advanced flight control systems. Viewing these systems as a collection of tasks, schedulability analysis allows to optimize usage of resources, such as processor load, and to ensure that tasks finish before their deadline. A traditional approach in preemptive priority-based scheduling is that of the worst-case response time (WCRT) analysis [5,12]. It involves estimating worst case scenarios for both the execution time of a task and the blocking time a task may have to spend waiting for a shared resource. Apart from certain applicability limitations, classical response time analysis is known to be over-approximate which may lead to pessimistic conclusions in that a task may miss its deadline, even if in practice such a scenario could be unrealizable. Model-based approach is a prominent alternative for verification of schedulability [2–4,16] as it considers such parameters as offsets, release times, exact scheduling policies, etc. Due to this, the model-based approach is able to provide a more exact schedulability analysis.

We continue the effort in using a model-based approach and the model checker UPPAAL to perform a Stopwatch Automata based schedulability analysis of systems [6]. Specifically, we re-revisit the industrial case study of the ESA Herschel-Planck satellite system [8,16]. The Danish company Terma A/S [19] developed the control software and performed the WCRT analysis for the system. The case we analyse consists of 32 individual tasks being executed on a single processor with the policy of fixed priority preemptive scheduling. In addition, a combination of priority ceiling and priority inheritance protocols is used, which in essence makes the priorities dynamic. Preemptive scheduling is encoded in the model with the help of stopwatches which allow to track the progress of each task and stop it when the task is preempted. In UPPAAL, existing symbolic reachability analysis for models with stopwatches is over-approximate, which may provide spurious traces. In such models, our randomized reachability analysis allows to obtain exact, non-spurious traces to target states.

In the previous work of [16] the schedulability of Herschel-Planck was "successfully" concluded, but with an unrealistic assumption of each task having a fixed execution time (ET). To improve on this, the analysis of [8] was carried out with each of the tasks given a non-deterministic execution time in the interval of [WCET, BCET]. Unfortunately, interval based execution times, preemption and shared resources that impose dependencies between tasks, makes schedulability of systems like Herschel-Planck undecidable [9].

Even in the presence of unschedulability, two model-checking (MC) techniques were used in [8] to either verify or disprove schedulability for certain intervals of possible task execution times. First, the symbolic, zone-based, MC was used. Even though for stopwatch automata it is implemented as an over-approximation in UPPAAL which still suffices for checking of safety properties, e.g. if the deadline violation can never be reached. However, this technique cannot be used to disprove schedulability of the system as resulting traces may possibly be spurious. Second, the statistical model-checking (SMC) technique was used to provide concrete counterexamples witnessing unschedulability of the model in cases where symbolic MC finds a potential deadline violation and cannot conclude on schedulability. The idea of SMC [15,20] is to run multiple *sample traces* from a model and then use the traces for statistical analysis which, among all, estimates the probability of a property to be satisfied on a random run of a model. The probability estimate comes with some degree of confidence that can be set by the user among a number of other statistical parameters. Several SMC algorithms that require stochastic semantics of the model have been implemented in UPPAAL SMC [7].

Table 1. Summary of schedulability of Herschel-Planck system.

$f = \frac{BCET}{WCET}$	0–71%	72–80%	81–86%	87–90%	90–100%
Symbolic MC:	maybe	maybe	maybe	n/a	**Safe**
Statistical MC:	**Unsafe**	maybe	maybe	maybe	maybe
Randomized MC:	**Unsafe**	**Unsafe**	maybe	maybe	maybe

Our contribution to the Herschel-Planck case study is to use our proposed under-approximate randomized reachability analysis techniques in hope to witness unschedulability in places where previously not possible. The summary of (un)schedulability of Herschel-Planck that includes the new results is shown in Table 1. Symbolic MC finds no deadline violation with over-approximate analysis and is able to conclude schedulability for $\frac{BCET}{WCET} \geq 90\%$. SMC find a witness of unschedulability for $\frac{BCET}{WCET} \leq 71\%$. Finally, our randomized reachability methods are able to further "breach the wall" of undecidable problem by discovering concrete traces proving unschedulability for $\frac{BCET}{WCET} \leq 80\%$. Moreover, for the same $\frac{BCET}{WCET}$, randomized reachability finds the deadline violation by three orders of magnitude faster than SMC: the case that took 23 h for SMC now only takes 23 s with randomized methods.

To further verify the proposed efficient development process, we look at several different models of the *Gossiping Girls* problem made by the Master's thesis students – future model developers – and explore the potential of our randomized method. We also perform experiments on a range of other (timed and stopwatch automata) models and compare the performance of our randomized reachability analysis in "rare event" detection to that of existing verification techniques of UPPAAL: Breadth First Search (BFS), Depth First Search (DFS), Random Depth First Search (RDFS) and SMC. The results are extremely encouraging - randomized reachability methods perform up to several orders of magnitude faster and scale significantly better with increasing model sizes. Furthermore, randomized reachability uses constant memory w.r.t. the size of the model and typically requires only up to 25 MB of memory. This is a notable improvement in comparison to the symbolic verification of upscaled and industrial sized models. Each of the experiments in this study was given 16 GB of memory.

The main contributions of the paper are:

- A new randomized reachability analysis technique implemented in UPPAAL
- Detection of "rare event" states up to several orders of magnitude faster than with other existing model-checking techniques
- Possibility to analyze previously intractable models, including particular settings for the Herschel-Planck case study
- Searching for *shorter* or *faster* traces with randomized reachability analysis.

The rest of the paper is structured as follows: In Sect. 2 we describe the different randomized methods we tried in this study. Section 3 presents the new results on the Herschel-Planck industrial case study and Sect. 4 provides more experimental results on other schedulability models. Section 5 demonstrates the efficiency of our randomized method applied on student models of the *Gossiping Girls* problem and Sect. 6 gives the results on other upscaled models. Finally, Sects. 7 and 8 give conclusions and future work.

2   Randomized Reachability Analysis

The purpose of the randomized methods is to explore the state-space quickly and be less affected by the state-space explosion. The method is based on a repeated execution of concrete-state based *random walks* through the system. Each random walk is quick and lightweight as it avoids expensive computations of symbolic zone-based abstractions and does not store any information about already visited states in memory. The flaw of such analysis is its under-approximate nature of exploration which does not allow to conclude on reachability if the target state has never been found. However, the results of [13] hint that randomized reachability analysis has a potential to provide substantial performance improvements in comparison to existing model-checking techniques.

An already existing method of SMC tries to give valid statistical predictions based on stochastic semantics. SMC is very similar to the randomized method as it performs cheap, non-exhaustive simulations of the model. In cases where symbolic model-checking techniques of UPPAAL are expensive or even inconclusive (for stopwatch automata), SMC is often used as a remedy to provide concrete traces to target states. The stochastic semantics SMC operates on allows for a model to mimic the behavior of a real system; however, this may not be efficient for detection of "rare event" states. Consider the timed automaton model in Fig. 1 with the Goal location representing the target state we want to discover. The guard x<=1 on the edge leading to Goal requires clock x to be at most of 1 time unit. According to stochastic semantics, at the starting location Init SMC would select a delay uniformly in range $[0, 1000]$, which is bounded by the invariant x<=1000. This leaves a probability of $\frac{1}{1000}$ to discover Goal in 1 step; Alternatively, the "loop" edge is taken which resets clock x with the update x=0 thus resetting all the progress back to the initial state.

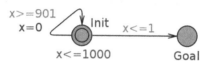

Fig. 1. Timed Automaton model with a Goal target state.

We aim to improve the efficiency of detecting "rare event" states with our new randomized method by experimenting with several different randomized heuristics and examining their efficiency through extensive experimental evaluation. A heuristic in this case dictates how a random walk is performed, i.e.

Table 2. Randomized reachability analysis heuristics.

Acronym	Name	Origin	Status
SEM	Semantic exploration	New	Only experiments
RET	Random Enabled Transition	[13]	Implemented in UPPAAL
RLC	Random Least Coverage	New	Only experiments
RLC-A	Random Least Coverage Accumulative	New	Only experiments

how delays and transitions are chosen. The summary of the heuristics and their status is given in Table 2. We now explain each heuristic in detail.

SEM. An intuitive heuristic we tried, denoted as SEM, is based on the natural semantic exploration of the system. A meaningful delay, i.e. a delay that leads to an enabled transition, is selected uniformly at random and then a transition is picked uniformly from those available after the chosen delay has been made. In the model from Fig. 1, SEM would choose a delay uniformly from two ranges – $[0,1]$ and $[901,1000]$, thus having a probability of $\frac{1}{100}$ to reach Goal in 1 step. Overall, we believe this heuristic will struggle the most in systems where certain specific delays are required to reach a target state, e.g. delaying exactly the lower or upper bound of the transition's availability range.

Differently from SEM, the heuristics we describe further (RET, RLC and RLC-A) require selecting a *target transition* first. The exact delay is then chosen only from that target transition's range of available delays. Selecting transition first makes exploration of the state-space more uniform and removes a bias towards transitions with larger availability range. The mechanism for choosing delays is common between the heuristics presented below and will be described later in this section.

RET. As a continuation of our work on randomized techniques from [13] we implement them in UPPAAL for both Timed and Stopwatch Automata. The study proposed two different heuristics for selecting a target transition. A heuristic denoted as RET (Random Enabled Transition) selects one of the eventually enabled transitions, i.e. transitions that are either currently enabled or will become such after a delay, uniformly at random. This means that at each step each transition is equally likely to be selected. When used in the model from Fig. 1, RET would first choose one of the two transitions at random, having a probability of $\frac{1}{2}$ to reach the Goal location in 1 step.

RLC, RLC-A. Here we introduce a heuristic denoted as RLC that chooses a transition with the *least coverage* for the sending edge. If there is more than one such transition, RLC picks one uniformly at random. In systems that are cyclic or contain multiple loops, RLC provides a more uniform exploration of the state-space which may be useful for some models. Consider the model from Fig. 2 that uses two integer variables i and j. The only initially available edge is the bottom loop edge at the Init location which increments the variable i by 1 upon each traversal. Once i==2, the leftmost loop edge can be taken, resulting in a reset of i and increment of j (i=0,j++). Crucially, if the variable i is incremented above the value 2, the leftmost loop edge becomes permanently unavailable. Hence, to reach Goal the leftmost edge has to be taken as soon as it becomes available and at least 7 times (j>=7) in one run. Since the coverage of the leftmost edge is always lower, the probability for RLC heuristic to discover Goal in 1 random walk is 100% while for RET it is less than 1%. The coverage counters, however, are reset at the start of a random walk, making each subsequent run independent of the previous one. We also experiment with a similar heuristic that does not reset the coverage counters and instead keeps them shared among all of the random walks. We denote such *accumulative* heuristic as RLC-A.

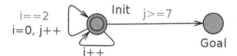

Fig. 2. Timed Automaton model of a difficult case for RET heuristic.

Other Randomized Methods Investigated. A number of tokenized heuristics, inspired by [14], have been attempted with the intent of storing a small, fixed number of tokens in a clever way to increase the likelihood of reaching the target state faster. Unfortunately, as no considerable improvements have been observed we decided to exclude these heuristics and leave them as future work.

We have also tried using traces of symbolic MC of Uppaal from verification of the Herschel-Planck model to guide the random walks towards the target state. However, even with the RDFS search strategy, all of the symbolic traces have appeared to be spurious due to the over-approximate analysis of stopwatch automata. Hence, we could not gain any useful results with this approach.

To reduce resource demands for the most expensive operation in a random walk – computation of eventually enabled transitions – an alternative heuristic to RET was used in [13] denoted as RCF (Random Channel First). Instead of computing all eventually enabled transitions, RCF first randomly picks a channel and only computes transitions labeled with that channel. However, during implementation of these techniques in Uppaal it became clear that the RCF does not give performance advantages over RET due to the differences in the underlying data structures of Uppaal and Java prototype from [13]. Therefore, we got rid of the RCF heuristic.

Choosing Delay. A naive way of choosing delays – uniformly at random from a given range – is likely to not be very efficient. While in some systems that are either small or not sensitive to specific delay values reaching target state can be doable, in more complex models such a strategy may not be optimal. In [13] we experimented with a few different strategies for choosing delay values, such as (1) uniformly at random, (2) based on predefined probability distribution and 3) based in changing (adapting) delay probability distributions. The experiments have shown the first strategy to be the least efficient, whereas the third one has shown the most potential. Hence, we reuse the third strategy here with slight modifications for RET, RLC and RLC-A heuristics.

The idea behind the adaptive delay choice algorithm is the following: the delays are drawn in accordance to some predefined delay probability distribution which changes on each unsuccessful random walk. Such distribution in this case defines probability for lower bound (LB), upper bound (UB) or the values in between the bounds to be chosen. For example, a distribution of

40% *LB*/40% *UB* means that it is equally probable that either LB or UB will be selected as a delay, while leaving 20% chance for intermediate delay to be chosen uniformly at random from the range that excludes the bounds. Table 3 shows the sequence delay probability distributions used in this study. Upon reaching the last distribution in the sequence, the next random walk starts from the first one.

Table 3. Delay probability distributions used for RET, RLC and RLC-A.

Sequence	1	2	3	4	5	6	7	8	9	10	11
Lower bound	60%	70%	80%	90%	100%	0%	10%	20%	30%	40%	40%
Uniform	0%	0%	0%	0%	0%	0%	0%	0%	0%	0%	20%
Upper bound	40%	30%	20%	10%	0%	100%	90%	80%	70%	60%	40%

Previously, the cycle of delay probability distributions did not leave any room for intermediate time delays, considering only LB or UB values. The downside is that for some systems it means that parts of the state-space become unreachable by the algorithm; however, experiments have shown this strategy to be surprisingly efficient. To eliminate the flaw of intermediate delay values never being chosen, here we add a 40% *LB*/40% *UB* probability distribution, leaving 20% chance to select an intermediate time value. As the result, a target state, if one exists, will be eventually found in any system.

Random Walk Depth. To explore the state-space gradually and reduce the risk of a random walk being stuck in an isolated part of the state-space with no target state, we increase the random walk depth dynamically as the exploration continues. Specifically, the first batch of random walks at most can perform 2^4 steps. After the full cycle of delay probability distributions is completed, the random walks in the next cycle have their maximum allowed depth doubled, but no further than 2^{18} steps. Should one have some apriori knowledge of the system, it is also possible to manually set the maximum allowed depth in UPPAAL that is a constant value used for all of the conducted random walks.

Shorter or Faster Trace. Since our techniques cannot disprove reachability of a target state due to under-approximate analysis, searching for errors in large systems, where symbolic techniques struggle, is one of the main expected applications. To aid developer in analyzing error traces and fixing systems, we implement an option to search for an optimal trace being the either *shortest*, in the size of steps, or the *fastest*, in the amount of total delay. With either one of these options selected, the algorithm searches for the initial trace and afterwards restricts all subsequent random walks to the current smallest amount of steps or delay discovered. Every randomized heuristic can be used with the *shortest* or *fastest* option and we refer to those by appending "-S" or "-F", e.g. RET-S.

In symbolic model-checking, searching for an optimal trace requires an exhaustive exploration of the state-space. Thus, for larger systems, it often drastically increases time and memory demands up to an extent where it becomes impractical. As opposed to that, our randomized techniques do not require more memory as the old trace is being discarded as soon as the new, more optimal one is discovered. On the down side, being a non-exhaustive technique the randomized search cannot guarantee that any discovered trace is indeed the most optimal, endlessly continuing the search. In UPPAAL we let the user provide *timeout* value (in seconds) which is defaulted to 300 s.

3   New Results on Herschel-Planck

According to previous results on Herschel-Planck model [8], symbolic MC confirmed schedulability for $f = \frac{BCET}{WCET} \geq 90\%$. However, symbolic MC cannot be used for disproving schedulability due to over-approximate analysis of automata with stopwatches, used to encode preemption. Thus, SMC was used to generate concrete counterexamples, disproving schedulability for $f \leq 71\%$. For the rest of $f \in (71\%, 90\%)$ both symbolic and statistical MC were inconclusive due to either over-approximation or burden in computation time, respectively. All of the models used in the experiments are made available at: http://people.cs.aau.dk/~ulrik/submissions/874325/FMICS2021.zip.

Table 4. Average time to detect non-schedulability in Herschel-Planck (in seconds). SMC search is limited to 160, 640 or 1280 cycles of 250 ms.

f (%)	SMC (160)	SMC (640)	SMC (1280)	SEM	RET	RLC	RLC-A
68	3378.82	3656.0	2626.11	nf	**14.1**	14.35	14.48
69	6087.64	3258.13	3565.49	nf	15.91	14.32	**13.7**
70	19408.04	16875.89	24322.69	nf	17.59	14.47	**14.77**
71	85837.23	nf	nf	nf	22.54	**16.56**	16.75
72	nf	nf	nf	nf	27.81	**18.42**	18.96
73	nf	nf	nf	nf	31.56	**20.66**	20.68
74	nf	nf	nf	nf	52.53	**38.08**	40.31
75	nf	nf	nf	nf	72.16	**61.98**	68.35
76	nf	nf	nf	nf	**83.12**	328.03	327.32
77	nf	nf	nf	nf	**375.08**	nf	nf
78	nf	nf	nf	nf	**1155.50**	nf	nf
79	nf	nf	nf	nf	**2009.01**	nf	nf
80	nf	nf	nf	nf	**11194.43**	nf	nf
81	nf	nf	nf	nf	nf	nf	nf

In our experiments we compare SMC to our randomized reachability analysis techniques in attempt to detect non-schedulability in Herschel-Planck model for varying execution times in the interval of $[f \cdot \text{WCET}, \text{WCET}]$. The results are shown in Table 4 with each test case given 48 h. As the f value gets higher we see the expected growth in computational demands with $f = 71\%$ requiring just under 24 h for SMC to disprove schedulability, confirming results of [8]. On the other hand, 3 out of 4 of our randomized heuristics were able to detect an error for the same setting of $f = 71\%$ in less than 23 s, improving on performance of SMC by three orders of magnitude. Furthermore, RET heuristic appeared to give the best results, witnessing unschedu-

Table 5. Trace length comparison.

f (%)	RET	RET-S	Timeout
68	6882	560	1 h
69	7619	568	1 h
70	8285	572	1 h
71	10411	570	1 h
72	12394	571	1 h
73	15937	578	1 h
74	26605	1549	1 h
75	41003	1546	1 h
76	40154	1529	1 h
77	97258	1536	1 h
78	119939	1540	5 h
79	129387	1536	5 h
80	145493	6455	20 h

lability for values of f up to and including 80%. We have also tried running longer experiments of up to 7 days for $f = 81\%$, but no errors were discovered which hints at possibility of the Herschel-Planck system being schedulable for $f > 80\%$. The SEM heuristic turned out to be the least efficient one, failing to discover any errors, which is likely due to the exponentially small probability of hitting the "right" time windows with chosen delays. Overall, these experiments showcase the strength of randomized reachability analysis being fit as a part of an efficient development process that speeds up falsification of models.

Once a trace leading to an error is discovered, it might be in the interest of a developer to analyze it to find the cause for the error. The trace, however, can be arbitrarily long, especially for larger systems, making its analysis difficult in practice. In our next experiment we look at the average length of traces

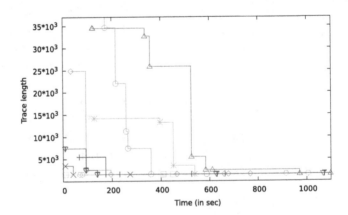

Fig. 3. 10 runs of RET-S for Herschel-Planck with $f = 75\%$.

found for Herschel-Planck system and compare RET heuristic from experiments in Table 4 against the version of RET with the shortest trace option enabled - RET-S. In order for non-exhaustive exploration of RET-S to terminate, we specify the Timeout value and increase it w.r.t. to the average time required by RET to find an error. The results are shown in Table 5. With the given timeout, RET-S shortens the length of the trace by a factor of 12 at minimum. Note that for $f \in [75\%, 79\%]$ the length of the shortest discovered trace is approximately the same – just under 1600 – while the effort to discover such trace is roughly proportional to the average time to detect the first trace (as shown in Table 4).

The exact value of the timeout has to be decided on by the user which may not be an easy parameter to estimate in the setting of randomized and unpredictable exploration. To better understand how RET-S behaves, we plot 10 runs of RET-S for Herschel-Planck system with $f = 75\%$ in Fig. 3. In average it took 263.14 s to find a trace of sub 1600 steps, while the longest run took 970 s.

4 More Schedulability

As already stated, application of symbolic techniques to stopwatch models may provide spurious traces due to over-approximate analysis of UPPAAL. If the target state in these models is potentially reachable, we can use SMC to generate concrete and exact traces witnessing the reachability of the goal state. However, SMC can only be applied to systems with broadcast channels as required by stochastic semantics SMC operates on. In stopwatch models that use handshake channels, our randomized methods become the only solution that can perform a more exact reachability analysis.

Table 6. Average time to find target state in stopwatch automata models. Symbolic MC techniques provide potentially spurious traces.

Model	#loc	BFS	DFS	RDFS	SMC	SEM	RET	RLC	RLC-A
IMAOptim-0	88	0.09	0.1	0.07	**0.04**	0.07	0.1	0.1	0.08
IMAOptim-1	88	0.21	0.2	0.08	**0.05**	**0.05**	0.08	0.08	0.06
IMAOptim-2	88	0.21	0.26	0.09	**0.06**	0.08	0.11	0.11	0.1
md5-jop	594	0.25	10.8	6.53	n/a	0.15	0.18	0.18	**0.12**
md5-hvmimp	476	0.41	0.85	0.49	n/a	0.1	0.14	0.14	**0.09**
md5-hvmexp	11901	oom	oom	oom	n/a	14.17	19.85	20.18	**8.71**
MP-jop	371	0.39	0.14	0.12	n/a	**0.08**	0.12	0.12	0.09
MP-hvmimp	371	0.35	0.14	0.12	n/a	**0.08**	0.12	0.12	0.09
MP-hvmexp	4388	oom	oom	oom	n/a	13.49	22.95	21.99	**8.59**
simplerts-opt	409	oom	oom	oom	n/a	2.43	**1.48**	nf	nf

We consider more schedulability systems modelled as stopwatch automata. Table 6 shows experiments for two different sets of schedulability problems:

ARINC-653 partition scheduling of integrated modular avionics systems [11] (denoted as IMAOptim) and schedulability of Java bytecode systems, originating from TetaSARTS project [21], that are encoded as networks of automata and represent the original layered structure of Java bytecode systems. Our randomized methods discover the target state within 20 s even for a huge system with almost 12 thousands of locations, where other techniques are either not applicable or run out of memory.

5   Gossiping Girls

As claimed earlier, the randomized reachability analysis can serve as a useful tool particularly for an efficient development process. It can be used early in the development, as well as in late stages, for a quick falsification of models, i.e. discovery of errors or checking if another "rare event" state is actually reachable in practice.

To test the efficiency of our randomized methods and challenge them with different model development styles, we look at models of the same problem created by different developers. Specifically, we consider the *Gossiping Girls* problem, where a number of girls n each know a distinct secret and wish to share it with the rest of the girls. They can do so by calling each other and exchanging either only their initial or all of currently known secrets. The girls are organized as a total graph, allowing them to talk with each other concurrently, but with a maximum of 2 girls per call. Some variations of the problem have specific time constraints on the duration of the call or exhibit a different secret exchange pattern, but all with the same final goal of all the girls discovering all of the secrets. This is a combinatorial problem with each girl having a string of n bits which can at most take 2^n values. For a total of n girls this amounts to a string of n^2 with at most 2^{n^2} values. This makes it an incredibly hard combinatorial problem which, when scaled up, quickly exposes the limits of symbolic model-checking due to the state-space explosion problem.

We have gathered 10 models of the Gossiping Girls problem made by Master's thesis students as the final assignment for the course on model-checking at Aalborg University in Denmark. These students represent potential future model developers and we use their model to further experiment on applicability of the randomized methods. The implementation details vary from model to model, including timing constraints and secret exchange patterns. We leave the models unchanged and only scale them up to a certain amount of nodes to challenge both symbolic and randomized methods.

We first experiment on the models scaled up to 8 girls and look for a state with of all the girls having exchanged their secrets, while bounded by a certain global time constraint. The results are shown in Table 7 where each cell represent the average time for each found trace within 2 h. For 9 out of 10 of the models our randomized heuristic RET shows a massive improvement in performance compared to symbolic methods, whereas in 1 model the performance is on the same level. Since the problem is time constrained, the worst performance is that of SEM heuristic which fails to find our target state due to an inefficient way of selecting delays. Importantly, for some models some of the RDFS runs were "lucky" to discover the target state almost immediately, while other "unlucky" tries instead ran out of memory (oom). The oom attempts of RDFS contribute to the performance by noticeably dragging up the average time to find the goal state. Another important factor is memory: unlike symbolic methods, that are given 16 GB of memory, our randomized techniques do not run out of memory as its usage is constant w.r.t to the size of the model and amounts to at most 14 MB for any of the heuristics for this set of experiments.

Table 7. Gossiping Girls with 8 nodes. Each cell represent avg. time for each found trace within 2 h. Searching for a state with all secrets shared within a certain time.

Model	BFS	DFS	RDFS	SEM	RET	RLC	RLC-A
Gosgirls-1	oom	oom	697.13	nf	**0.39**	6949.95	nf
Gosgirls-2	oom	oom	**0.02**	nf	0.04	0.04	0.04
Gosgirls-3	oom	oom	44.49	nf	**0.02**	**0.02**	0.09
Gosgirls-4	oom	oom	28.35	nf	**0.03**	0.03	nf
Gosgirls-5	oom	oom	229.98	nf	**0.02**	**0.02**	**0.02**
Gosgirls-6	oom	oom	64.00	nf	**3.71**	167.44	1530.99
Gosgirls-7	oom	oom	55.61	nf	**0.17**	15.16	15.6
Gosgirls-8	oom	oom	13.96	nf	0.04	**0.03**	**0.03**
Gosgirls-9	oom	oom	2.08	nf	0.08	**0.07**	0.08
Gosgirls-10	oom	oom	598.64	nf	**0.24**	1.72	nf

Discovery of the state where all the secrets are known is arguably an easy target as such state will eventually always appear as we traverse the state-space. This also explains why RDFS was sometimes "lucky" to detect the searched state before it ran out of memory. We now experiment with searching for a particular configuration of secrets in models with 6 girls and show results in Table 8. Concretely, we divide the 6 girls into two clusters of 2 and 4 girls, and search for a state where each girl knows all the secrets of the other girls in the same cluster, but none from the other cluster. Such a state occurs less often in the state-space and is easy to miss, making it a more challenging problem; Hence, only 6 girls are considered. Unlike in previous experiments, the most efficient symbolic search strategy is different for each individual model due to

Table 8. Gossiping Girls with 6 nodes. Each cell represent avg. time for each found trace within 2 h. Searching for a particular configuration of secrets known.

Model	BFS	DFS	RDFS	SEM	RET	RLC	RLC-A
Gosgirls-1	16.98	oom	oom	2.17	**1.35**	1.60	0.23
Gosgirls-2	**0.04**	oom	360.43	**0.04**	**0.04**	**0.04**	**0.04**
Gosgirls-3	77.96	oom	oom	nf	1.44	0.19	**0.10**
Gosgirls-4	oom	oom	oom	nf	0.03	**0.02**	nf
Gosgirls-5	oom	oom	oom	nf	**0.02**	0.02	0.02
Gosgirls-6	oom	244.66	2596.62	**5.92**	7.10	nf	nf
Gosgirls-7	oom	oom	oom	nf	**0.14**	75.44	141.20
Gosgirls-8	32.63	oom	oom	nf	**0.11**	3.24	505.99
Gosgirls-9	oom	oom	199.77	**0.10**	13.04	3.65	2.07
Gosgirls-10	oom	oom	209.36	nf	**0.02**	0.03	0.04

the variance in model implementations. The randomized methods appear largely superior in almost all cases, with the RET heuristic being the most consistent and efficient across all the models. Note that even for 6 girls in a lot of cases symbolic techniques still run out of memory, whereas our random methods use less than 15 MB.

6   Scalability Experiments

We further investigate the efficiency of our randomized methods on a set of standard UPPAAL timed automata models. The models are scaled up in order to challenge both symbolic and randomized techniques and the results are provided in Table 9. The results are truly impressive – randomized methods perform up to 4 orders of magnitude faster and scale significantly better.

Even though the SEM heuristic shows the best performance of many models, its inefficient way of selecting delays causes it to completely miss target states on some models as demonstrated by all of the experiments in this study. Due to under-approximation, it is possible to construct "evil" examples for any heuristic, rendering it inefficient. We then make all of the heuristics available in UPPAAL.

Table 9. Average time to find target state in Timed Automata.

Model	BFS	DFS	RDFS	SEM	RET	RLC	RLC-A
csma-cd-20N	20.2	oom	**0.02**	0.03	0.07	0.06	0.21
csma-cd-22N	37.48	oom	oom	**0.03**	0.08	0.08	0.31
csma-cd-25N	91.0	oom	oom	**0.05**	0.09	0.1	0.55
csma-cd-30N	313.54	oom	oom	**0.05**	0.12	0.19	1.43
csma-cd-50N	oom	oom	oom	**0.46**	0.84	1.19	15.29
Fischer-10N	0.9	22.84	4.3	**0.04**	0.05	1.21	nf
Fischer-15N	8.35	6037.63	9038.96	**0.09**	**0.09**	5.06	nf
Fischer-20N	72.61	oom	oom	0.3	**0.28**	17.28	nf
Fischer-25N	452.45	oom	oom	**0.64**	0.73	36.93	nf
Fischer-50N	oom	oom	90.01	**21.78**	23.79	233.67	nf
FischerME-10N	7.15	0.14	0.02	0.01	0.02	**0.01**	0.02
FischerME-15N	oom	11.45	0.05	0.04	0.04	**0.03**	0.16
FischerME-20N	oom	970.33	0.4	0.11	0.09	0.05	**0.04**
FischerME-25N	oom	oom	83.29	0.25	0.21	0.08	**0.07**
FischerME-50N	oom	oom	174.32	14.87	15.26	**0.49**	4.04
LE-Chan-3N	0.03	0.35	0.04	**0.01**	**0.01**	**0.01**	**0.01**
LE-Chan-4N	oom	oom	107.7	0.95	0.54	4.36	**0.07**
LE-Chan-5N	oom	oom	1167.41	53.21	**31.38**	102.08	nf
LE-Hops-3N	0.02	0.02	0.02	**0.01**	**0.01**	**0.01**	**0.01**
LE-Hops-4N	oom	oom	oom	49.40	**14.57**	428.96	1588.33
LE-Hops-5N	oom	oom	1108.15	63.44	**35.15**	36.49	49.00
Milner-N100	0.45	0.16	2.72	nf	**0.11**	**0.11**	0.12
Milner-N500	44.44	10.56	1619.75	nf	**1.19**	1.2	1.43
Milner-N1000	488.41	110.35	36455.73	nf	**4.44**	4.45	4.59
Train-200N	oom	5.64	6.06	5.91	**5.4**	16699.98	nf
Train-300N	oom	28.19	30.28	**25.62**	26.53	nf	nf
Train-400N	oom	85.22	90.66	**67.91**	70.87	nf	nf
Train-500N	oom	210.89	223.13	**181.99**	188.9	nf	nf
Train-1000N	nf	3461.17	3542.08	**2192.12**	2541.57	nf	nf
Train-2000N	nf	71286.92	oom	**19229.02**	23233.21	nf	nf

7   Conclusion

We have presented a new method of randomized reachability analysis in the domain of model-based verification. The method excels at detection of "rare event" states, such as errors, by means of quick and lightweight random walks through the system. Randomized reachability analysis explores the state-space in an under-approximate manner and can only conclude on reachability if the target state is discovered. However, in many cases this method significantly outperforms other existing techniques at reachability checking. Randomized reachability analysis is therefore a very useful addition to the process of model development: it provides an efficient way of checking models for potential bugs or violations during the development and can be followed by exhaustive and expensive symbolic verification at the very end. The randomized method also supports the search for either *shorter* or *faster* trace to the target state, which improves the process of debugging the model. The randomized reachability analysis is implemented and made available for use in the model checker UPPAAL.

To validate the efficiency of our method, we have performed extensive experiments on models of varying size and origin. The results are extremely encouraging: randomized reachability analysis discovers "rare event" states up to several orders of magnitude faster. In particular, a case that could previously be analyzed by SMC in 23 h now only takes 23 s. Moreover, our randomized methods discover traces to target states in cases that were previously intractable by any of the existing techniques either due to state-space explosion or inconclusiveness in verification of stopwatch models.

8   Future Work

Further investigations into tokenized, coverage-based and guided methods can be done to improve the efficiency of the method. Some combinations of static analysis of the models with either fixed or dynamic look-ahead for the random walk could result in better performance of the method.

One future goal is to perform a more thorough and independent user evaluation of the benefits of the randomized reachability analysis. This could indicate the need for more parameters to be manually set by the user, such as custom delay probability distribution, or could highlight other areas for improvement of randomized methods.

Automatic sanity checks is another improvement that can noticeably enhance the user experience and aid during model development. An implementation [17] for UPPAAL of such sanity checks has been undertaken as a master thesis project [18] in the Formal Methods & Tools group at University of Twente. This report demonstrates the usefulness of such sanity checks and highlights the need for quick feedback to the tool user. Our randomized method is highly suitable for this purpose.

References

1. Behrmann, G., David, A., Larsen, K.G.: A tutorial on UPPAAL. In: Bernardo, M., Corradini, F. (eds.) Formal Methods for the Design of Real-Time Systems, SFM-RT 2004. LNCS, vol. 3185, pp. 200–236. Springer, Heidelberg (2004). https://doi.org/10.1007/978-3-540-30080-9_7
2. Boudjadar, A., et al.: Statistical and exact schedulability analysis of hierarchical scheduling systems. Sci. Comput. Program. **127**, 103–130 (2016). https://doi.org/10.1016/j.scico.2016.05.008
3. Boudjadar, A., et al.: A reconfigurable framework for compositional schedulability and power analysis of hierarchical scheduling systems with frequency scaling. Sci. Comput. Program. **113**(3), 236–260 (2015). https://doi.org/10.1016/j.scico.2015.10.003

4. Brekling, A., Hansen, M.R., Madsen, J.: MoVES—A framework for modelling and verifying embedded systems. In: 2009 International Conference on Microelectronics - ICM, pp. 149–152 (2009). https://doi.org/10.1109/ICM.2009.5418667

5. Burns, A.: Preemptive Priority-Based Scheduling: An Appropriate Engineering Approach, pp. 225–248. Prentice-Hall Inc., Hoboken (1995)

6. David, A., Illum, J., Larsen, K.G., Skou, A.: Model-based framework for schedulability analysis using UPPAAL 4.1. Model-Based Des. Embed. Syst. 1(1), 93–119 (2009)

7. David, A., Larsen, K.G., Legay, A., Mikucionis, M., Poulsen, D.B.: UPPAAL SMC tutorial. Int. J. Softw. Tools Technol. Transf. 17(4), 397–415 (2015)

8. David, A., Larsen, K.G., Legay, A., Mikucionis, M.: Schedulability of Herschel-Planck revisited using statistical model checking. In: Margaria, T., Steffen, B. (eds.) Leveraging Applications of Formal Methods, Verification and Validation, ISoLA 2012. LNCS, vol. 7610, pp. 293–307. Springer, Heidelberg (2012). https://doi.org/10.1007/978-3-642-34032-1_28

9. Fersman, E., Krcal, P., Pettersson, P., Yi, W.: Task automata: schedulability, decidability and undecidability. Inf. Comput. 205(8), 1149–1172 (2007). https://doi.org/10.1016/j.ic.2007.01.009, https://www.sciencedirect.com/science/article/pii/S0890540107000089

10. Grosu, R., Smolka, S.A.: Monte Carlo model checking. In: Halbwachs, N., Zuck, L.D. (eds.) Tools and Algorithms for the Construction and Analysis of Systems, TACAS 2005. LNCS, vol. 3440, pp. 271–286. Springer, Heidelberg (2005). https://doi.org/10.1007/978-3-540-31980-1_18

11. Han, P., Zhai, Z., Nielsen, B., Nyman, U.: Model-based optimization of ARINC-653 partition scheduling. Int. J. Softw. Tools Technol. Transf. (2021). https://doi.org/10.1007/s10009-020-00597-6

12. Joseph, M., Pandya, P.: Finding response times in a real-time system. Comput. J. 29(5), 390–395 (1986). https://doi.org/10.1093/comjnl/29.5.390

13. Kiviriga, A., Larsen, K.G., Nyman, U.: Randomized refinement checking of timed I/O automata. In: Pang, J., Zhang, L. (eds.) Dependable Software Engineering. Theories, Tools, and Applications, SETTA 2020. LNCS, vol. 12153, pp. 70–88. Springer, Cham (2020). https://doi.org/10.1007/978-3-030-62822-2_5

14. Larsen, K., Peled, D., Sedwards, S.: Memory-efficient tactics for randomized LTL model checking. In: Paskevich, A., Wies, T. (eds.) Verified Software. Theories, Tools, and Experiments, VSTTE 2017. LNCS, vol. 10712, pp. 152–169. Springer, Cham (2017). https://doi.org/10.1007/978-3-319-72308-2_10

15. Legay, A., Delahaye, B., Bensalem, S.: Statistical model checking: an overview. In: Barringer, H., et al. (eds.) Runtime Verification, RV 2010. LNCS, vol. 6418, pp. 122–135. Springer, Heidelberg (2010). https://doi.org/10.1007/978-3-642-16612-9_11

16. Mikučionis, M., et al.: Schedulability analysis using UPPAAL: Herschel-Planck case study. In: Margaria, T., Steffen, B. (eds.) Leveraging Applications of Formal Methods, Verification, and Validation, ISoLA 2010. LNCS, vol. 6416, pp. 175–190. Springer, Heidelberg (2010). https://doi.org/10.1007/978-3-642-16561-0_21

17. Onis, R.: UrPal. https://github.com/utwente-fmt/UrPal. Accessed 18 May 2021

18. Onis, R.: Does your model make sense?: Automatic verification of timed systems (2018). http://essay.utwente.nl/77031/

19. Palm, S.: Herschel-Planck ACC ASW: sizing, timing and schedulability analysis. Technical report, Terma A/S (2006)

20. Sen, K., Viswanathan, M., Agha, G.: Statistical model checking of black-box prob-abilistic systems. In: Alur, R., Peled, D.A. (eds.) Computer Aided Verification, CAV 2004. LNCS, vol. 3114, pp. 202–215. Springer, Heidelberg (2004). https://doi.org/10.1007/978-3-540-27813-9_16

21. Søe Luckow, K., Bøgholm, T., Thomsen, B.: A Flexible Schedulability Analysis Tool for SCJ Programs. http://people.cs.aau.dk/~boegholm/tetasarts/. Accessed 07 May 2021

Verifying the Mathematical Library of an UAV Autopilot with Frama-C

Baptiste Pollien[1]([✉]), Christophe Garion[1], Gautier Hattenberger[2],
Pierre Roux[3], and Xavier Thirioux[1]

[1] ISAE-SUPAERO, Université de Toulouse, Toulouse, France
`baptiste.pollien@isae-supaero.fr`
[2] ENAC, Toulouse, France
[3] ONERA, Toulouse, France

Abstract. Ensuring safety of critical systems is crucial and is often attained by extensive testing of the system. Formal methods are now commonly accepted as powerful tools to obtain guarantees on such systems, even if it is generally not possible to formally prove the safety and correctness of the whole system. This paper presents an ongoing work on the formal verification of the Paparazzi UAV autopilot using the Frama-C verification platform. We focus on a Paparazzi mathematical library providing different UAV state representations and associated conversion functions and manage to prove the absence of runtime errors in the library and some interesting functional properties on floating-point conversion functions.

Keywords: Proof of program · Critical systems · Deductive methods · Abstract interpretation

1 Introduction

Formal methods are verification techniques based on mathematics which facilitate the formal verification of properties of hardware, software or models. They are nowadays widely accepted as an efficient complement to testing, particularly for critical systems, see for instance the DO-330 supplement to DO-178C. There are many formal methods and they can be distinguished by the properties they can help to verify, the efforts required to specify the system in order to use the verification tools, or their automation level. For instance, *abstract interpretation* is often used to prove the absence of runtime errors and is an automatic tool. *Deductive verification* is another tool that can be used to prove more complex properties, like correctness of a program given a formal specification, and generally uses automated solvers, though sometimes needs to use a proof assistant and requires human intervention.

This work is supported by the Defense Innovation Agency (AID) of the French Ministry of Defense (research project CONCORDE N 2019 65 0090004707501).

A. Lluch Lafuente and A. Mavridou (Eds.): FMICS 2021, LNCS 12863, pp. 167–173, 2021.
https://doi.org/10.1007/978-3-030-85248-1_10

The goal of this ongoing project is to review different formal verification techniques to define an analysis process taking advantage of these tools in order to verify properties of an UAV autopilot. This analysis process is applied on the Paparazzi autopilot developed at ENAC and implemented in the C programming language [6,9].

Frama-C [7] is a C code analysis tool facilitating formal verification. Verification with Frama-C require the addition of annotations in the C code as special comments to specify the expected properties: definition of contracts for functions (*preconditions*, *postconditions* and frame specification (i.e., all the memory elements that will be modified during the execution of the function), and the definition of *invariants* and *variants* for loops and assertions. Frama-C has many plugins but three were of particular interest: WP (*Weakest Precondition*) which uses the weakest preconditions calculus, RTE (*RunTime Errors*) that automatically add assertions to verify the absence of runtime errors, and EVA (*Evolved Value Analysis*) using abstract interpretation to compute sets of possible values for each variable of the program.

Verification of the Paparazzi autopilot is currently done using the Frama-C platform (version 23.0 Vanadium) and mainly automatic provers[1]. We focused on verifying a mathematical library presented in Sect. 2. Section 3 details the analysis concerning the absence of runtime errors. The second part of the analysis covers the verification of functional properties for some state representation transformation functions. Section 4 details the verification process using only automatic provers. As automatic provers were not able to prove some of these functions, Sect. 5 presents how we proved such functions using the interactive prover Coq [12]. Finally, Sect. 6 gives a conclusion and some perspectives.

2   The Paparazzi Autopilot

Paparazzi [6] is an open-source autopilot under GPL license developed at ENAC since 2003. Paparazzi supports various types of drones and permits the control of several of them simultaneously. Paparazzi has also various built-in modes and offers the ability to create personalized flight plans. The mathematical library studied here provides functions converting different representations of vector rotations as rotation matrices, Euler angles, or quaternions. It also defines elementary operations on these representations. This library is written in the C programming language and each function is available in three versions: one using `double` values, another one with `float` values and the last one using `int` values to represent fixed point values.

3   Proving the Absence of Runtime Errors

The studied library defines C structures for the different representations (rotation matrices, quaternions, vectors, etc.). The library functions take only pointers

---

[1] Complete specified code of Paparazzi, tools versions, and installation instructions are available on https://gitlab.isae-supaero.fr/b.pollien/paparazzi-frama-c/-/tree/fmics-2021.

on such structures as inputs and always return pointers. Preconditions ensuring the validity of pointers have been added in the contracts as the functions are not designed to work with invalid pointers. It has also been necessary to specify which variables will be modified during the execution of the function. Finally, invariants on `for` loop have been added to help the provers to ensure the absence of runtime errors.

The WP plugin of Frama-C offers different models of arithmetic that take into account more or less precisely C semantics. The verification of the `int` flavor of the functions was made using 32-bits integer arithmetic with overflows. When using the RTE plugin to verify the absence of runtime errors, assertions are automatically added to check that there is no overflow for each arithmetical operation. To verify this, each function was manually analyzed to determine the maximum possible value for the different variables. When bounds of the variables have been determined, they were added as preconditions in the function contracts. Unfortunately, WP associated with automatic provers is not able to verify these new contracts. Even if the complete memory separation of structures used in a function is specified as precondition, the solvers are unable to prove that the modification of a field in a structure does not change any other part of the memory.

To overcome this problem, we decided to associate the EVA plugin to WP. EVA has no issue dealing with pointers nor aliasing and is able to compute accurate intervals of possible values for each variable. The result is then passed to WP by Frama-C, which makes it easier to conclude some proofs. This WP limitation when pointers are extensively used as input and output parameters was also found by Vassil Todorov during his PhD thesis [13]. He also used a static analysis tool using abstract interpretation, Astrée [3], to solve the same problem. To conclude, the association of EVA and WP enables the verification of absence of runtime errors for the functions using `int` values.

WP has also an arithmetical model `real` for real arithmetic. We decided to use this model for the verification of the library functions working on floating-point values. Using the same precondition used for the `int` version of the functions, and such a model permits us to verify the absence of division by zero and that real variables do not take the `NaN` value. To perform these verifications, it was only necessary to add as preconditions the fact that each pointer refers to a valid address. The absence of these two kind of runtime errors as well as the termination of the functions have been proven, using WP and EVA, for the `float` and `double` versions of the library. Unfortunately, our verification does not offer any guarantee on the risk of floating-point overflow or on rounding errors. Moreover, the properties proven for the `real` model can only serve as an hint, but not a guarantee, that they hold for floating-point values. However, this model was particularly useful to verify functional properties as presented in Sect. 4. Indeed, even if the model is semantically incorrect and we cannot get functional guarantees during execution, it permits at least to verify that the code is correct in the mathematical sense.

4   Functional Verification Using Automatic Provers

The goal of functional verification is to ensure properties about the behavior of functions. We will first focus here on the function float_rmat_of_quat to explain the process used. This function takes a normalized quaternion as input and returns the corresponding rotation matrix.

In order to specify the functional properties of such a function, types and predicates have been defined in the logic provided by ACSL [1], the language used to express Frama-C annotations. We defined types for matrices and quaternions, as well as elementary algebraic operations. We specified lemmas and then verified them to ensure that these operations are correct (e.g., we verified that matrix transposition is idempotent). Then, a logical function that converts a quaternion to a rotation matrix has been defined independently of the C code from the library. This function is based on the mathematical equation that expresses the conversion of a quaternion to a rotation matrix [5,8]. In the following, we will note rmat_of_quat the function that represents this conversion. rmat_of_quat's semantics is expressed in ACSL as a mathematical, model-based specification. This function takes as parameter a unitary quaternion q and returns a rotation matrix. Frama-C is able to verify automatically that for any given unitary quaternion q, the rotation matrix computed by rmat_of_quat corresponds to the same rotation as described by the quaternion. Verification of this property has required to verify the following lemma: $\forall q \in \mathbb{H}, v \in \mathbb{R}^3, q(0,v)q^* = (0, \text{rmat\_of\_quat}(q).v)$. This lemma states that given a quaternion q and a vector v, applying the rotation with the quaternion q on vector v is equivalent to applying the rotation matrix obtained from q by rmat_of_quat on v.

The contract for the function float_rmat_of_quat has then been established using these ACSL functions. Assuming that the quaternion passed as parameter is normalized, we wanted to verify two functional properties. The first one is that the returned matrix does indeed correspond to the conversion of the quaternion passed as a parameter: our post-condition verifies that the rotation matrix generated by the C code is equal to the rotation matrix generated by our logical function rmat_of_quat. As presented in the previous section, we use the WP real model for the verification of this property, thus ignoring the differences in the results between the C version and the mathematical version which could have been introduced by rounding errors. The second verified property is that the generated matrix is indeed a rotation matrix, i.e. the transpose of the matrix is its inverse, and its determinant is equal to 1.

Despite the use of the real arithmetic model, WP could not verify this contract. It was therefore necessary to manually review the code. We noticed that the C code used a constant M_SQRT2 to represent $\sqrt{2}$. By analyzing the calculations done in the code, we realized that the constant M_SQRT2 was every time multiplied by itself. We therefore suggested a code modification that replaces M_SQRT2 * M_SQRT2 by 2. This modification does not change the number of multiplications in the C code but permits to reduce the rounding errors propagated by the function. With this code change and the arithmetic model `real`, WP verifies the contract of the function `float_rmat_of_quat`.

5   Functional Verification Using Interactive Provers

The same verification has been attempted for the inverse function `float_quat_of_rmat` that converts a rotation matrix into a quaternion. There are different equations to perform this conversion in the literature but we use the four formulae using Shepperd's method [10, 11]. These equations are directly deduced from the formula that converts a quaternion into a rotation matrix and are defined according to the diagonal values of the rotation matrix: one is defined when the trace is strictly positive, the three other ones are defined when the trace is negative and correspond to the possible choices for the greatest element of the diagonal of the matrix. We defined each of these formulae by an ACSL logical function. When defining postconditions of C functions, we uses ACSL `behavior` feature to specify one sub-contract per Shepperd's case, specifying as preconditions in the sub-contract the conditions for which the corresponding Shepperd's function is defined. For instance, we defined a behavior that requires as precondition that the trace of the input matrix is positive. These behaviors then ensure, as postconditions, that the quaternion computed by the C function is equal to the quaternion computed using the corresponding logical function. Another feature offered by Frama-C is the possibility to verify that the behaviors are disjoint and complete. I.e. for every input matrix, there is one and only one behavior such that its preconditions are fulfilled by the matrix. With this contract, we were able to verify that the function returns a quaternion that corresponds to the same rotation as the matrix used as input.

Let us denote by `quat_of_rmat` the mathematical function that returns the quaternion corresponding to a given rotation matrix. Let us consider here the case where the rotation matrix used as input has a positive trace. Verifying that `quat_of_rmat` is correct in this case is equivalent to verifying that the property described on the following lemma holds: $\forall R \forall q\ ||q|| = 1 \wedge Tr(R) > 0 \rightarrow (R = $ `rmat_of_quat`$(q) \leftrightarrow q = $ `quat_of_rmat`$(R))$. This lemma can be read as follows: for all rotation matrices R with a positive trace and for all unitary quaternions q, R represents the rotation matrix obtained from `rmat_of_quat`(q), if and only if the function `quat_of_rmat` will return q when applied to R. It has then been translated into an ACSL lemma, as well as the similar equations resulting from the three other cases.

Unfortunately, Frama-C is not able to prove these lemmas using only automatic SMT solvers, even after extending the timeout value considerably. The proof requires specific transformations, such as factorization, that the solvers might not be able to find. We therefore had to use the interactive mode of WP. This mode generates incomplete proof scripts for each unproven goal. The scripts contain all the definitions and lemmas that have already been proved by Frama-C and the solvers. The theorem corresponding to an unproven goal needs to be verified with some interactive prover where in our case, we use Coq [12].

The implication that if R is obtained from rmat_of_quat(q), then the function quat_of_rmat will return q has been verified with Coq for the four lemmas. The reverse implication has not been proved yet. However, by considering the verification of the function rmat_of_quat, this proof is sufficient to guarantee that the result of the function quat_of_rmat describe the same rotation than the input matrix.

We also wanted to verify the function implementing the conversion from the Euler representation of a rotation to a rotation matrix. In the library, there are two functions, float_rmat_of_eulers_321 and float_rmat_of_eulers_312, that implement this conversion. These two functions differ on the order of Euler angles (given the $(\vec{z}, \vec{y}, \vec{x})$ axis for the 321 function and given the $(\vec{z}, \vec{x}, \vec{y})$ axis for the 312 function). The contracts defined for these functions ensure that the matrix must be special orthogonal, i.e., a rotation matrix. In order to verify these contracts, we started using only automatic SMT solvers. The first problem we faced was that the code for the conversion uses the cosf and sinf trigonometric functions from the C standard library. Frama-C equips these built-in functions with contracts, but these contracts do not provide enough information. We decided to add an hypothesis in the contract stating that the result of these functions was equal to the result obtained with the corresponding mathematical trigonometric function of ACSL (defined by \cos and \sin). This hypothesis might not be correct. However, as we use the real model, this hypothesis permits to use properties of trigonometric functions (for instance $\forall a \in \mathbb{R}$, $\cos a^2 + \sin a^2 = 1$).

Unfortunately, Frama-C was not able to prove the postcondition of the conversion functions, even with this hypothesis and WP tactics. WP tactics are a feature offered by WP that applies basic transformations on the goals to simplify them in order to discharge the solvers (for instance, definitions can be unfolded or goals splitted into subgoals). Even by using tactics, there were remaining unproven subgoals. Instead of using Coq to verify the whole postcondition, we decided to define generic lemmas in ACSL which correspond to the subgoals unproven by SMT solvers and verify them in Coq. Such a lemma is for instance $\forall a, b, c \in \mathbb{R}$ $\sin a^2 * \cos b^2 + (\sin a * \sin b * \cos c - \sin c * \cos a)^2 + (\cos c * \cos a + \sin a * \sin b * \sin c)^2 = 1$, which can easily be proved by hand using factorization and properties of trigonometric functions.

6 Conclusion

We have presented in this paper an ongoing work on formal verification of a mathematical library of the open-source autopilot Paparazzi. We have mainly focused on the verification of the absence of runtime errors, but also have proven interesting properties of rather complex functions.

In future work, we plan on completing the proof remaining presented in Sect. 5. Some functional properties of other functions from the same mathematical library of Paparazzi should also be verified. We want especially to focus on verifying rounding errors, and therefore do not use WP real model but rather using a model that represents accurately the floating-point numbers. We should also compare our approach to *autoactive proofs*, where interactive provers are not used, but SMT solvers are guided by assertions inserted by developers to help the provers [2,4]. Finally, we plan to tackle formal verification of the Paparazzi flight plan generator.

References

1. Baudin, P., Filliâtre, J., Marché, C., Monate, B., Moy, Y., Prevosto, V.: ACSL: ANSI/ISO C Specification Language (2008)
2. Blanchard, A., Loulergue, F., Kosmatov, N.: Towards full proof automation in Frama-C using auto-active verification. In: Badger, J., Rozier, K. (eds.) NASA Formal Methods, NFM 2019. LNCS, vol. 11460, pp. 88–105. Springer, Cham (2019). https://doi.org/10.1007/978-3-030-20652-9_6
3. Cousot, P., Cousot, R., Feret, J., Mauborgne, L., Miné, A., Rival, X.: Why does Astrée scale up? Formal Methods in System Design 35(3), 229–264 (2009)
4. Dross, C., Moy, Y.: Auto-active proof of red-black trees in SPARK. In: Barrett, C., Davies, M., Kahsai, T. (eds.) NASA Formal Methods, NFM 2017. LNCS, vol. 10227, pp. 68–83. Springer, Cham (2017). https://doi.org/10.1007/978-3-319-57288-8_5
5. Grubin, C.: Derivation of the quaternion scheme via the Euler axis and angle. J. Spacecraft Rockets **7**(10), 1261–1263 (1970). https://doi.org/10.2514/3.30149
6. Hattenberger, G., Bronz, M., Gorraz, M.: Using the Paparazzi UAV system for scientific research. In: International Micro Air Vehicle Conference and Competition 2014, IMAV 2014, Delft, Netherlands, pp. 247–252 (2014). https://doi.org/10.4233/uuid:b38fbdb7-e6bd-440d-93be-f7dd1457be60, https://hal-enac.archives-ouvertes.fr/hal-01059642
7. Kirchner, F., Kosmatov, N., Prevosto, V., Signoles, J., Yakobowski, B.: Frama-C: a software analysis perspective. Formal Aspects Comput. **27**, 573–609 (2015). https://doi.org/10.1007/s00165-014-0326-7
8. Klumpp, A.R.: Singularity-free extraction of a quaternion from a direction-cosine matrix. J. Spacecraft Rockets **13**(12), 754–755 (1976). https://doi.org/10.2514/3.27947
9. Paparazzi UAV Team: Paparazzi - the free autopilot (2021). https://paparazzi-uav.readthedocs.io/en/latest/
10. Sarabandi, S., Thomas, F.: Accurate computation of quaternions from rotation matrices. In: Lenarcic, J., Parenti-Castelli, V. (eds.) Advances in Robot Kinematics 2018, ARK 2018. SPAR, vol. 8, pp. 39–46. Springer, Cham (2019). https://doi.org/10.1007/978-3-319-93188-3_5
11. Shepperd, S.W.: Quaternion from rotation matrix. J. Guidance Control **1**(3), 223–224 (1978). https://doi.org/10.2514/3.55767b
12. The Coq Development Team: The Coq Proof Assistant, version 8.8.0 (2018). https://doi.org/10.5281/zenodo.1219885, https://hal.inria.fr/hal-01954564
13. Todorov, V.: Automotive embedded software design using formal methods. Ph.D. thesis, Université Paris-Saclay (2020). https://tel.archives-ouvertes.fr/tel-03082647

Formal Analysis of the UNISIG Safety Application Intermediate Sub-layer
Applying Formal Methods to Railway Standard Interfaces

Davide Basile[1]([ID]), Alessandro Fantechi[1,2]([ID]), and Irene Rosadi[2]

[1] ISTI–CNR, Pisa, Italy
davide.basile@isti.cnr.it
[2] University of Florence, Florence, Italy

Abstract. The combined use of standard interfaces and formal methods is currently under investigation by Shift2Rail, a joint undertaking between railway stakeholders and the EU. Standard interfaces are useful to increase market competition and standardization whilst reducing long-term life cycle costs. Formal methods are needed to achieve interoperability and safety of standard interfaces and are one of the targets of the 4SECURail project funded by Shift2Rail. This paper presents the modelling and analysis of the selected case study of the 4SECURail project: the Safe Application Intermediate sub-layer of the UNISIG RBC/RBC Safe Communication Interface. The adopted formal method is Statistical Model Checking of a network of Stochastic Priced Timed Automata, as provided by the UPPAAL SMC tool. The main contributions are: (i) rigorous complete and publicly available models of an official interface specification already in operation, (ii) identification of safety and interoperability issues in the original specification using Statistical Model Checking, (iii) quantification of costs for learning the adopted formal method and developing the carried out analysis.

1   Introduction

Despite the large number of successful applications of formal methods in the railway domain [14], no universally accepted technology has emerged. Indeed, if applicable standards (e.g. CENELEC EN 50128 for the development of software for railway control and protection systems) mention formal methods as highly recommended practices [13], they do not provide clear guidelines on how to use them in a cost-effective way. The absence of a clear idea of which benefits can result from the adoption of formal methods is one of the aspects that act as an obstacle to the widespread use of formal methods [16,17]. This is witnessed also by the current efforts undertaken by Shift2Rail.

The Shift2Rail Joint Undertaking was established in 2014 under Horizon 2020 R&I program for pursuing research and innovation activities in the railway domain. As mentioned in the technology demonstrator TD2.7 "Formal methods and standardisation for smart signalling systems", Shift2Rail "has identified the

© Springer Nature Switzerland AG 2021
A. Lluch Lafuente and A. Mavridou (Eds.): FMICS 2021, LNCS 12863, pp. 174–190, 2021.
https://doi.org/10.1007/978-3-030-85248-1_11

use of formal methods and standard interfaces as two key concepts to enable reducing the time it takes to develop and deliver railway signalling systems, and to reduce costs for procurement, development and maintenance. Formal methods are needed to ensure correct behaviour, interoperability and safety, and standard interfaces are needed to increase market competition and standardization, reducing long-term life cycle costs" [24]. One of the two workstreams of the 4SECURail (FORmal Methods and CSIRT for the RAILway sector) project deals with investigating the benefits of a formal method approach to the specification of standard interfaces. Moreover, 4SECURail aims to perform a costs and benefits analysis for the adoption of formal methods in the railway environment.

In this paper we present recent efforts in the context of the 4SECURail project. We present the formal modelling and analysis of the selected case study of the project that is the UNISIG Subset-098 - RBC/RBC (Radio Block Centre) Safe Communication Interface [25], and in particular the Safe Application Intermediate (SAI) sub-layer, concerning the protection against specific threats identified by CENELEC standards [12]. We exploit formal methods to build a fully defined mathematical model, in particular a network of Stochastic Priced Timed Automata. We verify the specified protection mechanisms against safety requirements identified by CENELEC standards, that are formalized using temporal logics. Our model enhances the existing standard interface with unambiguous, fine-grained modelling of the natural language requirements. The model can be exploited as starting point for other model-based activities such as model-based development or model-based testing. The identified benefits are also represented by a series of issues that emerged from the formal verification, mostly due to undefined or ambiguous aspects, tampering both safety and interoperability of the system. We also traced the costs in terms of man-hours needed to learn formal methods and to develop the model and analysis presented. Such data can be validated against publicly available documents and regulations [27]. All models and logs of experiments are publicly available at [22].

Related Work. A subset of authors have experience in applying UPPAAL to study the upcoming ERTMS/ETCS Level 3 specification in the context of the Shift2Rail ASTRail project in [2,3,5,6]. Whilst those papers are exploring new requirements of an envisioned system, here we verify an official specification (dated 2012) already realised. Concerning the Shift2Rail 4SECURail project, in [4] the design of a formal methods demonstrator is discussed, which is based upon behavioural UML models. Here we provide a further contribution by adopting UPPAAL SMC. In [19] the handover in Communication Based Train Control systems is analysed with UPPAAL SMC and a novel method of probability evaluation. Similar to our work, they consider probabilistic failures (with probability weights set to 10^{-5}), assuming the presence of probabilistic communication failures. They analyse the scenarios of handover request and border point crossing from the front and rear end of a train, to show that the overall probability of a successful handover is high (0.99985). In [9] the RBC/RBC handover is analysed using run-time monitoring algorithms enforcing modal sequence charts. They report a concrete accident scenario where two trains collided. The accident was due to incorrect interactions between interlocking and RBC, where basically the trains movement authority were independently generated by both the RBC (using Level 3) and the track circuits (using Level 2), thus unfortunately allocating the same track portion to two different trains. Compared to these papers, we study the current ERTMS/ETCS Level 2 handover. We do not focus on the exchange of application messages (e.g. crossing the border), but on a lower level, ensuring protection against threats due to open radio communications. Moreover, we do not focus on providing a precise evaluation of the probability of the handover to fail, nor to provide run-time monitors. We provide a qualitative analysis of the requirements in [25], identifying both safety and interoperability issues in the current operating specification. We use SMC to scale to the real-world case study size of our model, and probabilities of communications errors are inflated to drive the simulations toward faulty scenarios to analyse the protections.

Structure of the Paper. UPPAAL SMC and the case study are briefly introduced in Sect. 2. The model and the analysis are in, respectively, Sect. 3 and Sect. 4. Section 5 concludes the paper.

2   Background

Statistical Model Checking and UPPAAL. Statistical Model Checking [1,20] (SMC) is concerned with running a controlled number of (probabilistically distributed) simulations of a system model to obtain a statistical evaluation (with a predefined level of statistical confidence) of some formula φ. The Monte Carlo estimation with Chernoff-Hoeffding bound executes $N = \lceil (ln(2) - ln(\alpha))/(2\epsilon^2) \rceil$ simulations ρ_i, $i \in 1...N$, to provide the interval $[p' - \epsilon, p' + \epsilon]$ with confidence $1 - \alpha$, where $p' = (\#\{\rho_i \mid \rho_i \models \varphi\})/N$, i.e., $\Pr(|p' - p| \leq \epsilon) \geq 1 - \alpha$ where p is the unknown value of φ being estimated statistically [20]. SMC offers advantages over exhaustive (probabilistic) model checking. Most importantly: SMC scales better, since there is no need to generate and possibly explore the full state space of the model under scrutiny, thus avoiding the combinatorial state-space explosion problem typical of model checking. Indeed, the parameter N is *independent* from the size of the state-space. Moreover, the required simulations can easily run in parallel. This comes at a price: contrary to exhaustive model checking, exact results are out of reach, especially for formulae evaluated with very low probability, called rare events. Another advantage of SMC is its uptake in industry: compared to model checking, SMC is very simple to implement, understand and use, due to the widespread adoption of Monte Carlo simulation.

UPPAAL SMC [11] extends UPPAAL [7], a well-known toolbox for the verification of real-time systems modelled by (extended) timed automata. UPPAAL SMC models are network of Stochastic Priced Timed Automata: Timed Automata are finite state automata enhanced with real-time modelling through *clock* variables; their stochastic extension replaces non-determinism with probabilistic choices and time delays with probability distributions (uniform for bounded time and exponential for unbounded time). These automata may communicate via (broadcast) channels and shared variables. UPPAAL SMC allows to check (quantitative) properties over simulation runs of a UPPAAL SMC model. These properties must be expressed in a dialect of the Metric Interval Temporal Logic (MITL) [8]. In particular, all formulae φ_i evaluated in Sect. 4 follow a specific form, which is the probability that the configuration identified by the propositional formula `conf` is reached before `bound` units of time, written `Pr[<=bound](<>conf)`.

RBC/RBC Safe Communication Interface. The selected case study is the RBC/RBC handover interface as specified by UNISIG Subset-098 − RBC/RBC Safe Communication Interface in [25], which provides a public standardized interface that specifies the requirements for the handover protocol between neighbouring RBCs in natural language.

Each RBC supervises all the trains moving within its responsibility area. The handover procedure is used to manage the interchange of train supervision between two neighbouring RBCs. This protocol is based on a layered structure. The higher layer corresponds to an application process that addresses high-level functionalities, such as the generation and the reception of information to communicate with peer RBC entities, or the re-establishment of the safe connection when it is lost due to errors in lower layers. This layer communicates with an underlying layer, the Safety Functional Module (SFM) which specifies the requirements related to the safety of the communications. The SFM layer consists of two distinct sub-layers, the SAI (Safe Application Intermediate) sub-layer and the Euroradio SL (Euroradio Safety Layer), and their combination provides a safe protection strategy for the open transmission system. The SAI layer provides adequate protection against the threats identified by CENELEC and specified in the EN 50159 European Standard [12], specifically: repetition (a message already sent is sent again in the message stream); deletion (a message is removed from the message stream); insertion (an additional message is implanted in the message stream) and re-sequencing (the ordering of messages in a stream is changed). The Euroradio SL protects the system against corruption, masquerade and insertion threats. The SAI sub-layer protection is achieved with a sequence number for deletion, re-sequencing and repetition threats. Basically, it consists of inserting a consecutive number to each message and computing the difference between such numbers. The delay defence technique is achieved with the TTS (Triple Time Stamp) procedure, consisting in storing in each message three timestamps information for checking that the transmission delay is within a computed offset. An alternative delay defense technique in [25], namely, the execution cycle, is not addressed in our model. Due to lack of space, we refer to [12,20,25] for more details on, respectively, SMC, Subset-098 and EN 50159.

3   The Model

We now discuss the model of the case study. Due to lack of space, some aspects will not be detailed. The model is defined through template automata. Each template automaton may have a set of parameters and local declarations of constants, variables, user functions and clocks. Global declarations are instead accessible from all the templates and can include clocks, constants, variables, functions and channels. The templates are parameterised with an identifier id to identify which device each template belongs to, i.e. the Initiator or the Responder device. The system is defined as a network of processes that interact with each other in parallel; a process is instantiated from a template where all its parameters, if any, are set. The synchronizations between different processes of the system are obtained through broadcast channels, which are required to perform statistical model checking. All the safety service primitives specified in the requirements are modelled as arrays of channels where the indexing allows to identify the synchronized process. Since UPPAAL channel synchronization does not support value passing, this is encoded with the use of global shared variables. State invariants are used to ensure that the communications through shared variables used for the value-passing are atomic. This implies that signals are always received and never lost, overcoming the undetected loss of messages.

The system is composed of two communicating devices, an Initiator device that sends the request to establish a connection and a Responder device that receives the connection request. When referring to the partner device, we consider the Responder device as the partner of the Initiator device, and vice versa. In Fig. 1, the overall architecture of the system is shown. Only one component (i.e. the initiator or the responder) is displayed whilst the other is specular. Each device is modelled using three modules: the SAI User, the SAI and the Euroradio SL modules. The SAI User and SAI modules are adjacent and can communicate with each other. The same applies also to the SAI and Euroradio SL modules. Both the Initiator and the Responder devices are composed of all these three modules. Finally, the Euroradio SL modules of both devices can receive failure notifications from the Communication System module, a component of the system that abstracts both the Euroradio SL lower layers and the physical transmission system. In particular, this component models the occurrence of a disruptive connection release communicated to both the Initiator and the Responder devices, as specified in the requirements.

The communications between adjacent modules of the same device are modelled using channels synchronizations. Instead, the two partner devices interact asynchronously using two queues of messages. Their interactions are affected by stochastic delays, simulating the transmission delays that characterize the radio communications. UPPAAL does not natively support asynchronous communication through queues, which are implemented in the model using arrays. Probabilistic failures are used to simulate communication errors and are implemented by functions modifying data in the arrays (e.g., removing, swapping elements). These injected faults are not to be confused with the low-level channels synchronizations that are guaranteed by invariants to be received.

While both the SAI User module and the Euroradio module functionalities are implemented through single templates, the SAI module is split into multiple sub-modules to reduce the complexity of each of them. Indeed, the responsibilities of both the SAI User and the Euroradio modules were abstracted away

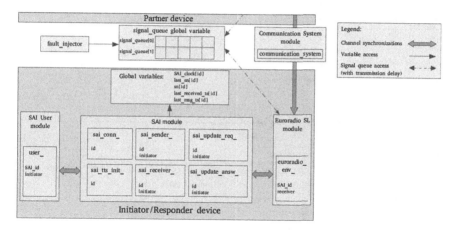

Fig. 1. The model architecture, the partner device is specular to the one displayed

and only the interface with the SAI is implemented. They are the external entities interacting with the SAI module target of our model, whose functionalities are instead completely modelled. The SAI module is divided into different submodules. The TTS technique is implemented in the TTS initialisation and the TTS update procedure modules. The following list shows the templates that make up a single device:

The SAI_User template abstracts the SAI User module behaviour, implementing the triggering of a connection and periodically sending Application messages. It is instantiated specifying the `SAI_id` parameter and the `initiator` parameter;

The Euroradio_SL_Env template abstracts the Euroradio SL module behaviour implementing the stochastically delayed message exchange with the partner device. It is instantiated by specifying the `id` parameter and the `receiver` parameter;

The SAI_Conn_Ini/SAI_Conn_Res templates model the connection establishment according to the role of the device. The templates are instantiated specifying the `id` parameter corresponding to the device they belong to;

The SAI_TTS_Init_Ini/SAI_TTS_Init_Res templates model the TTS initialisation, depending on the role of the device. They exchange messages to estimate the minimum and maximum offset delay of messages. Their parameter is the same as SAI_Conn_Ini/SAI_Conn_Res;

The SAI_Update_Req templates implement the offset estimations update requests, to update the minimum and maximum offset delay. Its parameters are the same as the SAI_Sender template;

The SAI_Update_Answ template models the TTS update procedure by sending the offset estimations update answers to SAI_Update_Req. Its parameters are the same as the SAI_Sender template;

The SAI_Sender template models the SAI defence techniques, by inserting into each message the three timestamps of TTS and the sequence number,

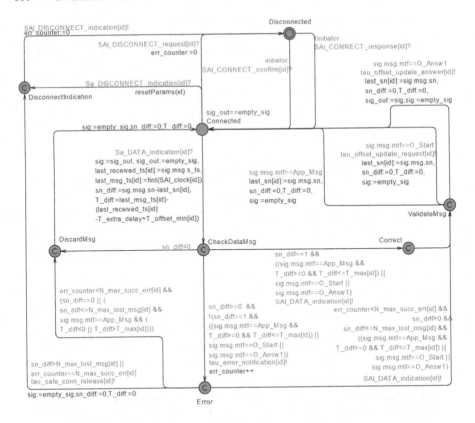

Fig. 2. The SAI_Receiver template

implementing the message sending procedure. It is instantiated with the `id` and the `initiator` parameters identifying its device and role;

The SAI_Receiver templates implement the check procedure for all the incoming messages. It has the same parameters as the SAI_Sender.

We discuss in details the template implementing the check of messages for the protections and the fault injection implementing the various CENELEC threats.

SAI_Receiver. The SAI_Receiver template implements the protection against the repetition, deletion, resequencing and delay threats that can occur in a transmission system, commanding itself the connection release if certain unsafe conditions are met, and it is shown in Fig. 2. It performs functionalities related to the protection against delay, by checking the timestamps of messages. In state `Connected`, if a data message from the partner device is received (i.e. `Sa_DATA_indication[id]?`), the `last_received_ts` and `last_msg_ts` variables are updated. Then, the sequence number difference (referred to as `sn_diff`) between the sequence number received in the message and the last sequence number stored in the `last_sn` variable is computed. Also the freshness of the

received message (referred to as T_diff) is computed as the difference between
the timestamp at the message reception (the last_msg_ts value just updated)
and the estimation of the message time transmission in term of the SAI_Receiver
clock, i.e. the sum of the last received timestamp (the last_received_ts value
just updated) and the minimum offset estimation computed by the Receiver
device during the TTS initialization, with the extra delay subtracted. The
sn_diff computed values determine the SAI_Receiver behaviour according to
the three outgoing transitions from state CheckDataMsg. If sn_diff==1 and 0
$\leq$ T_diff $\leq$ T_max for an Application Message (i.e. a message to the SAI User),
the received data message is not affected by sequencing errors and the transmission delay is acceptable. Assuming that also the conditions for no delay errors
occur, the SAI_Receiver notifies its adjacent SAI_User of the correct message
reception through the SAI_DATA_indication, moves first to the Correct location and then to the ValidateMsg location. Here, according to the message
type field of the received message, the SAI_Receiver can forward a signal to the
SAI_Update_Answ or the SAI_Update_Req templates respectively when concerning offset update request or offset update answer messages. Otherwise, in case
of an Application message, the Connected location is entered without further
actions. If sn_diff < 0, the message is discarded (location DiscardMsg) without notifying the SAI_User. If sn_diff $\geq$ 0 and the previous conditions are not
verified (i.e. sn_diff $\neq$ 1 or the transmission delay is not acceptable, i.e. either
T_diff < 0 or T_diff > T_max), the SAI_Receiver notifies the SAI_User, updates
its error counter and then enters the Error location. Here, if the maximum number of either successive errors N_max_succ_err or lost messages N_max_lost_msg
is reached, the SAI_Receiver immediately sends a safe connection release (i.e.
tau_safe_conn_release) to the SAI_Sender, which in turn sends a discon-
nect request to the peer entity, and from location DisconnectIndication a
SAI_DISCONNECT_indication is sent to the SAI_User to command the release
of the connection. Instead, if the maximum number of successive errors is not
reached and the received message is a repetition of the last accepted message
(i.e. sn_diff==0), or its transmission delay is not acceptable, the message is
discarded. Anyway, the message can be validated if both its transmission delay
and the number of lost messages are acceptable (i.e. 0 $\leq$ T_diff $\leq$ T_max and
1 < sn_diff $\leq$ N_max_lost_msg).

Moreover, from state Connected the SAI_Receiver synchronizes with the
Sa_DISCONNECT_indication signal from the Euroradio_SL_Env. When a discon-
nect indication is received, the SAI_Receiver forwards the communication to
the SAI_User before entering the Disconnected location and also all the other
SAI templates of the same device that by synchronizing through the channel
SAI_DISCONNECT_indication move to the Disconnected locations.

Fault_Injector. The Fault_Injector template shown in Fig. 3 models all the possible threats that can affect the communication system. This template acts as a
fault injector in the signal queue of the two communicating devices, determining the occurrence of communication errors or simulating transmission problems
that could lead to unacceptable delays. This could also be considered as a model

of an external attacker artificially injecting failures [12]. This template provides a minimum waiting time to model the probability of occurrence. Two probabilistic branches decide whether the attempt to perform a fault injection is successful or not. By fine-tuning the `fault` and `noFault` weights associated with the probabilistic branches, the probability of the desired fault occurrence can be adjusted.

Only if the signal queue of the non-deterministically chosen device to perform the fault injection is not empty, all the devices are connected and the attempt is successful, a probabilistic branching decides which threat to perform. The possible threats are: *deletion threat* (the first signal of the queue is removed), *repetition threat* (the first signal is repeated if the queue is not full, otherwise no repetition is performed), *resequencing threat* (the first signal is shifted of one or two positions inside the queue, if at least another signal is present, otherwise no resequencing is performed), and *transmission delay threat* (the `msgDelay` variable of the selected device is updated with the `msgDelayInjected` value).

The transmission delay is based on the update of the `msgDelay` variable,

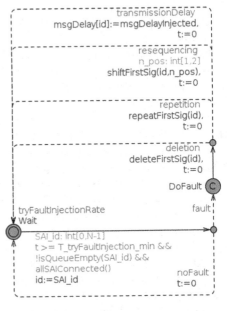

Fig. 3. The Fault_Injector template

which defines the rate for the exponential distribution of the edge performing the signal dequeue. The injected rate is lower than the standard rate assigned to `msgDelay`, and during the sampling of the exact delay, the smaller the rate is specified, the longer the delay is preferred. Hence, with the injected rate it is possible to simulate a longer transmission delay, increasing the probability to exceed the validity time for the incoming messages.

4   The Analysis

In this section we discuss the analysis of the model and the issues found. As required by Subset-039 [26] (ref. 4.2.1.2) only one RBC/RBC communication between a pair of RBCs must be active at one time. Thus, we focus on analysing a single pair of communicating devices. The specification suggests which parameters values to use with particular systems (for example highly-available systems), whereas the definition of other parameters is left to the specific application settings. Our experiments consider a high probability of fault injection success, and diminishing the rates allows to model longer delays. This allows to observe faults with fewer simulations, thus quickly verifying the defence techniques against such faults. Finally, the configuration of certain parameters is done according to the need for a stable connection where both the probability of the SAI_User to send a disconnection request, the Communication_System to perform a disruptive connection release and the Euroradio_SL_Env to fail are very low. We remark that the purpose of our analysis is not the accurate quantification of measures such as performance or reliability. This would require a realistic, less extreme set-up of parameters with lower fault probabilities and time-expensive verification. We address the qualitative verification of the protection mechanisms. Nonetheless, threats for open systems [12] are also considering attackers artificially injecting faults into the communication system.

All the verified properties are related to the probability estimation of the occurrence of a specific hazard. If the probability of occurrence of the hazards is close to zero (i.e. $p' = 0$, see Sect. 2) the model satisfies its safety requirements with a certain degree of confidence $(1 - \alpha)$ dictated by the parameters of the statistical model checker (probability of false negatives $\alpha = 0.0005$ and probability uncertainty $\epsilon = 0.005$). We recall that all evaluated formulae are of the form:

$$\varphi_i = \text{ Pr[<=bound]}(\text{<>conf\_i}).$$

We set `msg_freq=8` time units (i.e. the period in which SAI_User attempts to send a new Application message) and `bound=1000` (i.e. trace length), thus allowing to perform faster simulations but still inclusive of a non-negligible message exchange. With this formula "template" only the logical conditions are left to be specified thus making easier the formalisation of the properties also for users not expert in temporal logics. In the following we only provide the specific configuration conditions `conf_i` of each formula indexed by i, and for improving readability we use the names of the templates, even though the names of the corresponding instantiations have been used in UPPAAL.

Model Checking. We start by checking some properties that the model should meet and that are not related to the specification. Only for these formulae, we set α and ϵ to 0.05 to have a faster evaluation ($N = 738$, see Sect. 2). Firstly, since the queue of messages is bounded, an excessive message delay could cause the queue to be filled if the size of the queue is not properly set. To ensure that this event does not occur, we measure the probability that there exists a full queue within 1000 time units using `conf_1 = exists(id: id_t) isQueueFull(id))`. The probability is evaluated to be close to zero (based on α and ϵ).

The next formula concerns the connection procedure, and in particular the parameter `T_conn_max` that is the maximum waiting time between two connection requests. The requirements specify that during the TTS initialization procedure, a `T_start_max` maximum waiting time for the incoming offset messages from the Responder device is provided. Thus it is important to issue new connection requests only if the TTS initialization procedure has exceeded its time limit. If this is not the case, a specific location `ConnectionFailure` is entered by the SAI_TTS_Init_Ini. Thus we set `T_conn_max = c*T_start_max` and we experimentally find the threshold value for the constant c beyond which the probability to enter the `ConnectionFailure` location is not close to zero. This is evaluated with the formula `conf_2=SAI_TTS_Init_Ini.ConnectionFailure` performing several experiments at the varying of the constant c. The degradation of the model occurs for c≤3, hence we set c=4. Concerning the possibility of undetected message loss, we recall that we used state invariants to ensure that all synchronous signals are received. Finally, we verify the high probability of fault injection that happens when the Fault Injector template enters the `DoFault` location with the formula `conf_3=Fault_Injector.DoFault`. The evaluation of φ_3 is evaluated with a value close to one, thus meaning that at least one fault is always injected in each simulation of the system.

Verifying Safety. We now discuss the verification of the safety properties related to the effectiveness of the defence techniques described in the specification and implemented in our model. The hazards are modelled as "bad" configurations (expressed by `conf`) of the system and have been identified by a manual review of the model based on the requirements. We followed a schematic methodology where first the probability of occurrence for a particular threat, among those specified in the requirements, is evaluated. Then we evaluate the probability that the system does not behave as expected when that particular threat occurs. This second probability evaluation makes sense only if the first probability evaluation is non-negligible (i.e. $p' > 0.1$), thus meaning that the system is actually verified when the threat has a non-negligible probability to occur. Note that identifying the severity of each hazard is out of scope.

The first two analysed hazards concern the probability of either receiving a correct message that is considered erroneous or treating a message affected by some communication errors as a correct message. The φ_4 formula checks if the SAI_Receiver of both the Initiator and the Responder devices receives a correct message, i.e. the configuration where the sequence number difference with the previous message is 1 (`sn_diff==1`) and its delay is acceptable (`T_diff` $\geq$ 0 && `T_diff` $\leq$ `T_max`), and the system treats it as an error, i.e. the SAI_Receiver template enters the `Error` the `DiscardMsg` location. Formula φ_5 checks if the SAI_Receiver of both the Initiator and the Responder devices receives an erroneous Application Message, i.e. the sequence number difference with the previous message is not 1 (`sn_diff!=1`) or its delay is unacceptable (`T_diff` < 0 || `T_diff` > `T_max`), and the system considers it as a correct message, i.e. the SAI_Receiver enters the `Correct` location. Note that this location is necessary to distinguish the correct messages from the messages that are validated despite the sequence number difference with the previously accepted message is different from 1. Both φ_4 and φ_5 are evaluated with a value close to zero.

Concerning the threats that can occur in a communication system, we measure the probability of occurrence of six possible hazards caused by the CENELEC threats (formulae/subformulae with even id numbers), and we measure the probability of the corresponding protection to fail (with odd id numbers). Due to lack of space, we do not fully report the formulae. All the formulae are predicating over locations and variables of the SAI_Receiver (see Fig. 2). All threats probabilities were evaluated with a non-negligible probability of occurrence, confirming the fault injection. The corresponding probabilities of protection failure were all evaluated with values close to zero. Concerning the resequencing threat we found two hazards. Condition conf_6 checks if a message earlier than the last accepted one is received (sn_diff < 0); and conf_7 checks if under this condition the SAI_Receiver does not discard this message (does not visit the location DiscardMsg). Another condition conf_8 checks if a message with the same sequence number of the last accepted one is received, and conf_9 checks if it is validated (location ValidateMsg). For the resequencing threat we found one hazard, and another one is obtained by combination with the delay threat. Condition conf_10 (resp. conf_12) is satisfied if a message arrives with both an acceptable (resp. unacceptable) delay and with a sequence number difference between 2 and N_max_lost_msg. Condition conf_11 checks if under conf_10 the message is discarded or accepted (resp. locations DiscardMsg or Correct), whilst condition conf_13 checks if under conf_12 the error location is not entered by the SAI_Receiver. Note that for entering such location, it is required that both the delay is unacceptable and sn_diff is positive (see Fig. 2), thus the necessity of mixing the two threats. For the deletion threat condition conf_14 checks if a message with a sequence number difference greater than N_max_lost_msg is received, and conf_15 checks if it is discarded or validated. In this case it was also required the possibility of tolerating one communication error. Finally, for the delay threat we have one hazard: condition conf_16 checks if a message with a correct sequence number (sn_diff=1) but with an unacceptable delay is received, and conf_17 checks if it is valid (location ValidateMsg).

We verified three additional safety properties for further validation of the model. Condition cond_18 is used for ensuring that the TTS initialization is completed before receiving any application message. Condition cond_19 verifies that only correct messages are forwarded from the SAI to the user, and condition cond_20 verifies if the SAI module correctly commands the release of the connection when reaching the maximum number of successive errors during the message exchange with the partner device. These last three formulae are evaluated in scenarios where the system can reach unsafe configurations due to the fault injection of communication errors, and are all satisfied. The results presented so far meet our expectations, augmenting our confidence that both the model and the adopted defence techniques are correct.

Issues Detected. We report the most relevant issues discovered with the analysis, which have been confirmed by our industrial partners in the 4SECURail project. Whilst some issues were already known and are due to negotiations among the UNISIG members for compatibility with their legacy solutions, others are new and will possibly lead to request for changes of the Subset-098.

Zero-Crossing. The first problem we met concerns the implementation of both the sequence number defence and TTS technique. Indeed, in the Subset-098 specification, for both protection techniques (sequence number and TTS) it is not specified how to behave in the presence of zero-crossing (i.e., overflow of the assigned bytes), and the specification only considers the case without overflow. We only detail the sequence number problem in the following. Through the formula φ_{21}, we verify if the above unsafe scenario is reachable for the SN_max parameter (bound of the sequence number) set to a lower value, e.g. 100.

Condition conf_21 checks if the SAI_Receiver enters either the Error location or the DiscardMsg location when receiving an incoming message (sig !=empty_sig) with sequence number 0 (sig.msg.sn==0) and its last accepted message had sequence number last_sn[id]==SN_max. This formula refers to the scenario in which the Sender device performs the zero-crossing of the sequence number. Even if the message stream is correct, the Receiver device behaves as if a communication error occurred, an undesired scenario. The formula is evaluated (where both the probability of false negatives α and the probability uncertainty ϵ are set to 0.05) with $p' = 0.847987$. An example of mitigation of this sequence number zero-crossing problem is to force the release of the safe connection from the SAI module when the maximum value for the sequence number is reached. We refer to domain experts for more efficient solutions to this problem. Note that without bounding the maximum number of consecutive lost messages, when approaching the zero-crossing it is not possible to distinguish between the reception of an earlier message or the loss of consecutive messages. The Subset-098 leaves this aspect of the protection open, which could potentially lead to unsafe scenarios in case of communication errors.

TTS Initialisation. We identified an undefined scenario of the system that could lead to possible unsafe configurations if no specific actions are implemented. Briefly, if during the TTS initialisation a specific notification message (i.e. OffsetStart) sent to the Responder device is lost, the Responder is stuck until a new connection request arrives from the Initiator. In the Subset-098, there is no mention of this scenario: it is not included in the SAI initial procedures at the error handling section (ref. 5.4.10.1.3 [25]) as no TTS initialization for the Responder is started yet. Moreover, no communication with the SAI User can be assumed, as the interactions between the SAI and the SAI User modules of the Responder device start after the successful TTS initialization. In our model, in this scenario the failed connection procedure is interrupted to restart a new one from the beginning. Obviously, this implies that the Initiator must send again a connection request. Another possible solution would be for the Responder to answer again to the connection request.

TTS Offset Update. Another undefined aspect concerns the type fields of the offset update messages. It is only mentioned in ref. 5.4.8.7.3 and Figure 21 of [25] that two messages are exchanged. Since the two communicating devices can both start the update procedure and the two distinct update procedures can overlap, it could be the case that one device, after sending a request for offset update, cannot discern whether the received message is an answer to the previous request or a new request of the same type. In our model, we re-used the TTS initialization message type fields to distinguish the two types of update messages, and in particular the OffsetStart for the update request message and the OffsetAnsw1 for the update answer message. These implementation choices were made necessary to model a working offset update procedure despite the lack of details in the specification. The fact that different suppliers could implement these aspects independently could compromise the interoperability of their RBCs. Moreover, the Subset-098 [25] does not specify the actions to perform in case the timestamps of the offset update answer and request messages (used for relating them) do not correspond, a condition necessary to update the offset estimation. We identified two possible behaviours for the SAI module in this case: either it reissues a new request without waiting, or it can wait for the right answer, and reissues a new request only at the expiration of the timer. We opted for the second case. Indeed, the first case could cause a loop where the answering device keeps sending answer messages but they arrive when another request has already been sent, so the timestamps would not correspond again. The subset leaves both implementations possible, whilst only the second case should be allowed for avoiding unnecessary disconnections with errors.

Error Tolerance. Finally, we discuss the configuration choice of the maximum number of successive errors (N_max_succ_err) parameter, which [25] specified to have values either 1 or 2 (thus allowing a maximum tolerance of one error). By analysing the model, we noted that a transmission delay causes a rejection of the message, thus incrementing the error counter and triggering a subsequent sequence number error due to the discarding of the previous message. This means that the ability of the system to tolerate the occurrence of one communication error is tied to the type of the error being detected: if the error is a transmission delay, then the system is no longer able to accept the next incoming message as correct, even if the tolerance is set to do so.

The formal verification step helped in identifying the problems reported in this section, thus resulting very useful. It has been used to check the correctness of the model by debugging modelling errors during its development, as well as to formally validate the requirements of the system defined in the specification and discovering corner cases where both protections are ineffective.

Quantifying the Learning and Development Efforts. We provide a rough but indicative estimation of the costs for training and development. We considered the effort in terms of CFU (Crediti Formativi Universitari, corresponding to ECTS − European Credit Transfer and Accumulation System − credits) sustained by the third author for developing her Master thesis (containing the presented results) under the supervision of the first two authors. The training in formal methods has been provided during the *Software Dependability* university course in Florence University, provided by the second author, where the basis for the modelling aspects and the logic required to understand the model checking algorithm have been studied, which are almost 7 CFU [15].

Concerning the work presented in this paper, it can be quantified in the 24 CFU of the Master thesis. There is no clear division between the modelling and the verification phases because since the beginning of the modelling phase, a constant activity of verification of the model was made. Indeed, useful counterexamples from the verification allowed to debug modelling errors in the first model prototypes. Considering that each CFU conventionally corresponds to 25 working hours, we can estimate an effort of 775 working hours to reach the result we described in this paper, starting from no knowledge of formal methods, which we report to adhere to the actual effort. Thus, an indicative division of the working hours required for each activity is: *Learning* - 169 h, *Modelling and Verification* - 606 h. These data can be validated by consulting the online regulations of the Degree Course [27] and the Master thesis [23]. Finally, assuming a fresh and already trained graduate as the third author, a fitting payment (in Italy) could be a professionalising grant (*assegno professionalizzante* [10]). In this specific case, she/he would have an annual gross cost of 21343 euro (as per the time of writing this paper), with a cost per hour of 15.56 euro, which roughly gives us a gross cost of 9400 euro for producing both the artifacts and the analysis described in this paper.

5   Conclusion

We have formalised and analysed an existing industrial specification already in operation: the UNISIG Subset-098 [25], and in particular the Safety Application Intermediate sub-layer, whose goal is to protect the system from the CENELEC 50159 [12] threats of open transmission systems. The analysis has discovered corner cases where the protections are not effective, due to unspecified scenarios or ambiguous requirements. We discussed simple mitigations to such issues, not detailed in the specification. Since different interpretations of these undefined aspects could be given as well by different suppliers (especially for newcomers, rather than the original members of the consortium that issued these subsets), this could lead to non-interoperability between RBCs developed and provided by different suppliers. This appears to be the current situation for this standard interface, as reported in [21], where interoperability issues during the handover procedure were encountered in the Milano-Bologna line containing three RBCs produced by different suppliers (Alstom and Ansaldo) using the same requirements analysed in this paper. Finally, considering that formal methods are still a subject of study in the field of railway industrial applications [14,18], as witnessed by several Shift2Rail projects, this paper represents a further contribution to evaluate the usefulness in terms of costs of learning and development, as well as benefits deriving from the adoption of formal methods in this domain. The model and analysis for the various scenarios are publicly available in [22].

We argue that the benefits derived from the work described in this paper are not only limited to the identified safety and interoperability issues. Indeed, the provided formal model and the safety properties analysed can enrich the existing documentation. By simply tuning the parameters to realistic, less extreme values it is possible to have evaluations of other dependability aspects of the system such as performance, reliability. The presented model could also be the starting point for other model-based development approaches, e.g., by translating the SAI models into state machines (e.g., RT-UML) for code generation or model-based testing. A subset of the authors already provided a translation from RT-UML machines to UPPAAL models in [2]. As future work it could also be of interest to enrich the model with full formalisation of the other layers as well as the execution cycle protection technique.

Acknowledgements. This work has been partially funded by the H2020 Shift2Rail 4SECURail project, grant agreement No 881775 in the context of the open call S2R-OC-IP2-01-2019, programme H2020-S2RJU-2019.

References

1. Agha, G., Palmskog, K.: A survey of statistical model checking. ACM Trans. Model. Comput. Simul. **28**(1), 6:1–6:39 (2018). https://doi.org/10.1145/3158668
2. Basile, D., ter Beek, M.H., Ciancia, V.: Statistical model checking of a moving block railway signalling scenario with UPPAAL SMC. In: Margaria, T., Steffen, B. (eds.) ISoLA 2018. LNCS, vol. 11245, pp. 372–391. Springer, Cham (2018). https://doi.org/10.1007/978-3-030-03421-4_24
3. Basile, D., Fantechi, A., Rucher, L., Mandò, G.: Statistical model checking of hazards in an autonomous tramway positioning system. In: Collart-Dutilleul, S., Lecomte, T., Romanovsky, A. (eds.) RSSRail 2019. LNCS, vol. 11495, pp. 41–58. Springer, Cham (2019). https://doi.org/10.1007/978-3-030-18744-6_3
4. Basile, D., et al.: Designing a demonstrator of formal methods for railways infrastructure managers. In: Margaria, T., Steffen, B. (eds.) ISoLA 2020. LNCS, vol. 12478, pp. 467–485. Springer, Cham (2020). https://doi.org/10.1007/978-3-030-61467-6_30
5. Basile, D., ter Beek, M.H., Ferrari, A., Legay, A.: Modelling and analysing ERTMS L3 moving block railway signalling with simulink and UPPAAL SMC. In: Larsen, K.G., Willemse, T. (eds.) FMICS 2019. LNCS, vol. 11687, pp. 1–21. Springer, Cham (2019). https://doi.org/10.1007/978-3-030-27008-7_1
6. Basile, D., ter Beek, M.H., Legay, A.: Strategy synthesis for autonomous driving in a moving block railway system with UPPAAL STRATEGO. In: Gotsman, A., Sokolova, A. (eds.) FORTE 2020. LNCS, vol. 12136, pp. 3–21. Springer, Cham (2020). https://doi.org/10.1007/978-3-030-50086-3_1
7. Behrmann, G., et al.: UPPAAL 4.0. In: Proceedings of the 3rd International Conference on the Quantitative Evaluation of SysTems (QEST 2006), pp. 125–126. IEEE (2006). https://doi.org/10.1109/QEST.2006.59
8. Bulychev, P., David, A., Larsen, K.G., Legay, A., Li, G., Poulsen, D.B.: Rewrite-based statistical model checking of WMTL. In: Qadeer, S., Tasiran, S. (eds.) RV 2012. LNCS, vol. 7687, pp. 260–275. Springer, Heidelberg (2013). https://doi.org/10.1007/978-3-642-35632-2_25
9. Chai, M., Wang, H., Tang, T., Liu, H.: Runtime verification of train control systems with parameterized modal live sequence charts. J. Syst. Softw. **177**, 110962 (2021). https://doi.org/10.1016/j.jss.2021.110962
10. CNR: Assegni di ricerca. https://www.urp.cnr.it/page.php?level=15&pg=1522
11. David, A., Larsen, K.G., Legay, A., Mikučionis, M., Poulsen, D.B.: UPPAAL SMC tutorial. Int. J. Softw. Tools Technol. Transf. **17**(4), 397–415 (2015). https://doi.org/10.1007/s10009-014-0361-y
12. European Committee for Electrotechnical Standardization: CENELEC EN 50159 - Railway applications - Communication, signalling and processing systems - Safety-related communication in transmission systems (2010). https://standards.globalspec.com/std/14256321/EN50159
13. European Committee for Electrotechnical Standardization: CENELEC EN 50128 - Railway applications - Communication, signalling and processing systems - Software for railway control and protection systems (2020). https://standards.globalspec.com/std/14317747/EN2050128

14. Fantechi, A.: Twenty-five years of formal methods and railways: what next? In: Counsell, S., Núñez, M. (eds.) SEFM 2013. LNCS, vol. 8368, pp. 167–183. Springer, Cham (2014). https://doi.org/10.1007/978-3-319-05032-4_13

15. Fantechi, A.: Software Dependability course. University of Florence. https://www.unifi.it/p-ins2-2018-502809-0.html

16. Ferrari, A., Mazzanti, F., Basile, D., ter Beek, M.H., Fantechi, A.: Comparing formal tools for system design: a judgment study. In: Proceedings of the 42nd International Conference on Software Engineering (ICSE), pp. 62–74. ACM (2020). https://doi.org/10.1145/3377811.3380373

17. Ferrari, A., Mazzanti, F., Basile, D., ter Beek, M.H.: Systematic evaluation and usability analysis of formal tools for system design. arXiv:2101.11303 [cs.SE] (2021). https://arxiv.org/abs/2101.11303

18. Garavel, H., Beek, M.H., Pol, J.: The 2020 expert survey on formal methods. In: ter Beek, M.H., Ničković, D. (eds.) FMICS 2020. LNCS, vol. 12327, pp. 3–69. Springer, Cham (2020). https://doi.org/10.1007/978-3-030-58298-2_1

19. Huang, J., Lv, J., Feng, Y., Luo, Z., Liu, H., Chai, M.: A novel method on probability evaluation of ZC handover scenario based on SMC. In: Qian, J., Liu, H., Cao, J., Zhou, D. (eds.) ICRRI, vol. 1335, pp. 319–333. Springer, Singapore (2020). https://doi.org/10.1007/978-981-33-4929-2_22

20. Legay, A., Lukina, A., Traonouez, L.M., Yang, J., Smolka, S.A., Grosu, R.: Statistical model checking. In: Steffen, B., Woeginger, G. (eds.) Computing and Software Science. LNCS, vol. 10000, pp. 478–504. Springer, Cham (2019). https://doi.org/10.1007/978-3-319-91908-9_23

21. Morselli, S.: Il nuovo servizio ferroviario ad Alta Velocità "Frecciarossa": analisi delle performance. Master's thesis, University of Bologna (2009). http://amslaurea.unibo.it/435/

22. Rosadi, I.: Repository for reproducing the experiments (2021). https://github.com/IreneRosadi/UppaalModels

23. Rosadi, I.: Analysing a safe communication protocol in the railway signaling domain with Timed Automata and Statistical Model Checking. Master's thesis, University of Florence (2021)

24. Shift2Rail: Annual Work Plan and Budget (2021). https://shift2rail.org/about-shift2rail/reference-documents/annual-work-plan-and-budget/

25. UNISIG: RBC-RBC safe communication interface, Subset-098, v3.0.0 (2012). https://www.era.europa.eu/sites/default/files/filesystem/ertms/ccs_tsi_annex_a_-_mandatory_specifications/set_of_specifications_3_etcs_b3_r2_gsm-r_b1/index063_-_subset-098_v300.pdf

26. UNISIG: FIS for the RBC/RBC handover, Subset-039, v3.2.0 (2015). https://www.era.europa.eu/sites/default/files/filesystem/ertms/ccs_tsi_annex_a_-_mandatory_specifications/set_of_specifications_3_etcs_b3_r2_gsm-r_b1/index012_-_subset-039_v320.pdf

27. University of Florence: Regulations of the M.Sc. degree. https://www.informaticamagistrale.unifi.it/vp-165-regulations.html

Tools

PROB2-UI: A Java-Based User Interface for ProB

Jens Bendisposto$^{(\boxtimes)}$ ⓘ, David Geleßus$^{(\boxtimes)}$, Yumiko Jansing,
Michael Leuschel$^{(\boxtimes)}$ ⓘ, Antonia Pütz, Fabian Vu$^{(\boxtimes)}$ ⓘ, and Michelle Werth

Institut für Informatik, Universität Düsseldorf, Universitätsstr. 1,
40225 Düsseldorf, Germany
{bendisposto,dagel101,leuschel,fabian.vu}@hhu.de

Abstract. PROB2-UI is a modern JavaFX-based user interface for the animator, constraint solver, and model checker PROB. We present the main features of the tool, especially compared to PROB's previous user interfaces and other available tools for B, Event-B, and other formalisms. We also present some of PROB2-UI's history as well as its uses in the industry since its release in 2019.

1 Introduction and Motivation

This paper presents PROB2-UI, a JavaFX-based user interface for the animator, constraint solver, and model checker PROB. The core of PROB is written in SIC-Stus Prolog and supports formalisms such as B, Event-B, Z, TLA$^+$ and Alloy. Initially, PROB had a Tcl/Tk interface, first presented in 2003 [28], but with roots dating back to around 2000. Later the command-line interface PROBCLI was developed, which is still being heavily used for testing, data validation, and batch verification. For example, PROBCLI is used for data validation of railway systems, see [7,27] or Sect. 4 of [3].

Around 2005 we started to integrate PROB into the Rodin tool for Event-B, requiring integration with Java and the Eclipse user interface. For this purpose, an interface was added to PROBCLI, allowing Java code to control PROB by sending commands over a socket. This resulted in the first version of PROB for Rodin. Its user interface was more intuitive, appealing and modern than PROB for Tcl/Tk, but did only provide a limited set of features (e.g., it had no state space visualisation or projection features).

At that moment we had to decide whether to fully focus on Rodin and Eclipse, or keep PROB and its user interface independent of it. In the end, we decided to develop a new lightweight Java API allowing end-users to customize PROB independent of Eclipse. This resulted in the development of the PROB2 Java API, which was available in 2014 (cf. Sect. 2 of [20]). After several unfruitful attempts at developing a new user interface, we started to work on a JavaFX user interface in 2016. The first stable version 1.0.0 was released in 2019. PROB2-UI has been used within our team for a variety of case studies, e.g., for an automotive case study [29]. It has also already been used for several industrial applications

© Springer Nature Switzerland AG 2021
A. Lluch Lafuente and A. Mavridou (Eds.): FMICS 2021, LNCS 12863, pp. 193–201, 2021.
https://doi.org/10.1007/978-3-030-85248-1_12

(many confidential). In particular, PROB2-UI was used successfully during the demonstration of the ETCS hybrid level 3 concepts [13,14] at runtime. Here, model traces were captured during field tests and could be replayed along with a visualisation plugin for fine-grained retrospective analysis. Another use was made for modelling key properties of a CBTC zone controller in [6].

2   Features of PROB2-UI

Figure 1 shows the main window of PROB2-UI. On the right-hand side, you can see the *project view*. A project contains a group of (related) models along with preference settings and configurations for validation and verification tasks. This lets the user easily re-check these tasks, e.g., after modifying a model, without having to re-enter the parameters. The project information is stored in a project file; it contains a list of models and tasks with their status, a list of preference settings along with visualisation, simulation, and trace files. An overview of the status of all verification tasks is shown in the "status" tab of the project view.

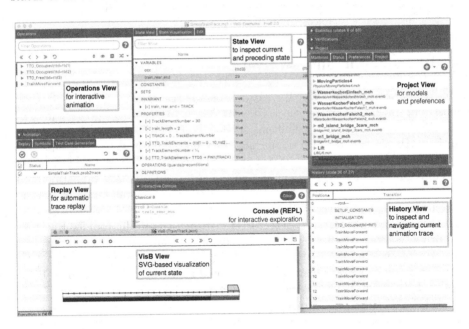

Fig. 1. Main window of PROB2-UI

Animation. After a model has been loaded, the user can animate the model. In contrast to simulation, an animator allows the user to interactively select the execution steps. This is done in the *operations view*, where PROB has precomputed all enabled operations (up to a user-provided limit). By clicking on an operation, the current state of the model is changed, which can be seen in the state view. It is also possible to enter some of the operation's parameters and an optional post-condition to execute an operation. This is for example useful when not all operations were precomputed by PROB.

The *state view* displays the current and previous state of the model, highlighting differences. In addition to variables and constants, the view also shows predicates such as the properties (aka axioms), invariants, or the guards of operations. Complex expressions and predicates can be expanded to inspect the values of individual sub-expressions/predicates.

During the interaction with the model, a trace of all executed operations and visited states is maintained. One can navigate through this trace in the *history view*, e.g., to return to a previous state and then execute an alternate operation. The history can be saved to a file. The saved trace files are shown in the *replay view* on the left-hand side, where they can be replayed by a simple click. These trace files contain the exact parameter and variable values for each animation step, which allows replaying the trace exactly even if some operations are not deterministic.

Visualisation. PROB2-UI provides various ways to *visualise* the currently animated model. For example, it is possible to visualise the state space, the machine hierarchy, event hierarchy, formula trees etc. Figure 2 shows a state space projection [25] of the model from [29] on the right-hand side.

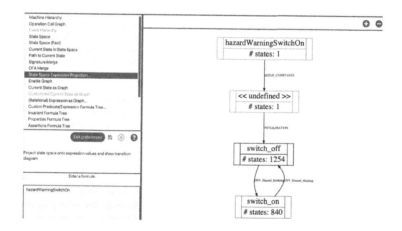

Fig. 2. Graph visualisation window of PROB2-UI with projected state space

The visualisation tool VISB [39] can be used to create interactive visualisations using SVG images and a glue file. It was previously a PROB2-UI plugin, but is now available in the regular *VisB view*, as shown at the bottom of Fig. 1. In the view, the user can see a visual rendering of the current state and execute operations by clicking on visual elements (as stipulated in the glue file). A very recent feature is the export of an animation trace as a stand-alone HTML file containing the visualisations. This HTML file can, e.g., be sent via email to domain experts and they can inspect the trace with its states in a regular browser, without any need for PROB2-UI.

Using PROB2-UI's plugin support, custom visualisations can be implemented using Java and JavaFX. Developing such a visualisation requires more effort and knowledge than VISB, but offers greater flexibility via arbitrary GUI elements and code. Such a visualisation plugin was developed as part of a demonstration of the ETCS Hybrid Level 3 concept [13,14], and was instrumental in domain experts understanding the model and discovering issues. More figures and screenshots of PROB2-UI can be seen in [13,14] (Fig. 3).

Figure 3 of [6] shows another PROB2-UI visualisation plugin for an Alstom CBTC system. The plugin mechanism was also used to provide custom views for a domain-specific extension of B for data validation [15].

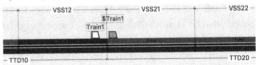

Fig. 3. Figure 3 from [13] with physical train and train image

Verification. As explained before, a modeller can save verification tasks for each model, which is particularly useful during development. It is possible to re-check all verification tasks on an updated model.

PROB2-UI supports various model checking techniques, including exhaustive model checking [28], LTL model checking [32], and symbolic model checking [22] (Fig. 4).

Regarding explicit-state model checking, one can choose different search strategies, e.g., breadth-first, depth-first, and mixed. Furthermore, one can define the properties to be checked in each state. These include the invariant, deadlock-freedom, assertions, well-definedness, and precondi-

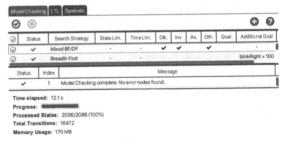

Fig. 4. Model checking view

tions. It is also possible to provide a goal predicate to specify desired states, or limit the number of states explored or the time spent. In the case that an error or a goal is found, the counterexample is shown in the history view of the animator.

LTL model checking can be used to verify temporal properties of a model. Here, the user can define LTL formulas combining state predicates with the standard LTL operators. In addition, operators of Past-

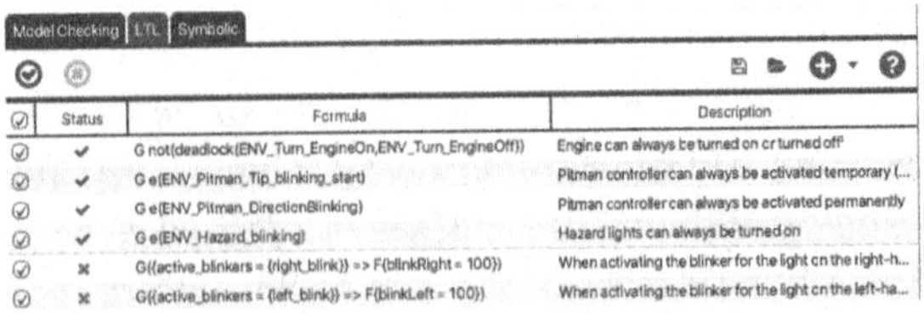

Fig. 5. LTL model checking view

LTL are available, as well as operators for fairness, deadlock, determinacy, and enabledness of operations. Finally, it is possible to declare LTL patterns, which can be reused in multiple formulas. Similar to explicit-state model checking, counterexamples are also stored and can be displayed in the history view.

Simulation. Recently, PROB2-UI has been extended by a simulator called SIMB [38]. It is based on lightweight annotation files that specify how events activate each other along with timing, priorities, and probabilistic annotations as well as possible start and end conditions. The user can then perform simulations, where the model is simulated live in real-time. In combination with the other views, in particular the VISB view, one can see how the model's state changes in real-time. It is also possible to perform Monte Carlo simulations in accelerated time. Based on the simulations, statistical techniques such as hypothesis testing and estimation can then be applied to validate probabilistic and timing properties. Every single simulation can be saved as a *timed trace*, or be replayed in real-time afterwards (Fig. 5).

Other Features. In addition to the features presented so far, PROB2-UI also provides an editor to modify the models in the project. Furthermore, there are three consoles: a B console in which formulas in B or Event-B can be evaluated, a Groovy console in which one has access to the objects of the ProB2 API, and a Prolog console to inspect debugging or performance messages of the PROB kernel. In addition to high-level languages such as B, Event-B, Z, TLA+, Alloy or CSP, PROB also supports XTL files, which contain a raw Prolog encoding of the transition system to be checked. Here, the modeller has to implement the interface to PROB consisting of the predicates `start/1` (calculating the initial states), `trans/3` (calculating transitions and resulting states outgoing from every state), and `prop/2` (calculating the properties of every state). We have used it for teaching, e.g., by encoding the rules of chess in Prolog and illustrate game-playing algorithms. It is also possible to provide a Prolog interpreter for another specification language and extend PROB and PROB2-UI in this way. For example, we have such interpreters for Promela [40], SMV, and Lustre [37] models.

3   Related Work

In this section, we compare PROB2-UI with other formal methods tools that come with a graphical user interface. The reader may also consult various recent studies [8–10, 35] about tools and also their usability.

Atelier-B [5] and Rodin [1] have a strong focus on the refinement-based software development process of the B method. They both provide a project or workspace concept, with a convenient way for managing and discharging proof obligations. As mentioned, PROB can also be run within [1], but with a much-reduced feature set compared to PROB2-UI. It is also possible to start PROB2-UI from [1] for a given model. From Atelier-B it is also possible to start ProB Tcl/Tk for a model, or use PROB as an alternate prover. At the moment, PROB2-UI is complementary to Atelier-B and Rodin: PROB2-UI focuses on validation and model checking, Atelier-B and Rodin on proof and proof obligations.[1] Other animation tools for B, such as Brama [34], AnimB [30] or JeB [41] provide convenient visualisation features, but lack many of the features of PROB2-UI.

The TLA Toolbox is an IDE for the modelling language TLA+ which is widely used for distributed systems. Both the TLC model checker [42] and the TLA+ proof system are integrated into the TLA Toolbox [23]. In practice, most users will use the TLC features, where similar to PROB2-UI, one can save various model checking configurations. Counterexample traces can be inspected and a REPL has been added recently to the toolbox. However, at the moment, there are no interactive animation or visualisation features available. Here, a PROB plugin for the TLA toolbox was implemented to support animation and visualisation [12], but it is now superseded by PROB2-UI which can also open TLA+ files.

Overture [26] is an Eclipse-based IDE for the VDM formal method with a large feature set, particularly as far as simulation is concerned. The Maestro [36] INTO-CPS tool is an evolution targeting cyber-physical systems, containing unique features such as three-dimensional rendering of systems. PVSio-Web [31] for PVS is a tool particularly well-suited for domain-specific visualisations, e.g., for medical user interfaces. Many other formal specification languages and tools come with powerful user interfaces, such as Spin [16] or extensions thereof [33] for Promela, UPPAAL [2] and PRISM [24] for (probabilistic) timed automata, Alcoa [18] for Alloy [17], NuSMV [4] for SMV, or FDR4 [11] for CSP.

4   Conclusion

As presented above, PROB2-UI has some special features not available in its predecessor PROB Tcl/Tk. Still, there are some features of PROB Tcl/Tk that are not yet implemented in PROB2-UI, such as the LTSmin [19] integration [21]. Indeed, we have learned that one should not underestimate the time for a complete rewrite. Catching up with a still-evolving feature set of an existing tool is hard. Furthermore, it was not easy to achieve a performance as good as PROB Tcl/Tk. In initial versions of PROB2-UI, both memory usages and runtimes were considerably higher, and it took a while to identify and correct the bottlenecks. On the one hand, the Tcl interface of SICStus Prolog is relatively limited, only supporting simple values such as atoms and numbers, and lists thereof. This actually forced us to write an efficient UI API design from the start in PROB Tcl/Tk (e.g., not sending formulas back and forth between Tcl and Prolog). On the other hand, the Tcl interface of SICStus Prolog has less latency than the communication via sockets in PROB2. This meant that we had to group requests in PROB2 in order to improve the performance.

Two recent surveys [10,35] have investigated the formal methods tools used in the railway sector and have found the B-Method tools (in particular ATELIERB and PROB) to be the most mature and widely used. We hope that PROB2-UI provides another step forward, in the form of a feature-rich and intuitive user

---

[1] See Sect. 5 of [9]: "Atelier-B and PROB are the right choice for top-down development of mainly monolithic systems, with complementary verification capabilities".

interface, which helps the modeller develop, verify, validate, debug, and understand formal models.

Our tool's homepage with download links and a video presentation is available at: https://prob.hhu.de/w/index.php/ProB2-UI.

Acknowledgements. We want to thank Christoph Heinzen who has elaborated the plugin mechanism in his Master's thesis. Many more persons were involved in the implementation of PROB2-UI, notably Dominik Hansen, Jessica Petrasch, Daniel Plagge, and Sebastian Stock. Thanks also to Olga Iudina for the Russian translations and anonymous referees for their useful corrections and suggestions. PROB2-UI is currently being extended within the DFG funded project IVOIRE.

References

1. Abrial, J.-R., Butler, M., Hallerstede, S., Hoang, T.S., Mehta, F., Voisin, L.: Rodin: an open toolset for modelling and reasoning in Event-B. Int. J. Softw. Tools Technol. Transf. **12**(6), 447–466 (2010)

2. Bengtsson, J., Larsen, K., Larsson, F., Pettersson, P., Yi, W.: UPPAAL — a tool suite for automatic verification of real-time systems. In: Alur, R., Henzinger, T.A., Sontag, E.D. (eds.) HS 1995. LNCS, vol. 1066, pp. 232–243. Springer, Heidelberg (1996). https://doi.org/10.1007/BFb0020949

3. Butler, M., et al.: The first twenty-five years of industrial use of the B-Method. In: ter Beek, M.H., Ničković, D. (eds.) FMICS 2020. LNCS, vol. 12327, pp. 189–209. Springer, Cham (2020). https://doi.org/10.1007/978-3-030-58298-2_8

4. Cimatti, A., et al.: NuSMV 2: an opensource tool for symbolic model checking. In: Brinksma, E., Larsen, K.G. (eds.) CAV 2002. LNCS, vol. 2404, pp. 359–364. Springer, Heidelberg (2002). https://doi.org/10.1007/3-540-45657-0_29

5. ClearSy, A.B.: User and Reference Manuals. Aix-en-Provence, France (2016). http://www.atelierb.eu/

6. Comptier, M., Leuschel, M., Mejia, L.-F., Perez, J.M., Mutz, M.: Property-based modelling and validation of a CBTC zone controller in Event-B. In: Collart-Dutilleul, S., Lecomte, T., Romanovsky, A. (eds.) RSSRail 2019. LNCS, vol. 11495, pp. 202–212. Springer, Cham (2019). https://doi.org/10.1007/978-3-030-18744-6_13

7. Falampin, J., Le-Dang, H., Leuschel, M., Mokrani, M., Plagge, D.: Improving railway data validation with ProB. In: Romanovsky, A., Thomas, M. (eds.) Industrial Deployment of System Engineering Methods, pp. 27–43. Springer, Berlin, Heidelberg (2013). https://doi.org/10.1007/978-3-642-33170-1_4

8. Ferrari, A., Mazzanti, F., Basile, D.: Systematic evaluation and usability analysis of formal tools for system design. CoRR, abs/2101.11303 (2021)

9. Ferrari, A., Mazzanti, F., Basile, D., ter Beek, M.H., Fantechi, A.: Comparing formal tools for system design: a judgment study. In: Rothermel, G., Bae, D. (eds.) ICSE 2020: 42nd International Conference on Software Engineering, Seoul, South Korea, 27 June–19 July, 2020, pp. 62–74. ACM (2020)

10. Ferrari, A., et al.: Survey on formal methods and tools in railways: the ASTRail approach. In: Collart-Dutilleul, S., Lecomte, T., Romanovsky, A. (eds.) RSSRail 2019. LNCS, vol. 11495, pp. 226–241. Springer, Cham (2019). https://doi.org/10.1007/978-3-030-18744-6_15

11. Gibson-Robinson, T., Armstrong, P., Boulgakov, A., Roscoe, A.W.: FDR3 — a modern refinement checker for CSP. In: Ábrahám, E., Havelund, K. (eds.) TACAS 2014. LNCS, vol. 8413, pp. 187–201. Springer, Heidelberg (2014). https://doi.org/10.1007/978-3-642-54862-8_13

12. Hansen, D., Bendisposto, J., Leuschel, M.: Integrating ProB into the TLA Toolbox. In: TLA Workshop (2014)

13. Hansen, D., et al.: Validation and real-life demonstration of ETCS hybrid level 3 principles using a formal B model. Int. J. Softw. Tools Technol. Transf. **22**(3), 315–332 (2020)

14. Hansen, D., et al.: Using a formal B model at runtime in a demonstration of the ETCS hybrid level 3 concept with real trains. Proceedings ABZ **2018**, 292–306 (2018)

15. Hansen, D., Schneider, D., Leuschel, M.: Using B and ProB for data validation projects. In: Butler, M., Schewe, K.-D., Mashkoor, A., Biro, M. (eds.) ABZ 2016. LNCS, vol. 9675, pp. 167–182. Springer, Cham (2016). https://doi.org/10.1007/978-3-319-33600-8_10

16. Holzmann, G.: The SPIN Model Checker: Primer and Reference Manual. Addison-Wesley Professional, 1st edition (2011)

17. Jackson, D.: Alloy: a lightweight object modelling notation. ACM Trans. Softw. Eng. Methodol. **11**, 256–290 (2002)

18. Jackson, D., Schechter, I., Shlyakhter., I.: Alcoa: the alloy constraint analyzer. In: Proceedings of the 2000 International Conference on Software Engineering. ICSE 2000 the New Millennium, pp. 730–733 (2000)

19. Kant, G., Laarman, A., Meijer, J., van de Pol, J., Blom, S., van Dijk, T.: LTSmin: high-performance language-independent model checking. In: Baier, C., Tinelli, C. (eds.) TACAS 2015. LNCS, vol. 9035, pp. 692–707. Springer, Heidelberg (2015). https://doi.org/10.1007/978-3-662-46681-0_61

20. Körner, P., Bendisposto, J., Dunkelau, J., Krings, S., Leuschel, M.: Embedding high-level formal specifications into applications. In: ter Beek, M.H., McIver, A., Oliveira, J.N. (eds.) FM 2019. LNCS, vol. 11800, pp. 519–535. Springer, Cham (2019). https://doi.org/10.1007/978-3-030-30942-8_31

21. Körner, P., Leuschel, M., Meijer, J.: State-of-the-Art model checking for B and Event-B using PROB and LTSMIN. In: Furia, C.A., Winter, K. (eds.) IFM 2018. LNCS, vol. 11023, pp. 275–295. Springer, Cham (2018). https://doi.org/10.1007/978-3-319-98938-9_16

22. Krings, S.: Towards infinite-state symbolic model checking for B and Event-B. Ph.D. thesis, Heinrich Heine Universität Düsseldorf, August 2017

23. Kuppe, M.A., Lamport, L., Ricketts, D.: The TLA$^+$ toolbox. Electron. Proc. Theoret. Comput. Sci. **310**, 50–62 (2019)

24. Kwiatkowska, M., Norman, G., Parker, D.: PRISM: probabilistic symbolic model checker. In: Field, T., Harrison, P.G., Bradley, J., Harder, U. (eds.) TOOLS 2002. LNCS, vol. 2324, pp. 200–204. Springer, Heidelberg (2002). https://doi.org/10.1007/3-540-46029-2_13

25. Ladenberger, L., Leuschel, M.: Mastering the visualization of larger state spaces with projection diagrams. In: Butler, M., Conchon, S., Zaïdi, F. (eds.) ICFEM 2015. LNCS, vol. 9407, pp. 153–169. Springer, Cham (2015). https://doi.org/10.1007/978-3-319-25423-4_10

26. Larsen, P., Battle, N., Ferreira, M., Fitzgerald, J., Lausdahl, K., Verhoef, M.: The overture initiative: integrating tools for VDM. ACM SIGSOFT Softw. Eng. Not. **35**, 1–6 (2010)

27. Lecomte, T., Burdy, L., Leuschel, M. :Formally checking large data sets in the railways. CoRR, abs/1210.6815. Proceedings of DS-Event-B 2012, Kyoto (2012)
28. Leuschel, M., Butler, M.: ProB: a model checker for B. In: Araki, K., Gnesi, S., Mandrioli, D. (eds.) FME 2003. LNCS, vol. 2805. Springer, Heidelberg (2003). https://doi.org/10.1007/b13229
29. Leuschel, M., Mutz, M., Werth, M.: Modelling and validating an automotive system in classical B and Event-B. In: Raschke, A., Méry, D., Houdek, F. (eds.) ABZ 2020. LNCS, vol. 12071, pp. 335–350. Springer, Cham (2020). https://doi.org/10.1007/978-3-030-48077-6_27
30. Métayer, C.: AnimB 0.1.1 (2010). http://wiki.event-b.org/index.php/AnimB
31. Oladimeji, P., Masci, P., Curzon, P., Thimbleby, H.: PVSio-web: a tool for rapid prototyping device user interfaces in PVS. In: Proceedings FMIS, vol. 69 (2013)
32. Plagge, D., Leuschel, M.: Seven at a stroke: LTL model checking for high-level specifications in B, Z, CSP, and more. Int. J. Softw. Tools Technol. Trans. **12**, 9–21 (2007)
33. Ruys, T.C.: Xspin/Project - integrated validation management for Xspin. In: Dams, D., Gerth, R., Leue, S., Massink, M. (eds.) SPIN 1999. LNCS, vol. 1680, pp. 108–119. Springer, Heidelberg (1999). https://doi.org/10.1007/3-540-48234-2_8
34. Servat, T.: BRAMA: a new graphic animation tool for B models. In: Julliand, J., Kouchnarenko, O. (eds.) B 2007. LNCS, vol. 4355, pp. 274–276. Springer, Heidelberg (2006). https://doi.org/10.1007/11955757_28
35. ter Beek, M.H., et al.: adopting formal methods in an industrial setting: the railways case. In: ter Beek, M.H., McIver, A., Oliveira, J.N. (eds.) FM 2019. LNCS, vol. 11800, pp. 762–772. Springer, Cham (2019). https://doi.org/10.1007/978-3-030-30942-8_46
36. Thule, C., Lausdahl, K., Gomes, C., Meisl, G., Larsen, P.G.: Maestro: the INTO-CPS co-simulation framework. Simul. Model. Pract. Theory **92**, 45–61 (2019)
37. Vu, F.: Simulation and verification of reactive systems in Lustre with ProB. Master's thesis, Heinrich Heine Universität Düsseldorf, June 2020
38. Vu, F., Leuschel, M., Mashkoor, A.: Validation of formal models by timed probabilistic simulation. In: Raschke, A., Méry, D. (eds.) ABZ 2021. LNCS, vol. 12709, pp. 81–96. Springer, Cham (2021). https://doi.org/10.1007/978-3-030-77543-8_6
39. Werth, M., Leuschel, M.: VisB: a lightweight tool to visualize formal models with SVG graphics. In: Raschke, A., Méry, D., Houdek, F. (eds.) ABZ 2020. LNCS, vol. 12071, pp. 260–265. Springer, Cham (2020). https://doi.org/10.1007/978-3-030-48077-6_21
40. Winter, D.: Validating promela models with the ProB model chcker. Master's thesis, Institut für Informatik, Universität Düsseldorf (2008)
41. Yang, F., Jacquot, J., Souquières, J.: JeB: safe simulation of Event-B models in JavaScript. In: Proceedings APSEC, vol. 1, pp. 571–576. IEEE (2013)
42. Yu, Y., Manolios, P., Lamport, L.: Model checking TLA$^+$ specifications. In: Pierre, Laurence, Kropf, Thomas (eds.) CHARME 1999. LNCS, vol. 1703, pp. 54–66. Springer, Heidelberg (1999). https://doi.org/10.1007/3-540-48153-2_6

Intrepid: A Scriptable and Cloud-Ready SMT-Based Model Checker

Roberto Bruttomesso[✉]

Via Castronno, 48, 21040 Morazzone, VA, Italy

Abstract. Intrepid is an SMT-based model checker that provides a rich set of APIs for creating, simulating, and verifying state machines expressed as circuits (just like Simulink or Lustre models). Intrepid may be further used in its Docker container version to be deployed on a local or in a cloud-based infrastructure. The container exposes an equivalently powerful REST API for operating with the model checker. Verification of safety properties in Intrepid is performed in a bit-precise manner, including operations involving integers and floating point arithmetic. Intrepid features standard verification engines as well as multi-property optimizing engines which are suitable for automated test generation tasks, such as MC/DC test generation for avionics.

1 Introduction

Model Checking has been successfully employed for decades in industrial environments such as Electronic Design Automation (e.g., equivalence checking for RTL power reduction [2]) and Control Engineering (e.g., automated test generation for avionics and automotive [6,13]), or modern re-implementations of established techniques for network security such as the derivation of attack graphs [1,16,27,29].

Oftentimes companies do not have the resources, the knowledge, or the interest in building an in-house model checker to use as a backend for a new application. Rather, they tend to rely on a free academic tool [7–9,15,17,23,25,30] or to buy licenses for a commercial product from a third-party company [22]. In either case the user of the chosen tool is immediately confronted with the task of translating an instance of her problem into the particular language accepted by the backend, as well as parsing a counterexample for mapping it back to the original problem. While in some contexts the translation effort is not an issue, in some scenarios it represents a major hurdle, especially from a performance and usability perspective. This issue is particularly evident in applications that require a high degree of interaction between the application and the model checker, such as Automated Test Generation [13] or attack graph generation [1,29].

Intrepid aims to tackle these problems by providing a rich Python-based API where input models and the verification steps are executable Python scripts[1],

---

A demonstration video is available at https://youtu.be/n-0Y_iJqkqY.

[1] E.g.: `[ctx.mk_input('i' + str(i)) for i in range(100)]` to create 100 inputs.

© Springer Nature Switzerland AG 2021
A. Lluch Lafuente and A. Mavridou (Eds.): FMICS 2021, LNCS 12863, pp. 202–211, 2021.
https://doi.org/10.1007/978-3-030-85248-1_13

which can be imported, reused, and extended. Counterexamples can be stored as Python dictionaries or as pandas dataframe, one of the most popular representation for tabular data in Python. Intrepid can be thus used as a rapid-prototyping tool, where the heavy solving tasks are silently delegated to an underlying efficient C++ library. Intrepid can also be started as a server running in a Docker container, on a local or remote machine. The server exposes a rich REST API that can be used to construct, simulate, and solve model checking problems. Under the hood, Intrepid relies on the powerful SMT-solver Z3 [24] for solving satisfiability queries and for performing quantifier elimination required by the model checking engines.

Intrepid is distributed as a library for Python-3.8. It can be installed by issuing the command `pip3 install intrepyd`[2]. The REST API relies on the Docker container `robertobruttomesso/intrepid`. The Python code is available at https://github.com/formalmethods/intrepid and can be used under the liberal BSD-3 license.

2   Constructing Models

In Intrepid models are standard, word-level sequential circuits defined as follows:

```
circuit : constant | input | latch | circuit op circuit
```

where constants, inputs, and latches can be of type Boolean, signed or unsigned integers of size in $\{8, 16, 32, 64\}$, floating point of size in $\{16, 32, 64\}$, or real (the only infinite-precision type). `op` is an arithmetic operator, a comparison relation, or a Boolean gate, applied to the proper circuit types, essentially following the typing rules of the SMT-LIB language [3]. Constants, inputs, latches, and operators can be created using an instance of the `Context` object. Intrepid's language is similar in semantic and expressiveness to the BTOR2 format for hardware model checking [25].

Figure 1 shows the creation of a circuit representing a clock signal (a signal that toggles at each time step). The `Context` is created at line 3 and stored in variable `ctx`. At line 6 and 7 the `input` and a `latch1` of type Boolean are created. At lines 8–10 `latch1` is given an initial and a next state: this step is performed after the latch creation to allow the specification of sequential loops (i.e., loops that involve at least a latch. Combinational loops are not allowed). Lines 11–15 perform the creation and initialization of `latch2`.

Because models are Python scripts, they can be placed into convenient functions or classes inside Python modules. The clock model above, for instance, can be imported from the `intrepyd.components.eda` submodule.

---

[2] Notice the "y" in the name of the Python package: the name "intrepid" was already taken.

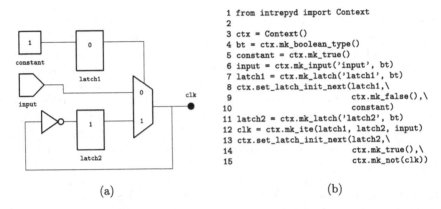

```
1  from intrepyd import Context
2
3  ctx = Context()
4  bt = ctx.mk_boolean_type()
5  constant = ctx.mk_true()
6  input = ctx.mk_input('input', bt)
7  latch1 = ctx.mk_latch('latch1', bt)
8  ctx.set_latch_init_next(latch1,\
9                          ctx.mk_false(),\
10                         constant)
11 latch2 = ctx.mk_latch('latch2', bt)
12 clk = ctx.mk_ite(latch1, latch2, input)
13 ctx.set_latch_init_next(latch2,\
14                         ctx.mk_true(),\
15                         ctx.mk_not(clk))
```

(a)   (b)

Fig. 1. The encoding of a clock signal, starting with a random value: (a) the schematic of the circuit (b) the encoding in Intrepid, `clk` being the output.

2.1 Translating Industrially-Relevant Models

Intrepid is intended to be used via its API, however, in order to facilitate the processing of existing industrial models, Intrepid comes with two submodules `intrepyd.lustre2py` and `intrepyd.iec611312py`. The first one translates Lustre models [18], while the second one translates the IEC-61131-3 Structured Text language models in OpenPLC format, into Intrepid's scripts. Both translators, based on the ANTLR parser [26], do not fully support all the aforementioned languages' constructs (e.g.: arrays are not supported).

The Lustre frontend has been tested with a subset of the models available from [20] (see Sect. 4.1). The Structured Text encoder is currently in an earlier proof-of-concept stage: its main purpose is to demonstrate that the translation is possible, by providing an initial implementation. It has been tested on an OpenPLC model[3], in turn translated from a Simulink/Stateflow model of an infusion pump, using the Simulink PLC Coder tool[4]. The infusion pump model is part of the CocoSim tool [7] test suite[5].

3 Simulating Models

Since models are circuits, they can be simulated for a given number of time steps. The result of the simulation is a `Trace` object. For each simulation step the trace assigns a value to the sub-circuits that are being watched.

Figure 2 shows the simulation of the clock circuit of Fig. 1, conveniently imported from the `eda` module. The simulator is created at line 7. Both the clock output and input are "watched" at lines 8 and 9: watched signals are those that will show up in the trace. Line 10 creates a new empty trace, and line 11

---

[3] Available at https://bit.ly/3hggxgV.
[4] Simulink PLC Coder is a Mathwork's proprietary tool.
[5] Available at https://bit.ly/3qw4osy.

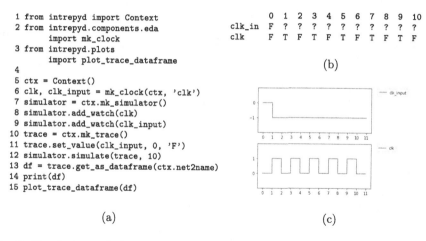

(a)

(b)

(c)

Fig. 2. Simulating a clock signal over 10 time steps: (a) the encoding in Intrepid, (b) the pandas dictionary printed at line 14, (c) the signal values graphs generated at line 15.

initializes the first value of the input to **F**. If an input value is not specified for a time step, the simulator will assign to a "don't care" value ?. During the simulation, at line 12, these values are propagated through the circuit, but, if irrelevant, will not show up at the circuit output: this is exactly the case in our example. At line 13 the trace is converted in a pandas dataframe, and then printed and plotted at lines 14 and 15. In the plots, **F** is mapped to 0, **T** to 1, and ? to −1.

4   Model Checking

Model Checking in Intrepid consists in defining reachability `targets`, i.e., Boolean signals for which the tool tries to find a `trace`. In standard terminology a target is a bad state corresponding to the negation of a safety property, and a trace is a counterexample that disproves its validity. Safety properties are the only ones supported by Intrepid. In order to support a wider range of properties a user could rely on the approach of [11] to create monitor circuits, by constructing them using Intrepid's basic APIs. It is important to notice that Intrepid's engines attempt to reach multiple targets at once.

Bounded Model Checking and Temporal Induction. Bounded Model Checking (BMC) is the process of reaching a target by unrolling the circuit for finite number of steps. The unrolling is performed in a backward manner, from the targets to the inputs. Latches are recursively replaced with their unrolled next state signal. Optionally, Temporal Induction (TI) can be enabled to prove target's unreachability. Intrepid essentially follows the "Zig-zag" approach of [12], as well as its strategy of dynamically adding difference constraints.

Optimizing Bounded Model Checking. Some applications such as Automated Test Generation require to find traces that satisfy the most number of targets at once. Since each trace is turned into a test, and each test might need to undergo manual revision, it is important to produce a small number of traces that cover all the targets. The Optimizing Bounded Model Checking (OBMC) engine aims at solving exactly this problem. By relying on the optimization procedure of Z3 [5], it is possible to simply use the MAX-SMT solver instead of the default one to find traces that satisfy the maximum number of active targets (a sample application is presented in Sect. 5.2).

Backward Reachability. Backward Reachability (BR) is inspired to the exploration algorithm behind the MCMT model checker [16], which is adapted for Intrepid's circuit-like models. The algorithm keeps a frontier of states to explore, and a set of blocked states. Blocked states are states that have been already explored, and therefore do not need to be enumerated again. The frontier is initialized with the targets to reach. Then the main loop starts. At each iteration a state S is popped from the frontier: if it intersects the initial states, then some target is reachable, otherwise the pre-image states of S that are not blocked already are added to the frontier, and S is added to the blocked states. The loop exits when the frontier is empty. Backward Reachability relies on Z3's quantifier elimination to rule out non-Boolean inputs from the enumerated states.

4.1   A Comparison of the Engines

Table 1 reports an evaluation of the engines on a subset of the benchmarks from [20]. Overall we run 848 divided in 6 families. Each benchmark contains either a safe or an unsafe property. The experiments show that BMC solves

Table 1. A comparison on the lustre models from [20]. The tests have been run on an Intel i7-8565U 1.80 GHz machine, with 32 GB of RAM, running Ubuntu Linux and Intrepid version 0.10.3. The timeout was set at 60 s. The column "TO" reports the number of timed-out benchmarks. The column "Best" indicates on how many benchmarks the tool was the fastest to find the answer. Full raw data is available at https://bit.ly/3duFd4a. The benchmarks and the scripts to run the tests are available under the folder **benchmarks** of the Github repository). Bold-face fonts highlight the best performing solver per each benchmark family.

Family	BMC				BMC+TI				BR			
	Safe	Unsafe	TO	Best	Safe	Unsafe	TO	Best	Safe	Unsafe	TO	Best
Protocol	0	**14**	22	14	**16**	**14**	6	**16**	15	7	14	0
Simulation	0	**58**	132	57	**68**	52	70	**68**	64	43	83	6
Memory1	0	**110**	172	**108**	10	109	163	8	**17**	10	255	11
Memory2	0	**98**	84	**97**	25	96	61	22	**35**	57	90	15
Misc	0	62	48	**54**	18	**62**	30	22	34	62	**14**	21
Large	0	0	48	0	12	0	36	**7**	13	0	**35**	6
Total	0	**342**	506	**330**	149	333	**366**	143	**178**	179	491	59

the most unsafe benchmarks, as expected, while BR solves the most safe ones. BMC+TI solves the most benchmarks overall (it reports the least number of timeouts). A comparison with other model-checkers is left as future work.

5   Sample Applications

5.1   Equivalence Checking for Clock-Gating

Sequential clock gating is an important technique used in EDA to reduce the power consumption of digital circuits [4]. The idea of clock-gating is to reduce flip-flop value toggles, which is known to be draining a substantial amount of power, by adding extra logic to the circuit, in such a way that the power used for the new logic is highly compensated by the reduced toggles.

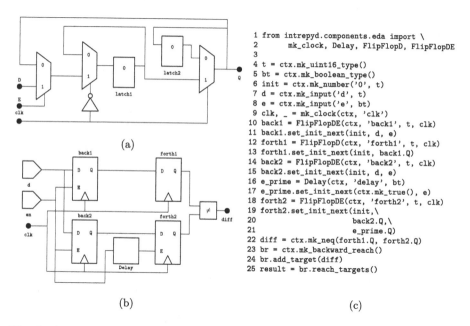

```
 1 from intrepyd.components.eda import \
 2        mk_clock, Delay, FlipFlopD, FlipFlopDE
 3
 4 t = ctx.mk_uint16_type()
 5 bt = ctx.mk_boolean_type()
 6 init = ctx.mk_number('0', t)
 7 d = ctx.mk_input('d', t)
 8 e = ctx.mk_input('e', bt)
 9 clk, _ = mk_clock(ctx, 'clk')
10 back1 = FlipFlopDE(ctx, 'back1', t, clk)
11 back1.set_init_next(init, d, e)
12 forth1 = FlipFlopD(ctx, 'forth1', t, clk)
13 forth1.set_init_next(init, back1.Q)
14 back2 = FlipFlopDE(ctx, 'back2', t, clk)
15 back2.set_init_next(init, d, e)
16 e_prime = Delay(ctx, 'delay', bt)
17 e_prime.set_init_next(ctx.mk_true(), e)
18 forth2 = FlipFlopDE(ctx, 'forth2', t, clk)
19 forth2.set_init_next(init,\
20                     back2.Q,\
21                     e_prime.Q)
22 diff = ctx.mk_neq(forth1.Q, forth2.Q)
23 br = ctx.mk_backward_reach()
24 br.add_target(diff)
25 result = br.reach_targets()
```

(a)   (b)   (c)

Fig. 3. An an equivalence checking problem for a power reduction technique called Stability Condition [14]: (a) the encoding of a register with enable, (b) the schematic of the problem, where the enable signal **en** is propagated to the register **forth**, delayed by one cycle, and (c) the encoding of the problem in Intrepid.

Figure 3b shows a transformation of a chain of a pair of registers back1-forth1 into a more power-efficient one back2-forth2. Due to the changes in the design, clock-gating opportunities must be proven correct: in the schematic above the pin diff must never evaluate to 1. diff is be passed as a target to the backward reachability an engine for proving its unreachability.

The SMT-like language of Intrepid allows the definition of clock-gating checks at the "word level", thus operating on the original registers as a whole rather than on their individual flip-flops (in the example we are running the check for a 16-bits register).

5.2   Automated Test Generation of MC/DC

The avionics standard DO-178C [28] dictates that every Level-A control software must be fully covered by a test suite using the Modified Condition/Decision (MC/DC) coverage metric [10]. Encoding of MC/DC conditions as Boolean or SMT formulas is a well-studied topic: the interested reader may refer to [6] for a simple logical formulation of the problem. Essentially the idea is to create reachable targets such that their traces correspond to tests that satisfy the coverage. Intrepid implements a simple ATG algorithm using only 300 LOC of Python that roughly follows the approach of [13], and is based on repeated calls to the OBMC engine, as shown in Fig. 4.

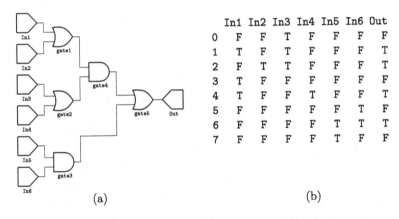

	In1	In2	In3	In4	In5	In6	Out
0	F	F	T	F	F	F	F
1	T	F	T	F	F	F	T
2	F	T	T	F	F	F	T
3	T	F	F	F	F	F	F
4	T	F	F	T	F	F	T
5	F	F	F	F	F	T	F
6	F	F	F	F	T	T	T
7	F	F	F	F	T	F	F

(a)   (b)

Fig. 4. An example of an execution of ATG on a simple combinational circuit (a) taken from [19]. Each row of the table (b) is an assignment to the inputs representing a test. Pair of tests show the satisfaction of the MC/DC coverage criterion for a specific input. For example $(0, 1)$ is a pair of tests that shows MC/DC for In1 (a so-called independence pair): In1 toggles between the two tests, all the other inputs keep the same value, and Out toggles. This is a proof that In1 can affect the behavior of the circuit.

6   A REST API for Model Checking

Intrepid is also available as a Docker container, that can be (downloaded and) run with `docker run -p 8000:8000 -d robertobruttomesso/intrepid`[6].

---

[6] The `docker` framework can be obtained from https://www.docker.com/.

The command starts a local server at port 8000 that exposes a rich REST API that roughly wraps the Python API so far described. The API is still experimental (it lacks for instance a mechanism for authentication), but it is fully operational for constructing, simulating, solving, and retrieving traces.

Figure 5 shows a sample interaction that creates an **and** gate using a command-line tool; similar interactions can be programmed and automated with popular languages such as Python, Ruby, or Javascript. Beside increasing the tool's interoperability with other frameworks and languages, having a containerized application with a REST API is a first step towards the embedding of Model Checking in a cloud environment such as AWS, Azure, or Digital Ocean: these providers can easily host and orchestrate multiple containers with frameworks like Docker-compose or Kubernetes.

One application that we envision for this setting is that of solving large problems that can be partitioned and dispatched to several different engines: the application described in Sect. 5.1, for instance, can be often tackled by partitioning the global equivalence checking problem into thousands of independent smaller ones, one per each clock gating opportunity discovered, using the notion of cut-points [21]. However, several challenges needs to be considered, such as the dispatching of problems and the reconstruction of the results. We leave the investigation of the feasibility of this research direction for a future work.

```
1 c> curl --location --request POST 'localhost:8000/api/v1/contexts/create' \
2         --header 'Content-Type: application/json' \
3         --data-raw '{"name": "default"}'
4 s> {"result":"default"}
5 c> curl --location --request POST 'localhost:8000/api/v1/inputs/create' \
6         --header 'Content-Type: application/json' \
7         --data-raw '{"context": "default", "type": "bool"}'
8 s> {"result":"__i0"}
9 c> curl --location --request POST 'localhost:8000/api/v1/inputs/create' \
10         --header 'Content-Type: application/json' \
11         --data-raw '{"context": "default", "type": "bool"}'
12 s> {"result":"__i1"}
13 c> curl --location --request POST 'localhost:8000/api/v1/nets/ands/create' \
14         --header 'Content-Type: application/json' \
15         --data-raw '{"context": "default", "x": "__i0", "y": "__i1"}'
16 s> {"result":"__n10"}
```

Fig. 5. A client-server interaction using the popular command-line tool `curl` (`c>` is the client's query, `s>` is the server's response): lines 1–3 create a new context named `default`, lines 5–7 and lines 9–11 create two inputs, and lines 13–15 create an **and** gate using them. Further documentation for the REST APIs is available at https://bit.ly/3bn2h42.

7 Conclusion

We have introduced Intrepid, a scriptable SMT-based Model Checker. We have presented a sketch of its Python API by applying it to a concrete industrially relevant sample application. Intrepid is additionally shipped as a Docker container, and it exposes a REST API that enables the deployment of the model checker on a remote server, a first step towards the employment of Model Checking in a cloud-based environment.

References

1. Al Ghazo, A.T., et al.: A2G2V: automatic attack graph generation and visualization and its applications to computer and SCADA networks. IEEE Trans. Syst. Man Cybern. Syst. **50**(10), 3488–3498 (2020). https://doi.org/10.1109/TSMC.2019.2915940

2. Babighian, P., Benini, L., Macii, E.: A scalable ODC-based algorithm for RTL insertion of gated clocks. In: Proceedings of the Design, Automation and Test in Europe Conference and Exhibition, vol. 1, pp. 500–505 (2004). https://doi.org/10.1109/DATE.2004.1268895

3. Barrett, C., Fontaine, P., Tinelli, C.: The SMT-LIB standard: version 2.6. Technical report, Department of Computer Science, The University of Iowa (2017). http://www.smt-lib.org/

4. Benini, L., et al.: Symbolic synthesis of clock-gating logic for power optimization of control-oriented synchronous networks. In: Proceedings of the European Design and Test Conference, ED TC 1997, pp. 514–520 (1997). https://doi.org/10.1109/EDTC.1997.582409

5. Bjørner, N., Phan, A.-D., Fleckenstein, L.: vZ - an optimizing SMT solver. In: Baier, C., Tinelli, C. (eds.) TACAS 2015. LNCS, vol. 9035, pp. 194–199. Springer, Heidelberg (2015). https://doi.org/10.1007/978-3-662-46681-0_14

6. Bloem, R.P., et al.: Model-based MCDC testing of complex decisions for the Java card applet firewall. In: VALID Proceedings. Ed. by IARIA, pp. 1–6 (2013)

7. Bourbouh, H., Brat, G., Garoche, P.-L.: CoCoSim: an automated analysis framework for Simulink/Stateflow. In: Model Based Space Systems and Software Engineering - European Space Agency Workshop (MBSE 2020) (2020)

8. Cavada, R., et al.: The NUXMV symbolic model checker. In: Biere, A., Bloem, R. (eds.) CAV 2014. LNCS, vol. 8559, pp. 334–342. Springer, Cham (2014). https://doi.org/10.1007/978-3-319-08867-9_22

9. Champion, A., Mebsout, A., Sticksel, C., Tinelli, C.: The KIND 2 model checker. In: Chaudhuri, S., Farzan, A. (eds.) CAV 2016. LNCS, vol. 9780, pp. 510–517. Springer, Cham (2016). https://doi.org/10.1007/978-3-319-41540-6_29

10. Chilenski, J.J.: An investigation of three forms of the modified condition decision coverage (MCDC) criterion. Technical report. DOT/FAA/AR-01/18, Boeing Commercial Airplane Group, April 2001

11. Claessen, K., Eén, N., Sterin, B.: A circuit approach to LTL model checking. In: FMCAD, pp. 53–60 (2013). http://ieeexplore.ieee.org/xpl/freeabsall.jsp?arnumber=6679391

12. Eén, N., Sörensson, N.: Temporal induction by incremental SAT solving. Electron. Notes Theor. Comput. Sci. **89**(4), 543–560 (2003). BMC 2003. ISSN: 1571-0661

13. Ferrante, O., Ferrari, A., Marazza, M.: Model based generation of high coverage test suites for embedded systems. In: 19th IEEE European Test Symposium, ETS, pp. 1–2 (2014). https://doi.org/10.1109/ETS.2014.6847843

14. Fraer, R., Kamhi, G., Mhameed, M.K.: A new paradigm for synthesis and propagation of clock gating conditions. In: 2008 45th ACM/IEEE Design Automation Conference, pp. 658–663 (2008)

15. Gacek, A., Backes, J., Whalen, M., Wagner, L., Ghassabani, E.: The JKIND model checker. In: Chockler, H., Weissenbacher, G. (eds.) CAV 2018. LNCS, vol. 10982, pp. 20–27. Springer, Cham (2018). https://doi.org/10.1007/978-3-319-96142-2_3 ISBN: 978-3-319-96142-2

16. Ghilardi, S., Ranise, S.: MCMT: a model checker modulo theories. In: Giesl, J., Hähnle, R. (eds.) IJCAR 2010. LNCS (LNAI), vol. 6173, pp. 22–29. Springer, Heidelberg (2010). https://doi.org/10.1007/978-3-642-14203-1_3

17. Goel, A., Sakallah, K.: AVR: abstractly verifying reachability. In: TACAS 2020. LNCS, vol. 12078, pp. 413–422. Springer, Cham (2020). https://doi.org/10.1007/978-3-030-45190-5_23 ISBN: 978-3-030-45190-5

18. Halbwachs, N., et al.: The synchronous data flow programming language LUSTRE. In: Proceedings of the IEEE 1991, pp. 1305–1320 (1991)

19. Hayhurst, K.J., et al.: A Practical Tutorial on Modified Condition/Decision Coverage. TM 2001-210876. Langley Research Center. NASA, Hampton, May 2001

20. Kind2 benchmarks. https://github.com/kind2-mc/kind2-benchmarks

21. Kuehlmann, A., Eijk, C.A.J.: Combinational and sequential equivalence checking. In: Hassoun, S., Sasao, T. (eds.) Logic Synthesis and Verification. SECS, vol. 654, pp. 343–372. Springer, Boston (2002). https://doi.org/10.1007/978-1-4615-0817-5_13

22. Mathworks: Simulink Design Verifier. https://www.mathworks.com/products/sldesignverifier.html

23. Mattarei, C., et al.: CoSA: integrated verification for agile hardware design. In: FMCAD. IEEE (2018)

24. de Moura, L., Bjørner, N.: Z3: an efficient SMT solver. In: Ramakrishnan, C.R., Rehof, J. (eds.) TACAS 2008. LNCS, vol. 4963, pp. 337–340. Springer, Heidelberg (2008). https://doi.org/10.1007/978-3-540-78800-3_24

25. Niemetz, A., Preiner, M., Wolf, C., Biere, A.: BTOR2, BtorMC and Boolector 3.0. In: Chockler, H., Weissenbacher, G. (eds.) CAV 2018. LNCS, vol. 10981, pp. 587–595. Springer, Cham (2018). https://doi.org/10.1007/978-3-319-96145-3_32

26. Parr, T.: The Definitive ANTLR 4 Reference, 2nd edn. Pragmatic Bookshelf, Raleigh (2013). ISBN: 978-1-93435-699-9. https://www.safaribooksonline.com/library/view/the-definitive-antlr/9781941222621/

27. Ritchey, R.W., Ammann, P.: Using model checking to analyze network vulnerabilities. In: Proceeding of the 2000 IEEE Symposium on Security and Privacy, SP 2000, pp. 156–165 (2000)

28. RTCA: DO-178C: Software Considerations in Airborne Systems and Equipment Certification

29. Sheyner, O., et al.: Automated generation and analysis of attack graphs. In: Proceedings of the 2002 IEEE Symposium on Security and Privacy, pp. 273–284 (2002). https://doi.org/10.1109/SECPRI.2002.1004377

30. Vizel, Y., Gurfinkel, A.: Interpolating property directed reachability. In: Biere, A., Bloem, R. (eds.) CAV 2014. LNCS, vol. 8559, pp. 260–276. Springer, Cham (2014). https://doi.org/10.1007/978-3-319-08867-9_17 ISBN: 978-3-319-08867-9

Merit and Blame Assignment with Kind 2

Daniel Larraz[1]([✉]), Mickaël Laurent[1,2], and Cesare Tinelli[1]

[1] Department of Computer Science, The University of Iowa, Iowa City, USA
daniel-larraz@uiowa.edu
[2] IRIF, CNRS—Université de Paris, Paris, France

Abstract. We introduce two new major features of the open-source model checker Kind 2 which provide traceability information between specification and design elements such as assumptions, guarantees, or other behavioral constraints in synchronous reactive system models. This new version of Kind 2 can identify minimal sets of design elements, known as *Minimal Inductive Validity Cores*, which are sufficient to prove a given set of safety properties, and also determine the set of *MUST* elements, design elements that are necessary to prove the given properties. In addition, Kind 2 is able to find minimal sets of design constraints, known as *Minimal Cut Sets*, whose violation leads the system to an unsafe state. We illustrate with an example how to use the computed information for tracking the safety impact of model changes, and for analyzing the tolerance and resilience of a system against faults.

Keywords: SMT-based model checking · Inductive validity cores · Traceability · MUST-set generation · Minimal Cut Sets

1 Introduction

KIND 2 [6] is an open-source[1] SMT-based model checker for safety properties of finite- and infinite-state synchronous reactive systems. It takes as input models written in an extension of the Lustre language [11]. The extension allows the specification of assume-guarantee-style contracts for the modeled system and its components which enables modular and compositional reasoning and considerably increases scalability. KIND 2's contract language [5] is expressive enough to allow one to represent any (LTL) regular safety property by recasting it in terms of invariant properties. KIND 2 runs concurrently several model checking engines which cooperate to prove or disprove contracts and properties. In particular, it combines two induction-based model checking techniques, k-induction [16] and IC3 [4], with various auxiliary invariant generation methods.

One clear strength of model checkers is their ability to return precise error traces witnessing the violation of a given safety property. In addition to being invaluable to help identify and correct bugs, error traces also represent a checkable unsafety certificate. Similarly, some model checkers are able to return some form of corroborating evidence when they declare a safety property to be satisfied by a system under analysis.

Work partially funded by DARPA grant #N66001-18-C-4006 and by GE Global Research.
[1] KIND 2 is distributed under the Apache 2.0 License at http://kind.cs.uiowa.edu.

A. Lluch Lafuente and A. Mavridou (Eds.): FMICS 2021, LNCS 12863, pp. 212–220, 2021.
https://doi.org/10.1007/978-3-030-85248-1_14

For instance, KIND 2 can produce an independently checkable proof certificate for the properties that it claims to have proven [14]. However, these certificates, in the form of a k-inductive invariant, give limited user-level insight on what elements of the system model contribute to the satisfaction of the properties.

Contributions. We describe two new diagnostic features of KIND 2 that provide more insights on verified properties: (1) the identification of minimal sets of model elements that are *sufficient* to prove a given set of safety properties, as well as the subset of design elements that are *necessary* to prove the given properties; (2) the computation of minimal sets of design constraints whose violation leads the system to falsify one of more of the given properties.

Although these two pieces of information are closely related, each of them can be naturally mapped to a typical use case in model-based software development: respectively, *merit assignment* and *blame assignment*. With the former the focus is on assessing the quality of a system specification, tracking the safety impact of model changes, and assisting in the synthesis of optimal implementations. With the latter, the goal is to determine the tolerance and resilience of a system against faults or cyber-attacks.

In general, proof-based traceability information can be used to perform a variety of engineering analyses, including vacuity detection [12]; coverage analysis [7,9]; impact analysis [15], design optimization; and robustness analysis [17,18]. Identifying which model elements are required for a proof, and assessing the relative importance of different model elements is critical to determine the quality of the overall model (including its assume-guarantee specification), determining when and where to implement changes, identifying components that need to be reverified, and measure the tolerance and resilience of the system against faults and attacks.

2 Running Example

We will use a simple model to illustrate the concepts and the functionality of KIND 2 introduced in this paper. Suppose we want to design a component for an airplane that controls the pitch motion of the aircraft, and suppose one of the system requirements is that the aircraft should not ascend beyond a certain altitude. The controller must read the current altitude of the aircraft from a sensor, and modify the next position of the aircraft's nose accordingly. Moreover, we want the system to be fault-tolerant to sensor failures. One way to improve system fault-tolerance is to introduce some redundancy. In particular, we can equip the system with three different altimeters so the controller receives three independent altitude values. Then the controller, with the help of a dedicated component, a *triplex voter*, takes the average of the two altitude values that are closest to each other—as they are more likely to be close to the actual altitude. For simplicity, we will ignore other relevant signals that should be considered in a real setting to control the elevation of the aircraft.

Following a model-based design, we model an abstraction of the system's environment to which the aircraft's controller will react. We also model the fact that the system relies on possibly imperfect readings of the current altitude by the sensors to decide the next pitch value. Finally, we provide a specification for the controller's behavior so that it satisfies the system requirement of interest.

```
1  node SystemModel (const TH, UB, ERR: real; alt1, alt2, alt3: real)
2  returns (act_alt: real);
3  (*@contract
4    assume "C1" TH > 0.0; assume "C2" UB > 0.0; assume "C3" ERR >= 0.0;
5    assume "S1" abs(0.0 -> pre act_alt - alt1) <= ERR;
6    assume "S2" abs(0.0 -> pre act_alt - alt2) <= ERR;
7    assume "S3" abs(0.0 -> pre act_alt - alt3) <= ERR;
8    guarantee "R1" act_alt <= TH;
9  *)
10    var pitch, alt: real;
11  let
12    alt = TriplexVoter(alt1, alt2, alt3);
13    pitch = Controller(TH, UB, ERR, alt);
14    act_alt = Environment(UB, pitch);
15  tel
16
17  node imported Controller (const TH, UB, ERR: real; alt: real) returns (pitch: real);
18  (*@contract
19    const LIMIT: real = TH - (UB + ERR);
20    guarantee "L1" alt > LIMIT => pitch < 0.0;
21  *)
```

Fig. 1. System model and subcomponents. Operators $->$, abs and $=>$ are respectively the initialization operator, the absolute value function, and Boolean implication.

Our model is described in Fig. 1 in KIND 2's input language where system components are called *nodes*. The main component, SystemModel, is an *observer* node that represents the full system consisting in this case of just three subcomponents: one node modeling the controller, one modeling a triplex voter, and another one modeling the environment. The observer has three inputs: alt1, alt2, and alt3, representing the altitude values from each altimeter, and an output act_alt, representing the current altitude of the aircraft, which we are modeling as a product of the environment in response to the pitch value generated by the controller.

KIND 2 allows the user to specify contracts for individual nodes, either as special Lustre comments added directly inside the node declaration, or as the instantiation of an external stand-alone contract that can be imported in the body of other contracts. The contract of SystemModel, included directly in the node, specifies assumptions on the altitude values provided by the sensors and on a number of symbolic constants (TH, UB and ERR) which act in effect as model parameters. The contract assumes at line 4 that those constants are positive, or non-negative for ERR. The assumptions at lines 5–7 account for fact that, while the altitude value produced by each altimeter is not 100% accurate in actual settings, its error is bounded by a constant (ERR)[2]. The contract

---

[2] The initialization operator $->$ is used to specify initial state values. Operationally, a node has a cyclic behavior: at each tick t of an abstract global clock it reads the value of each input stream at time t, and instantaneously computes the value of each output stream at time t. For streams x and y, the value $(x -> y)(t)$ for stream $x -> y$ equals $x(t)$ for $t = 0$ and $y(t)$ for $t > 0$.

```
1  node TriplexVoter (alt1,alt2,alt3: real) returns (r: real);
2    var ad12,ad13,ad23,m,avg1,avg2,avg3: real;
3  let
4    (ad12, ad13, ad23) = (abs(alt1 − alt2), abs(alt1 − alt3), abs(alt2 − alt3));
5    m = min(ad12, min(ad13, ad23));
6    (avg1, avg2, avg3) = (alt1 + alt2) / 2.0, (alt1 + alt3) / 2.0, (alt2 + alt3) / 2.0));
7    r = if m = ad12 then avg1 else if m = ad13 then avg2 else avg3;
8  tel
```

Fig. 2. Low-level specification of the Triplex voter.

```
1  node imported Environment (const UB: real; pitch: real) returns (alt: real);
2  (*@contract
3    guarantee "E1" (alt = 0.0) −> true;
4    guarantee "E2" alt >= 0.0;
5    guarantee "E3" true −> (pitch < 0.0 => alt <= pre alt);
6    guarantee "E4" true −> (pitch < 0.0 => alt >= pre alt − UB);
7    guarantee "E5" true −> (pitch > 0.0 => alt >= pre alt);
8    guarantee "E6" true −> (pitch > 0.0 => alt <= pre alt + UB);
9    guarantee "E7" true −> (pitch = 0.0 => alt = pre alt);
10  *)
```

Fig. 3. Contract specification for the Environment component of SystemModel.

includes a guarantee (line 8) that formalizes the requirement that aircraft maintain its altitude below a certain threshold TH at all times. The body of SystemModel is simply the parallel composition of a triplex voter, that takes the sensor values and computes an estimated altitude for the controller as explained above, the controller component, and the environment node.

A full specification for the TriplexVoter is given in Fig. 2. We do not specify the body of the Controller and the Environment nodes in our model because their details are not important for our purposes. Instead, we abstract their dynamics with an assume-guarantee contract that captures the relevant behavior. In the Controller's case, we model the guarantee that the controller will produce a negative pitch value whenever the sensor altitude indicates that the aircraft is getting too close to the threshold value TH—with "too close" meaning that the difference between the current altitude and the threshold is smaller than UB + ERR where UB represents an upper bound on the change in altitude from one execution step to the next (see below).

The declaration of the Environment component and its contract are shown separately in Fig. 3. With alt representing the actual altitude of the aircraft, the contract's guarantees capture salient constraints on the physics of our model by specifying that a positive pitch value (which has the effect of raising the nose of the aircraft and lowering its tail) makes the aircraft ascend, a negative value makes it descend, and a zero value keeps it at the same altitude.[3] The contract also states that the actual altitude starts at

---

[3] We are ignoring here that, in reality, the altitude also depends on aircraft speed.

zero, is alway non-negative, and does not change by more than a constant value (UB) in one sampling frame, where a sampling frame is identified with one execution step of the synchronous model (one global clock tick) for simplicity. The latter constraint on the altitude change rate captures physical limitations on the speed of the aircraft.

KIND 2 can easily prove that property (guarantee) R1 of SystemModel is invariant. However, a few interesting questions arise: (1) Is property R1 satisfied because of the conditions we imposed on the behavior of Controller, or does the property trivially hold due to the stated assumptions over the environment and the sensors? (2) Are all the assumptions over the environment and the sensors in fact necessary to prove the satisfaction of property R1? (3) How resilient is the system against the failure of one or more assumptions? We present in the following the new features of KIND 2 that help us answer these questions. A demo video associated to this paper can be found here [1].

3   The New Features

The first of the two new features offered by KIND 2 consists in identifying which parts of the input model were used to construct an inductive proof of invariance for R1. The new functionality relies on the concept of inductive validity core introduced by Ghassabani et al. [8]. Generally speaking, given a set of *model elements M* and an invariant property P, an *inductive validity core* (IVC) for P is a subset of M that is enough to prove P invariant. Kind 2 allows the user to choose among four sets of model elements: assumptions/guarantees, node calls, equations in node definitions[4], and assertions[5]. In our running example, we consider $P = R1$ and $M = S_1 \cup C_2 \cup E_3 \cup \{L1\}$ where $S_1 = \{S1, S2, S3\}$, $C_2 = \{C1, C2, C3\}$, and $E_3 = \{E1, E2, E3, E4, E5, E6, E7\}$. In particular, note that M is an IVC, although not a very interesting one. In practice, for complex enough models, smaller IVCs exist. In particular is often possible to compute efficiently a smaller IVC that contains few or no irrelevant elements. We can ensure that the elements of an IVC for a property P are necessary by requiring it to be *minimal*, that is, to have no proper subset that is also IVC for P. KIND 2 offers the option to compute a *small* but possibly non-minimal IVC, *a minimal* IVC (MIVC), or *all minimal* IVCs.

IVCs for Coverage and Change Impact Analysis. If a property P of a system S has multiple MIVCs, inspecting all of them provides insights on the different ways S satisfies P. Moreover, given all the MIVCs for P, it is possible to partition all the model elements into three sets [15]: a *MUST* set of elements which are required for proving P in every case, a *MAY* set of elements which are optional, and a set of elements that are irrelevant. This categorization provides complete traceability between specification and design elements, and can be used for coverage analysis [9] and tracking the safety impact of model changes. For instance, a change to one of the elements in the *MAY* set for P will not affect the satisfaction of P but will definitely impact some other property Q if it occurs in the *MUST* set for Q.

IVCs for Fault-Tolerance or Cyber-resiliency Analysis. Another use of IVCs, is in the analysis of a system's tolerance to faults [18] or resiliency to cyber-attacks [17].

---

[4] Note that a node is Lustre is defined declaratively by a set of equations.

[5] In Lustre, assertions are (unchecked) assumptions on a node's input.

For instance, an empty MUST set for a system S and its invariant P indicates that the property is satisfied by S in various ways, making the system fault tolerant or resilient against cyber-attacks as far as property P is concerned. In contrast, a large MUST set suggest a more brittle system, with multiple points of failure or a big attack surface.

Quantifying a System's Resilience. To help quantify the resilience of a system, KIND 2 also supports the computation of minimal cut sets (aka, *minimal correction sets*) for an invariance property. Given a set of model elements M and an invariant property P, a *cut set C* for P is a subset of M such that P is no longer invariant for $M \setminus C$. A *minimal cut set* (MCS) for P is a cut set none of whose proper subsets is a cut set for P. A *smallest cut set* is an MCS of minimum cardinality. KIND 2 provides options to compute a (single) smallest cut set, all the MCSs, and all the MCSs up to a given cardinality bound. In the context of fault or security analyses, the cardinality of an MCS for a property P represents the number of design elements that must fail or be compromised for P to be violated. The smaller the MCS, or the higher the number of MCSs of small cardinality, the greater the probability that the property can be violated.

Running Example. If we ask KIND 2 to generate an IVC for the invariant R1 of the system presented in Sect. 2, KIND 2 generates a IVC with 9 elements: assumptions S1, S2, S3, and C1 from SystemModel's contract, the (only) guarantee L1 in Controller's contract, and all guarantees in the contract of Environment except for E2, E4, and E5. This tells us already that E2, E4, and E5 are not necessary to satisfy property R1 and is enough to answer the second of the questions listed at the end of Sect. 2. Moreover, since the guarantee L1 of Controller is part of the IVC, it is likely that the controller's behavior is relevant for the satisfaction of R1. However, we can not be sure because the generated IVC is not necessarily minimal.

To confirm that L1 is indeed necessary we can ask KIND 2 to identify a true MIVC, a more expensive task computationally. When we do that, KIND 2 returns the same set. This confirms the necessity of the guarantee L1 but only for the specific proof of R1's invariance found by KIND 2. It might still be the case that the guarantee is not required in general, that is, there may be *other* proofs that do not use L1, which would be confirmed by the discovery of a different MIVC that does not contain it. In other words, at this point we do not know whether L1 is a *must* element for R1. To determine that, we can ask KIND 2 to compute the MUST set for property R1 in addition to the MIVC. In that case, KIND 2 will return the same set as the MUST set, which confirms that all the included elements are required and the excluded ones are irrelevant.

Note that the last result also means that assumptions S1, S2, and S3 are always necessary, and thus, property R1 requires *all three* sensors to behave accordingly to their specification. Put differently, the analysis shows that the introduced redundancy mechanism *does not* actually make the system more fault tolerant. After reviewing the model, however, one can conclude that to benefit from the triplex voter we must decrease the safety limit value LIMIT in the controller's contract. Specifically, it is enough to decrease it as follows, doubling the error bound value:

```
const LIMIT: real = TH − (UB + 2.0 ∗ ERR);
```

After this change, KIND 2 stops classifying assumptions S1, S2, and S3 as MUST elements. It computes a new MIVC of 8 elements which differs from the one computed for the previous version of the model for the absence of S3. To confirm that this MIVC is not the only solution, we can ask KIND 2 to compute all the MIVCs instead of a single one. This makes KIND 2 show two additional MIVCs that are symmetric to the computed MIVC: one set that contains S1 and S3 rather than S1 and S2, and another one that contains S2 and S3 instead S1 and S2. In alternative, we could ask KIND 2 to compute all the MCSs for the revised model. In that case, KIND 2 will find the following MCSs: {E1}, {E3}, {E6}, {E7}, {C1}, {L1}, {S1,S2}, {S1,S3}, {S2,S3}. This confirms that the system can now tolerate the failure of one of its three altimeters.

The exercise above illustrates how the new traceability feature in KIND 2 could be used to detect a subtle flaw in our enhanced model that prevented it from making the system fault-tolerant despite the triplication of the altitude sensors. We stress how a simple safety analysis, verifying the invariance of R1 would not help detect such flaw.

4   Implementation Details

KIND 2 is written in OCaml. All logical reasoning done by KIND 2 eventually reduces to queries to an external SMT solver. The implementation of the new features required around 2.8 KLOC. The computation of a small IVC for a property P is based on algorithm IVC_UC by Ghassabani et al. [8]. It consists of three main steps: (*i*) reducing the value of k for the k-inductive proof of property P (obtained by finding a k-inductive strengthening $Q = Q_1 \wedge \cdots \wedge Q_n$ of P); (*ii*) reducing the number of conjuncts in invariant Q by removing those not needed in the proof; (*iii*) computing an UNSAT core over the model constraints in the same query to the backend SMT solver that checks that Q is a k-inductive strengthening of P. The computation of a single MIVC is based on algorithm IVC_UCBF, also by Ghassabani et al. [8]. The main idea is to generate a small IVC first, and then minimize it using a brute-force approach that removes one model element at a time and (model) checks that the property P still holds.

To compute all MIVCs we adapted algorithm UMIVC by Berryhill and Veneris [3] which in turn is a generalization of previous work [2,10]. It basically explores in an efficient way the power set of model elements. The algorithm implemented in KIND 2 can be seen as an instantiation of UMIVC where all MCSs of cardinality 1 are precomputed. The major difference with UMIVC is that our algorithm is able to identify the MUST set from the generated set of MCSs, which can be use to check for early termination of the algorithm and to enhance the minimization of the intermediate IVCs generated during the process.

The problem of finding one cut set for a system S and a property P with at most k model elements is reduced to a model checking problem. Every violation of property P in this problem leads to a cut set. KIND 2 keeps solving this model checking problem using smaller and smaller bounds until there is no more violations. When that happens, it can extract a cut set of minimal cardinality. KIND 2 is also able to find all possible MCSs with cardinality smaller than a given bound by incrementally adding constraints that block the previous solutions. When there are no more minimal sets within the current cardinality bound, it increases that bound by one and repeats the process. It ends this process when the cardinality bound equals the number of model elements considered, having computed at that point all possible MCSs.

We refer the interested reader to a related technical report [13] for further implementation details and experimental results.

References

1. Demo video. https://doi.org/10.5281/zenodo.5070546. Accessed 5 July 2021
2. Bendík, J., Ghassabani, E., Whalen, M., Černá, I.: Online enumeration of all minimal inductive validity cores. In: Johnsen, E.B., Schaefer, I. (eds.) SEFM 2018. LNCS, vol. 10886, pp. 189–204. Springer, Cham (2018). https://doi.org/10.1007/978-3-319-92970-5_12
3. Berryhill, R., Veneris, A.G.: Chasing minimal inductive validity cores in hardware model checking. In: Barrett, C.W., Yang, J. (eds.) 2019 Formal Methods in Computer Aided Design, FMCAD 2019, San Jose, CA, USA, 22–25 October 2019. pp. 19–27. IEEE (2019). https://doi.org/10.23919/FMCAD.2019.8894268
4. Bradley, A.R.: SAT-based model checking without unrolling. In: Jhala, R., Schmidt, D. (eds.) VMCAI 2011. LNCS, vol. 6538, pp. 70–87. Springer, Heidelberg (2011). https://doi.org/10.1007/978-3-642-18275-4_7
5. Champion, A., Gurfinkel, A., Kahsai, T., Tinelli, C.: CoCoSpec: a mode-aware contract language for reactive systems. In: De Nicola, R., Kühn, E. (eds.) SEFM 2016. LNCS, vol. 9763, pp. 347–366. Springer, Cham (2016). https://doi.org/10.1007/978-3-319-41591-8_24
6. Champion, A., Mebsout, A., Sticksel, C., Tinelli, C.: The KIND 2 model checker. In: Chaudhuri, S., Farzan, A. (eds.) CAV 2016. LNCS, vol. 9780, pp. 510–517. Springer, Cham (2016). https://doi.org/10.1007/978-3-319-41540-6_29
7. Chockler, H., Kroening, D., Purandare, M.: Coverage in interpolation-based model checking. In: Sapatnekar, S.S. (ed.) Proceedings of the 47th Design Automation Conference, DAC 2010, Anaheim, California, USA, 13–18 July 2010. pp. 182–187. ACM (2010). https://doi.org/10.1145/1837274.1837320
8. Ghassabani, E., Gacek, A., Whalen, M.W.: Efficient generation of inductive validity cores for safety properties. In: Zimmermann, T., Cleland-Huang, J., Su, Z. (eds.) Proceedings of the 24th ACM SIGSOFT International Symposium on Foundations of Software Engineering, FSE 2016, Seattle, WA, USA, 13–18 November 2016. ,p. 314–325. ACM (2016). https://doi.org/10.1145/2950290.2950346
9. Ghassabani, E., Gacek, A., Whalen, M.W., Heimdahl, M.P.E., Wagner, L.G.: Proof-based coverage metrics for formal verification. In: Rosu, G., Penta, M.D., Nguyen, T.N. (eds.) Proceedings of the 32nd IEEE/ACM International Conference on Automated Software Engineering, ASE 2017, Urbana, IL, USA, 30 October–03 November 2017, pp. 194–199. IEEE Computer Society (2017). https://doi.org/10.1109/ASE.2017.8115632
10. Ghassabani, E., Whalen, M.W., Gacek, A.: Efficient generation of all minimal inductive validity cores. In: Stewart, D., Weissenbacher, G. (eds.) 2017 Formal Methods in Computer Aided Design, FMCAD 2017, Vienna, Austria, 2–6 October 2017, pp. 31–38. IEEE (2017). https://doi.org/10.23919/FMCAD.2017.8102238
11. Halbwachs, N., Lagnier, F., Ratel, C.: Programming and verifying real-time systems by means of the synchronous data-flow language LUSTRE. IEEE Trans. Software Eng. 18(9), 785–793 (1992). https://doi.org/10.1109/32.159839
12. Kupferman, O., Vardi, M.Y.: Vacuity detection in temporal model checking. Int. J. Softw. Tools Technol. Transf. 4(2), 224–233 (2003). https://doi.org/10.1007/s100090100062
13. Larraz, D., Laurent, M., Tinelli, C.: Merit and blame assignment with kind 2. CoRR abs/2105.06575 (2021). https://arxiv.org/abs/2105.06575

14. Mebsout, A., Tinelli, C.: Proof certificates for SMT-based model checkers for infinite-state systems. In: Piskac, R., Talupur, M. (eds.) 2016 Formal Methods in Computer-Aided Design, FMCAD 2016, Mountain View, CA, USA, 3–6 October 2016, pp. 117–124. IEEE (2016). https://doi.org/10.1109/FMCAD.2016.7886669

15. Murugesan, A., Whalen, M.W., Ghassabani, E., Heimdahl, M.P.E.: Complete traceability for requirements in satisfaction arguments. In: 24th IEEE International Requirements Engineering Conference, RE 2016, Beijing, China, 12–16 September 2016, pp. 359–364. IEEE Computer Society (2016). https://doi.org/10.1109/RE.2016.35

16. Sheeran, M., Singh, S., Stålmarck, G.: Checking safety properties using induction and a SAT-solver. In: Hunt, W.A., Johnson, S.D. (eds.) FMCAD 2000. LNCS, vol. 1954, pp. 127–144. Springer, Heidelberg (2000). https://doi.org/10.1007/3-540-40922-X_8

17. Siu, K., et al.: Architectural and behavioral analysis for cyber security. In: 2019 IEEE/AIAA 38th Digital Avionics Systems Conference (DASC), pp. 1–10. IEEE (2019)

18. Stewart, D., Liu, J.J., Whalen, M.W., Cofer, D., Peterson, M.: Safety annex for the architecture analysis and design language (2020)

Test Generation and Probabilistic Verification

PSY-TaLiRo: A Python Toolbox
for Search-Based Test Generation
for Cyber-Physical Systems

Quinn Thibeault[✉], Jacob Anderson, Aniruddh Chandratre, Giulia Pedrielli,
and Georgios Fainekos

Arizona State University, Tempe, AZ 85281, USA
qthibeau@asu.edu

Abstract. In this paper, we present the Python package PSY-TaLiRo
which is a toolbox for temporal logic robustness guided falsification of
Cyber-Physical Systems (CPS). PSY-TaLiRo is a completely modular
toolbox supporting multiple temporal logic offline monitors as well as
optimization engines for test case generation. Among the benefits of
PSY-TaLiRo is that it supports search-based test generation for many
different types of systems under test. All PSY-TaLiRo modules can be
fully modified by the users to support new optimization and robustness
computation engines as well as any System under Test (SUT).

Keywords: Falsification · Cyber-Physical Systems · Search-based test
generation

1 Introduction

Requirements falsification for Cyber-Physical Systems (CPS) has gained promi-
nence in recent years as a practical way to test and debug industrial complexity models and systems [18,22,24,27]. Since the automotive industry was an
early adopter of the falsification technology [16], many of the benchmark CPS
models driving the research were MATLAB/Simulink models [8,14,15,23]. As a
result, some of the academic falsification tools are MATLAB tools: Breach [10],
S-TaLiRo [5], and ARIsTEO [18]. Other academic falsification tools that partic-
ipate in the ARCH falsification competition [11] are FALSTAR [28] (Java/Scala),
zlscheck [3] (OCaml with Zelus models), and falsify [4] (ChainerRL [1] Python
Library for reinforcement learning calling MATLAB functions).

However, as the autonomy and robotics research communities (and even
industry) increasingly adopt Python as the preferred language for prototyping,
there is a need for a falsification toolbox natively in Python. An all Python/C++
falsification framework would resolve any computational inefficiencies and compatibility issues of calling Python from MATLAB and/or vice versa. A native
Python toolbox also helps to resolve incompatibilities which can be encountered

© Springer Nature Switzerland AG 2021
A. Lluch Lafuente and A. Mavridou (Eds.): FMICS 2021, LNCS 12863, pp. 223–231, 2021.
https://doi.org/10.1007/978-3-030-85248-1_15

when attempting to merge modules written in Python into other software ecosystems (for example, using MATLAB to call an optimizer written in Python that calls a Simulink model). The PSY-TaLiRo (or Ψ-TaLiRo) toolbox, which stands for Python SYstems' TemporAl LogIc RObustness, addresses exactly this need. It is a fully modular and extensible toolbox for temporal logic guided falsification which mirrors the S-TaLiRo [5] structure. Namely, the users can easily call different temporal logic robustness computation engines (e.g., TLTk [9], RTAMT [20]), optimizers (SciPy), and Systems under Test (SUT) while still offering a common interface and specification language syntax. PSY-TaLiRo supports multiple libraries to compute temporal logic robustness, referred to as robustness computation backends, out of the box without any additional effort. When using the RTAMT robustness computation engine, PSY-TaLiRo supports all major operating systems.

In summary, PSY-TaLiRo makes the following contributions:

1. it is an open source fully modular toolbox in Python,
2. it provides a common syntax for the temporal logic monitors, and
3. it enables testing of Software and Hardware in the loop systems.

With PSY-TaLiRo, users will be able to quickly compare different optimization and robustness computation engines without any other changes to the test setup. Currently, the PSY-TaLiRo toolbox supports only basic functionality including defining and executing models, optimizers, and specifications. Future goals for the toolbox are to support the more advanced features of S-TaLiRo, including parameter mining and time varying control points for input signal parameterization.

This toolbox is open-source and publicly available at:

$$\boxed{\text{https://gitlab.com/sbtg/pystaliro}}$$

Additional materials, examples, and a quick-start guide can be found on the documentation site available at:

$$\boxed{\text{https://sbtg.gitlab.io/pystaliro}}$$

2   Architecture

The toolbox is organized into several modules: the SUT, the specification, the optimizers, and the options (see Fig. 1). Each module defines a **Protocol** interface as defined in [17] or **Abstract Base Class (ABC)** which may be implemented or extended respectively to create specialized implementations for a particular domain. A Python protocol is used to define the expected shape of an object but implementations are not required to be sub-classes, while an ABC requires sub-classing to implement. The life-cycle of a test is started by providing a specification, a SUT, an optimizer and options object to the toolbox entry-point. Using the SUT and the specification, the toolbox generates an objective

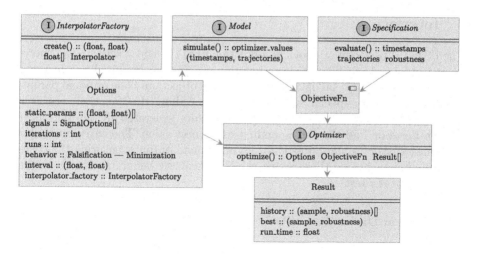

Fig. 1. Component diagram of PSY-TaLiRo architecture

function that accepts a 1-D sequence of inputs and returns a robustness value. The generated objective function and the options object are then passed as parameters to the optimizer. The optimizer executes the objective function several times, generating and storing the input sample and the output robustness for each execution. When a sample is provided to the objective function, it is decomposed into a sequence of static parameters and a sequence of signals that are used as inputs to the system model. The output of the system model is passed to the specification, which evaluates the result and produces a robustness value, which is returned to the optimizer. When the optimizer terminates its execution, a *Result* object is returned for every execution of the optimizer in case multiple experiments are performed.

Type Checking. Optional static type checking was introduced to the Python language in version 3.6 as type annotations defined in [21]. The benefit of static type checking is that multiple classes of errors can be caught before the program is executed by using a static type checker which traces the types of values through a program to ensure consistency. Python supports incremental typing, where a code-base can gradually add more type annotations over time instead of requiring the entire project to be typed immediately. PSY-TaLiRo makes extensive use of type annotations in both the internal and public APIs. Internally, annotations help ensure consistency between modules, reduce the difficulty of reasoning about functionality, and make it easier to implement additional features. For users, the annotations indicate the proper usage of the API for constructing system tests and a static type checker can provide immediate feedback.

3   Interface

The PSY-TaLiRo toolbox provides a function `staliro` which serves as an entry-point to the package. The `staliro` function accepts four required parameters - a specification, a SUT, an optimizer, an options object, and one optional parameter – an optimizer-specific options structure. Calling this function returns a sequence of `Result` objects that store the values generated by the optimizer at each iteration and the corresponding robustness value. The entry-point also implements basic validation logic for its inputs and outputs, ensuring the types of each component and their return values are correct before moving on to the next stage of the test.

3.1   System Under Test (SUT)

A SUT must provide the domain-specific information required to execute or simulate a system. It can be a simulation model e.g., (Python, MATLAB/Simulink, etc.), software-in-the-loop (SiL) (e.g., PX4, Webots, etc.), or even hardware-in-the-loop (HiL). A SUT is responsible for accepting inputs generated by the optimizer and returning the output trajectory of the execution along with the timestamps. The inputs generated by the optimizer are: static parameters, signal interpolators, and the simulation time interval. Static parameters are time-invariant inputs to the system which are often used to represent initial conditions. The simulation time interval dictates the range of time for which signals will be generated and the simulation should be executed. Signal interpolators are further described in the *Interpolation* section below.

Currently, PSY-TaLiRo provides two ways to run a SUT: a Blackbox class and an ODE integrator. The Blackbox class provides the most general way to execute a SUT because it makes no assumptions about the underlying architecture of the system it represents. To construct a Blackbox, a user needs to provide a function that accepts a vector of static parameters and/or initial conditions X, a sequence of time values T, and an array of signal values U corresponding to each time value. The Blackbox function must return the time values and corresponding output/state trajectory of the SUT. In contrast, an ODE model assumes the underlying system is represented as an ordinary differential equation and attempts to simulate the system by solving an initial-value problem. To construct an ODE model, a user must provide a function that accepts a time t, and the state at and the values of the input signal at t, and returns the derivatives of the system dynamics at time t.

Interpolation. In addition to time-invariant inputs to the SUT, PSY-TaLiRo also supports time-varying inputs referred to as signals. To generate a signal for a model, a `SignalOptions` object is created and included in the test options. A `SignalOptions` object defines an interval for the value of the signal as well as a number of **control points** which dictates how many values the optimizer should generate over the simulation interval. The optimizer-generated control points and a set of equally-spaced time values are provided to an `InterpolatorFactory` also defined in the `SignalOptions` to create an interpolator which can generate a signal value for any time in the simulation time interval. The generated interpolators are then passed to the model under test. Currently, the PSY-TaLiRo toolbox provides factories for **PChip, Piecewise Linear**, and **Piecewise constant** interpolators. Should a user want to implement a custom interpolator, defining a class that implements the `InterpolatorFactory` and providing it to the `SignalOptions` object is sufficient.

3.2 Specifications

The PSY-TaLiRo toolbox supports multiple robustness computation libraries, referred to as backends by providing a uniform interface implemented as the `Specification` class. The `Specification` interface defines the `evaluate` method, which accepts the time and signal values from the SUT and returns the robustness value. It is important to note that even though PSY-TaLiRo currently supports TLTk [9] and RTAMT [20], PSY-TaLiRo's modular architecture allows the user to utilize any other robustness computation engine, or, in general, any other reward or cost function. By implementing the `Specification` interface, a user can define and use any specification language or analysis logic they choose.

To construct a specification, a user must provide a system requirement written in STL, a dictionary structure specifying the requirement data. When the TLTk library is selected, the `Specification` class is responsible for parsing the discrete time STL requirement into a corresponding TLTk object representation. ANTLRv4 is used to generate a Python parser from a discrete time Signal Temporal Logic (STL) grammar [6]. When the RTAMT library is selected, no processing is done to the requirement and the both discrete and continuous time requirements are supported.

Table 1 provides an overview of the supported common operators and syntax between the two backends. Beyond the common syntax, each robustness computation backend has different capabilities and the user is advised to read the respective documentation. For example, TLTk supports parallel computation for scaling up to very large signals and distance based robustness [12] for less conservative robustness estimates. On the other hand, RTAMT supports past-time operators and dense time semantics.

Table 1. Common TLTk [9] and RTAMT [20] syntax supported in PSY-TaLiRo.

Specification constructs	Syntax
Next*	`next, X`
Eventually	`eventually, F`
Globally	`always, G`
Until	`until, U`
Time constraints on operator OP	`OP[ ... , ... ]`
Predicates	*varName* (`<=` | `>=`) *float*

*Only supported in discrete time STL

3.3 Optimizers

An optimizer in the PSY-TaLiRo toolbox is defined as a protocol that implements a method named optimize, which accepts an objective function, an options object, and an optional object with additional configuration options that are specific to the optimizer. The optimizer is also responsible for maintaining the history of samples and robustness values generated during execution and packaging them into a Result object when completed. Common optimizer behavior is configured using the options object and specific optimizer behavior is configured using the optimizer-specific options object. PSY-TaLiRo also defines two search behaviors: falsification and minimization. Under falsification, the optimizer stops when the first negative robustness value is found, while minimization allows the optimizer to continue searching for lower robustness values until the execution budget is exhausted. The PSY-TaLiRo toolbox provides a Uniform Random Sampling optimizer and it also includes wrappers for Dual Annealing and Basinhopping [26] optimizers implemented in the SciPy [25] package. PSY-TaLiRo also provides support for the PartX family of optimization algorithms [7] which comes with probabilistic guarantees on the absence or presence of falsifying behaviors.

3.4 Options

To customize the behavior of the toolbox, an options object must be created and provided to the staliro function. Constructing a minimally valid options object can be accomplished by providing either the static_parameters or *signals* keyword argument to the constructor. The static_parameters attribute defines a sequence of intervals which represent the bounds of the input variables that do not change with respect to time. The *signals* attribute represents the opposite: a sequence of signal options objects which define system inputs that vary with time. Other important attributes are iterations which defines the optimizer execution budget, runs which specifies the number of times to execute the optimizer, and interval which specifies the interval of time for which the system should run.

4 Examples

PSY-TaLiRo includes as Python demo an instance of the AircraftODE benchmark [19] as well as the test setup scripts for the Python version of the F16 GCAS benchmark problem [13]. In the following, we review how PSY-TaLiRo can interface with SUT external to Python using the Blackbox template.

4.1 MATLAB/Simulink

The Simulink toolbox that is provided as a part of the MATLAB software package is useful for representing complex systems using block diagrams. MATLAB additionally provides a Python library to enable access to the MATLAB engine from a Python application. A PSY-TaLiRo test using a Simulink model is implemented by defining a Blackbox function which uses the MATLAB Python library to pass the parameters and signal values to the Simulink simulation engine. The data returned by Simulink can then be parsed into native Python data types by the Blackbox function before returning from the `simulate` method.

There are a few considerations when implementing a Blackbox that requires the MATLAB Python library. Since the `simulate` method of the Blackbox is called many times by the optimizer, it is very inefficient to start a new instance of the MATLAB engine every time. There will also be an unavoidable time cost when interfacing with MATLAB due to the inter-process communication between the Python interpreter and the MATLAB engine. Finally, any exception that is raised during a simulation will halt the entire execution of the test, so care must be taken to ensure that any errors produced during a simulation are properly handled.

4.2   PX4

The strategies used to implement a Blackbox model that can interface with the MATLAB/Simulink engine can also be applied for communication with more complex systems such as the PX4 autopilot stack [2]. The PX4 is a commercial-grade autopilot software package used to control small aircraft like quad-rotors, and is capable of both SiL and HiL execution using one of several publicly available simulators. A successful integration of the PSY-TaLiRo toolbox and PX4 simulation environment was accomplished by using Docker to containerize the simulator and custom ground-control software to create and upload missions to the simulated drone. Some examples of requirements that were tested using the PX4 were to avoid exclusion zones when executing a mission, and another was to achieve a takeoff altitude within a threshold before landing.

5   Conclusions

We have presented the open-source Python toolbox PSY-TaLiRo (Ψ-TaLiRo). PSY-TaLiRo implements search-based test generation for falsifying temporal logic requirements over Cyber-Physical Systems (CPS). The toolbox is fully modular and extensible in order to accommodate different algorithms for optimization and temporal logic robustness (or arbitrary cost functions). Hence, PSY-TaLiRo can provide test automation support for CPS (and in particular autonomous systems) which are natively developed in Python.

Acknowledgements. This research was partially supported by DARPA (ARCOS FA8750-20-C-0507, AMP N6600120C4020) and NSF 1932068.

References

1. The ChainerRL Library. https://github.com/chainer/chainerrl
2. Open source autopilot for drones - px4 autopilot. https://px4.io
3. zlscheck: A random testing tool for Zelus. https://github.com/ismailbennani/zlscheck
4. Akazaki, T., Liu, S., Yamagata, Y., Duan, Y., Hao, J.: Falsification of cyber-physical systems using deep reinforcement learning. In: Havelund, K., Peleska, J., Roscoe, B., de Vink, E. (eds.) FM 2018. LNCS, vol. 10951, pp. 456–465. Springer, Cham (2018). https://doi.org/10.1007/978-3-319-95582-7_27
5. Annpureddy, Y., Liu, C., Fainekos, G., Sankaranarayanan, S.: S-TaLiRo: a tool for temporal logic falsification for hybrid systems. In: Abdulla, P.A., Leino, K.R.M. (eds.) TACAS 2011. LNCS, vol. 6605, pp. 254–257. Springer, Heidelberg (2011). https://doi.org/10.1007/978-3-642-19835-9_21
6. Bartocci, E., et al.: Specification-based monitoring of cyber-physical systems: a survey on theory, tools and applications. In: Bartocci, E., Falcone, Y. (eds.) Lectures on Runtime Verification. LNCS, vol. 10457, pp. 135–175. Springer, Cham (2018). https://doi.org/10.1007/978-3-319-75632-5_5
7. Cao, Y., Thibeault, Q., Chandratre, A., Castillo-Effen, M., Fainekos, G., Pedrielli, G.: Work-in-progress: towards assurance case evidence generation through search based testing. In: International Conference on Embedded Software (EMSOFT) (2021, to appear)
8. Chutinan, A., Butts, K.R.: Dynamic analysis of hybrid system models for design validation. Technical report, Ford Motor Company (2002)
9. Cralley, J., Spantidi, O., Hoxha, B., Fainekos, G.: TLTk: a toolbox for parallel robustness computation of temporal logic specifications. In: Deshmukh, J., Ničković, D. (eds.) RV 2020. LNCS, vol. 12399, pp. 404–416. Springer, Cham (2020). https://doi.org/10.1007/978-3-030-60508-7_22
10. Donzé, A.: Breach, a toolbox for verification and parameter synthesis of hybrid systems. In: Touili, T., Cook, B., Jackson, P. (eds.) CAV 2010. LNCS, vol. 6174, pp. 167–170. Springer, Heidelberg (2010). https://doi.org/10.1007/978-3-642-14295-6_17
11. Ernst, G., et al.: ARCH-COMP 2020 category report: falsification. In: 7th International Workshop on Applied Verification of Continuous and Hybrid Systems. EPiC Series in Computing, vol. 74, pp. 140–152 (2020). https://doi.org/10.29007/trr1
12. Fainekos, G.E., Pappas, G.J.: Robustness of temporal logic specifications for continuous-time signals. Theoret. Comput. Sci. **410**(42), 4262–4291 (2009)
13. Heidlauf, P., Collins, A., Bolender, M., Bak, S.: Verification challenges in f-16 ground collision avoidance and other automated maneuvers. In: 5th International Workshop on Applied Verification of Continuous and Hybrid Systems (ARCH), vol. 54, pp. 208–217 (2018)
14. Hoxha, B., Abbas, H., Fainekos, G.: Using S-TaLiRo on industrial size automotive models. In: Frehse, G., Althoff, M. (eds.) ARCH14-15. 1st and 2nd International Workshop on Applied veRification for Continuous and Hybrid Systems. EPiC Series in Computing, vol. 34, pp. 113–119. EasyChair (2015)
15. Jin, X., Kapinski, J., Deshmukh, J.V., Ueda, K., Butts, K.: Powertrain control verification benchmark. In: 17th International Conference on Hybrid Systems: Computation and Control (2014)

16. Kapinski, J., Deshmukh, J.V., Jin, X., Ito, H., Butts, K.: Simulation-based approaches for verification of embedded control systems: an overview of traditional and advanced modeling, testing, and verification techniques. IEEE Control Syst. Mag. **36**(6), 45–64 (2016)

17. Levkivskyi, I., Lehtosalo, J., Langa, Ł.: Protocols: structural subtyping (static duck typing). PEP 544, Python Foundation (2017). https://www.python.org/dev/peps/pep-0544/

18. Menghi, C., Nejati, S., Briand, L.C., Parache, Y.I.: Approximation-refinement testing of compute-intensive cyber-physical models: an approach based on system identification. In: ACM/IEEE 42nd International Conference on Software Engineering (ICSE) (2020)

19. Nghiem, T., Sankaranarayanan, S., Fainekos, G.E., Ivancic, F., Gupta, A., Pappas, G.J.: Monte-Carlo techniques for falsification of temporal properties of non-linear hybrid systems. In: Proceedings of the 13th ACM International Conference on Hybrid Systems: Computation and Control, pp. 211–220. ACM Press (2010)

20. Nickovic, D., Yamaguchi, T.: RTAMT: Online robustness monitors from STL (2020)

21. van Rossum, G., Lehtosalo, J., Langa, Ł.: Type hints. PEP 484, Python Foundation (2014). https://www.python.org/dev/peps/pep-0484/

22. Sankaranarayanan, S., Kumar, S.A., Cameron, F., Bequette, B.W., Fainekos, G., Maahs, D.: Model-based falsification of an artificial pancreas control system. ACM SIGBED Rev. (Special Issue on Medical Cyber Physical Systems workshop (MedicalCPS 2016)) **14**(2), 24–33 (2017)

23. Strathmann, T., Oehlerking, J.: Verifying properties of an electro-mechanical braking system. In: Frehse, G., Althoff, M. (eds.) ARCH14-15. 1st and 2nd International Workshop on Applied veRification for Continuous and Hybrid Systems. EPiC Series in Computing, vol. 34, pp. 49–56. EasyChair (2015)

24. Tuncali, C.E., Hoxha, B., Ding, G., Fainekos, G., Sankaranarayanan, S.: Experience report: application of falsification methods on the UxAS system. In: Dutle, A., Muñoz, C., Narkawicz, A. (eds.) NFM 2018. LNCS, vol. 10811, pp. 452–459. Springer, Cham (2018). https://doi.org/10.1007/978-3-319-77935-5_30

25. Virtanen, P., et al.: SciPy 1.0 contributors: SciPy 1.0: fundamental algorithms for scientific computing in Python. Nature Methods **17**, 261–272 (2020). https://doi.org/10.1038/s41592-019-0686-2

26. Wales, D.J., Doye, J.P.K.: Global optimization by basin-hopping and the lowest energy structures of Lennard-Jones clusters containing up to 110 atoms. J. Phys. Chem. A **101**(28), 5111–5116 (1997). https://doi.org/10.1021/jp970984n

27. Yamaguchi, T., Kaga, T., Donzé, A., Seshia, S.A.: Combining requirement mining, software model checking and simulation-based verification for industrial automotive systems. In: 16th Conference on Formal Methods in Computer-Aided Design (2016)

28. Zhang, Z., Ernst, G., Sedwards, S., Arcaini, P., Hasuo, I.: Two-layered falsification of hybrid systems guided by Monte Carlo tree search. IEEE Trans. Comput.-Aided Des. Integr. Circ. Syst. **37**(11), 2894–2905 (2018)

Probabilistic Verification for Reliability of a Two-by-Two Network-on-Chip System

Riley Roberts[1]($\boxtimes$)(iD), Benjamin Lewis[1]($\boxtimes$)(iD), Arnd Hartmanns[2](iD),
Prabal Basu[3](iD), Sanghamitra Roy[1](iD), Koushik Chakraborty[1](iD),
and Zhen Zhang[1]($\boxtimes$)(iD)

[1] Utah State University, Logan, UT, USA
{riley.roberts,benjamin.lewis}@aggiemail.usu.edu,
{sanghamitra.roy,koushik.chakraborty,zhen.zhang}@usu.edu
[2] University of Twente, Enschede, The Netherlands
a.hartmanns@utwente.nl
[3] Cadence Design Systems, San Jose, CA, USA
bprabal@cadence.com

Abstract. Modern network-on-chip (NoC) systems face reliability issues due to process and environmental variations. The power supply noise (PSN) in the power delivery network of a NoC plays a key role in determining reliability. PSN leads to voltage droop, which can cause timing errors in the NoC. This paper makes a novel contribution towards formally analyzing PSN in NoC systems. We present a probabilistic model checking approach to analyze key features of PSN at the behavioral level in a 2×2 mesh NoC with a uniform random traffic load. To tackle state explosion, we apply incremental abstraction techniques, including a novel probabilistic choice abstraction, based on observations of NoC behavior. The MODEST TOOLSET is used for probabilistic modeling and verification. Results are obtained for several flit injection patterns to reveal their impacts on PSN. Our analysis finds an optimal flit pattern generation with zero probability of PSN events and suggests spreading flits rather than releasing them in consecutive cycles in order to minimize PSN.

Keywords: Probabilistic model checking · Network-on-chip · Formal methods · Abstraction

1 Introduction

As the complexity advances in designing reliable distributed many-core systems, *network-on-chip* (NoC) has become the de-facto standard for on-chip communication. In general, their architecture composes of topologically homogeneous routers operating synchronously in a decentralized manner, and communication is governed by a predefined routing protocol. While sharing similarity with conventional computer networks, a NoC design faces unique reliability challenges, such as *process variation*, the variation in the transistor attributes (oxide thickness, width, etc.) due to the imperfection in the manufacturing process and

© Springer Nature Switzerland AG 2021
A. Lluch Lafuente and A. Mavridou (Eds.): FMICS 2021, LNCS 12863, pp. 232–248, 2021.
https://doi.org/10.1007/978-3-030-85248-1_16

environmental variation, which refers to the change in the supply voltage and temperature that can influence the performance of the transistor devices. Precise evaluation of the NoC early in the design flow is paramount to establish rigorous reliability and performance guarantees. NoC reliability analysis has to capture and quantify the design's inherent distributive and reactive characteristics.

Existing literature lacks probabilistic verification of the NoC. NoC formal verification has focused primarily on functional correctness [1–4], checking performance [5–7], and security [8,9]. Advances in probabilistic verification have produced mature tools such as the MODEST TOOLSET [10], which includes the MCSTA probabilistic model checker and the MODES statistical model checker [11], Storm [12], and PRISM [13]. However, these existing works in the formal verification of probabilistic systems have not focused on the NoC domain.

Building on the previous success in the probabilistic verification of a NoC central router [14], we present probabilistic verification of the power supply noise for a 2×2 mesh NoC system under uniform random traffic loads. We cumulatively apply abstraction techniques to tackle state space explosion for a 2×2 mesh NoC model. This includes a novel abstraction technique based on changing probabilistic choices derived from critical observations under design constraint assumptions. Verification results show significant scalability of our abstraction techniques, which reduce the state space growth from exponential to polynomial. They reveal extremely low *power supply noise* (PSN) related activity in the 2×2 NoC under an every other clock cycle flit injection pattern, while showing relatively high PSN under a burst style flit injection. This indicates the large impact design decisions have on PSN. Additionally, we report on an efficient flit generation pattern that incurs *zero* probability for PSN events and make recommendations for flit generation patterns to minimize PSN.

2 Motivation

PSN in the power delivery network of a NoC is created by simultaneous switching of logic devices, causing a drop in the effective power supply voltage. PSN is composed of two major components: (a) resistive noise—the product of the current drawn and the lumped resistance of the circuit ($i \times r$); and (b) inductive noise—proportional to the rate of change of current through the inductance of the power grid ($\frac{\Delta i}{\Delta t}$). The latter plays a central role [15] for a NoC.

A high inductive noise is responsible for the intermittent peaks in the cycle-wise noise profile of a NoC. It has been substantially growing with technology scaling. In an 8×8 NoC, it has been shown that the peak PSN can increase from 40% of the supply voltage at the 32-nm technology node to about 80% at the 14-nm technology node, while running a uniform-random synthetic traffic pattern [15]. Such a droop can radically degrade the delay of various on-chip circuit components causing timing errors in the pipe-stages of the NoC routers. Hence, PSN worsens the reliability and performance of the on-chip communication. The impact of technology on PSN is discussed in detail in [15].

Existing approaches to mitigate PSN are a far cry from a truly reliable NoC design paradigm that can be deployed in mission-critical systems, as they do not guarantee the worst-case peak PSN [15,16]. These works do not provide any bounds on the temporal PSN profile for a router, given an application execution. Hence, temporal high peak PSNs may still exacerbate the NoC reliability across different operating conditions. To address this critical reliability challenge, we show that probabilistic verification can offer precise bounds on the performance and reliability of the NoC.

3   Concrete Formal Model for NoC

This work analyzes the synchronous 2×2 mesh NoC shown in Fig. 1. All formal models described in this paper are available on Github[1]. There are four symmetric routers, each with three channels: one in the horizontal X direction, one in the vertical Y direction, and a local channel. Each channel has a buffer with the capacity of storing four network flits. Each router has an arbiter which resolves conflicts, i.e., multiple input flits competing for the same output direction, and forwards the winning flit in one clock cycle. The arbiter uses round-robin protocol to resolve multiple simultaneous requests to ensure fairness in each direction. The NoC uses X-Y routing, where a flit is first routed in the X direction until it is at the destination router or in the same column as the destination. It is then routed in the Y direction to the destination. For example, in Fig. 1, if router 0 were to receive a flit destined for router 3 on the local channel, the flit would be sent first in the X direction to router 1, then in the Y direction to router 3.

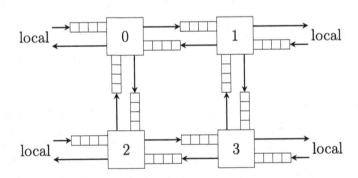

Fig. 1. Architecture of the 2×2 NoC model.

When a new flit is generated in each router's local channel, its destination is uniformly randomly selected among the other three routers. The routers then route all flits simultaneously. First, a flit's next forwarding direction is determined by the X-Y routing protocol by comparing its destination and the current router. The arbiter then forwards the flit to the neighboring router and resolves

---

[1] https://github.com/formal-verification-research/Modest-Probabilistic-Models-for-NoC.

conflicts if they arise. We use a priority queue in the arbiter to implement the round-robin scheduling mechanism in order to maintain fairness when resolving conflicts. Figure 2 illustrates how the priority queue works. When two channels conflict, the one closer to the front of the priority queue is serviced by the arbiter and the other is marked as unserviced. A channel that fails to send due to the receiving buffer being full is also marked as unserviced. At the end of the current clock cycle, the priority queue updates by shifting all unserviced channels to the front and pushing those serviced to the end, while maintaining their relative ordering. We use the high-level formal modeling language MODEST [10] to specify the probabilistic NoC model in Fig. 1.

Data types of the concrete NoC model are shown in Listing 1.1. The buffers are modeled as a FIFO queue with a capacity of four. Each channel is modeled as a datatype containing a buffer, the channel's priority, the forwarding direction for the front flit of the queue, the ID of the channel, and a Boolean variable indicating whether the channel was serviced or not. Each router is modeled as a datatype with an array of three channels, the order of which determines the priority, and two counters `unserviced` and `totalUnserviced` that keep track of the number of unserviced channels and are used by the arbiter. The NoC model has an array of four routers.

Listing 1.1. Channel and router datatypes.

```
datatype  channel = {int direction,
          int id, bool serviced, int priority,
          queue buffer};
datatype  router = {int unserviced,
          int totalUnserviced, channel[] channelArray};
```

All formal models described in this work have been formulated at a higher behavioral level. Therefore, it is necessary to map circuit-level behavior characterizing PSN onto the same behavioral level as these models, in order to quantitatively check PSN-related properties. The two components of PSN are modeled as follows. Resistive noise is measured by accumulating the clock cycles with high router activity, i.e., all three buffers: X direction, Y direction, and local, in a router are able to forward flits. This is represented by a variable *resistiveNoise*, which increments every time a router encounters a cycle with high activity. Inductive noise is measured by accumulating cycles with high rate of change of current drawn. This directly corresponds to cycles where a router switches between forwarding all flits to forwarding no flits and vice versa. Represented by the variable *inductiveNoise*, it increments on the cycles of abrupt change in router activity. Left unbounded, these variables would accumulate to infinity, adding to state explosion. However, we forcibly stop the execution of the models after a predetermined number of clock cycles to avoid state explosion of other variables, which in turn places a limit on the accumulation of these new variables.

The relation between the two PSN components, *resistiveNoise* and *inductiveNoise*, and their associated real-world applications is discussed in [15,17]. We rely on the analysis presented there as the foundation. The purpose of specifying and checking these properties is to understand the likelihood of PSN at a behavioral level under a given routing protocol. The intermittent peaks in the cycle-wise noise profile of the NoC is strongly correlated to the NoC router activities. Hence, understanding PSN behaviorally can help with the design of routing protocols and other higher-level NoC designs independent of the physical hardware implementation of the NoC.

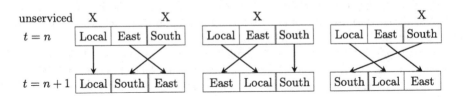

Fig. 2. Three priority queue examples.

4   Need for Abstraction

The state spaces of all probabilistic formal models presented in this work are large *discrete-time Markov chains* (DTMC), and they are analyzed by the tools in the MODEST TOOLSET, namely, MCSTA and MODES. The concrete model presented in the previous section incurs an exponential state space growth as the number of considered clock cycles increases. This is due to the combinations of flits in all twelve buffers in the model. To address this issue, we investigate several abstraction techniques. These abstraction techniques are performed *cumulatively*: results labeled using the name of one technique are the results of that technique applied on top of all previous abstractions.

4.1   Predicate Abstraction to Simplify Complex Data Structures

Predicate abstraction is applied first to the concrete model. It works by formulating predicates that capture critical decision points in the concrete model, and then transforming the model to include only predicate variables. In our model, the predicate abstraction converts all complex data structures into predicate variables. For example, the two predicate variables in Listing 1.2 are defined as the two possible forwarding directions of the front flit in the local channel buffer of router 0. Performing predicate abstraction in this manner significantly simplifies the complex data structures in the concrete model, and it also preserves the properties *resistiveNoise* and *inductiveNoise*, since router and arbiter activity remain unchanged after abstraction. Note that predicate abstraction is only applied to simplify complex data structures in our concrete model to turn them into predicate variables, instead of the entire concrete model. Therefore, it does not introduce nondeterministic behavior as a result. Unfortunately, the predicate abstracted model still incurs significant state space explosion with 7 or more clock cycles.

Listing 1.2. Example predicate variables after predicate abstraction.

```
bool rOL1;//noc[0].channel[local].direction==east
bool rOL2;//noc[0].channel[local].direction==south
```

4.2 Probabilistic Choice Abstraction

Next, we present a novel *probabilistic choice abstraction* technique that builds on the previous predicate abstraction. The idea comes from the following observation. The flit's destination is selected by a uniform random distribution when it is input into the local buffer of each router, but the destination information is not checked *until* the flit enters the router, where it is used to decide the flit forwarding direction. This implies that, when generating states, enumeration of all possible values for the destination variable does not need to happen at its initial assignment, but can be delayed until the location where its value is first checked. Furthermore, the destination variable is not in use beyond this point. Consequently, this variable can be entirely replaced by a probabilistic choice when its value is evaluated, i.e., when the router decides the flit's direction, while preserving the model behavior. The noteworthy state reduction comes from delaying the enumeration of all of the possible values until it is evaluated. For the purpose of this work, the abstraction was applied manually to the model, but we plan to automate the process in our future work.

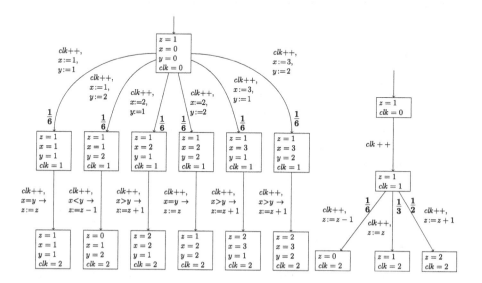

Fig. 3. Probabilistic choice abstraction

Figure 3 compares state graphs for an illustrative model before and after applying probabilistic choice abstraction. The left one is the fully expanded state space of a concrete model, which determines the update of z by comparing two uniform random integer variables $x \in [1, 3]$ and $y \in [1, 2]$. This results in six unique states when the clock reaches 2. Variables x and y are only compared at this row, but not evaluated in any of the six states in the middle row, and are not used after the comparison. Thus, we can apply probabilistic choice abstraction by replacing x and y with a probabilistic choice with explicit probabilities as the state graph on the right illustrates. The abstract model creates only five states and preserves the behavior of the observable variables z and clk.

Figure 3 is similar to our predicate-abstracted NoC model. In this figure, the observable variables are z and clk. Variables x and y are just used to determine the behavior of z. Similarly in our model, the observable variables are *resistiveNoise*, *inductiveNoise* and *clock*. All other variables are used to determine the update behavior of *resistiveNoise* and *inductiveNoise* in between clock cycles. The destinations of the flits are the only probabilistically updated variables in the model. Using this abstraction, we are able to remove the destination variables from the state space, and replace them with a probabilistic choice. This abstraction preserves the behavioral activities of the flits, which determine *resistiveNoise* and *inductiveNoise*. We have experimentally observed that for as many cycles as the concrete and abstract models can run, the behaviors of *resistiveNoise* and *inductiveNoise* are identical across the concrete, predicate abstract, and probabilistic choice abstract models.

Applying probabilistic choice abstraction to non-observable and probabilistically updated variables, such as x and y in Fig. 3, causes states of the concrete model to merge into abstract states, altering the branching structure of the state graph. However, we expect that the probability of reaching each target abstract state is equivalent to the sum of probabilities of reaching its corresponding concrete states, therefore, preserving trace distribution equivalence. We are working on developing theories and correctness proofs for this abstraction technique.

Probabilistic choice abstraction can be directly applied to a formal model without first generating the state graph of the concrete model. This idea is applied to the NoC model in the following way. Any flit coming from the local channel in router 0 can be destined for router 1, 2, or 3 as shown in Fig. 1. Given that the NoC uses X-Y routing and uniform random distribution of destinations, if the destination is router 1 or 3, the flit is forwarded east with probability $\frac{2}{3}$. If the destination is router 2, the flit is forwarded south with probability $\frac{1}{3}$. Any incoming flit coming from the east buffer of router 0 must have been generated in router 1 and is destined for either router 0 or router 2 with equal probability $\frac{1}{2}$. Similarly, any incoming flit in the south buffer of router 0 is generated by either router 2 or 3, and can only be destined for this router. Due to the symmetric nature of the NoC, this same pattern is true for all routers. Because the exact destination of the flit is no longer required knowledge, the buffers can be further abstracted as detailed in the next section.

4.3 Boolean Queue Abstraction

With three buffers in each router, there are a total of six possible orders that determine the priority in servicing each buffer in the case of conflict. Our analysis indicates that, for the 2 × 2 NoC with X-Y routing, the north/south buffer can *never* be in conflict with the local buffer. Therefore, the model only needs to keep track of the local and north/south buffers priority relative to the east/west buffer but not to each other. This allows us to abstract the six possible orders into four, further reducing the state space.

Further, because all buffers operate as FIFOs, an empty buffer element can only exist either after a non-empty element if the buffer is neither full nor empty, or at the front of the buffer if it is empty. Rather than keeping track of the buffer's contents, we only need to store the length of flit occupancy in a buffer, i.e., the number of non-empty elements. This length is represented as a bounded integer ranging between 0 and 4. In general, a buffer storing maximally n Boolean variables incurs 2^n states, but only $n + 1$ states if its occupancy is recorded. In order to maintain correct behavior through this abstraction, the four arbiter processes were synchronized on one action, rather than run sequentially.

Figure 4 depicts the decision procedure in a router after Boolean queue abstraction. It first checks for a possible conflict by testing if the east/west buffer is empty. If it is not empty (i.e., `ewLen` $\neq 0$), the decision procedure goes into one of four branches, depending on whether the two Boolean variables `localPriority` for the local buffer and `nsPriority` for the north/south buffer have priority over the east/west buffer. The router then makes a decision based on the Boolean lock variables. If the local buffer tried to send in the north/south direction, but could not due to a conflict or a full buffer, the lock variable `localLns` would become `true`, ensuring that the flit is sent in the same direction next cycle. The probabilistic decisions have probability values marked on the edges. The router then tries to service the buffers in the order listed in the figure. If a buffer fails to win the conflict resolution in sending a flit, it is locked in the same direction and its priority is advanced. Accumulation of *resistiveNoise* is labeled by `RNoise++` when all three buffers send their flits in a cycle. Figure 4 depicts branches 1 and 2 of the four branches. Branch 3 is identical to branch 1, except the order of buffer updates changes from "local, ns, ew" to "ns, ew, local". Similarly, branch 4 changes branch 2's order from "ew, local, ns" to "local, ew, ns".

5 Results

Assuming uniform random flit destination generation at each router, we report verification results for flit injection at the rate of one flit every two clock cycles first, followed by a bursty mode injection. We then report findings of an optimal flit injection pattern that minimizes PSN. All results presented in this section were generated on a machine with an AMD Ryzen Threadripper 12-core 3.5 GHz Processor and 132 GB memory, running Ubuntu Linux v18.04.3.

We consider the following two transient probabilistic properties: (1) the probability that the number of *resistiveNoise* is lower-bounded by a constant $K \in \mathbb{Z}^+$

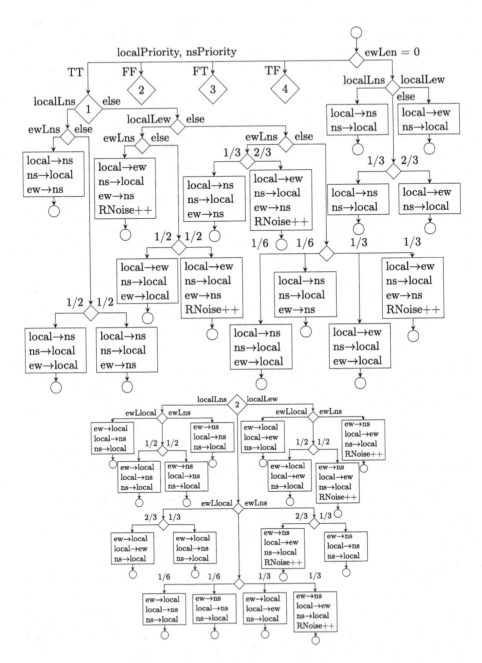

Fig. 4. Decision procedure for the router model after Boolean queue abstraction.

within n cycles; and (2) the probability that the total number of *inductiveNoise* is lower-bounded by a constant $K \in \mathbb{Z}^+$ within n cycles. High router activity, characterized by property (1), is a key indicator of local congestion in the network, and a highly congested network leads to high PSN due to an unbalanced power density [17]. Property (2) reflects an abrupt load change in a router that causes a large inductive drop in the power delivery network [15].

5.1   Every Other Cycle Flit Injection

The operation of the NoC, namely, flit injection/ejection into/from a router, is synchronous with a global clock. We first consider flits to be injected into the network once in every two consecutive clock cycles, which we refer to as the "every other clock cycle flit injection" pattern.

State Reduction from Abstraction. Figure 5 illustrates the impact of applying the aforementioned abstraction techniques on state growth. The exponential cycle-wise growth of the concrete model dramatically reduces to a polynomial growth after Boolean queue abstraction, with other abstraction methods in between. Note that state growth for the presented abstraction techniques are cumulative: probabilistic choice abstraction is applied after predicate abstraction, and it is the base for Boolean queue abstraction. The exponential state growth of the concrete model is due to the probabilistic input. Every other clock cycle, four new flits are generated each with three different possible destinations. This means that if variable x were to increase every other clock cycle, the states, due to just this combination, would be 3^{4x}. This analysis is confirmed by calculating the R^2 values of regression of the state space growth of the different abstractions. The closer the R^2 value is to 1, the better the regression is as an approximation. The R^2 value for the exponential regression is closer to 1 than the polynomial regression for the concrete and predicate abstract models, and the R^2 value for polynomial regression is closer to 1 than the exponential regression for both probabilistic choice abstraction and Boolean queue abstraction.

In addition, we also performed exponential and polynomial regression on the state growth of the probabilistic choice and Boolean queue abstractions using only the values from the first ten clock cycles, in order to see how accurately each regression would predict the values from the next 5 clock cycles. The polynomial regression was a more accurate prediction of the values for the next five clock cycles than the exponential regression. Figure 5 also illustrates the effectiveness of the cumulative abstraction steps detailed in Sect. 4. No property verification results could be obtained on the concrete model regarding the *resistiveNoise* property, as it is impossible for at least one *resistiveNoise* to occur within the 4 to 5 clock cycles before state explosion occurs. The same reasoning applies to the *inductiveNoise* property.

We keep an integer variable *clk* as a cycle counter, which contributes to the state growth. On the other hand, by gradually increasing its upper bound, state space generation is manageable. This is because state generation only needs to represent model behaviors up to the upper bound of *clk*.

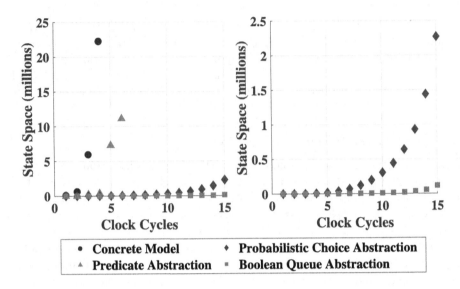

Fig. 5. State count comparison.

Probabilistic Model Checking (PMC). We used MCSTA, an explicit-state probabilistic model checker, to calculate the probabilities of *resistiveNoise* and *inductiveNoise* occurring within a given bounded number of clock cycles using the final Boolean queue abstraction model. The results are shown in Fig. 6. The more abstract models perform an increasing amount of "work"—calculating, communicating, and updating transient and state variables—on every transition. Thus, as state space explosion is alleviated, the runtime for state space exploration rises. An attempt to run the Boolean queue abstraction model for 35 clock cycles ran for 22 h and generated 150.5 million states. When MCSTA attempted to merge these states, it failed due to a segmentation fault indicating an out-of-memory error.

Due to the inability of the concrete model to produce any verification results, it is impossible to compare it's results with that of the abstract models. Comparing the *resistiveNoise* property checking results between the probabilistic choice delay and Boolean queue abstract models, a difference of 1E-7, i.e., a 0.15% difference, starts to manifest after 20 clock cycles. It is possible that this difference is due to floating-point error in the transition probabilities, which can be complicated due to the probabilistic behavior of all four arbiters being compounded. These small rounding errors can then accumulate over several clock cycles. With fewer state transitions in the Boolean queue abstracted model, it is possible that the floating-point errors accrue at a different pace. The concrete model is too large to model check for this many cycles, and a manual calculation would be infeasible due to the scale and complexity of this model. Therefore, we are unable to reconcile this difference at this point. We are currently working on automating the probabilistic choice abstraction and expect that it will provide insight into whether this difference could have been caused by an error in the manual abstraction of the models, as this process was quite arduous, with the final model being several thousand lines long.

Binary decision diagrams (BDDs) have been highly successful in hardware verification [18]. We thus also explored the use of BDD-based symbolic model checking for our NoC models by exporting them to the JANI model interchange format [19] and applying the Storm model checker's *hybrid* and *dd* engines. Unfortunately, with both supported BDD libraries—CUDD and SYLVAN [20]—Storm quickly ran out of memory. This may be due to probabilistic models requiring multi-terminal BDDs to store probability values, which often does not lead to a memory-efficient representation.

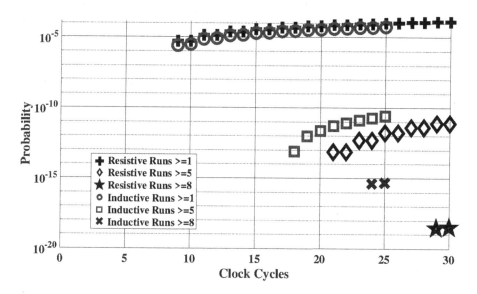

Fig. 6. Probabilities for *resistiveNoise* and *inductiveNoise* in every other cycle input configuration

Statistical Model Checking (SMC). Since our models represent DTMC, we can also apply the Monte Carlo simulation-based statistical model checking technique. In contrast to PMC, it avoids state space explosion entirely, but only delivers statistical guarantees and is problematic for rare events. However, because we could only apply PMC to a relatively few number of clock cycles, we applied SMC to a larger number of cycles in order to analyze the longer-term behavior of the models. We checked the *resistiveNoise* property using SMC with MODES. Running 10000 simulations, MODES reported 643 had at least one optimal run, while 345 had at least one noise run, after 10000 clock cycles. These values correspond to statistical probabilities of 0.0643 and 0.0345 respectively.

5.2   Burst Flit Injection

To more accurately model flit injection patterns in real-world applications and measure their impact on PSN, we gathered verification results for a bursty mode packet injection, where for every 10 cycles, the first 3 consecutive cycles each have a flit injected, followed by 7 idle cycles in all four routers. A surprising observation is that this input pattern drastically increases the scalability to allow verification for significantly longer clock cycles. Our analysis indicates that the NoC empties out flits completely within the 7 idle cycles before it receives the next burst of 3 flits. Other than the priority orderings, the NoC has completely reset itself to the initial condition by the end of the idle cycles. Consequently, the number of reachable states is significantly reduced, compared to the every other cycle injection pattern. This reduction leads to the generation of the entire state space for the 2×2 NoC model whereas the clock variable clk is no longer used to forcibly stop the model checking after a certain number of cycles as in the every other cycle packet injection pattern. A simple 0 to 9 counter was added to maintain the 10-cycle injection pattern. Consequently, we made clk a *transient* variable in order to continue to check properties in relation to clock cycles. A transient variable is only "live" during the assignments execution when taking a transition, which excludes it from the state vector. In this way, clock cycle progress becomes a *reward* annotation to certain transitions instead of being encoded in the structure of an expanded state space. We can then formalize properties (1) and (2) as reward-bounded reachability queries:

$$(1) \quad \mathbf{P}_{=?}\big(\diamond^{[\mathrm{accumulate}(clk) \leqslant N]}\ \textit{resistiveNoise} \geqslant K\big)$$

$$(2) \quad \mathbf{P}_{=?}\big(\diamond^{[\mathrm{accumulate}(clk) \leqslant N]}\ \textit{inductiveNoise} \geqslant K\big)$$

Probabilistic model checking of the bursty mode with MCSTA scales to hundreds of clock cycles. In order to prevent the infinite accumulation of *resistiveNoise*, it is upper bounded by 20, resulting in a total of 16,581,401 reachable states explored in about 3.5 h. Similarly, *inductiveNoise* is upper-bounded by 8, resulting in 10,251,017 states generated in 2.16 h. A smaller upper bound is required due to the addition of helper variables for accurately tracking the high-to-low and low-to-high activities for *inductiveNoise*. The helper variables are required because the behavior of the previous cycle, not just the current, need to be known in order to determine if an *inductiveNoise* event has occurred.

This input configuration results in only 3 flits every 10 cycles for each arbiter to service in a router, as opposed to 5 for the every-other-cycle injection. However, the ability of each arbiter to receive flits during consecutive cycles has a major impact on the PSN behavior of the NoC. The likelihood of having both *resistiveNoise* and *inductiveNoise* increases significantly. Figure 7 shows the plots of the *cumulative distribution function* (CDF) for *resistiveNoise* being greater than or equal to 1, 5, 10, and 20, and the CDF for *inductiveNoise* being greater than or equal to 1, 5, and 8. Comparing these *resistiveNoise* and *inductiveNoise* probabilities with that of the every other cycle injection shows that PSN is much more likely with bursty style injection, within the same number of clock cycles, despite fewer packets entering the NoC every 10 cycles.

5.3 Minimizing PSN with Flit Generation Pattern

We parameterized the bursty mode model so that it could accept a burst lasting any number of cycles, followed by any number of idle cycles. Under our memory constraints, we were able to model check bursts lasting 1, 2, or 3 cycles long, with the requirement that the number of idle cycles must be at least twice as long as the number of cycles in the burst. When testing various burst configurations, we made a critical observation that the input configuration of 1 flit every 3 cycles incurred *zero* probability of a *resistiveNoise* event, and, by extension, zero probability of an *inductiveNoise* event. This is of particular note, because 1 every 3 flit injection results in more flits being injected over time than 3 every 10 injection, but with no occurrence of high-PSN events. Additionally, 1 every 3 flit injection allows considerable number of cycles to be verified compared to every other cycle flit generation and yet it still incurred zero probability of PSN.

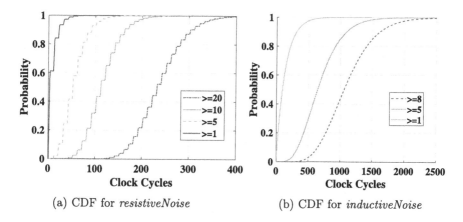

(a) CDF for *resistiveNoise*   (b) CDF for *inductiveNoise*

Fig. 7. CDF for *resistiveNoise* and *inductiveNoise* in burst of three input configuration

5.4 Results Summary and Discussion

The experiments on every other cycle injection suggest that applying PMC on the Boolean queue abstract model is the only viable option to verify PSN-related probabilistic properties at longer cycles with reasonable accuracy, given the rarity of the properties. Verification results indicate extremely low probabilities in observing a *resistiveNoise* event within 30 clock cycles. Since *inductiveNoise* accumulates cycles with high-to-low or low-to-high activities, rare occurrences of *resistiveNoise* consequently lead to extremely low probabilities in *inductiveNoise* verification. On the other hand, PMC on the 3 every 10 burst flit injection scales it to allow much longer cycles and results in considerably higher PSN due to significantly increased *resistiveNoise* and *inductiveNoise* probabilities. Under our memory constraints, 1 of every 3 flit injection is the most effective packet injection pattern that minimizes PSN probability to zero.

The drastically different PSN behaviors can be explained by analyzing local buffer and arbiter activities of each router. Since the entire NoC only includes four corner routers, each flit has a relatively short distance to its destination router, which reduces the number of buffers it has to visit. Therefore, it is unlikely that all three buffers can contain a flit at the same time, a condition necessary for a *resistiveNoise* cycle to occur. In addition, with X-Y routing, flits tend to exit the NoC quickly without filling up buffers in a way that is conducive to *resistiveNoise*. For the burst mode flit injection, because all three buffers in a router simultaneously start three cycles of burst of flits, it is more likely to incur high router activities and switching between high and low router activities. The burst mode is more prone to cycles of high activity when the NoC has consecutive cycles of flit injection, because it does not have cycles to clear out the buffers before another injection. This causes more traffic in the buffers during the burst, leading to more cycles of high router activity overall, despite the seven cycles of idle behavior. An optimal compromise is to have 1 flit every 3 cycles where the occurrence of the high PSN events we are tracking reduces to none.

Our findings indicate that spreading flits over a small number of cycles, rather than releasing them in consecutive ones, drastically reduces PSN. In this work, we assume each router generates flits. In real NoC design, network flits are generated and scheduled externally. Traditional techniques (e.g., IcoNoClast [15]) enhance the router microarchitecture to delay the flit traversal within a NoC, thus effectively curbing the maximum noise of the communication fabric. However, such schemes incur additional design complexity and hardware overheads that are prohibitive for low-power edge applications. Based on our PMC analysis, we set a more cost-effective approach to tackling the communication noise in the low-power domains. Our findings suggest that while scheduling network flits, the scheduler should try to insert empty cycles to separate flits in succession in order to minimize PSN. We leave the design decisions on how to best implement inserting these empty cycles, e.g. inserting busy waits, to further research.

6   Conclusion

This paper describes our experience in formally modeling a 2×2 NoC system and applying probabilistic verification to quantitatively verify the frequency of PSN. Probabilistic model checking using MCSTA was used to evaluate the properties. The concrete model incurs severe state explosion that prevents property checking. Several abstraction techniques, including a novel probabilistic choice abstraction, are applied to alleviate the rapid state-space explosion and allow for successful verification. Results indicate that bursty flit injection in consecutive cycles yields high likelihood of PSN-causing behavior, while spreading flits over a small number of cycles achieves PSN reduction. This shows that flit injection patterns affect PSN drastically, and that by using certain flit injection patterns, such as 1 flit every 3 cycles, more flits can be injected while also minimizing PSN. While the presented PSN probability verification results cannot be directly applied to larger NoCs, due to exclusion of edge and central routers in a 2 × 2 NoC, the abstraction methods, including the novel probabilistic choice abstraction, are independent of the NoC size and therefore are applicable to larger NoC models. For further work, we will extend the PSN analysis to larger NoCs, analyze different flit generation rates, and investigate expected long-run probabilities for PSN. In order to scale probabilistic model checking to larger NoCs, we plan to pursue probabilistic assume-guarantee reasoning to combat state explosion. Additionally, we plan to work on a formal proof for the probabilistic choice abstraction. Finally, we plan to investigate methods to make the use of BDDs more successful in analyzing this NoC.

Acknowledgments. Arnd Hartmanns was supported by NWO VENI grant 639.021.754. Riley Roberts, Benjamin Lewis, Koushik Chakraborty, and Sanghamitra Roy were supported in part by National Science Foundation (NSF) grants CAREER-1253024, CNS-1421022, and CNS-1421068. Any opinions, findings, and conclusions or recommendations expressed in this material are those of the authors and do not necessarily reflect the views of the NSF. Riley Roberts and Benjamin Lewis were supported in part by donations from Adobe Systems.

References

1. Verbeek, F., Schmaltz, J.: A decision procedure for deadlock-free routing in wormhole networks. IEEE Trans. Parallel Distrib. Syst. **25**(8), 1935–1944 (2014)
2. Zhang, Z., Serwe, W., Wu, J., Yoneda, T., Zheng, H., Myers, C.: Formal analysis of a fault-tolerant routing algorithm for a network-on-chip. In: Lang, F., Flammini, F. (eds.) FMICS 2014. LNCS, vol. 8718, pp. 48–62. Springer, Cham (2014). https://doi.org/10.1007/978-3-319-10702-8_4
3. Salamat, R., Khayambashi, M., Ebrahimi, M., Bagherzadeh, N.: A resilient routing algorithm with formal reliability analysis for partially connected 3D-NoCs. IEEE Trans. Comput. **65**(11), 3265–3279 (2016)
4. Zhang, Z., Serwe, W., Wu, J., Yoneda, T., Zheng, H., Myers, C.: An improved fault-tolerant routing algorithm for a Network-on-Chip derived with formal analysis. Sci. Comput. Program. **118**, 24–39 (2016). Formal Methods for Industrial Critical Systems (FMICS 2014). http://www.sciencedirect.com/science/article/pii/S0167642316000125
5. Zaman, A., Hasan, O.: Formal verification of circuit-switched Network on Chip (NoC) architectures using SPIN. In: 2014 International Symposium on System-on-Chip, SoC 2014, Tampere, Finland, 28–29 October 2014, pp. 1–8 (2014)
6. Chen, Y.-R., Su, W.-T., Hsiung, P.-A., Lan, Y.-C., Hu, Y.-H., Chen, S.-J.: Formal modeling and verification for Network-on-Chip. In: 2010 International Conference on Green Circuits and Systems (ICGCS), pp. 299–304 (2010)
7. Holcomb, D.: Formal verification and synthesis for quality-of-service in on-chip networks. Ph.D. dissertation, EECS Department, University of California, Berkeley, December 2013. http://www2.eecs.berkeley.edu/Pubs/TechRpts/2013/EECS-2013-228.html

8. Wassel, H.M.G., et al.: Networks on chip with provable security properties. IEEE Micro **34**(3), 57–68 (2014)
9. Sepúlveda, J., Aboul-Hassan, D., Sigl, G., Becker, B., Sauer, M.: Towards the formal verification of security properties of a Network-on-Chip router. In: 23rd IEEE European Test Symposium, ETS 2018, Bremen, Germany, 28 May–1 June 2018, pp. 1–6 (2018)
10. Hartmanns, A., Hermanns, H.: The modest toolset: an integrated environment for quantitative modelling and verification. In: Ábrahám, E., Havelund, K. (eds.) TACAS 2014. LNCS, vol. 8413, pp. 593–598. Springer, Heidelberg (2014). https://doi.org/10.1007/978-3-642-54862-8_51
11. Budde, C.E., D'Argenio, P.R., Hartmanns, A., Sedwards, S.: A statistical model checker for nondeterminism and rare events. In: Beyer, D., Huisman, M. (eds.) TACAS 2018. LNCS, vol. 10806, pp. 340–358. Springer, Cham (2018). https://doi.org/10.1007/978-3-319-89963-3_20
12. Dehnert, C., Junges, S., Katoen, J.-P., Volk, M.: A **STORM** is coming: a modern probabilistic model checker. In: Majumdar, R., Kunčak, V. (eds.) CAV 2017. LNCS, vol. 10427, pp. 592–600. Springer, Cham (2017). https://doi.org/10.1007/978-3-319-63390-9_31
13. Kwiatkowska, M., Norman, G., Parker, D.: PRISM 4.0: verification of probabilistic real-time systems. In: Gopalakrishnan, G., Qadeer, S. (eds.) CAV 2011. LNCS, vol. 6806, pp. 585–591. Springer, Heidelberg (2011). https://doi.org/10.1007/978-3-642-22110-1_47
14. Lewis, B., et al.: Probabilistic verification for reliable Network-on-Chip system design. In: Larsen, K.G., Willemse, T. (eds.) FMICS 2019. LNCS, vol. 11687, pp. 110–126. Springer, Cham (2019). https://doi.org/10.1007/978-3-030-27008-7_7
15. Basu, P., Shridevi, R.J., Chakraborty, K., Roy, S.: IcoNoClast: tackling voltage noise in the NoC power supply through flow-control and routing algorithms. IEEE Trans. VLSI Syst. **25**(7), 2035–2044 (2017)
16. Shridevi, R.J., Ancajas, D.M., Chakraborty, K., Roy, S.: Tackling voltage emergencies in NoC through timing error resilience. In: ISLPED, pp. 104–109 (2015)
17. Dahir, N., Mak, T.S.T., Xia, F., Yakovlev, A.: Modeling and tools for power supply variations analysis in Networks-on-Chip. TC **63**(3), 679–690 (2014)
18. Chaki, S., Gurfinkel, A.: BDD-based symbolic model checking. In: Clarke, E., Henzinger, T., Veith, H., Bloem, R. (eds.) Handbook of Model Checking, pp. 219–245. Springer, Cham (2018). https://doi.org/10.1007/978-3-319-10575-8_8
19. Budde, C.E., Dehnert, C., Hahn, E.M., Hartmanns, A., Junges, S., Turrini, A.: JANI: quantitative model and tool interaction. In: Legay, A., Margaria, T. (eds.) TACAS 2017. LNCS, vol. 10206, pp. 151–168. Springer, Heidelberg (2017). https://doi.org/10.1007/978-3-662-54580-5_9
20. van Dijk, T., van de Pol, J.: Sylvan: multi-core framework for decision diagrams. STTT **19**(6), 675–696 (2017). https://doi.org/10.1007/s10009-016-0433-2

Author Index

Printed in the United States
by Baker & Taylor Publisher Services